D1596805

MAURICE BISHOP SPEAKS

To the memory of **Maurice Bishop, Unison Whiteman, Fitzroy Bain, Jacqueline Creft, Vincent Noel, and Norris Bain** *whose accomplishments and living political heritage form part of the imperishable revolutionary continuity of the world's working people in their struggle against imperialist oppression and exploitation and for the establishment of socialism.*

To **George Louison, Kenrick Radix, Don Rojas, and other leaders and cadres of the New Jewel Movement and Grenada revolution** *who maintain their commitment to the struggle for the revolutionary transformation of their own country, the entire Caribbean and Central America, and the world.*

To **the Grenadian and Cuban working people** *who gave their lives in Grenada in combat against U.S. imperialism's first direct use of U.S. troops in its effort to halt the advancing socialist revolution in the Americas.*

MAURICE BISHOP SPEAKS

The Grenada Revolution 1979-83

PATHFINDER PRESS/NEW YORK

Edited by Bruce Marcus and Michael Taber
Copyright © 1983 by Pathfinder Press

Library of Congress Catalog Card Number 83-63309
ISBN cloth 0-87348-611-0; ISBN paper 0-87348-619-6

Manufactured in the United States of America
First edition, 1983

Pathfinder Press
410 West Street
New York, NY 10014

Write for a free catalog of books and pamphlets

Contents

Introduction

Grenada's Workers' and Farmers' Government:
Its Achievements and Its Overthrow

by Steve Clark

On October 12, 1983, Maurice Bishop, prime minister of Grenada and founding leader of the New Jewel Movement, was placed under house arrest at the orders of a clique of army, government, and party officials organized by Deputy Prime Minister Bernard Coard.

On October 19, Bishop and five other central leaders of Grenada's revolutionary government and the New Jewel Movement were murdered in cold blood, again at the order of Coard's clique.

On October 25, thousands of U.S. Marines and Army Rangers landed in Grenada to establish a military occupation of the island and brutally reverse the far-reaching popular advances gained as a result of the March 13, 1979, revolution.

In less than two weeks, the Grenada revolution had been betrayed, its workers' and farmers' government overthrown by renegades, and the island nation invaded and occupied by U.S. imperialism.

Pathfinder Press is publishing this new collection entitled *Maurice Bishop Speaks* because Bishop's own words are the best available record of the accomplishments and inspiring perspectives of that revolution, which for four and a half years marched forward arm in arm with revolutionary Nicaragua and Cuba. Making this material accessible to the widest possible audience is an elementary responsibility of all those engaged in the struggle against world imperialism and for freedom and justice for the vast majority of humanity.

Maurice Bishop's speeches and interviews provide political weapons not only for revolutionary-minded fighters in Central America and the Caribbean, nor even just for those in other oppressed nations of Latin

---

Steve Clark is editor of the socialist newsmagazine *Intercontinental Press*. His articles also appear regularly in the U.S. newspapers the *Militant* and *Perspectiva Mundial*.

America, Africa, the Middle East, and Asia. They also form part of the revolutionary continuity and political arsenal of fighters for national liberation, democracy, peace, and socialism throughout the world, including working people in the United States, Britain, Canada, and other imperialist countries. Bishop himself stressed this international significance of the Grenada revolution during a July 1980 interview reprinted here from the socialist newsmagazine, *Intercontinental Press*. The interview was conducted by Andrew Pulley, Diane Wang, and myself.

Bishop told us that the New Jewel Movement understood "the importance of progresssive forces worldwide joining together. We see that struggle as being *one* struggle, indivisible. And what happens in Grenada, we recognize its importance for all struggles around the world."

"We certainly place a great deal of importance on the activity, the potential, and the possibilities for the American working-class movement," Bishop said. Not only its potential for solidarity with national liberation struggles and opposition to Washington's war moves, but also "in terms of the potential of doing mortal damage to the international capitalist and imperialist system from within the belly of the main imperialist power on earth."

Both in this 1980 interview, and again very forcefully in his June 1983 speech to more than 2,500 people in New York City, Bishop emphasized the historic importance and potential impact of the Grenada revolution on the Black population of the United States. The island is 95 percent African in origin, he reminded the New York audience, and it is also English-speaking, thus facilitating direct communication with U.S. Blacks.

What Bishop wanted to communicate above all was the indissoluble connection between the battles for national liberation and socialism, and the worldwide interdependence of peoples engaged in those struggles. He understood that the March 1979 victory in Grenada, together with that in Nicaragua the following July, represented the extension of the American socialist revolution opened two decades earlier in Cuba. He told a May Day 1980 rally in Havana that "we recognize in Grenada just as the imperialists recognize, that without the Cuban revolution of 1959 there could have been no Grenadian revolution, nor Nicaraguan revolution in 1979."

Bishop also recognized what this meant for U.S. imperialism; the stakes were very high, involving the preservation of the capitalist system of exploitation and oppression right on its own doorstep. Washington has "certainly put Cuba, Nicaragua, and Grenada as being the key countries to get at," Bishop explained during the July 1980 interview.

"Cuba for obvious reasons. It is obviously the vanguard in this region. Nicaragua because of its *tremendous* importance for Central America. Everybody in Central America wants to be a Sandinista." And Grenada, in addition to the special reasons already cited, because it was part of this unfolding revolutionary process.

As Fidel Castro put it, Grenada, Nicaragua, and Cuba were "three giants rising up to defend their right to independence, sovereignty, and justice on the very threshold of imperialism."

The November 1983 U.S. invasion of Grenada marks the first direct use of Washington's own military forces in the new Vietnam-style war that the U.S. rulers have begun to carry out in Nicaragua and El Salvador, as well. Rolling back the socialist revolution in the region is top priority for the U.S. capitalist class, its government, and its two political parties. That is why virtually all Democratic and Republican politicians, both liberals and conservatives, fell in line behind the Reagan administration's militarily successful onslaught against Grenada, despite a few initial tactical misgivings.

The world relationship of class forces has shifted further to the detriment of the U.S. imperialists over the past decade. Since their military defeat at the hands of Vietnamese liberation forces in 1973-75, and the break in one of the longest capitalist economic booms, the U.S. rulers have sustained further blows — in Indochina, Iran, and in Central America and the Caribbean.

These blows have increased the political price Washington will pay at home and internationally when it directly uses U.S. troops and planes against revolutionary struggles. Opposition to military interventions abroad, which became widespread among U.S. working people during the Vietnam War, will come more quickly and go deeper as the deaths and setbacks of the next war unfold. Recognition that this will occur has put important obstacles in Washington's path. It has already been of decisive importance to the workers and peasants of Nicaragua, Grenada, El Salvador, and Cuba. It has bought them precious time to consolidate their revolutions and to prepare to defend their conquests against the inevitable escalation of Washington's aggression.

The U.S. rulers, however, do not intend to wait until they have achieved majority support at home before launching military action against the Central American and Caribbean revolutions. They cannot accept the extension of the socialist revolution to Nicaragua, then El Salvador, followed by other countries. For Washington, the events that opened wide the door to an invasion of Grenada created a golden opportunity to make a first decisive move. The prior beheading of the revolutionary forces and disarming of the people there meant that military victory would come relatively cheap in U.S. lives and dollars. The accomplished fact of the invasion was then used to whip up greater support for Washington's political and military objectives. The justifications for the invasion were presented after it had already taken place. The propaganda of the deed came first, then propaganda of the word.

The response in the United States to the invasion showed that such actions by the rulers can succeed, at least for a time, in spreading confusion and even winning an important measure of acceptance. At the same time, the polarized character of the response, the debates and discussions in thousands of workplaces, and the immediate nationwide protests against the invasion all testified to the profound changes in consciousness of the U.S. working class over the past decade. These changes are the result not only of the Vietnam War, but also of escalating attacks on jobs, living conditions, racial equality, and political rights in the United States.

Polls confirming majority opposition to U.S. military intervention in Central America will not stop Washington from aiding the counterrevolutionary war already under way against Nicaragua and the Salvadoran freedom fighters. Nor will antiwar opinion alone halt the steady buildup of U.S. military forces in Honduras and throughout the region, or the use of these U.S. troops, planes, and ships in what could escalate into a new Vietnam-style war.

But the changed political consciousness of the U.S. working class and labor movement *will* play a much more decisive role much more rapidly than even during the late stages of the Vietnam War in helping to ensure defeat of the U.S. invading forces and victory for the workers and peasants of those countries.

That is one reason why Nicaraguan leader Tomás Borge told visiting Canadian trade unionists last summer that while he was "not optimistic in regards to peace," he was "absolutely optimistic in terms of victory."

Behind Borge's confidence in victory is his conviction that the armed workers and peasants of Nicaragua are determined to defend their revolution, their social conquests, and their national sovereignty.

Prior to the events culminating in the arrest and subsequent murder of Bishop and other NJM leaders, this same conviction about the readiness of the Grenadian workers and farmers to defend their social gains gave reason for confidence that if imperialism ever invaded, it could only conquer after a mighty battle. As Bishop often warned, it would be far easier for U.S. invaders to come onto Grenada than to get off it alive.

"As we begin the fourth year of our revolution," Bishop told the third anniversary rally on March 13, 1982, "it is very clear that the great strength of the revolution, first and foremost, lies in the unbreakable link between the masses and the party; between the masses and the government; between the masses and the state. That is what gives our revolution invincible force, because the masses see the party, see the state and the government as theirs; not something foreign or strange, or apart or isolated from them, but living, throbbing entities that embody their aspirations, their interests, and their hopes."

When the U.S. invasion actually came October 25, however, Grenada's workers' and farmers' government had already been overthrown thirteen days earlier. On October 12, the Coard group placed Maurice Bishop under house arrest and organized to use whatever deadly force was necessary to establish its own total domination. One week later, the revolution suffered another devastating blow, when Bishop, five other NJM leaders, and other Grenadians were gunned down by Coard's supporters. The very first proclamation of the new, self-appointed "Revolutionary Military Council" was a four-day round-the-clock curfew, with the warning that violators would be "shot on sight." The entire population of Grenada was placed under house arrest.

"In our view, Coard's group objectively destroyed the revolution and opened the door to imperialist aggression," President Fidel Castro explained to more than 1 million people gathered in Havana November 14 to honor the Cuban volunteer construction workers killed during the U.S. invasion of Grenada.

"As soon as the internal dissensions, which came to light on October 12, became known," Castro explained, "the Yankee imperialists decided to invade."

As a result of these events, Castro said, the new Grenadian government had become "morally indefensible. And, since the party, the government, and the army had divorced themselves from the people, it was also impossible to defend the nation militarily, because a revolutionary war is only feasible and justifiable when united with the people."

The U.S. imperialists, Castro said, "wanted to kill the symbol of the Grenadian revolution, but the symbol was already dead. The Grenadian revolutionaries themselves destroyed it with their split and their colossal errors.

"We believe that, after the death of Bishop and his closest comrades, after the army fired on the people, and after the party and the government divorced themselves from the masses and isolated themselves from the world, the Grenadian revolutionary process could not survive.

"In its efforts to destroy a symbol," he said, "the United States killed a corpse and brought the symbol back to life at the same time."

Imperialism brought the Grenada revolution to the attention of millions of workers and farmers around the world. It had to try to destroy the example of that revolution, to obliterate the "symbol" it had become. But the lessons contained in this collection, *Maurice Bishop Speaks*, prove that this example has importance far beyond Grenada and the Caribbean. These are *living* lessons for those committed to learning from and continuing the worldwide fight that Maurice Bishop was part of.

Grenada's Workers' and Farmers' Government

As Cuban journalist Arnaldo Hutchinson explains in the historical review of Grenada that follows this introduction, the island had been a colony — first of France, later Britain — for more than 300 years prior to obtaining formal political independence in 1974. The French colonialists exterminated the native Carib and Arawak Indian population, replacing it with slave labor shipped in chains from Africa. Britain maintained Grenada as a source of agricultural products processed and packaged by British companies, which walked off with virtually all the profits. Little industry was permitted to develop on the island beyond tiny handicraft workshops, and the lush and fertile island was kept dependent on imported food. A small number of plantation owners and prosperous merchants served the colonial power as a base of local support and stability.

Little changed for the people following independence. The neocolonial government of dictator Eric Gairy, already ensconced under direct colonial administration, remained in power. In the early 1950s, Gairy had won wide popular support as a leader of the fight for independence and to unionize agricultural workers. He had subsequently misused his influence, however, to sell out Grenada's working people and build up his own holdings in real estate, tourism, and commerce. His government served the profit needs of a handful of wealthy Grenadians, above all his own. The island's economy remained subordinate to British, Canadian, and U.S. finance capital. Gairy used the government to gain an edge on his local business competitors and advance his own personal interests and eccentric obsessions. He pushed through antistrike and other repressive measures. To defend his corrupt and exploitative regime in the face of rising protests, Gairy unleashed the thugs of his feared and hated Mongoose Gang to murder and brutalize opponents.

In 1973 the New Jewel Movement was formed, primarily through the merger of two organizations that had been established the previous year: the Movement for Assemblies of the People (MAP), whose best-known leader was Maurice Bishop, and the Joint Endeavour for Welfare, Education and Liberation (JEWEL), whose most prominent spokesperson was Unison Whiteman. The new organization quickly showed its capacity to mobilize mass support through two rallies of more than 10,000 people each that same year. Over the rest of the decade, the NJM helped initiate and lead repeated struggles for democratic rights, against imperialist domination, and for improved conditions for workers and farmers. NJM members won leading positions in several island trade unions, as well as three seats in Grenada's parliament.

Maurice Bishop and Unison Whiteman explained the NJM's political evolution and perspectives in a 1977 interview with Cuba's main weekly magazine, *Bohemia*, retranslated into English for this collection. The initial political inspiration for the organization, Bishop said, came from "the ideas of 'Black Power' that developed in the United States and the freedom struggle of the African people in such places as Angola, Mozambique, and Guinea-Bissau."

"But unquestionably," Bishop added, "through the Cuban experience we got to see scientific socialism close up." This, above all, he explained, "has been teaching us, on the practical level of day-to-day political struggle, the relevance of socialism as the only solution to our problems. Our party began to develop along Marxist lines in 1974, when we began to study the theory of scientific socialism."

In the weeks leading up to March 13, 1979, NJM leaders learned of a plot by Gairy to assassinate them while he was out of the country. The revolutionists thwarted the planned massacre by organizing a successful armed takeover of the True Blue army barracks and of the island's sole radio station. An appeal for mass support over the renamed Radio Free Grenada brought the people into the streets by the tens of thousands, occupying the police station and other strategic points and ensuring victory.

The revolutionary government born in this triumphant popular insurrection was politically independent of both the imperialists and local Grenadian capitalists and plantation owners, basing itself instead on the workers and farmers. The New Jewel Movement took the initiative in establishing a People's Revolutionary Government (PRG), composed primarily of NJM leaders but also of representatives from other sectors of the anti-Gairy opposition, including some professionals and businessmen. Maurice Bishop became prime minister.

The New Jewel Movement immediately carried out a measure proven by history to be indispensable to the survival and advance of every genuine workers' and farmers' revolution. As Bishop explained in a 1981 interview with Cuba's *Granma Weekly Review*, "It is our firm belief that no revolution has a right to call itself that if it does not have or does not develop a capacity to defend itself. This is why the Gairy army was disbanded and a new army, the People's Revolutionary Army, was created. This is also why we have been building the People's Revolutionary Militia so that the people of our country will themselves be involved in the defense of what they have fought for and what they are trying to build."

The March 1979 revolution was a radical popular uprising. In its direct impetus and immediate tasks, it was a democratic, anti-oligarchical, anti-imperialist revolution. Like the Cuban revolution twenty years earlier, and the Nicaraguan revolution a few months later, however, the Grenada revolution was at the same time profoundly anticapitalist from the outset. Deeply influenced by the Cuban revolution, the NJM leaders recognized that consistent efforts to carry out democratic tasks and throw off imperialist domination would inevitably bring the workers and farmers into conflict with the profit needs of both foreign and local capitalists.

Starting from the organization and mobilization of Grenada's working people to combat imperialist oppression and establish democratic liberties, the new government began laying the foundation for working people to carry out the transition from the domination of capitalist property relations to the establishment of a workers' state based on state-owned industry, economic planning, and a government monopoly of foreign trade. That was how the Cuban revolution had developed, making possible enormous gains for the Cuban workers and peasants in education, health, life expectancy, elimination of discrimination against Blacks and women, and growing democratic participation in administering their own affairs.

That is what the New Jewel Movement set out to achieve on March 13, 1979. "With the working people we made our popular, anti-imperialist, and democratic revolution," Bishop explained. "With them we will build and advance to socialism and final victory."

The new workers' and farmers' government was an indispensable instrument at the service of the Grenadian masses to deepen their mobilization, organization, education, and class consciousness. It put an end to the political dictatorship of the imperialist-backed capitalist minority in Grenada, replacing it with the opening stage of what Marxists call the dictatorship of the proletariat — that is, political rule by, and in the class interests of, the workers and poor farmers, the laboring majority.

The Grenadian capitalists, landowners, and some imperialist interests retained substantial property holdings in agriculture, real estate, commerce, tourism, and industry. But they no longer held *political* power. They could no longer dictate that the government and state in Grenada would act to defend profits over the needs of the workers and farmers.

Still ahead of the revolution was the task of breaking the economic power of the remaining big capitalists and landlords. Bishop and the NJM leadership correctly sought to lead this transition in a manner that would maximize development of productive jobs and social benefits, and minimize unnecessary hardship for working people.

Following the house arrest and subsequent murder of Maurice Bishop, the big-business press in the United States and elsewhere began peddling speculation that this course carried out under Bishop's leadership had been too "moderate" for "more Marxist" figures such as Coard, and had not been to the liking of Cuba either.

First, there is no indication that any explicit fundamental economic or social policy question was at the root of the betrayal by Coard and other NJM renegades. The factors behind their treachery will be discussed shortly.

Second, there is no evidence that Cuban leaders disagreed with the "mixed economy" course followed by Bishop and the NJM. More importantly, the Cubans would not have meddled in the internal affairs of the Grenadian government and party even if such differences had existed.

As Fidel Castro explained in his November 14 speech, reprinted as an appendix in this book, "Socioeconomically, Grenada was actually advancing satisfactorily. The people had received many benefits, in spite of the hostile policy of the United States, and Grenada's Gross National Product was growing at a good rate in the midst of the world crisis.

"Bishop was not an extremist," Castro said. "Rather he was a true revolutionary — conscientious and honest. Far from disagreeing with his intelligent and realistic policy, we fully sympathized with it, since it was rigorously adapted to his country's specific conditions and possibilities."

Those "specific conditions and possibilities" in Grenada involved advancing the socialist course charted by the New Jewel Movement in the face of enormous objective problems. Grenada's revenues were largely dependent on the export of three agricultural commodities — bananas, cocoa, and nutmeg — and on tourism and the wholesale and retail trade generated by it. The revolution met intense economic and military pressure from U.S. imperialism right from the outset. Moreover, Grenada is a very small island of some 110,000 people, with very little industry and a small working class.

All this created objective limits to the pace of economic development needed to undergird permanent advances in social conditions and to free the country from imperialist domination and the legacy of colonial oppression. Moreover, the revolution came at a time when the demand and prices for its agricultural products were slumping on the world market, while outlays for needed industrial, consumer, and energy imports were steadily climbing.

The NJM leaders understood that it would take organization, education, and discipline for the working class to prepare itself and its allies, the small farmers, to administer the entire society and all the industrial, agricultural, and commercial enterprises that made it up. It would take time for the new government to build up an infrastructure of roads, new plant and equipment, state farms and cooperatives, and administrative and scientific know-how to lay a solid basis to begin development along socialist lines. Even over the longer haul, there were no plans to expropriate small shops or tourist homes, let alone small farms.

The revolutionary leaders of the Nicaraguan workers' and farmers' government, too, have so far left many shops, factories, and agricultural holdings in private hands, while declaring socialist property relations to be their goal and taking important steps toward a workers' state as they consolidate their workers' and peasants' government.

Of course, for a revolutionary leadership to follow this path means facing the challenge and responsibility to organize working people to advance their own class interests in the ongoing struggle between exploiters and exploited. Capitalists and landlords can be expected to engage in speculation, black-market operations, and other profiteering — even sabotage and decapitalization. They will use their remaining economic clout to attempt to rebuild their lost political power.

The question for a revolutionary leadership of the working class in any such situation is not how quickly in the abstract to move toward expropriation. The tempo and methods necessary for carrying out a fundamental social transformation are determined by objective material realities and class relations. Acting on a preconceived schema could bring the economy to a screeching halt, send potential allies of the workers fleeing to the counterrevolution, and decimate and demoralize the working class and poor farmers themselves.

A nationalized factory won't produce more than a privately owned one if the skills don't yet exist to run it or if sufficient resources have not yet been accumulated to invest in new equipment, raw materials, upkeep, and wages. An expropriated foreign bank won't marshal more funds for socialist construction if the banks' assets were largely kept outside the country and the impact of the expropriation is to cut off access to grants and loans from capitalist governments and financial institutions before alternative aid has been secured. An expropriated plantation will neither provide decent lives for the landless nor provide products needed for export income until the government can provide the credit, tools, fertilizer, and elementary farming skills to carry out a successful agrarian reform. And expropriating the whole thing will produce nothing but chaos until at least minimal methods of control, accounting, and planning can be instituted from the individual farm and enterprise up to the national level.

Even after the workers and farmers hold state power, in other words, wealth is still produced by applying human labor to land, machinery, and raw materials, not by applying signatures to decrees.

As Bishop explained in the July 1980 interview with *Intercontinental Press*, it is wrong to think that "a revolution is like instant coffee; you just throw it in a cup and it comes out presto."

The challenge confronting the revolutionary leadership in Grenada was how to prepare, educate, and organize the working population to run that society given the existing material conditions in that small country. The answers could only be determined by a concrete assessment of the level of Grenada's economic and social development; the political relationship of class forces at home and internationally; the prospects for economic assistance from the USSR, Cuba, and other workers' states and from other sources; the class consciousness and organization of the working class; and the firmness of its alliance with working farmers and other nonproletarian working people.

That required political leadership capacity and experience, not ultraleft haste and administrative methods.

Two years prior to the revolution, Maurice Bishop presented a sober but optimistic assessment of the prospects facing Grenadian socialists in the 1977 interview with the Cuban magazine *Bohemia.*

"Socialism is the future we would like to see in Grenada," Bishop explained in that interview. "At present the reality is that the most backward forms of capitalist exploitation exist in Grenada. We have to remember that Grenada — with its small territory, high unemployment, great poverty and misery, with the small size and low level of consciousness of its working class, with all its commercial ties to imperialism, and with a profoundly repressive government — must accomplish democratic advances in step with the march of the other countries of the region.

"We know how poor and backward our country is," Bishop said. "And we know how difficult it would be to resist the general economic and political pressures that imperialism would unleash against Grenada if it tried to break the bonds of domination without first making serious attempts to develop true and significant links with the socialist camp.

"However, despite all the difficulties," he concluded, "we feel that the perspectives for the cause of social revolution in Grenada are good."

Two years later, the New Jewel Movement would begin to put in practice the socialist course it had charted for Grenada.

Bishop, Whiteman, and other NJM leaders were quite aware of the snares and traps involved in leading a social revolution in tiny and poor Grenada. One conceivable response to this recognition could have been to conclude, as many "official" Communist parties have done in the colonial world, that the workers and farmers are simply not ready to take power there. That the only "realizable" goals must be limited to democratic reforms, and therefore the capitalist class or some sector of it must still play the leading role in any revolutionary government.

That was *not* the response of the New Jewel Movement, however. Bishop and the other NJM leaders correctly saw the Grenada revolution as part of the world struggle against imperialism, and for national liberation and socialism. They had the courage to take the power and chart a course toward the construction of socialism. But they also had the political sense to understand the real conditions and immediate tasks in Grenada, as well as the steps needed to prepare the working class and its allies to rebuild their society on the foundation of state property and democratic planning.

The Russian Experience

The Grenadian revolutionists, of course, were not the first to confront the difficult tasks of leading the working class and its allies through the transition from the decaying capitalist social system toward socialism. On a world scale, the workers' first historical experience in this regard was the Russian revolution.

In 1919 the new Soviet government took the initiative in launching the Communist International. During its first five years as a revolutionary leadership of the world working class, the Comintern, as it was called for short, discussed the lessons of this first experience in conquering and wielding power; it drew important conclusions for revolutionary strategy and tactics. Extensive discussions of this question were held at the Comintern's fourth world congress in December 1922, and at a meeting of its international executive committee the following July.

At the July 1923 gathering, a resolution on workers' and farmers' governments was adopted. It stressed that following the conquest of power, the working class must remember "the necessity to harmonize its movements with the sentiments of the peasantry in their respective countries, to establish a correct coordination between the victorious proletariat and the peasantry, and to observe a rational policy in the gradual introduction of the economic measures of the proletariat, such as was arrived at by the victorious proletariat of Russia in that period of the Russian revolution which is called the New Economic Policy."

What was Russia's New Economic Policy? Why in his speech to the 1922 Comintern congress did Bolshevik leader V. I. Lenin say that the NEP was rich in "important practical conclusions for the Communist International" and "of first-rate importance to all the Communist parties"?

Lenin explained that following the October 1917 victory, the new Soviet government had "made an attempt to pass, as gradually as possible, breaking up as little of the old as possible, to the new social relations. . . ."

By mid-1918, however, the onslaught of imperialist invasion and full-scale civil war had forced the Russian revolutionary leaders to abandon this initial course toward as efficient and gradual as possible a transformation of property relations. Faced with escalating economic sabotage by the capitalists and the imperatives of producing food and industrial goods for the war, the Bolsheviks carried out sweeping nationalizations and centralized virtually all trade through the state.

By the end of 1920, however, both domestic counterrevolutionary forces and imperialist invaders had been largely defeated by the new Red Army. On the other hand, the capitalists elsewhere in Europe had succeeded in defeating revolutionary struggles in Hungary, Germany, and Italy, tightening the isolation of the world's first workers' state. Moreover, the civil war had taken a heavy toll inside Russia. Many of the most class-conscious workers and poor peasants, who were the vanguard of the Red Army soldiers, had fallen in battle or died from disease and starvation at the front. The economic and social dislocation from the war was exacerbated by drought and famine.

As Lenin explained at the Comintern's 1922 congress, "after we had passed through the most important stage of the Civil War — and passed through it victoriously — we felt the impact of a grave — I think it was the gravest — internal political crisis in Soviet Russia.

"This internal crisis," Lenin said, "brought to light discontent not only among a considerable section of the peasantry but also among the workers. This was the first and, I hope, the last time in the history of Soviet Russia that feeling ran against us among large masses of peasants, not consciously but instinctively."

The source of this crisis, Lenin explained, was not just the war-caused destruction. It was also a consequence of the too-rapid economic and social transformations that had been imposed on the young workers' and farmers' republic by its struggle for survival. While the peasants had supported this fight against the reimposition of landlordism and tsarism, their alliance with the working class was now near the breaking point as a result of the policies of the previous few years. And this alliance, Lenin stressed, was key to the defense of the Soviet republic and its advance toward socialism.

"In this respect," Lenin said at the party's tenth congress in 1921, "we are very much to blame for having gone too far; we overdid the nationalisation of industry and trade, clamping down on local exchange of commodities. Was that a mistake? It certainly was."

Lenin explained this again the following year at the fourth Comintern congress. "The reason for [the crisis]," he said, "was that in our economic offensive we had run too far ahead, that we had not provided ourselves with adequate resources, that the masses sensed what we ourselves were not then able to formulate consciously but what we admitted soon after, a few weeks later, namely, that the direct transition to purely socialist forms, to purely socialist distribution, was beyond our available strength, and that if we were unable to effect a retreat so as to confine ourselves to easier tasks, we would face disaster."

That was the origin of the New Economic Policy adopted by the Russian revolutionists in early 1921. The NEP made it possible for peasants to sell a portion of their produce on the open market inside Russia. Restrictions on private trade were relaxed to supplement state-organized exchanges. To help revive industrial production, the Soviet republic sought to lease nationalized factories, mines, forests, and oil fields to foreign and domestic capitalists.

In introducing the NEP, a resolution adopted by the fourth congress explained, "the Soviet government is following an economic path which it would doubtless have pursued in 1918-19 had not the implacable demands of Civil War obliged it to expropriate the bourgeoisie at one blow. . . ." The resolution was drafted on behalf of the Russian delegation by Comintern leader Leon Trotsky.

Such measures, Lenin pointed out, were even more important for nations less economically advanced than Russia itself. In a 1921 letter to

communists in Azerbaijan, Armenia, Georgia, and several other nations
oppressed under the old tsarist empire, Lenin advised: "You will need to
practise more moderation and caution, and show more readiness to make
concessions to the petty bourgeoisie, the intelligentsia, and particularly
the peasantry. You must make the swiftest, most intense and all possible
economic use of the capitalist West through a policy of concessions and
trade."

In other words, Lenin explained, these allied soviet republics must
"effect a slower, more cautious and more systematic transition to
socialism."

On the basis of the NEP experience, Lenin drew some general conclusions for Marxist revolutionists in an article written at the end of 1921.
"True revolutionaries have mostly come a cropper," he said, "when they
began to write 'revolution' with a capital R, to elevate 'revolution' to
something almost divine, to lose their heads, to lose the ability to reflect,
weigh and ascertain in the coolest and most dispassionate manner . . . at
what moment, under what circumstances and in which sphere you must
turn to reformist action."

The last two words of Lenin's statement may appear a bit jarring.
What did he mean by recommending "reformist action"? Lenin
explained himself as follows:

"Marxism alone has precisely and correctly defined the relations of reform to revolution, although Marx was able to see this relation from only
one aspect — under the conditions preceding the first to any extent permanent and lasting victory of the proletariat, if only in one country.
Under those conditions," Lenin stressed, "the basis of the proper relation
was that reforms are a by-product of the revolutionary class struggle of
the proletariat. Throughout the capitalist world this relation is the foundation of the revolutionary tactics of the proletariat — the ABC."

After the victory of the proletariat," however, Lenin said, "if only in
one country, something new enters into the relation between reforms and
revolution. In principle, it is the same as before, but a change in form
takes place." Under such conditions, he said, reforms can represent "a
necessary and legitimate breathing space when, after the utmost exertion
of effort, it becomes obvious that sufficient strength is lacking for the
revolutionary accomplishment of some transition or another."

Based on the experience of the world's first proletarian revolution, the
Comintern's fourth congress drew some conclusions about the tasks of a
victorious workers' and farmers' government, which it defined as a government which "is born out of struggle of the masses, is supported by
workers' bodies which are capable of fighting, bodies created by the
most oppressed sections of the working masses."

"The overriding tasks" of such a government, the congress resolution
on tactics explained, "must be to arm the proletariat, to disarm

bourgeois, counterrevolutionary organizations, to introduce the control of production, to transfer the main burden of taxation to the rich, and to break the resistance of the counterrevolutionary bourgeoisie."

Accomplishments of the Grenada Revolution

How had Grenada's workers' and farmers' government measured up to these kinds of challenges during its first four and a half years? The record shows that it had begun to do all this and more. The steps by the New Jewel Movement to dismantle the old state apparatus and army and replace it with a new government, army, and militia have already been explained. What about other political, social, and economic gains?

All of Gairy's repressive legislation was wiped off the books. New laws were adopted making it compulsory for employers to recognize unions and ensuring the right to strike. As a result, membership in the island's trade unions rose from about 30 percent of the labor force before the revolution to some 90 percent. Other organizations won thousands of members, as well. These included the National Women's Organisation, the National Youth Organisation, and the Productive Farmers' Union.

Along with these organizations, other bodies were formed at the initiative of the NJM leadership to begin the hard work of increasing the democratic involvement of working people in determining and administering the affairs of their country. Councils were set up in workplaces, parishes, villages, and neighborhoods. These councils discussed and debated proposed government policies, including the nation's 1982 and 1983 budget and plan. They had the power to summon government ministers and other officials to appear before them to be held accountable for their policies.

The New Jewel Movement leaders understood that these mass organizations and councils could not work miracles. Given the small size of Grenada's working class and the poverty and lack of education bequeathed by centuries of colonial oppression, it would take hard work and consistent attention to achieve effective participation by working people in running the affairs of their society. It was not enough to set up councils, encourage people to attend, and then hope the rest would take care of itself.

In order to focus attention on this important challenge, the New Jewel Movement designated 1983 the Year of Academic and Political Education. In his January 1983 speech launching this, Prime Minister Bishop explained that "our people must develop in the new year a mental grasp on the true nature of the international capitalist crisis which is holding back the progress of our revolution and the development of all poor countries in the world. They must know the causes and origins of this crisis. They must see clearly the link between politics and economics, between imperialist exploitation and persistent poverty, between the mad buildup of arms by imperialism and the economic crisis.

"With their political consciousness raised and broadened," Bishop explained, "our people will better understand the necessity to join and to strengthen those mass organizations and trade unions that already exist. Political education will help to identify from the ranks of our working people the future leaders of the revolution and it will help to prepare the working class to assume its historic role of transforming Grenada from backwardness and dependency to genuine economic independence."

At his public meeting in New York City in June 1983, Bishop announced that preparation of a draft constitution had begun, laying the groundwork for future island-wide elections. These elections, he stressed, would not replace but instead "institutionalize and entrench the systems of popular democracy" already established. The goal was the "involvement of our people in a participatory way from day to day and week to week," not "just the right to put an 'X' next to Tweedledum or Tweedledee" every few years, as in elections in the United States, Canada, Britain, or many East Caribbean islands.

On the economic front, Grenada's workers' and farmers' government had also registered impressive achievements. In 1982 its Gross National Product grew by 5.5 percent, for a total increase of nearly 14 percent since the 1979 revolution. This was at a time when the world capitalist system was suffering its worst downturn since the 1930s and the economies of most countries in the Western Hemisphere, including other Eastern Caribbean islands, were stagnating or declining.

Moreover, in line with the revolution's socialist goals, the state sector was increasingly taking the lead in the island's economic development. The single most ambitious government project was the new international airport to promote tourism and expedite export and import trade. Another priority was upgrading development of the island's agriculture and related "agro-industries." This involved both crop rehabilitation and the construction of factories to process, package, and market these products. Other major projects included new roads, including vital feeder roads to transport farm produce; several dozen buses for the island's first public transportation system; upgrading water, telephone, and electrical services, now all state-owned; and hotel and tourism development.

Whereas Gairy had spent only EC$8 million on such development projects the year before the revolution, the PRG had laid out EC$237 million since March 1979, which is equivalent to almost U.S.$88 million. In 1982, the thirty-two new state-owned enterprises produced about one-quarter of all goods and services on the island.

As Bishop cautioned in the July 1980 interview with *Intercontinental Press*, however, the bottom line for the progress of a workers' and farmers' government has to be measured, "Not in terms of how many industries you have or how many hotels you have when the profits are going to a very tiny elite, but in terms of what benefits are truly getting to the masses." The government, he said, must meet "the basic needs of the population — jobs, health, housing, food, clothing."

Here, too, the Grenada revolution had important accomplishments to its credit.

Real wages had risen by 10 percent over the 1981-82 period. Living standards actually improved more than suggested by this figure. For one thing, unemployment had fallen from about 50 percent to 12 percent during the first four years of the revolution, bringing higher family income. Most important, there had been a dramatic increase in the "social wage" — that is, the vital services and commodities available free or at low cost, as a *right*, to the population. In all, more than one-third of the country's operating budget went to health and education.

A land reform law empowered the government to take out a compulsory ten-year lease on any land above 100 acres that was underutilized to put it into production on a cooperative or state-owned basis. The government had expanded the supply of low-interest loans to small farmers and farm cooperatives and also initiated programs to help guarantee markets for their produce. A state-run tractor pool of forty-five machines was established, and the government sought to advance modern farming by establishing four new agricultural training schools, as well. These measures had begun not only to raise the income of farmers and agricultural workers, but also to provide jobs for the unemployed.

Medical and dental care became free. Medicine was provided without charge for hospital patients and at low cost for others. Clinics were built throughout Grenada, the central hospital modernized, and the number of doctors and dentists more than doubled.

Secondary school became a right for all Grenadians; under Gairy, tuition was required, making education a privilege for the rich. Free books, school uniforms, and hot lunches were provided to elementary school children from low-income families. In addition, hundreds of students received scholarships for university or advanced technical education, never before available to any but the wealthiest Grenadians. An adult education program had already made strides toward combating illiteracy, with the aim of wiping it out by 1985.

Free milk was distributed to thousands of families. Price controls were imposed on basic imported items such as sugar and cooking oil.

Some 75 percent of families had received interest-free loans and low-cost materials to repair their homes. The newly opened Sandino Housing Plant had gone into production with a potential output of 500 prefabricated housing units each year.

Some 30 percent of workers were exempted from taxation altogether, while new taxes and fees were imposed on local companies, import-export merchants, and profits of foreign-owned firms not reinvested in Grenada.

A social insurance plan was set up, Grenada's first on a national scale, covering workers employed in both private and public sectors. Benefits included retirement pensions, sickness and disability pay, maternity benefits, and payments to dependents of the deceased.

Special attention was placed on upgrading the rights and opportunities of Grenadian women. Legislation was adopted and implemented against sexual harassment of working women. Women workers were guaranteed equal pay for equal work. A maternity leave law compelled employers to give time off, most of it at full pay, to women both before and after childbirth.

Social programs such as these were a political choice that followed from the class interests the government defended. These programs were vital to the well-being of Grenadian workers and farmers. Since it is they who produce the island's wealth, their improved health, education, and welfare was an investment in Grenada's most important resource — its working people.

The costs and skills required for these social benefits and development projects would have put them out of reach for many years if Grenada had been limited to its own means. But it received substantial foreign aid. The most generous contributors were the government and people of Cuba. As Fidel Castro explained November 14, "Even though Cuba is a small underdeveloped country, it was able to help Grenada considerably, because our efforts — which were modest in quantity though high in quality — meant a lot for a country less than 400 square kilometers in size, with a population of just over 100,000."

Castro reported that the total over four years amounted to some $550 for every Grenadian. The biggest single Cuban contribution came in the form of materials, equipment, designs, and skilled volunteer construction workers for the Point Salines airport project. But Cuba also provided doctors, teachers, and technicians; financed and constructed the housing plant and other industrial projects; helped establish a fisheries school and fishing fleet; and assisted in training a professional army to safeguard the revolution's gains.

Other assistance came from Libya, Syria, the Soviet Union, several Eastern European workers' states, and North Korea. The U.S. government not only refused aid to Grenada, but also sought to prevent other capitalist governments and international financial institutions from providing any. Despite such sabotage, Grenada did get considerable help from the European Development Bank and from the Canadian and other governments.

Early on in the revolution, a U.S. diplomat offered Grenada a paltry

$5,000 — *if* the new government pledged not to develop economic or diplomatic relations with Cuba. The Grenadian revolutionists indignantly rejected this blackmail. Prime Minister Bishop gave a speech to the island's working people explaining that while the new government wanted cordial relations with Washington, "Grenada is no longer in anybody's backyard!" Grenada was a sovereign nation, he said, and would make up its own mind about both its affairs at home and its friends abroad.

From the start, the revolutionary government pursued an internationalist course. It established the warmest fraternal bonds with the government, leadership, and people of revolutionary Cuba and Nicaragua. Despite its own pressing tasks and limited cadres, the PRG sent young volunteer Grenadians to help with the literacy crusade on Nicaragua's English-speaking Atlantic Coast. It mobilized and educated Grenadians in solidarity with liberation struggles in the Caribbean and Central America, South America, Africa, Asia, the Mideast, and throughout the world. It joined the Movement of Nonaligned Countries. It established diplomatic and trade relations with Vietnam, the Soviet Union, the Eastern European workers' states, and North Korea.

"Because our own struggle is internationalist," Bishop said during the July 1980 interview, "we have over the years been giving our fullest support to all international causes that demand such support. We see that as our internationalist duty."

Washington Seeks "To Wipe Out All Vestiges"

These accomplishments set an example for the entire Caribbean and Central America, for Blacks and other working people in the United States, Britain, and Canada, and for the oppressed and exploited everywhere. They vindicated Fidel Castro's description of Grenada as "a big revolution in a small country." With each passing year, not only did Grenada's achievements grow, but also their power of attraction beyond its shores. Despite capitalist media efforts to blockade the truth, more and more people were learning about and being inspired by the Grenada revolution. Prime Minister Bishop's visit to the United States in June 1983 had a political impact on a small but important layer of U.S. working people, and a vanguard section of the Black population.

In order to stop the spread of this example, Washington was determined from day one to crush the Grenada revolution by armed might. The military and political groundwork for such aggression began to be laid by Carter's Democratic Party administration and continued under the Republican Reagan. U.S. military forces staged a trial run on a tiny island off Puerto Rico in 1981. This mock invasion was transparently named Operation Amber and the Amberdines, to echo the actual island chain of Grenada and the Grenadines. Even the pretexts for the practice invasion were the same as Reagan's phony justification in October 1983 — alleged danger to U.S. citizens, influence from a nearby "Country Red" (clearly Cuba), and a government that had destroyed democracy on "Amber" Island and was exporting subversion throughout the region.

Despite U.S. claims that it was "invited" into Grenada by the Organization of East Caribbean States, Prime Minister Tom Adams of Barbados admitted that the OECS governments were contacted about the operation by U.S. officials at the time Bishop's house arrest first became known. The invasion would have been carried out by the bipartisan cabal in Washington regardless of how many East Caribbean states agreed to "ask for it."

Having now carried out this invasion that has been in the works for four years, U.S. imperialism is setting about to use whatever force is necessary to dismantle every trace of the political, social, and economic accomplishments of the workers' and farmers' government.

Several days following the invasion, Don Rojas, an NJM leader who was Bishop's press secretary, told a British newspaper that Grenada would be "rapidly colonized" by the U.S. occupiers. "I think they will move very quickly to wipe out all vestiges of the revolution," Rojas said. "The local councils and other democratic structures that we put in place will be dismantled and kept that way by military force."

Washington intends to smash everything that remains from the revolution and to reimpose a puppet government directly subservient to U.S. imperialist interests. And that's exactly what it has been doing.

The central targets have been the cadres of the New Jewel Movement and mass organizations, whose consciousness remains the most durable conquest of the revolution. The occupiers are carrying out a systematic effort to intimidate and break these cadres, who numbered in the tens of thousands, especially in the working class and among the youth.

Support for the 1979 revolution and its gains remains strong on the island, posing a big problem for the occupiers. Due to the widespread disorientation caused by the Coard group's treachery and murderous violence against NJM leaders and the Grenadian people, many Grenadians mistakenly welcomed the U.S. troops as liberators. Even the big majority of these Grenadians, however, consider themselves supporters of Maurice Bishop and the People's Revolutionary Government — a fact that has perplexed reporters for the capitalist press.

"Will there still be free education in the schools?" asked one young Grenadian woman quoted by a U.S. newspaper. "Will there still be aid to buy [school] uniforms and books?"

"Some people here are beginning to ask themselves who is going to rescue us from our rescuers," another Grenadian reported.

The process of repression and dismantling began with the October 25 invasion itself — so much so that the U.S. government slapped a ban on press coverage of these initial days of terror. That has been followed by the arrest, detention, and grilling of more than 2,000 Grenadians, who were held in small wooden crates that they had to crawl into on their knees. Those who were released were given cards warning them to "refrain from participating in any anti-government activities." An unknown number have been jailed indefinitely.

Kenrick Radix, a leader of the New Jewel Movement who survived Coard's murder machine, was picked up by U.S. authorities and held for twenty hours in one of these isolation boxes. The occupiers claimed that Radix had been acting as "an instigator in spreading bad will among the people in public places." In other words, he had exercised his right to denounce the U.S. invasion and to call for immediate withdrawal of the occupiers in order to remove "the heavy boot of U.S. imperialism" from the neck of the Grenadian people.

A purge and blacklist of government employees has begun, based on CIA computer printouts. The U.S.-imposed puppet regime of British Commonwealth Governor-General Paul Scoon has curtailed political rights. The new government, allegedly needed to restore "democracy" to Grenada, quickly announced that even its trumpeted phony elections might not be held for several years.

The occupiers' degrading treatment of Coard and Gen. Hudson Austin, who are understandably hated by the Grenadian people, is nonetheless also aimed at intimidating supporters of the revolution. Coard and Austin were paraded half naked, blindfolded, and manacled on the island. U.S. military propaganda teams plastered Grenada with posters, printed in the United States, showing Austin with just a towel around his waist; below it was an anticommunist message. Coard and Austin deserve to be brought to justice for their crimes, but by the working people of Grenada, not in a kangaroo court set up by a U.S.-imposed puppet regime.

Along with this repression, initial steps have already been taken to strip the Grenadian people of the social and economic gains of the revolution. Free and low-cost distribution of milk and other necessities has ended. Adult education centers are shut down. Schools and hospitals have been deprived of teachers and doctors by the expulsion of Cuban and other overseas staff people. Unemployment has already doubled. And any remnants of mass organizations and democratic workplace and community councils are being crushed.

This is what it takes to try to stamp out the vestiges of Grenada's workers' and farmers' government and the popular revolution on which it stood.

Coard's Treachery and Betrayal

As already explained, Washington was able to carry off this counter-revolutionary onslaught with such apparent ease because the Grenadian workers' and farmers' government had been betrayed and overthrown. As surviving NJM leader George Louison put it, "the revolution was destroyed from within." Fidel Castro devoted a substantial portion of his November 14 speech to explaining the significance of this fact to the Cuban people and to revolutionists elsewhere in the Americas and throughout the world.

"Hyenas emerged from the revolutionary ranks," said Castro, referring to Coard's secret faction in the government, army, and New Jewel Movement.

"Were those who conspired against [Bishop] within the Grenadian party, army, and security forces by any chance a group of extremists drunk on political theory?" he asked. "Were they simply a group of ambitious, opportunistic individuals, or were they enemy agents who wanted to destroy the Grenadian revolution?

"History alone will have the last word," Castro said, "but it would not be the first time that such things occurred in a revolutionary process."

Castro is correct. Many details of the secret plotting and motivations of those involved may never be known. But Castro is also correct to explain that the most important facts and lessons *are* already known, and do not depend on yet unanswered questions.

"The fact is that allegedly revolutionary arguments were used," Castro said, "invoking the purest principles of Marxism-Leninism and charging Bishop with practicing a cult of personality and with drawing away from the Leninist norms and methods of leadership."

Castro correctly condemned these charges as "absurd." He explained how the capitalist press had made use of them to present the events in Grenada "as the coming to power of a group of hard-line communists, loyal allies of Cuba. Were they really communists?" Castro asked. "Were they really hard-liners? Could they really be loyal allies of Cuba? Or were they rather conscious or unconscious tools of Yankee imperialism?

"Look at the history of the revolutionary movement," Castro said, "and you will find more than one connection between imperialism and those who take positions that appear to be on the extreme left. Aren't Pol Pot and Ieng Sary — the ones responsible for the genocide in Kampuchea — the most loyal allies Yankee imperialism has in Southeast Asia at present?

"In Cuba, ever since the Grenadian crisis began," he said, "we have called Coard's group — to give it a name — the 'Pol Pot group.' "

Much of what happened in Grenada has been clarified in press interviews with surviving NJM and PRG leaders such as Don Rojas, Kenrick Radix, and George Louison, who have also given assessments of these events.*

A semisecret factional grouping or clique around Bernard Coard had managed, especially since mid-1982, to strengthen its influence and control inside the government apparatus, the officer corps of the army, and in the New Jewel Movement. It functioned more and more as a party within the party.

This grouping thrived on seeking to pin the blame for the revolution's very real difficulties on Bishop and other NJM leaders not in their faction, rather than trying to solve these problems and iron out differences in the course of loyal leadership collaboration and common practical work. Instead of functioning on the basis of political, objective, frank, honest, and selfless relations inside the leadership, the Coard group consolidated its position through favoritism, buddyism, privilege, and administrative control.

Coard's ability to carry out his catastrophic bid for power, if only for a few weeks, was not a matter of Lucifer somehow running amok amid the heavenly host. A materialist explanation for what happened in Grenada cannot rise or fall simply on an assessment of the actions of a single individual — even an individual whose role was unquestionably decisive. These events reflected the social consequences of objective difficulties from imperialist pressure, poverty, and small size already described. Coard exploited these real difficulties to gain a hearing from layers of politically inexperienced cadres in the NJM for his explanation that "the problem is Maurice."

In any revolution confronting such obstacles, the resulting pressures bear down with a different intensity and results on various social classes and layers within the working class itself. A small hotel owner is affected differently from a working person; a farmer differently from a

* Substantial quotations from interviews with Louison and Radix appeared in articles by Edward Cody in the November 9, 1983, *Wasington Post* and by Thomas E. Ricks in the November 8 *Wall Street Journal.* Radix was interviewed by Paul McIsaac for an article that appeared in the November 23 issue of New York's *Village Voice.* Articles in the October 31 *Washington Post* and October 30 *Sunday Sun* of Barbados centered on interviews with Rojas, and a major interview with Rojas appeared in the December 26 issue of *Intercontinental Press.* Articles by Morris S. Thompson interviewing Louison appeared in the November 6 and 7 issues of Long Island's *Newsday.* Articles based on interviews with Louison, Radix, and Lyden Ramdhanny, another PRG member, appeared in the November 6 issue of the *Sunday Guardian* of Trinidad. In addition, Louison conducted an extensive but yet-unpublished interview with a group visiting Grenada in mid-November sponsored by the Canadian University Service Organization (CUSO).

wage worker; a highly paid worker differently from one who has more directly benefited from the revolution's social achievements; and a person who has settled into a comfortable niche in the government apparatus differently from someone more closely attuned to the masses of the population. While there is no mechanical correlation between such underlying social differentiations and the lineup that developed inside the party, state apparatus, and army in Grenada, the strongest base of support for Bishop and the revolutionary government clearly came from working people, especially among the youth. Coard and his followers had become divorced from the Grenadian people and reflected attitudes of bureaucratism, careerism, and individual ambition characteristic of the petty bourgeoisie, not the working class.

It is important to add that CIA agents were undoubtedly operating at every level of the Grenadian government, army, party, and mass organizations, as they always do in any revolution or revolutionary organization. Nonetheless, imperialism and its agents did not create the divisions inside the revolutionary leadership. Instead, they were able to take advantage of weaknesses already there to exacerbate tensions and turn divisions to their own advantage.

The petty-bourgeois and bureaucratic modes of functioning by the Coard faction in the government, army, and party — not any thought-out alternative political course for Grenada — were at the root of this group's trajectory. Nonetheless, Fidel Castro chose his words well November 14 when he spoke of this outfit as the "Pol Pot group."

The point is not to imply that Coard was hell-bent on a wholesale expropriation policy, let alone on the extraordinarily brutal anti-working-class, antipeasant, and antisocialist measures imposed by Pol Pot.

As Don Rojas explained, however, "Bernard and his people . . . said they were dissatisfied with the pace at which the process was evolving. . . . Somehow the notion that this process was not going fast enough entered into the ideological discussion in the party and led to a kind of cleavage. Some people said we needed to push it forward more rapidly. Others argued for a more rational, scientific, and less idealistic assessment of this question."

Rojas said that this criticism had emerged rather suddenly, and that Coard himself had previously argued against such notions as the government's chief economic planning official.

Rather than recognizing *politically* that objective material conditions and class relations were above all responsible for the problems confronting the revolution in Grenada, Coard's followers acted as if it were somehow possible to leap over these factors in an *administrative* way.

The Coard and Pol Pot groups also shared, to however different an extent, a similar ultraleft, antidemocratic, and authoritarian brutality toward the workers and farmers. Unlike Bishop and other NJM leaders,

Coard's relations with the Grenadian workers and farmers were not based on promoting their organization, mobilization, and class consciousness, but on administrative dictates and persuasion of the gun.

To justify its maneuvers against Bishop, Whiteman, Radix, and other NJM leaders who did not share its penchant for dictates and commands, the Coard group began a campaign of gossip alleging that these individuals were "less Marxist" and "less proletarian." Suddenly, Rojas said, "we hear Maurice Bishop accused of being petty bourgeois. We hear Unison Whiteman accused of being social democratic, of representing the right wing within the party. This was the first time we heard that there was a right wing within the party."

Rojas explained that the Organization of Revolutionary Education and Liberation, the name of the organization forming the core of Coard's faction, went back to before the NJM was founded. In the early 1970s it had merged with Bishop's MAP and Whiteman's JEWEL to form the party, Rojas said, but "always maintained a kind of clique, an OREL clique, within the New Jewel Movement during the 1970s and even after the 1979 revolution."

In any genuine fusion of political organizations, it quickly becomes irrelevant who among the leadership and cadres of the new organization had his or her origins in one group or another. No one makes political judgments or assignments on the basis of whether or not someone in the party used to be "one of our people." While the MAP and JEWEL cadres had carried out such a successful fusion, it is now clear that Coard's OREL grouping had never adopted this attitude toward the New Jewel Movement.

Coard's campaign against Bishop and other NJM leaders took several concrete forms.

On one level, capable leaders of the revolution who were not Coard's "kind of guy" were pushed out of the leadership. Kenrick Radix, for example, was removed from the Central Committee. At the same time, Coard gradually managed to get more and more of his supporters onto the leadership bodies and into the apparatus of the party, the government, and the army. "He did this in a very systematic way," Rojas said, "so that when he decided to make his move for leadership of the party, he had already consolidated quite a power base."

In mid-1982, Coard and those around him began to complain about serious problems inside the party. In July 1982 Coard resigned from the Central Committee, attributing his decision to "slack and weak functioning" of the CC and the Political Bureau. He said that both leadership bodies were operating contrary to Marxist-Leninist principles of party building.

Charges began to be heard that Bishop's alleged political shallowness, lack of Leninist organizational skills and discipline, and insufficient grasp of party-building strategy and tactics were to blame for the "crisis" in the NJM. Coard himself, having stepped aside, never explicitly mentioned Bishop, leaving that to his collaborators. As Radix put it, "What he did was to hide behind his wife [Phyllis, who remained a CC member] and some of the younger fellows to work his way. Coard used slander, rumor, and deceit to slander Maurice. The worst of Stalinist tactics."

This campaign went on for more than a year. Then, in September 1983, an emergency meeting of the Central Committee was called together by Maj. Liam James, a follower of Coard in the army officer corps and a member of General Austin's shortlived "Revolutionary Military Council." Bernard Coard was not there, since he had resigned from the Central Committee.

Lt. Col. Ewart Layne, another Coard supporter in the army and later RMC member, opened the meeting. Layne explained that there was a big crisis in the country — lagging popular support, problems in the party, bad roads and electricity services, a deterioration of the revolution's international prestige, and so on. Phyllis Coard and Minister of Mobilization Selwyn Strachan, who also emerged as a Coard supporter, again spoke of the weakness in the Marxist-Leninist ideological development of the Central Committee.

According to George Louison, the initial portion of the meeting did not involve direct criticisms of Bishop, but discussion later shifted in that direction. James, Layne, and Maj. Leon Cornwall, also a Coard supporter and later RMC member, got the ball rolling. Phyllis Coard chimed in that many NJM members were scared to criticize Bishop, because he had been "hostile to criticism."

According to Louison, however, it was not until the last day of the two-and-a-half day meeting that "out of the blue a proposal came out: The main problem within the Central Committee is Maurice's weaknesses." No alternative political policies were put forward by Coard's supporters, Louison said.

Instead, Liam James placed a motion on the floor calling for Bishop to relinquish part of his leadership responsibilities to Coard. Bishop was to handle mass work and international relations; his strengths were allegedly limited to those arenas. Bernard Coard was to take over internal party work and overall strategy, since he was the "only" person who could "push the process forward."

Whiteman and Louison argued that the Central Committee should take collective responsibility for the problems facing the revolution, not attempt to place the blame on Bishop or any other single comrade in the leadership. Along with Bishop, they pointed to the material conditions in Grenada as the source of many difficulties, and stressed the need for more systematic efforts to strengthen relations between the party, the government, and the workers and farmers in Grenada.

When Louison asked how such an important change would be explained to the Grenadian people and to fraternal political parties, Coard's supporters answered that the decision would remain an internal secret of the NJM. Nothing would be said to the Grenadian people or other parties.

Of the thirteen members of the seventeen-person Central Committee in attendance, nine voted for this so-called joint leadership resolution; three abstained, including Bishop and Whiteman; and one — Louison — voted against.

Several more Central Committee meetings took place during the latter half of September; Coard began to attend. It was agreed that Bishop would take some time to consider the joint leadership proposal, and he did not attend most of these late September CC meetings. According to Louison, from that time on, Coard was actually "calling the shots." At a September 25 CC meeting, Bishop agreed to the joint leadership motion, "subject to clarification," Louison said.

Rojas, who although not a Central Committee member nonetheless worked very closely with Bishop, expanded on Bishop's attitude toward the CC proposal. "His position to the Central Committee," Rojas said, "and to the party was that he did not have any problems with the proposal in principle — that if it was a majority decision of the party, he would abide by the principle of democratic centralism and majority vote on this issue.

"But he would have liked more discussion of the practical application of this joint leadership proposal. He had difficulty understanding exactly how it was going to work, as did many members of the party. . . . And he felt, quite frankly, that the way it had been proposed would have effectively removed him from influence in the top decision-making organs of the party."

Bishop's attitude to the Coard group's talk about "more Leninist" functioning of the party was similar. "Maurice and the rest of the comrades had absolutely no difficulty in accepting the concept," Rojas said, "if it meant a more disciplined and more organized approach to party work; to the norms of party life; to study; to the application of the fundamental principles on which the party was built; to an understanding of democratic centralism," and so on.

"But I think Lenin was being used as a cover," Rojas said. "It appears that the call for a more Leninist organization was misused to cover up what was in its essence a bid for power."

At the end of September, Bishop, Whiteman, Louison, and Rojas left for Hungary and Czechoslovakia to try to obtain some additional electrical power generators for the island. It was then, Louison explained, that the Coard group took advantage of Bishop being out of the country to begin systematically disarming the militias. Coard and his followers knew what was coming, and they also knew that their base was in the army officer corps and a few trusted units, not in the armed workers and farmers of Grenada.

Bishop and the three other NJM leaders stopped in Cuba for a few days on his return trip from Eastern Europe. Castro explained in his November 14 speech that during this stopover, "In spite of his very close and affectionate links with our party's leadership, Bishop never said anything about the internal dissensions that were developing. On the contrary, in his last conversation with us he was self-critical about his work regarding attention to the armed forces and the mass organizations. Nearly all of our party and state leaders spent many friendly, fraternal hours with him on the evening of October 7, before his return trip to Grenada."

Contrary to all previous practice, only one other leader of the NJM and PRG was on hand at the airport to meet Bishop when he landed in Grenada October 8. For the next two days, Bernard Coard, who had served as acting prime minister during the trip, made no effort to contact Bishop about developments in the country during his absence.

When Coard learned of the meetings in Cuba with Castro and other top CP leaders, however, he charged that Bishop, Louison, Whiteman, and Rojas had taken internal NJM affairs outside the party and had sought to obtain Cuban backing for their position. The four NJM leaders denied this charge.

Coard and his backers "went so far as to say Fidel had made himself a little god in Cuba," Louison reported, implying that this was happening in Grenada as well. This marked the opening salvo of a new campaign against Bishop, this one centering on his alleged "one-manism" and the dangers of a personality cult.

"That was perhaps the weakest charge of all," Rojas commented. "The people who knew Maurice Bishop knew him to be perhaps the most modest and least arrogant of all the top leaders of the party. He was the most accommodating and probably the number one adherent to the principle of collective leadership."

As a result of these developments, according to Louison, Bishop informed other members of the Central Committee that he would like to schedule a review in the CC or the Political Bureau of the joint leadership proposal and its practical application and consequences.

Then, on October 12, a chain of events was set into motion that would result, before the day was out, in a de facto coup and the overthrow of Grenada's workers' and farmers' government.

Those events began just after midnight, when Bishop's security detail was awakened and brought together for a meeting while Bishop was sleeping. According to Louison, they were told that Bishop was "becoming a dictator" and that "their responsibility is to defend the working people and not to defend any leader." This was the set-up for Bishop's house arrest, which was to come later in the day.

At 7 a.m., the members of the New Jewel Movement in the army met and passed a resolution claiming that Bishop and Louison were trying to reverse the earlier Central Committee decision and demanding that these "opportunists" be expelled from the party.

At 9 a.m., the New Jewel Movement Political Bureau met. The two main points on its agenda were discussion of the armed forces resolution, and a motion to expel Louison from the Political Bureau and Central Committee for alleged violations of democratic centralism.

Later in the day, the Central Committee met. It expelled George Louison, and members leveled yet another charge against Bishop. They claimed that Bishop was spreading a rumor that Bernard and Phyllis Coard were plotting to kill him. Louison stated that this "was a complete lie . . . made up by Bernard in order to try to justify his position." Rojas and Radix agree.

The Central Committee demanded that Bishop tape a radio statement that the alleged rumor was untrue, which Bishop did. At the end of the meeting, the CC voted to place Bishop under house arrest. His phones were cut off, and any security guards suspected of loyalty to him were disarmed and replaced. George Louison's brother, Einstein Louison — who as the army chief of staff was the highest officer not lined up with Coard's grouping — was also placed under house arrest.

As news of Bishop's detention began to leak out to the workers and farmers of Grenada, the walls began to be covered with the slogan, "No Bishop, No Revo." And that immediate and widespread sentiment among the masses reflected the reality. The workers' and farmers' government that they had established in March 1979 had been overthrown through a coup that day.

The next day, October 13, a meeting of 400 New Jewel Movement cadres was held. Bishop was brought before it, confronted with the false charges, especially the alleged rumor, and told to comment on them. Bishop strongly denied having spread the rumor.

Coard, who attended the meeting, did not speak. Once again, he let his supporters do the dirty work. One after another, they took the floor to denounce Bishop. "They called him a dangerous individual," Louison recalled. Rojas reported that proposals were made to expel Bishop from the party altogether, even to court-martial him.

"We all thought certainly the point of the meeting was to vote on the question and come up with some consensus within the party," Rojas said, "some line of march to explain to the masses why Maurice Bishop was being placed under house arrest."

But no vote was taken on the proposals. Coard's group on the Central

Committee explained that the purpose of the meeting was to inform the members of actions already taken by the CC so they could begin taking these decisions to the population the following day.

The atmosphere at the meeting was "intimidating, really intimidating," Louison said. "Maurice's head has already rolled and so has mine. These would be good deterrents to further offenses."

Bishop was returned to house arrest following the meeting.

On the next day, October 14, Coard's supporters began meeting with various groups from the mass organizations, workplaces, and other sectors to justify their actions. Selwyn Strachan, for example, tried to hold a public meeting in downtown St. George's to announce that Bishop had been replaced as prime minister by Coard. A crowd gathered and chased Strachan off the street. A little later that day, Radio Free Grenada announced that Coard had resigned as deputy prime minister and finance minister in order to "clear the air" of the rumor that he was plotting to assassinate Bishop.

These events on October 14 were the first to be reported in the international press. From then on, Bernard and Phyllis Coard and Strachan evidently decided to lay low for a while, hoping to weather the storm of popular opposition — the depth of which they had misjudged — before making further public appearances. They were not heard about publicly again until the U.S. invasion and their subsequent arrest.

The following day, October 15, Kenrick Radix, together with union leader Fitzroy Bain, led the first street demonstration demanding the release of Bishop and his reinstatement as prime minister. And George Louison began a series of private meetings with Coard, hoping to find some way to resolve the worsening situation.

According to the Cuban government, Fidel Castro sent a message to the NJM Central Committee that day, as well. It was delivered directly to Coard. While Cuba had no intention of interfering in Grenada's internal affairs, the message said, Castro expressed his "deep concern that the division that had arisen could do considerable damage to the image of the revolutionary process in Grenada, both inside the country and abroad," including in Cuba. But Coard took no heed of the Cubans' concerns.

"This group of Coard's that seized power in Grenada expressed serious reservations toward Cuba from the very beginning," Castro explained in the November 14 speech, "because of our well-known and unquestionable friendship with Bishop."

On October 16, Gen. Hudson Austin gave a speech over Radio Free Grenada, attempting to diffuse and demobilize the mounting protest evidenced by the reaction to Strachan and the street demonstration. He now sought to reassure Grenadians that Bishop was not being challenged as prime minister, and that Bishop was just "at home and quite safe."

Then Austin got down to the actual point of the radio address — to present the slanders against Bishop for the first time publicly. The NJM, Austin said, had voted to expel Bishop from the party in order "to stop the steady growth of one-man rule in our party and country." The lie about the rumor and the other false charges were also repeated. Bishop had "disgraced" Grenada by these actions, Austin said, and had been expelled from the New Jewel Movement. At the same time, Austin stressed that "there has been no dispute" over the "political and economic policies of the party."

On October 18, Radix led a second street protest, following which he was picked up and jailed by Coard's backers. Unison Whiteman, who was foreign minister, returned to Grenada from the United States, where he had spoken before the United Nations General Assembly the previous week; he immediately began working with Louison, still in hopes of reaching a settlement with Coard. But the uncontrolled as well as controlled forces set in motion October 12 had already shattered that possibility.

Coard and his group "were completely contemptuous of the Grenadian people," Louison later said. "They believed that no matter what action they took, they could eventually explain it away." The Grenadian people "are bound to get tired and hungry," Coard told Louison, and then they would stop marching and go back to work. Things would return to normal. Gairy had let people demonstrate every day for almost two months straight in 1973-74, Coard reminded him.

Up until that point, Louison said, "I still believed a peaceful solution was possible." On October 18, however, he became convinced that the opposite was the case. "There was a distinct wing of the Central Committee that wanted a military solution," Louison explained. "That I'm clear of because I discussed it with them."

Whiteman called a Caribbean press agency later that day and announced that he, Louison, housing minister Norris Bain, and education minister Jacqueline Creft had all resigned from the government. Shortly afterwards, George Louison was jailed.

Then came October 19 — Coard's Bloody Wednesday. Unison Whiteman and Fitzroy Bain led another demonstration, this one of 5,000, while another 25,000-30,000 waited in the market place for Bishop to speak. That amounted to some 25-30 percent of Grenada's entire population, comparable to 60-75 million in the United States. The demonstrators went to Bishop's residence and managed to free him. Rojas spoke with Bishop, the last living NJM leader to have done so. He reports that Bishop told him that "those criminals up on the hill" were going to turn their guns on the people and that the people "must disarm them" first.

Bishop asked Rojas to lead a contingent to the central telephone exchange and to communicate several messages to the world. He asked Rojas to call on Grenadians overseas and on trade unions and progressive forces in the region to make known their support for the people's mass outpouring that day.

Rojas said that Bishop was concerned about efforts by a small handful of right-wingers in Grenada to use the protests against his house arrest as an opportunity to spread anti-Cuban and anticommunist propaganda. According to Rojas, Bishop "wanted the point made very clearly that President Fidel Castro and the Cuban people had absolutely no involvement in this crisis," and that nothing that might happen in Grenada should serve as a justification for U.S. intervention.

The mass demonstration marched to Fort Rupert, the army headquarters. Most of the soldiers in the garrison joined in the protest, turning over their weapons to members of the militia in the crowd. The plan was to arrange some kind of telephone hookup from inside the fort by which Bishop could address the Grenadian people over a public address system.

This was the last effort by Bishop, Whiteman, and other central New Jewel Movement leaders to salvage the revolution and restore a workers' and farmers' government to power. They sought to appeal to the army to refuse orders and, together with the people, to rise up and overthrow the illegitimate Coard regime that had strangled the revolutionary government. The response of the soldiers at Fort Rupert showed that this might well have happened if there had been sufficient time to get out Bishop's call for resistance and begin organizing on that basis. This attempt by Bishop was the only possible revolutionary course under the circumstances.

Shortly after the crowd arrived at Fort Rupert, however, Coard ordered three armored personnel carriers to the garrison. They fired automatic weapons into the crowd, killing an unknown number of participants and wounding many others. Bishop, Whiteman, Fitzroy Bain, Norris Bain, Jacqueline Creft, and union leader Vincent Noel surrendered themselves peacefully, in order to avoid a wholesale massacre. They were separated from the rest of the crowd and summarily murdered inside the fort.

"I am 100 percent sure [that Coard] ordered the killings," Louison later said. Radix agreed. Despite the fact that Coard dropped from public view hoping to deflect the Grenadian people's wrath, Radix said, "I want to make clear that the RMC [the Revolutionary Military Council officially headed by General Austin] was an extension of Bernard Coard. . . . He devised the thing."

These are the events, to the extent they are known at this time, that surrounded the overthrow of the workers' and farmers' government in Grenada. Coard's secret faction had moved from ambition and cliquism, to open treachery and betrayal of the revolution, and then to the murder of the revolutionary people and their leadership.

In the process, as Rojas put it, Coard handed Grenada "on a platter to the U.S. with all the trimmings." That is why the resistance by Grenadians to the U.S. invasion was limited — although, as Castro explained November 14, "despite these adverse circumstances, a number of Grenadian soldiers died in heroic combat against the invaders." Coard's actions are responsible for the confusion among many Grenadians about the counterrevolutionary goals of the U.S. intervention, as well for the fact that some Grenadians who had supported the revolution have now fallen for the lie, peddled both by Coard and the imperialists, that the betrayers were the "real Marxists."

With the arrest of Bishop, the U.S. rulers immediately recognized that this was the opening they had been waiting for, the chance to crush everything that was left of the revolution and the mass organizations. They had to move quickly to prevent a civil war from developing and the emergence of a new leadership of the New Jewel Movement that could topple the Coard regime and reestablish a revolutionary government. Radix, Louison, and Rojas are all convinced that the revolutionary majority in Grenada had at least a fighting chance of doing just that had Washington not invaded.

Of course, the United States government could have moved to crush the revolution militarily even if these events had not occurred. Perhaps it even could have succeeded, although that was far from certain. But the strength of the revolution had stayed Washington's hands for more than four years, and an invasion was not inevitable in the foreseeable future. Moreover, the political and military price that U.S. imperialism would have paid for such an assault would have been very high. As anyone who had visited Grenada and witnessed the popular commitment to that revolution can testify, the workers and farmers would have put up a mighty battle to defend *their* government.

But that government had been overthrown, and the people disarmed and demobilized. Coard's factionalism and splitting operation threw a decisive and fatal weight into the balance, tipping it toward Washington.

Cuba's Internationalist Leadership and Role

There is another important factor that would have weighed in favor of the Grenada revolution had not Coard toppled the revolutionary government. That is the help that Cuba could have rendered in the event of a U.S. invasion. The Cubans had long made clear their commitment to do whatever was necessary and possible to defend Grenada. Bishop told the May Day 1980 rally in Havana that, "Certainly we in Grenada will never forget that it was the military assistance of Cuba in the first weeks of the revolution that provided us with the basis to defend our own revolution."

At a press conference in Havana late at night October 25-26, just after the U.S. invasion, and again more briefly in his November 14 speech, Fidel Castro explained how the Cuban government had conducted itself in the days leading up to the aggression. Earlier, on October 20, the day after the murder of Bishop, the Cuban government had issued a public condemnation of the criminal actions by the so-called Revolutionary Military Council.

The Cuban revolutionists released these public statements not only to make clear their own position, but also because they recognized their responsibility to lead the working class and oppressed on a world scale, explaining these treacherous actions and laying out a perspective for supporters of the Grenada revolution.

While explaining that Coard's actions had made a U.S. invasion virtually inevitable, the Cubans conducted themselves in such a way as to make the U.S. imperialists pay the biggest possible price for such aggression. They sought to place the workers and farmers of Nicaragua, El Salvador, and Cuba in the best situation to defend their revolutions in the face of this escalation of U.S. military intervention in the region.

Despite the avalanche of bourgeois press smears throughout the Grenada events, the Cuban government and its leaders won international respect and recognition for their exemplary conduct. Many people today understand more clearly than before the revolutionary character and importance of the Cuban leadership in world politics. This has increased the authority of the Cuban revolution in sectors of the Black movement in the United States, for example.

Because of the significance of these October 20, October 25, and November 14 Cuban documents, all three have been reproduced here as appendices to this collection, *Maurice Bishop Speaks*. In these statements, the Cubans explained several fundamental principles of their proletarian internationalist approach to world politics.

First, the Cubans stressed that their international policy is based on the principle of noninterference in the internal affairs of other parties, governments, and countries. Whatever relations or agreements they enter into are only at the request of those parties and governments — with no political strings attached. The Cubans do not try to pick and choose among leaders, to pit them against each other, or to impose policies. They give advice with generosity, but only when it is asked for, and only as advice, never dictates.

"It is to our revolution's credit," Castro explained November 14, "that, in spite of our profound indignation over Bishop's removal from office and arrest, we fully refrained from interfering in Grenada's internal affairs. We refrained even though our construction workers and all our other cooperation personnel in Grenada — who did not hesitate to

confront the Yankee soldiers with the weapons Bishop himself had given
them for their defense in case of an attack from abroad — could have
been a decisive factor in those internal events.

"Those weapons," Castro explained, "were never meant to be used in
an internal conflict in Grenada and we would never have allowed them
to be so used. We would never have been willing to use them to shed a
single drop of Grenadian blood."

Second, the Cubans explained that despite their own limited resources, they do whatever they can to aid peoples throughout the world
who are oppressed by imperialism or engaged in struggle against it. In
his speech November 14, Fidel Castro stressed that despite Cuba's attitude toward Coard's government in Grenada, "We could not accept the
idea of leaving the Grenadians without doctors or leaving the airport,
which was vital to the nation's economy, unfinished."

Especially after Washington's dispatch of its naval armada to the seas
off Grenada, Castro said, the Cubans "couldn't psssibly leave the country. If the imperialists really intended to attack Grenada, it was our duty
to stay there. To withdraw at that time would have been dishonorable
and could have even triggered aggression in that country then and in
Cuba later on."

Under the impossible circumstances created by Coard's group, however, the Cuban government made the correct and necessary decision
that Cuban personnel would fight only if attacked by U.S. invading
forces. On October 22, the Cuban government sent a message with these
instructions to its mission in Grenada, to be communicated to the Cuban
construction workers and other personnel on the island. "We would thus
be defending ourselves," that message said, "not the [new Grenadian]
government and its deeds."

That same day Cuba sent a message to the Revolutionary Military
Council, rejecting an appeal by General Austin for additional military
aid. In a message to its embassy in Grenada the following day, the
Cuban government explained its decision to reject this request. It
pointed out that the members of the Revolutionary Military Council
"themselves are the only ones responsible for the creation of this disadvantageous and difficult situation for the revolutionary process politically and militarily." (Coard's group was spreading the slanderous
charge that blame for the impending U.S. aggression lay with Cuba because of its October 20 statement condemning the murder of Bishop.)

In its reply to the RMC leaders themselves, the Cuban government
stressed that while rejecting the military request, Cuba would conduct a
vigorous international political campaign to counter the U.S. threats. If
the invasion nonetheless took place, the Cubans said, it would be the
duty of the RMC officials "to die fighting, no matter how difficult and
disadvantageous the circumstances may be" — a duty they showed no

inclination to carry out. "It is noteworthy," Don Rojas explained, "that the fifteen members of the RMC and Coard, Strachan, and Austin all either surrendered to the Yankee invaders or were captured without resistance. This was the same group who . . . called on the Grenadian people to fight 'to the last man, woman, and child.' "

When the U.S. attack began, Cuban relations with the Coard-Austin government were so strained that there was no coordination between the Grenadian army and the Cuban construction workers. The Cuban volunteers, as instructed, began fighting only when attacked by the U.S. forces, and then they fought heroically and well. They gave their lives to provide Washington a small example of what would happen if U.S. forces invade El Salvador, Nicaragua, or Cuba.

"Not The First Time"

As Fidel Castro explained in Havana November 14, what took place in Grenada at Coard's hands was not "the first time that such things occurred in a revolutionary process."

Cuban Marxists have had their own direct experience, in 1962 and again in 1966-68, with the types of methods employed by Coard, and the dangers posed by them.

At the end of 1961, the July 26 Movement — which had led the workers and peasants to victory and to the consolidation of the first workers' state in the Americas — fused with the Popular Socialist Party (PSP), the traditional prerevolution Communist Party in Cuba, and with a third organization called the Revolutionary Directorate. The fused party took the name Integrated Revolutionary Organizations (ORI).

Aníbal Escalante, a longtime PSP leader, became organizational secretary of this new party. He abused his position by replacing cadres in the party and state apparatus almost exclusively with former associates from the PSP. Escalante then winked at the bureaucratic practices and the privileges and even corruption of these appointees.

Escalante also started a rumor-mill belittling the July 26 cadres and leaders. Fidel Castro, for example, was accused of not functioning as part of a collective leadership and of not being sufficiently Marxist. The popular support for Castro and other July 26 leaders was dismissed as signs of a developing personality cult. The PSP cadres, it was alleged, were the "real" party builders and Marxists.

To put a halt to these abuses, the ORI National Directorate held a series of discussions, removed Escalante from his positions, and instituted a number of other organizational changes. In March 1962, Castro presented a televised speech on behalf of the ORI leadership to explain to the people of the world what had happened, what had been done to correct it, and the lessons that could be learned from this experience.

The speech became known in Cuba and around the world by the title, "Against Bureaucracy and Sectarianism."

Castro pointed out that under Escalante, the party was being converted from what it should be, "an apparatus of the workers' vanguard," into a "nest of privilege," "favoritism," "immunities," and "favors." The workers and party cadres, Castro said, were beginning to ask: "Was [the ORI] a nucleus of revolutionists?" Or was it a "mere shell of revolutionists, well versed in dispensing favors"?

If the party did not reverse this process, Castro said, it would no longer "enjoy the prestige which a revolutionary nucleus should enjoy, a prestige born solely from the authority which it has in the eyes of the masses, an authority imparted to it by the example which its members set as workers, as model revolutionists."

In light of the bourgeois propaganda campaign around Grenada, it is interesting to note Castro's reference in the 1962 speech to similar disinformation efforts at that time. "It is logical to expect that the enemy will take advantage of these errors [by the Escalante grouping] to sow confusion, to go about saying that the Communists have taken over in Cuba; that Fidel has been replaced by Blas [Roca, another PSP leader] or Aníbal, or someone else, and Raúl [Castro] by another."

Concerning the charge of a developing cult of personality, Castro had this to say: "Those evils have not been a threat in our country. The only danger there was was the one that we did not see. How blind we were! What a difference between theory and practice! What a good lesson!"

"If we have one leader, two, ten with prestige, we should have more leaders with prestige," Castro said. "We should not destroy those leaders who have prestige," which has been gained because of what they have done for the revolution. That only ends up destroying the prestige of the revolution itself, Castro said. The task should be to develop more leaders known for their selfless activity and hard work.

Escalante's campaign of rumor had taken a toll on the revolution, Castro said. "Clearly this discouraged the masses," he explained. "No, the masses did not turn against the revolution," he said, "they're always with the revolution. . . . But this cooled the enthusiasm of the masses; this cooled the fervor of the masses."

What's more, Castro said, Escalante's factional activity fueled anticommunism, which still had a foothold in Cuba in those early years of the revolution. The leaders of the revolution had worked hard to combat anticommunism through patient education and experience, Castro said. But, confronted with the bureaucratic practices of the Escalante grouping, "many people will ask: 'Is this communism? Is this socialism? This abritrariness, this abuse, this privilege, all this, is this communism?' "

Castro also took up the charge that some ORI leaders were less "Marxist" than others because of their political origins. "The revolution is irrevocably defined as Marxist-Leninist," he said. "Let no one suffer from any fantasies or engage in any illusions on this score. Do not imagine that we are going to take a single step backwards. No, on the contrary, we are going to move forward!"

From "this moment on, comrades," Castro said, "all differences between the old and the new, between those who fought in the Sierra and those who were down in the lowlands, between those who took up arms and those who did not, between those who studied Marxism and those who did not study Marxism before, we feel that all these differences between them should cease. That from this moment on, we have to be one thing alone." That is, every party cadre was part of a common organization seeking to advance the revolution based on studying and applying the Marxist program and strategy in light of the living class struggle in Cuba and worldwide.

Following Castro's speech, Escalante was sent abroad to serve as a minor diplomatic official. Over the next few years, imperialist economic and military pressures against Cuba intensified, exacerbating shortages and other difficulties on the island. Attempts to extend the revolution in Latin America through support to several guerrilla war efforts failed, capped by the defeat of Che Guevara's forces in Bolivia, and some domestic measures aimed at accelerating economic development proved to be overambitious and ill-suited to the country's actual situation.

In 1964 Escalante returned to the island to be with an ailing relative. Later in the decade, amid the heightened social tensions, he began to carry out renewed secret factional activity, using the same methods of innuendo and slander.

Again reminiscent of Coard's charges against Maurice Bishop, the Escalante supporters began "passing themselves off as heroes of a battle against petty-bourgois leadership," as Cuban leader Carlos Rafael Rodríguez explained at a 1968 meeting of the party's Central Committee called to discuss the matter. One of Escalante's people complained to several lower-level Soviet officials in Cuba that, "Fidel wants Cuba to be the hub of the whole world . . . so that he can achieve a stature greater than that of Marx, Engels, and Lenin," and that in Cuba "policy is made by no one but Fidel Castro."

At the 1968 Central Committee meeting, Rodríguez — himself a former central leader of the PSP — explained what was at stake in combating Escalante's methods. The harm done by Escalante, Rodríguez said, "lies in the fact that he frustrated a process of unity that began by being, and could have been, a joyous, fraternal process in which comrades from various organizations, who had worked jointly or separately toward the same objective, were beginning to unite. He turned that into a bitter process, one that has since been painful."

The number of people involved in the second Escalante affair was small, but in one respect their activities were even more serious than in 1962. Escalante and his supporters tried to capitalize on strained relations that had developed between Cuba and the governments of the Soviet Union and several Eastern European countries over differences concerning aid to Vietnam and other international issues. The Escalante grouping urged personnel in the Soviet and Czech embassies to get their governments to bring pressure on the Cuban leadership to change its policies. They even went so far as to propose the withholding of economic aid and military aid from Cuba as a factional club against the revolution's leadership. Some officials from these two countries — who were later ordered to leave Cuba — cooperated with Escalante's maneuvers.

In 1968 Escalante and the core of his grouping were tried for violations of Cuban law committed in the course of their factional activity; they were convicted and sent to prison.

From both these rounds of the battle against the Escalante grouping, the Cuban leaders drew important lessons about leadership methods, bureaucracy, and the relationship between the party, the state apparatus, the army, the mass organizations, and the workers and farmers.

During his March 1962 speech, Castro proposed a new procedure for becoming a party member. From that time on, the majority of nominees were accepted into party membership only after having been elected a model worker by an assembly of their co-workers. This included all the workers in a given workplace — party members and non–party members alike — who knew the individual, and knew whether or not he or she was actually playing a leadership role as part of the communist vanguard of the Cuban working class. At the party's 1980 congress, Castro reported that the number of workers in the party had tripled since 1975, and that the party and its leadership bodies also had more women, more veterans of internationalist missions, and more peasants and agricultural workers. As a result, Castro said, the party had become "more Marxist-Leninist and more revolutionary," as well.

The 1968 events, in particular, drove home once more the principle that the Cubans have enunciated time and again in all their statements on Grenada — no interference in the internal affairs of other governments and other parties.

*   *   *

Combined with difficult objective circumstances, factional and administrative leadership methods such as those of the Coard grouping can split the vanguard party of the working class, separate it from the masses of working people, and lead to destruction of the revolution. In the process, the workers and farmers can be left wide open to direct imperialist intervention and repression.

As the example of Cuba proves, however, such a development is far from inevitable.

In his speech in Havana November 14, Fidel Castro warned the U.S. imperialists not to let their "victory in Grenada and their air of triumph ... go to their heads, leading them to commit serious, irreversible errors. They will not find in El Salvador, Nicaragua, and Cuba the particular circumstances of revolutionaries divided among themselves and divorced from the people that they found in Grenada."

Pointing to the determined resistance by Cuban construction workers at Point Salines, Castro asked the crowd of more than one million workers and farmers: "If in Grenada, the imperialists had to bring in an elite division to fight against a handful of isolated men struggling in a small stronghold, lacking fortifications, a thousand miles from their homeland, how many divisions would they need against millions of combatants fighting on their own [Cuban] soil alongside their own people?"

Nicaraguan leader Humberto Ortega told a gathering of Sandinista Youth in Managua, "The Yankees won't find us with our arms locked in storerooms. We have already distributed weapons and millions of bullets throughout the country."

And Vietnamese President Truong Chinh, after condemning the U.S. invasion of Grenada, warned that if Washington "were reckless enough to invade Cuba and Nicaragua, then many other Vietnams would emerge in Central America and Latin America."

Washington will certainly not find the job easy when it sends its troops and planes against the revolutionary peoples of Nicaragua and El Salvador, as it is right now preparing to do. As casualties mount and reverses accumulate, the U.S. capitalists will quickly find themselves fighting a second front at home, as well. U.S. workers don't want another Vietnam-style war. And they are growing increasingly angry over government and big-business attacks on their jobs, on their living and working conditions, on the rights of Blacks, Latinos, and women, and on democratic rights in general.

What's more, U.S. troops and firepower cannot erase the example and rich lessons of the Grenada revolution. Along with revolutionary Cuba and Nicaragua, the workers' and farmers' government brought to power in 1979 by the Grenadian people remains, as Fidel Castro once put it, one of the three giants of the Caribbean. Nor can the imperialists sweep away the contribution made by Maurice Bishop and the New Jewel Movement to the process of constructing a new revolutionary leadership of the working class and its allies in the Americas and internationally.

"Imperialism is bent on destroying symbols," Castro explained November 14, "because it knows the value of symbols, of examples, and of ideas. It wanted to destroy them in Grenada, and it wants to destroy them in El Salvador, Nicaragua, and Cuba.

"But symbols, examples, and ideas," he said, "cannot be destroyed. When their enemies think they have destroyed them, what they have done is made them multiply. . . . Grenada has already multiplied the patriotic conviction and fighting spirit of the Salvadoran, Nicaraguan, and Cuban revolutionaries."

Our aim in making available these speeches and interviews of Maurice Bishop is to help multiply the example and the lessons of the Grenada revolution as widely as possible among workers and the oppressed throughout the English-speaking world.

December 1983

GRENADA

CARRIBEAN SEA

CARRIACOU
Craigston
Hillsborough
Grand Bay

PETIT MARTINIQUE
PETIT TOBAGO

Argile
SALINE I.
LARGE I. FRIGATE I.

CARIBBEAN
SEA

Levera Bay LEVERA I. GREEN I.
Sauteurs
Duquesne Bay
Grenada Bay

Victoria
ST. MARKS MTS.
ST. MARK
ST. PATRICK
ST PATRICK
LAKE ANTOINE

Gouyave
(Charlotte Town)
Mt. St. Catherine
840 m (2757 ft.)

PEARLS AIRPORT

ST. JOHN
Mt. Granby
683 m (2240 ft.)
Great River Bay

Grand Bay
GRAND
Fedons Camp
766 m (2508 ft.)
GRAND ETANG
ETANG
ST. ANDREW
GREAT B

Grenville

Willis
FOREST
Mt. Lebanon
715 m (2347 ft.)
MARQUIS I.
St. Andrew's Bay

ST.
Sinai
703 m (2306 ft.)
RESERVE
Gt. Bacolet Bay

Grand Mal Bay
GEORGE
LA TANTER
Crochu Harbour

ST. GEORGE'S
Martin's Bay
ST. DAVID
St. David's

Grande Anse Bay
Morne Rouge Bay
Westerhall

Canoe Bay
Westerhall Bay

Lance aux Epines
HOG I.
GLOVER I.
CALIVIGNY I.

CARIBBEAN SEA

PRINCIPAL ROADS
PARISH BOUNDARIES
LAND OVER 304 m
(1000 ft.)

0 1 2 3 MILES
0 1 2 3 4 KILOMETRES

61°45'w
61°35'w
12°15'N
12°10'N
12°05'N
12°00'N
61°45'w

The Long Road to Freedom

by Arnaldo Hutchinson

The following article reviews some of the history of Grenada and of the Grenadian revolution. It is reprinted from the July 12, 1981, issue of Granma Weekly Review.

"Sisters and brothers, this is Maurice Bishop speaking. . . ." It was March 13, 1979. The present prime minister of Grenada and leader of the New Jewel Movement [NJM] party spoke to the people over a local radio station, which was renamed Radio Free Grenada, to report on the events which had led that day to the downfall of Eric Matthew Gairy. Gairy had dominated the political scene in Grenada for twenty-nine years.

Bishop said that at 4:15 a.m. the revolutionary forces had captured the True Blue barracks and the installations were set on fire and destroyed. After thirty minutes of fighting, Gairy's forces were surrounded and completely defeated. All soldiers surrendered and no member of the revolutionary forces was wounded.

The radio station, he said, had been captured without firing a shot, and shortly afterwards several ministers of the regime had been captured by revolutionary forces while they slept.

Bishop said that as he spoke to the people the white flag of surrender had already been raised over several police stations and revolutionary forces had been sent to cope with any resistance.

Bishop proclaimed that this was a revolution for work, food, housing, decent medical services, and a bright future for the children and grandchildren of the people of Grenada. He called on workers in various sectors, young people, and the middle class to join the revolutionary forces in their respective communitites and give them any help they required.

The support and participation of the people which had made possible the victory of the plan known as Operation Apple was once again reflected in the mass response to the call of the revolutionary leader.

Several witnesses reported that thousands of men, women, and children participated in the operations that day and in the period immediately afterwards which consolidated the victory of the insurrection.

1

They took up arms, backed the revolutionary army, went on patrol, gave information, and made arrests.

Proof of this overwhelming support lies in the fact that only three people were killed — one by accident — in the course of the events on March 13. Most of the police stations surrendered without a fight or were taken over by the people themselves.

Nevertheless, some people still characterize Gairy's overthrow as a coup carried out by a small group headed by Maurice Bishop, in which the people of Grenada were not involved.

This ignores the fact that the New Jewel Movement party, which headed the armed actions on March 13, was at that time an organization with a history of more than six years of struggle. It had survived Gairy's fierce repression and had grown and developed because it was, in fact, rooted in the people.

A look at the history of Grenada will demonstrate to the impartial observer that the development of the New Jewel Movement and the events on March 13 were the result of a process which started more than 350 years ago with the arrival of the French colonialists.

This was the theme of this year's Freedom March, held on February 7, the date of Grenada's independence from Great Britain. (The march was also held last year.)

The march started at Leapers Hill in the northern part of the island and went to Freedom Hill in the south. The organizers explained that the march linked the struggle of the indigenous population at the dawn of French colonialism with the most recent stage of struggle. Leapers Hill was where the Carib Indians chose to commit mass suicide by jumping into the sea rather than yield to the French, and Freedom Hill was where the revolutionaries gathered for the attack on Gairy's troops, marking the start of the operation which ended with the overthrow of the regime.

Although the island was sighted by Columbus on August 15, 1498, on his third trip to the Americas, it was not until April 1, 1609 that a group of 200 British adventurers landed on Grenada in order to establish a settlement; but the Caribs, with the help of the environment, were able to defeat them.

Thirty years later the French made a similar attempt and were also defeated by the local people. However, in June 1650, another group of 200 Frenchmen from neighboring Martinique landed and were able to trick the local chieftain into giving them the island in exchange for trinkets. A year later, however, fighting broke out and the Indians were slaughtered.

By 1657, according to Patrick Emmanuel in his book *Crown Colony Politics in Grenada — 1917-1951*, the genocide of the Indians had reached such a height that Grenada was one of the few English-speaking countries of the Caribbean where there were no indigenous survivors left.

The fighting between the European colonizing countries during the eighteenth and nineteenth centuries had an impact on the Caribbean. The British took over Grenada in 1762, and the following year the island was ceded to them by a treaty and they remained in control for the next sixteen years.

As a result of more fighting in Europe, the island went back under French control for four years starting in 1779 and was then returned to the British in 1783 by means of the Treaty of Versailles. The British governed from then on until February 7, 1974, when Grenada obtained formal political independence. Thus, British rule lasted 191 years.

The second half of the eighteenth century was a period of profound social turmoil. In 1776 the British colonies in North America proclaimed their independence after defeating the European colonialists, becoming the United States of America. In France, in 1789, with "Liberty, Equality, and Fraternity" as their motto, the revolutionaries dealt the death blow to the feudal monarchy. Closer by, in Haiti, the Black slaves rose up against their oppressors and set up the first free state in Latin America.

All of this had an impact in Grenada and gave rise to the rebellion headed by Julien Fedon.

On March 2, 1795, Fedon and supporters — mainly freemen and slaves from the French and English plantations — attacked Grenville, on the eastern coast of the island, in an attempt to capture it. Fedon had mobilized his supporters with a call for equality and freedom and demanded that the English abolish slavery.

An interesting point is that Fedon was able to recruit slaves, freemen, and whites, a fact which irked the British as much as their military defeats.

Except for St. George's, the capital, Fedon's forces gained control of most of the island. The British authorities were alarmed by the events in Grenada and feared a new Haiti, so they sent 2,000 men under the command of Gen. Ralph Abercromby to reinforce their troops. This shifted the situation in favor of the colonialists.

Little by little, Fedon's troops were forced to yield their positions, until they were finally defeated at Mount Qua Qua, in the area along Grand Etang Lake, nearly in the center of the island.

The industrial revolution in Great Britain led to changes in its colonial policy, which in turn had profound social and economic repercussions in Grenada during the nineteenth century. The development of the sugar industry, the use of steam engines, and the substitution of beet sugar for cane sugar made slave labor less necessary.

Meanwhile, slave rebellions and the slaves' resistance to the severe exploitation they were subjected to led the British to ban the slave trade in 1807 and then slavery itself in 1834.

The emancipation of the slaves and the growth of a Black middle class led to the upsurge of national feelings, in the face of which the prevailing colonial system was no longer effective. Thus, numerous contradictions arose.

In 1877, Britain decided to impose in Grenada the crown colony system, which gave all power to the governor. The metropolis opted for this system instead of the more liberal, so-called representative system that gave British citizens in the colony with a certain level of income the same political rights they would have had in Britain itself. The crown colony system lasted until 1951.

In its January 17, 1920, edition the newspaper the *West Indian* reported that Grenada, especially its capital St. George's, was affected by acts of "systematic violence" that included theft, arson, and destruction of homes, businesses, and government buildings. This occurred within the framework of the world economic crisis.

In Grenada, where the economy was based on the export of nutmeg and cocoa, the economic crisis made the lot of the wage workers and unemployed significantly worse.

All this notwithstanding, the first half of the century in Grenada was characterized by a struggle for reforms in the framework of the totalitarian crown colony system. Grenadians fought to obtain more decision-making power for the local population in matters of government.

Political campaigns from the thirties on were centered around the idea of a federation of English-speaking Caribbean states. This movement was chiefly promoted by the representatives of the growing middle class, which was caught between the large number of the exploited on one hand and the ruling class of big plantation owners and colonial officials on the other.

During the first half of this century a leading role in the federation movement was played by Theophilus A. Marryshow, a journalist born on November 7, 1887. His tenacious and eloquent campaigns directed towards this goal led him to be called the Father of Federation and be designated a national hero of the people of Grenada.

Marryshow founded the Association of Grenada Workers and in 1932 led a protest demonstration of 10,000 people against an official decision to increase import duties.

While the first half of the century was characterized by relatively calm political and social evolution, 1951 marked the start of an era of constant political turmoil in which the masses played a key role. The people of Grenada started the decisive stage of their drive towards freedom.

Patrick Emmanuel reports that the vast majority of the population lived in poverty and that the common denominators facing the working people were low wages, bad health and living conditions, and a shortage of clothing. There was a high rate of illiteracy and many people had a very limited education, with the resulting backwardness in their understanding of the world and natural phenomena.

Meanwhile, unions were not accepted until 1943, when workers were granted the right to organize and undertake peaceful demonstrations to press their demands.

In 1946 there were two unions: the General Workers' Union and the St. George's Workers' Union, both of which had a membership of mostly urban workers. However, the largest group of workers, and the most impoverished — the farm workers — lacked an organization to defend their interests.

This is where Eric Matthew Gairy came on the scene. For more than twenty-five years he was to cast a sinister shadow on the political life of Grenada.

Born in 1922, Gairy came from a poor background, had some formal education, and was a glib speaker. Unscrupulous and politically unprincipled, he was interested only in that which would contribute to his deeply felt need to be accepted and recognized by the ruling class. After having worked for years at oil refineries in the Caribbean, he returned home in December 1949, when the situation of the masses, especially those in the countryside, was at its worst.

Gairy sought to develop the image of an eagerly awaited leader, a messiah sent to save the oppressed masses. The way he dressed, the symbols he used, his voice, his evangelical language, were all aimed at creating that image.

Gairy plunged immediately into trade union work, and in July 1950 he established the Grenada Manual and Mental Workers' Union (GMMWU). Shortly afterwards he claimed it had 27,000 members.

After winning an eviction case and wage increases for sugar industry workers and with the fame of his union rising, Gairy demanded higher wages and better working conditions for farm workers.

When the bosses arrogantly refused to recognize the union and negotiate, Gairy called a general strike on February 19, 1951. The strike brought the economy of the island to a halt.

In an article entitled "The Political Situation in Grenada," published in the magazine *Socialism* in January 1975, Chris Holderness described the events surrounding the strike as a revolution, even though it started with simple demands for higher pay and better conditions for workers on nutmeg and cocoa plantations.

It became an in-depth attack on the plantation owners and the colonial ruling class, with general strikes, destruction or occupation of property belonging to the owners, and demonstrations against colonial rule.

There was also destruction of colonial government property.

It seemed that the events that began on February 19 would never end. It was an outburst of rage against racial oppression and colonial rule which had been held in check for centuries. The rebelling Black masses seemed determined to do away with the prevailing system, which reeled under their blows.

Neither Gairy's arrest nor his subsequent release, nor the local police which had been reinforced by contingents from nearby islands and the British navy, could control the situation.

The announcement that the union would be recognized didn't calm the situation either, nor did the start of talks on the demands raised by the workers.

This led the colonial regime to call on Gairy to help quell the unrest. Pleased by this opportunity, he threw himself into the effort.

He called on the workers to halt the uprising, but because of the deep-rooted unrest, the turmoil continued.

On March 15, the colonial government allowed Gairy to speak on the radio in an effort to convince the people to stop their protests. Part of his speech sheds light on what Gairy was like and on the magnitude of the challenge faced by the colonial system in 1951.

"I feel obligated morally and spiritually to do something to alleviate, to stop, and when I say stop, I mean stop, the burning of buildings and fields; interfering with people who are breaking your strikes (leave them alone); stop taking away things from the estates that are not belonging to you, particularly cocoa and nutmeg; I want you to stop and you must stop now, every act of violence and intimidation. . . . I told his excellency the governor that I have gained your respect and your implicit confidence and you will obey me without fail. Now don't let me down. I, Eric Matthew Gairy, am now making this serious appeal to you to start leading your normal peaceful life. Take my example and be a respectful decent citizen as I say, starting now. Let me make this point, however, everyone knows that I am a serious young man and when I say 'no' I mean 'no,' and when I say 'yes,' I mean 'yes.' Now listen to this: I am now in search for gangsters and hooligans, I ask every one of my people to help me, and if anyone is found setting fire to any place, breaking down or robbing or in any way interfering with people who are working, there will be nothing to save you, because the law will deal with you most severely, and 'Uncle Gairy' will turn you down completely. So join me now in saying 'no more violence.' Come on now, together, 'no more violence,' 'no more violence,' 'no more violence.' Thank you."

Gairy was used to divide and weaken the rebellion, while colonial officials increased arrests and violence against the people. After a month of constant turmoil, the situation returned to normal and the British, thanks to Gairy's betrayal, were able to gradually eliminate the colonial system at their leisure and introduce neocolonialism with independence on February 7, 1974.

According to Holderness, this rebellion was a redistribution of power under the colonial regime and represented a decline in the power of plantation owners. Several plantation owners sold their land and left the country or went to urban areas to engage in trade and business.

A new constitution for Grenada was approved in September 1951. The real power remained in the hands of the representatives of the crown, but an effort was made to integrate the masses into the system through the establishment of universal suffrage.

In addition to creating a union, Gairy had also set up the Grenada People's Party, which afterwards became the Grenada United Labour Party (GULP). It held seven of the eight seats in the colonial legislature in the first elections held on the basis of universal suffrage.

In 1955 the Grenada National Party (GNP) was set up. It subsequently became the political instrument of the old plantation-owning elite and its supporters in the professional field. Thus, both the GNP and the GULP represented the interests of ruling economic groups.

Gairy, the exploited, oppressed, and rejected young Black, had betrayed the masses from which he came to enter the world of the privileged.

As a result of the storm aroused by the process of decolonization which began after World War II and which gathered force in the sixties, the British gave Grenada the status of associated statehood as part of its plan to gradually replace colonial rule with neocolonialism. Under this new formula, Grenada was granted self-government in all fields except foreign policy and defense. The local government was also given the right to dissolve the association with Great Britain and seek independence whenever it so decided.

This new situation brought Gairy and his party back to power. They had lost the 1962 elections following an administrative corruption scandal in which he was the key figure. In the 1967 elections the GULP won seven out of ten seats and Gairy became prime minister.

Given the added power now at his disposal, he immediately moved to make sure that he stayed in office. Although he still had support among agricultural and farm workers, he did not have a following in urban areas, where the GNP was in control.

Gairy manipulated government employees through a skillful combination of patronage and political pressure and won the support of businessmen by granting them and their backers special concessions. Through these means, Gairy built up a much stronger urban base although his main source of support remained in the countryside.

What Grenadians began calling political victimization was instituted as a method of persecution and blackmail in public offices in order to silence all opposition, criticism, or challenge from public service employees. Political victimization meant dismissal, transfer, or rather exile, into obscure positions in remote places.

When Grenadians looked for a nickname to identify the special force set up by Gairy to terrorize the population, they soon hit upon one — the "Mongoose Gang." The characteristics of the mongoose fitted the members of the gang perfectly. The Mongoose Gang first came to public notice during the GULP campaign in the 1967 elections. From then on it grew in notoriety, reaching its peak in the seventies.

Two examples are sufficient to illustrate the kind of men that joined the gang: Norrel Belfon, alias "Tallboy," convicted thirty-four times between July 1955 and February 1970 for physical aggression, assault on the police, damage to public property, illegal possession of firearms, etc., and Crafton Fraser, alias "Tantie Gomez," convicted thirty-two times for crimes including robbery, physical aggression, burglary, and assault.

Now controlled by Gairy, the legislature began to pass a series of repressive laws like the Firearms Act (1968), which rescinded all firearms permits issued to members of the opposition; the Public Order Act (1974), which banned the use of loudspeakers not previously authorized by police; the Newspaper Act (1975), which required a deposit of 20,000 Eastern Caribbean dollars (EC$) [EC$1 = U.S.$.37] to be made prior to any newspaper being authorized to circulate, and which was obviously directed against the New Jewel Movement's publication; the Essential Public Services Act and the Port Authority Act, whereby the right to strike was virtually prohibited in these sectors.

Apart from the above, under the law in force at the time, it was up to the employers to determine which trade unions could lawfully negotiate on behalf of the workers. This allowed Gairy to exert pressure so that his trade union would be designated as the only representative of the workers, even if a majority of them belonged to another.

The sweeping changes in international politics which took place during the late fifties, the sixties, and seventies made a big impact on many social groups, particularly the youth, of the underdeveloped countries. Ghana's independence in 1957, the Cuban revolution in 1959, the war of liberation waged by Algeria against French colonialism, the Vietnamese struggle against U.S. aggression, the growing rebelliousness of the Black population in the United States, the unilateral declaration of independence by racist Rhodesia, the imperialist plot against Lumumba in the Congo, were some of the events that contributed to the postwar generation's political awakening.

In Grenada, three events directly reflected this popular, antiracist, anticolonialist, and anti-imperialist orientation, which grew stronger throughout that period, taking concrete shape in various emerging groups.

The first was a mass demonstration in solidarity with the Black Power movement that in 1970 shook Trinidad and Tobago society. One of the demonstrators was a young lawyer who had recently returned to his country and who would soon be playing a leading role in his country's affairs: Maurice Bishop.

Around that same date, a group of nurses working at the general hospital in St. George's took to the streets one day to protest against the awful working conditions, the lack of the most basic hygiene conditions, and the acute shortage of medicines at the hospital. Various sectors of the population, particularly high school students, joined the protest. Gairy hit back by arresting over thirty persons and charging them with conspiracy, sedition, and mutiny. Bishop, who was one of those arrested, undertook to defend the nurses, together with a group of prestigious regional attorneys. The case dragged on for close to seven months, but in the end everybody was acquitted.

Another demonstration was staged against British landowner Lord Brownslow, owner of the La Sagesse estate, who arbitrarily decided to ban local residents from a nearby beach. This provoked the wrath of the people, but the government turned a deaf ear to their complaints. Led by progressive young people, the residents then staged a public trial (in absentia) of Lord Brownslow, and after declaring him guilty of trampling upon the rights of the people, organized a popular demonstration and tore down the barrier to the beach road. Leading the action was a recently created group called JEWEL, headed by a young economist named Unison Whiteman.

Throughout the Caribbean, new progressive political organizations had begun to spring up, seeking to end dependency on foreign powers, wipe out racism, and improve living conditions. One such group, the New Jewel Movement, emerged in Grenada out of the merger of two separate organizations: the Joint Endeavour for Welfare, Education and Liberation (JEWEL), headed by Unison Whiteman, and the Movement for Assemblies of the People (MAP), headed by young attorneys Maurice Bishop and Kenrick Radix. JEWEL operated mainly in rural areas, while MAP worked in urban areas.

The New Jewel Movement, also popularly known as NJM, was set up on March 11, 1973, at a congress held by JEWEL and MAP. Maurice Bishop and Unison Whiteman were elected joint coordinating secretaries of the new political organization.

In its manifesto, the NJM put forward a series of noncapitalist measures to cope with the country's economic, social, and political problems. Regionally it advocated the economic integration of the Caribbean, specifically "an integration of the economies of the islands under popular ownership and control"; and internationally it adopted a nationalist, anti-imperialist, and anticolonialist stand.

It also voiced its support for the Movement of Nonaligned Countries and expressed its willingness to join that organization as soon as possible.

The NJM considered that apart from unemployment, then estimated at 50 percent of the population of working age, its main concerns should be "preventing daily rises in the price of food, clothing and other essential commodities, and developing a concrete program to improve housing, apparel, education, public health, food, and recreation for the people."

To carry out this program, the NJM urged the people to mobilize by means of a system of popular participation whose key element was the grassroots organizations.

The New Jewel Movement opened up a new horizon for the Grenadian people. The interest with which it was received was evidenced by, among other things, the fact that notwithstanding its rudimentary appearance and scant material resources, the newspaper *Jewel* — whose name was later changed to *New Jewel* — became the paper with the largest circulation in the country, selling three times as many copies as the other dailies that had been established decades earlier.

These new forces, their ideas, the fact that they were politically and economically uncommitted to the men in power and thus immune to flattery and bribery, and that in a short period of time they had succeeded in mobilizing significant sectors of the population, posed a real danger to Gairy and the interests he represented, and seriously threatened his plans to keep himself in power. It was against these popular forces that an implacable and systematic repression was unleashed.

After maneuvering to guarantee his own reelection in 1972, Gairy's next step was to ensure his control over the country by formalizing independence from Great Britain. Although all political organizations favored independence, they disagreed on the methods and the manner of achieving it.

The NJM objected to a formal independence devoid of content. It advocated "real independence, genuine independence, meaningful independence." Among the things that could be done to bring this about, it raised the demand that Britain pay at least EC$100 million as partial compensation for all the money stolen from the country and for the exploitation, misery, suffering, and degradation endured under its centuries-old domination.

Prompted by the tense atmosphere hanging over the question of independence, the telephone, electricity, and water workers called a strike on April 5 and 6, 1973, for their own sector's demands.

Shortly afterwards on the twentieth, the Gairy police murdered a young man, Jeremiah Richardson. This set off a wave of mass protests that led to the closing down of a police station and paralyzed the airport for two days.

On June 6, 1973, a scant two months after it was set up, the NJM called a People's Convention on Independence, attended by 10,000 persons, to denounce Gairy's plans.

On June 14 there were popular demonstrations to protest against a conference on Grenada's independence being held at the time in London, at which Gairy was trying to conclude with the British the details of a constitution for the island. Students, workers, and the business community took part, and the demonstrations led to a general strike.

On November 4, 1973, the NJM called a People's Congress held in Seamoon, St. Andrews, where Gairy was tried and found guilty of twenty-seven crimes against the people, ranging from murdering citizens, administrative incompetence, and corruption to ignoring legitimate popular demands.

The People's Congress handed a verdict of guilty and demanded that Gairy resign or else face a general strike. Clearly the people intended to topple his government before the independence date.

Attended by some 10,000 persons, the People's Congress at Seamoon was a great victory for the NJM, the more so because it was organized despite the aggression and intimidation of Gairy's Mongoose Gang. During the congress, Gairy ordered his followers to demonstrate a short distance away from the spot where the congress was being held, but only 2,000 people showed up. This failure infuriated Gairy and made him even more obstinate in his desire to bring the NJM and its leaders to heel. In a radio broadcast he replied to the charges against him and warned that he would "bring the NJM rebels to their senses and wake them up from their dreams in a very short time for fifty-four different reasons including treason and sedition."

On November 18, the day set for the general strike, six NJM leaders, including Maurice Bishop, Unison Whiteman, and Selwyn Strachan, were brutally attacked and beaten by policemen and the Mongoose Gang as they were visiting business establishments in Grenville in connection with the planned strike. Later, they were thrown into a filthy cell and denied medical attention or visits from their relatives.

The day became known as "Bloody Sunday." Grenadians were shocked, and the events led to numerous protests and, eventually, a new general strike.

A broad group of twenty-two organizations, including trade unions, businesses, civic organizations, and churches, signed a petition demanding the arrest of the perpetrators of the events on November 18, disbanding the Mongoose Gang, and an end to arbitrary searches and arrests.

Gairy hastened to announce that he would disband the gang, and reluctantly agreed to appoint a commission headed by Hubert Duffus, a well-known Caribbean attorney. Following this, the twenty-two organizations decided to call off the general strike. However, the new organization, institutionalized as the Committee of Twenty-two, insisted that all their demands be met or else that Gairy resign.

Seeing that Gairy adamantly refused to yield, the committee, after some hesitation, gave its support to the general strike originally proposed by the NJM — which incidentally had been excluded from participation in the committee. The strike began on January 1, 1974, and lasted nearly three months.

One of the most dramatic events that occurred in that period — later reported in minute detail by the Duffus Commission investigators — was the rifle and tear gas attack launched by the repressive forces against a peaceful demonstration on January 21, 1974. In the attack Rupert Bishop, Maurice's father, was killed. He had joined the protest demonstration together with his wife Alimenta and daughter Ann. Several other persons were wounded.

This popular show of force practically brought the country's economic life to a standstill and very nearly toppled the regime. It was the highest point in a period of political agitation originally prompted by the question of independence and marked by growing popular insurgency and the most brutal repression.

Gairy finally managed to regain control of the situation, using a combination of tactics: repression of the people, collusion with members of the Committee of Twenty-two, mustering support from abroad, and granting a few minor concessions.

The NJM, on the other hand, although it could count on the people's support, still lacked the institutional and organizational means to lead all opposition forces towards Gairy's overthrow, since it had only been functioning for one year.

Just as the NJM had predicted, independence did not bring about any change in the situation of the Grenadian people. However, it did allow Gairy greater control over the state apparatus, because he took charge of foreign affairs and defense, formerly under British control.

As an independent state, Grenada joined the OAS and the UN. However, Gairy soon became the laughingstock of the international community, solemnly presenting before these forums his eccentric ideas about UFOs and psychospiritual phenomena. He told the representatives of the UN that he had actually seen UFOs and proposed that the General Assembly establish an agency for the investigation of "UFOlogy."

This ridiculous image which Gairy created abroad was yet another reason for internal dissent and contributed to his isolation in the international sphere.

After the failure of the movement to overthrow Gairy in 1973-74, the NJM directed its efforts to strengthening the organization's structures and its ties with the various sectors of the population, particularly the workers, while forging an alliance with the different opposition forces. Meanwhile, it continued its campaign to denounce the regime and raise the people's political awareness.

The leadership of the NJM was convinced that, given the circumstances at the time, elections would not solve the country's problems. Furthermore, under Gairy, the parliament was merely a farce — a "pappyshow," as they called it. But the people, who still had faith in the electoral process, had to be made aware of this.

In anticipation of the 1976 elections, the NJM, along with the Grenada National Party and the United People's Party (an offshoot of the GNP), formed a "People's Alliance" on the basis of a minimum program of reforms.

On the ticket of the People's Alliance, the NJM nominated seven of the fourteen candidates, while the GNP nominated five and the UPP two. The proportion of candidates from each party served to demonstrate the development and prestige of the movement led by Maurice Bishop and Unison Whiteman.

In the elections held on December 7, the People's Alliance received 48.5 percent of the votes and six seats, with the NJM getting three, the GNP two, and the UPP one. Maurice Bishop became the leader of the parliamentary opposition.

Gairy's Grenada United Labour Party won nine seats in parliament and retained control of the government.

During the election campaign, Gairy resorted to a wide range of maneuvers, availing himself of the entire state apparatus in an attempt to curtail the opposition. A few examples suffice:

• names of dead persons were included on the voters' list, and many of his supporters were registered twice, while hundreds of opposition supporters were excluded;

• only government candidates had access to loudspeakers;

• all the poll clerks and other election officers were Gairy agents;

• the military apparatus was used to break up public meetings and terrorize neighborhoods where the opposition was strong;

• a vicious propaganda campaign, using the radio and other media, went so far as to charge that if the People's Alliance came to power, it would kill everyone over forty and turn the churches into discotheques!

In the light of this situation, the opposition's charges that the elections were rigged and that the People's Alliance was the true winner seem well grounded.

The NJM used its position in parliament to denounce and ridicule the regime. At the same time, the parliamentary forum gave the NJM the opportunity of presenting its ideas and programs to the entire nation, thus consolidating its position as a legitimate alternative to the Gairy government. As the legal opposition, it could also participate actively in international activities.

However, the major activity of the organization did not revolve around parliament, but around mass meetings, smaller strategy meetings restricted principally to party members, and activity conducted at the trade union level.

An example of the latter was the formation of the Bank and General Workers' Union under the leadership of Vincent Noel, a member of the Political Bureau of the NJM. On two occasions, the overwhelming majority of the workers in that sector voted to recognize this union as their legitimate representative in negotiations with management. In spite of this, Gairy continued to insist that the GMMWU, which he controlled, had jurisdiction.

As the regime became further discredited and the prestige of the NJM grew, Gairy relied more and more on repression in his desperate bid to stay in power.

A meeting of the General Assembly of the OAS was held in Grenada on June 19, 1977. The opposition forces, deprived of access to the radio and loudspeakers, decided to take advantage of the presence of foreign delegations and the international press to denounce the regime before the world.

Although Gairy denied permission to hold a rally, the NJM decided to go ahead with it, Kenrick Radix, an NJM leader, explained.

The army was mobilized and took the microphones away from the speakers. Then suddenly over 500 men, women, and children began a spontaneous demonstration through the city streets, demanding their rights. Without warning, the army opened fire on the people. Dozens were wounded and a twenty-year-old was killed.

Gairy also manipulated the people's religious beliefs for his own ends. As proof of his "devotion," he had a giant cross — fifty-four by sixteen feet and illuminated by 200 lights — erected at the top of one of the hills overlooking St. George's. On one occasion he declared before parliament that God had sent him to govern and therefore those that criticized him were criticizing God.

Aware of the growing isolation of his regime, Gairy established ties with the U.S. Mafia and the most reactionary forces of the international community, such as Pinochet's dictatorship in Chile and Pak Chung Hee's in South Korea.

His ties with the U.S. underworld can be seen in the case of Elmond Zeek, from Baltimore, Maryland. Wanted by the FBI for a million-dollar robbery, Zeek took refuge in Grenada, where he and his accomplices enjoyed Gairy's protection and friendship.

For seven years the NJM, in its effort to promote changes that would satisfy the demands and needs of the Grenadian population, used all forms of struggle, including strikes, peaceful mass demonstrations, elections, and the parliament. Given the mounting repression and political persecution and the impossibility of making changes peacefully, the organization resorted to armed struggle.

The NJM began to develop a clandestine wing trained in armed insurrection. This group was later to become the nucleus of the People's Revolutionary Army of Grenada which, on March 13, 1979, would join the people in eliminating the dictatorship. Time had run out for Eric Matthew Gairy, but for the people of Grenada, it was just beginning.

The Struggle for Democracy and against Imperialism in Grenada

August 1977

The following interview with Bishop and Unison Whiteman conducted by Pedro Pablo Rodríguez took place in Havana, Cuba. It was printed in the Cuban weekly Bohemia, *August 19, 1977, and has been retranslated to English for this book by Will Reissner.*

Situated at the far southern end of the crescent of the Antillean islands, very near the coast of South America, the island of Grenada has not been by-passed by the winds of renewal blowing over the lands of the Caribbean Sea since the 1960s.

The island, initially occupied by France, passed to England's control in 1762 when the British imperial lion consolidated its rule over what were called the Sugar Islands. This colonial phase lasted two centuries, until Grenada joined the community of independent nations in 1974.

The political freedom of this and other Caribbean countries, although late in terms of the rest of the Americas, has taken place in a world characterized by a confrontation between two social systems: victorious socialism and dying capitalism. As a result, among the most clearsighted leaders and disenfranchised sectors of the English-speaking Caribbean consciousness grew by leaps and bounds that real national sovereignty can be attained only through the elimination of colonialism in all its neocolonialist aspects and variants and through the destruction of its most basic cause: capitalism in its imperialist phase.

In a relatively short period of time, these truly progressive elements have understood that political independence can become a mere formality unless accompanied by an economic policy that promotes national development. And in following this road, some governments like those of Jamaica and Guyana have already found that they always encounter a stiff obstacle in the diverse forms of imperialist domination and penetration.

In Grenada, a young Marxist party feels that only through the socialist path can this national development be achieved. Maurice Bishop and Unison Whiteman, leaders of the New Jewel Movement and members

16

of the island's parliament, visited the offices of *Bohemia* to talk about the situation in their country.

Bishop, tall and slim, with a deliberate and convincing way of speaking, explained the positions of the party that he is the leader of.

"Our party, the New Jewel Movement, was formed in March 1973 through the unification of two political organizations that always took consistent democratic positions: one called JEWEL, which is an acronym for Joint Endeavour for Welfare, Education and Liberation; and the other called the Movement for Assemblies of the People.

"That year we held two conventions. The first [in May] dealt principally with the question of independence, which the party then in the government was taking steps toward. Our position was that the people should participate in the whole political process leading to independence. We wanted the government to take the popular sectors into account in working out the Constitution and the principles on which the economic system of independent Grenada would be based.

"The government focus, however, was to take up this whole question directly and exclusively with the British authorities.

"About 15,000 people attended this first convention.

"The second convention took place in November of the same year. There we examined problems such as the repressive situation created by the government, and we worked out an agreement on an economic program. In the period between the two conventions — between May and November 1973 — the government had forcibly repressed the democratic and progressive forces, so this was one of the central concerns of the second convention. In fact, just after this gathering closed, the police attacked a meeting in which six members of our party's Political Bureau took part."

Bishop went on to explain the difficult political conditions in which Grenada's independence took place.

"After the repression by the police, various organizations and institutions got together and formed the Committee of Twenty-two. In it there were representatives of workers and professional organizations, social welfare, religious, and student organizations. It was a combination of different political and class forces that did not have a socialist perspective, but were in agreement on the importance of getting rid of the government in power.

"This committee called a general strike that began January 1, 1974, and lasted about three and a half weeks. There were daily protest demonstrations. More than 24,000 people took part in the last one. That day, January 21, 1974, the government sent the regular police force, as well as the secret police and the army, to attack the demonstrators. Many people were killed, including my own father. This fierce repression stopped the demonstrations, and the government was able to declare independence on February 7, 1974, 'in peace.'

"From then on, we understood that along with mobilization of the masses we had to think about organization of the party and training and preparation of the cadres. That is, to try to build a party with the character of a vanguard party. To that end we maintained two organizational principles: the party had to have geographic structures, based on where the people lived, as well as structures in the work centers. We concentrated on that effort until 1976.

"In December of that year, our party participated in the general elections in alliance with two other opposition parties: the Grenada National Party and the United People's Party. The People's Alliance got 48.2 percent of the vote, and a big portion of that came from the young voters. (For this election the voting age was dropped from twenty-one to sixteen years old.) So of the fifteen seats in parliament, the People's Alliance won six of them. The New Jewel Movement held three of those seats and led the representation of the opposition."

In response to questions, Bishop discussed the reactionary, antidemocratic, and fascist-like character of the government of Grenada.

"The party in power, the Grenada United Labour Party [GULP], is led by the present Prime Minister Eric Gairy, who founded it in 1951. In that year, the GULP led an important movement of the agricultural workers, which won the party prestige in the Grenadian population. But despite their progressive beginnings, Gairy and his party turned into representatives of, and in part members of, the country's commercial bourgeoisie, closely tied to the interests of the big imperialist companies that exploit the island.

"During last year's election campaign the government constantly placed obstacles in the way of the People's Alliance opposition. Under Grenada's laws, you can hold a public meeting without having to ask for official permission. But you need official permission to use a sound system. Obviously you have to use such a system in those circumstances. For our election meetings, the police denied permission for the use of sound and we did not get access to the radio, which is in the government's hands. In addition, since 1975 we have had to put out our publication clandestinely because it was prohibited by a press law passed by the GULP government.

"The elections were marked by various frauds, beginning with the removal of about 10,000 voters favorable to the alliance from the rolls, while 13,000 nonexistent voters were registered. Nonetheless, as we said, the alliance received nearly half the votes.

"But despite this equilibrium of forces, the GULP government is continuing its repressive policy and this year it has sought out international support and aid. Prime Minister Gairy visited Santiago, Chile, and a

Chilean lieutenant colonel named García Zamorano, who is very close to Pinochet himself, was in the island. As a result of these contacts, the Chilean fascist junta is training and equipping Grenada's police and army.

"In addition, Gairy was in South Korea in 1975 and signed an agreement with that country's regime giving it unlimited fishing rights in Grenada's waters. These kinds of contacts explain why the GULP government offered the country as the site for the meeting of the Assembly of the Organization of American States.

"Furthermore, the government has developed ties with the Mafia. A man called John Clancy, whose real name is Eugene Zeck and who fled the United States in 1973, lives in Grenada. He has been given a monopoly over the lobster industry and over yachting services in St. George's harbor. This man, who is wanted in the United States by the Federal Bureau of Investigation for his illegal activities, is associated with Robert Vesco, also a fugitive from that country and known for his friendship and 'dealings' with former U.S. President Nixon.

"We have heard that Vesco, whose departure from Costa Rica is being demanded by public opinion there, is thinking about going to live in Grenada. His yacht has even been sighted on the island twice this year."

The presence of these figures, in whom the underworld, big business, and U.S. politics come together, led the conversation around to the U.S. interests in Grenada.

"The field in which Americans have penetrated Grenada," said Bishop, "is tourism. Together with Antigua and Barbados, Grenada has been the site of U.S. hotel investments. U.S. finance capital also controls the telephone company and is involved in the banking sector along with Canadian and British institutions.

"In addition, through the World Bank the U.S. government has told the GULP it would be willing to build an international airport in exchange for permission to use it for ninety-nine years. The importance of this installation for our country is obvious, given that it is an island. But its importance for the military circles in the Pentagon is also obvious, given Grenada's strategic position in the Caribbean and on the routes to Africa and Europe."

Bishop's remarks about the importance of U.S. tourism investments bring up the question of the significance of tourism in the Grenadian economy. It is Comrade Whiteman who responds. His tone of voice reflects his concern in reflecting upon and studying the island's problems. From a Marxist perspective, Whiteman explains the need to analyze the overall characteristics of Grenadian society and classes in order to gain a precise understanding of its economic problems.

"In terms of the ethnic origin of its population, our country is one of the most homogenous in the English-speaking Caribbean. Around 95 percent are of African descent, and the rest are Hindus, Portuguese, Syrians, Lebanese, and others. Undoubtedly this prevents the kind of fragmentation of the population along ethnic lines that colonialism has always tried to foster in other nations of the area.

"About one-third of Grenada's 100,000 inhabitants make up its work force. In terms of the distribution of the work force, Grenada has special characteristics in the region. It has the greatest number of small landowners in the English-speaking Caribbean. It is estimated that there are about 10,000 small farmers with landholdings of less than ten acres. This situation has been fostered through the sale of land by the GULP government, which has tried in this way to create a social base for itself and to reward its political followers.

"This sector is of decisive importance in the country's economy because it produces a large part of the exports like cocoa, bananas, and nutmeg. A significant number of seasonal workers also work in agriculture.

"We have a small working class because there is only one brewery, one cigarette factory, and a rum distillery on the island. When we add the commercial and hotel sector, and the infrastructure of the tourist trade, we have practically run the gamut of economic activity in Grenada. That's why there is such a high unemployment rate, comprising more than 55 percent of the population that could work.

"The economic picture is completed," Whiteman concluded, "if we note that the largest amount of income comes from the export of agricultural products, which exceeds the income from tourism."

The conversation continues in a free-wheeling dialogue. Both interviewees respond to the journalist's questions and proceed to outline the full picture of neocolonial exploitation, which was so well-known to Cubans during the pseudorepublic.

For more than two centuries Grenada has been known as the Spice Island, because it has supplied many condiments for Western Europe, and especially for the former mother country.

Bishop and Whiteman explain that after the Second World War producer cooperatives were formed to market Grenada's agricultural products and that since 1969 the island's GULP government began to take over these institutions and eliminated the process of elections through which the farmers had decided who would handle foreign sales of their products.

As a result the profits have remained exclusively in the hands of the government functionaries who control the cooperatives. And in addition, since none of Grenada's agricultural products are industrially processed on the island, these products can only be directly sold abroad as raw materials and, under the terms of unequal trade, the developed, purchasing countries obtain substantial profits.

For example, the Dutch name Van Geest is famous on many of the small Caribbean islands. The consortium by that name controls the sales of Grenada's bananas, which it transports in its own ships to England, the main consuming country. The institutions that sell cocoa and nutmeg operate in the same way. Whiteman summarizes the consequences of all this for Grenada.

"The imperialist sectors control our financial institutions as well as the insurance companies. All the large hotels are in imperialist hands, and the public services — electricity, telephone — are as well. All this is an important factor in the impoverishment of our population, which is shown, among other indexes, by the high and rising cost of living. The price we receive for our exports has remained the same for the last twenty or thirty years while the cost of imports has risen about 40 percent.

"The government has contributed to the deterioration of the situation. Committed to promoting the enrichment of its members and allies, it has given out monopoly rights to import rice, sugar, milk, televisions, and other lines of business. As you can imagine, in those cases the consumer has no choice but to pay the high prices fixed by these monopolies."

The main leader of the New Jewel Movement [Maurice Bishop] adds to the discussion, and explains how the party has confronted the various problems that the country and its different sectors are suffering.

"Since its formation, our party has tried to organize the people of Grenada. We have given priority to the organization of the working class through the unions. In Grenada there are sixteen unions, of which six are really important, and in four of those we have positions on the executive committees. In recent weeks the party directly formed the Bank and General Workers' Union.

"The second major priority has been organizing the youth, women, and the middle class. We have tried to create broad organizations for them, starting out with some existing organizations and founding some new ones with the participation of elements from different political organizations.

"As our third priority we have tried to organize the farmers. In this we have had some difficulties due to the fact that the farmers are dispersed in rural areas and due to the traditional influence of the Grenada United Labour Party. In addition to the small farmers, we want to organize the agricultural workers. Grenada's biggest union, the Grenada Mental and Manual Workers' Union [GMMWU] led by Prime Minister Gairy, was predominant among agricultural workers. In 1968 there was an attempt to organize a new agricultural union, but the police wiped it out. So we face this situation: when there have been attempts to organize the agricultural workers outside the official union, it has been shown that the government has used force to prevent that.

"Therefore when the party was created in 1973 we took the alternative of starting with other sectors of the workers before directly confronting the GMMWU, and since that year we have also tried to create a farmers' organization.

"In addition, the U.S. trade union organizations and the anticommunist and reactionary International Conference of Free Trade Unions are actively trying to penetrate the trade union movement in Grenada."

Maurice Bishop spoke to us about the evolution of ideas toward Marxism in Grenada.

"The English-speaking countries of the Caribbean began to gain consciousness of their real problems through the development of some currents of opinion among left-leaning sectors in the university or in government functions and among intellectual groups oriented toward what was called the Third-Worldist current.

"In Grenada's case, the ideas of 'Black Power' that developed in the United States and the freedom struggle of the African peoples in such places as Angola, Mozambique, and Guinea-Bissau powerfully contributed to providing an understanding that the problems of the Caribbean man were very different from those in the British mother country or the United States and Canada. But unquestionably, through the Cuban experience we got to see scientific socialism close up. This, together with the process that has taken place in recent years in Guyana and Jamaica, has been teaching us, on the practical level of day-to-day political struggle, the relevance of socialism as the only solution to our problems.

"Our party began to develop along Marxist lines in 1974, when we began to study the theory of scientific socialism."

The time we had available drew to an end. We used these last moments to talk about the possibilities of a socialist option for Grenada. Bishop's responses are realistic, indicating that the road selected by the New Jewel Movement is the fruit not of immature sentiments of social justice, but of deep reflection about the nature of this epoch and the Caribbean environment.

"The victory of socialism in our country will be possible only through firm ties with the socialist world and with the close cooperation of the most advanced governments of the region.

"Socialism is the future we would like to see in Grenada. At present the reality is that the most backward forms of capitalist exploitation exist in Grenada. We have to remember that Grenada — with its small territory, high unemployment, great poverty and misery, with the small size and low level of consciousness of its working class, with all its commercial ties to imperialism, and with a profoundly repressive government — must accomplish democratic advances in step with the march of the other countries of the region.

"We know how poor and backward our country is. And we know how difficult it would be to resist the general economic and political pressures that imperialism would unleash against Grenada if it tried to break the bonds of domination without first making serious attempts to develop true and significant links with the socialist camp.

"However, despite all the difficulties, we feel that the perspectives for the cause of social revolution in Grenada are good."

A Bright New Dawn

March 13, 1979

The following address to the Grenadian people, broadcast at 10:30 a.m. over the newly declared Radio Free Grenada, announced the defeat of Gairy's army and called on the people to rise up. From a text issued by the Grenadian government.

At 4:15 a.m. this morning, the People's Revolutionary Army seized control of the army barracks at True Blue.

The barracks were burned to the ground. After half-an-hour struggle, the forces of Gairy's army were completely defeated, and surrendered.

Every single soldier surrendered, and not a single member of the revolutionary forces was injured.

At the same time, the radio station was captured without a shot being fired. Shortly after this, several cabinet ministers were captured in their beds by units of the revolutionary army.

A number of senior police officers, including Superintendent Adonis Francis, were also taken into protective custody.

At this moment, several police stations have already put up the white flag of surrender.

Revolutionary forces have been dispatched to mop up any possible source of resistance or disloyalty to the new government.

I am now calling upon the working people, the youths, workers, farmers, fishermen, middle-class people, and women to join our armed revolutionary forces at central positions in your communities and to give them any assistance which they call for.

Virtually all stations have surrendered, I repeat. We restress, resistance will be futile. Don't be misled by Bogo DeSouze or Cosmos Raymond into believing that there are any prospects of saving the dictator Gairy.

The criminal dictator, Eric Gairy, apparently sensing that the end was near, yesterday fled the country, leaving orders for all opposition forces, including especially the people's leader, to be massacred.

Before these orders could be followed, the People's Revolutionary Army was able to seize power. This people's government will now be seeking Gairy's extradition so that he may be put on trial to face charges, including the gross charges, the serious charges, of murder, fraud, and the trampling of the democratic rights of our people.

In closing let me assure the people of Grenada that all democratic freedoms, including freedom of elections, religious and political opinion, will be fully restored to the people.

The personal safety and property of individuals will be protected. Foreign residents are quite safe, and are welcome to remain in Grenada.

And we look forward to continuing friendly relations with those countries with which we now have such relations.

Let me assure all supporters of the former Gairy government will not be injured in any way. Their homes, their families, and their jobs are completely safe, so long as they do not offer violence to our government.

However, those who resist violently will be firmly dealt with. I am calling upon all the supporters of the former government to realize that Gairy has fled the country, and to cooperate fully with our new government. You will not be victimized, we assure you.

People of Grenada, this revolution is for work, for food, for decent housing and health services, and for a bright future for our children and great-grandchildren.

The benefit of the revolution will be given to everyone regardless of political opinion or which political party they support.

Let us all unite as one. All police stations are again reminded to surrender their arms to the people's revolutionary forces.

We know Gairy will try to organize international assistance, but we advise that it will be an international criminal offense to assist the dictator Gairy.

This will amount to an intolerable interference in the internal affairs of our country and will be resisted by all patriotic Grenadians with every ounce of our strength.

I am appealing to all the people, gather at all central places all over the country, and prepare to welcome and assist the people's armed forces when they come into your area. The revolution is expected to consolidate the position of power within the next few hours.

Long live the people of Grenada. Long live freedom and democracy. Let us together build a just Grenada.

In Nobody's Backyard

April 13, 1979

The following address was broadcast nationally over Radio Free Grenada. From a text issued by the Grenadian government

Good evening sisters and brothers of free Grenada:

Today, one month after our historic people's revolution, there is peace, calm, and quiet in our country. Indeed, there has been a tremendous drop in the crime rate since our revolution. Foreign residents in the Levera-Bathway are feeling so comfortable and safe nowadays that they have advised the commissioner of police that he could close down the sub–police station in that area. An unusually high number of tourists for an off-season period are presently enjoying the beauty of our land and the warmth of our people, and this is so in spite of the fact that we have just had a revolution and that a real and present threat of mercenary invasion is faced by our country. In fact, it is almost impossible to rent a vehicle or to find an empty cottage at this point.

Tourists and visitors to our country have all been greatly impressed by the discipline of our troops and the respect that has been shown for the lives and property of local and foreign residents and visitors. From all over the island the same reports have come to us that the tourists are commenting on the warmth, friendliness, and discipline of our people and the People's Revolutionary Army. The same comments are being daily made by the hundreds of medical students studying in Grenada.

The annual boat race from Trinidad to Grenada took place as usual last night with a bigger than ever participation. The greast sense of relief and happiness of our people are obvious to all. In fact is is clear that there is no sense of panic here or hesitation by the tourists who daily continue to stream into Grenada.

For this reason we want the people of Grenada and the Caribbean to realize that if all of a sudden tourists start panicking and leaving the country, or stop coming to our country, then they should note that this came after veiled threats by the United States ambassador with respect to our tourist industy. The ambassador, Mr. Frank Ortiz, on his last visit to Grenada some days ago, went out of his way to emphasize the obvious importance of tourism to our country. He argued that as Grenada imported some $32 million a year in goods but exported only $13 million, we had a massive trade deficit of some $19 million which earnings from the tourist industry could substantially lessen. His point was, and we accept that point, that tourism was and is critical to the survival of our economy. The ambassador went on to advise us that if we continue to speak about what he called "mercenary invasions by phantom armies" we could lose all our tourists. He also reminded us of the experience which Jamaica had had in this regard a few years ago.

As some of you will undoubtedly recall, Jamaica at that time had gone through a period of intense destabilization. Under this process the people of Jamaica were encouraged to lose faith and confidence in themselves, their government and their country, and in the ability of their government to solve the pressing problems facing the country and meeting the expectations of their people. This was done through damaging news stories being spread in the local, regional, and international media, particularly newspapers, aimed at discrediting the achievements of the Jamaican government. It was also done through violence and sabotage and by wicked and pernicious attempts at wrecking the economy through stopping the flow of tourist visitors, and hence much needed foreign exchange earnings of the country. The experience of Jamaica must therefore remind us that the economies of small, poor, Third World countries which depend on tourism can be wrecked by those who have the ability and the desire to wreck them. In his official meetings with Minister of Finance Brother Bernard Coard, and then with me on Tuesday of this week, and in his unofficial discussions with a leading comrade of the People's Revolutionary Army at Pearls Airport on Wednesday, the ambassador stressed the fact that his government will view with great displeasure the development of any relations between our country and Cuba. The ambassador pointed out that his country was the richest, freest, and most generous country in the world, but as he put it, "We have two sides." We understood that to mean that the other side he was referring to was the side which stamped freedom and democracy when the American government felt that their interests were being threatened. "People are panicky and I will have to report that fact to my government," he advised us. However, the only evidence of panic given by the ambassador was the incident which took place last Monday when the People's Revolutionary Army, as a result of not having been warned before-hand, shot at a plane which flew very low, more than once over Camp Butler. He calls that panic. The people of Grenada call it alertness.

At the end of our discussion on Tuesday, the ambassador handed me a typed statement of his instructions from his government, to be given to us. The relevant section of that statement reads, and I quote: "Although my government recognizes your concerns over allegations of a possible counter-coup, it also believes that it would not be in Grenada's best interest to seek assistance from a country such as Cuba to forestall such an attack. We would view with displeasure any tendency on the part of Grenada to develop closer ties with Cuba."

It is well established internationally that all independent countries have a full, free, and unhampered right to conduct their own internal affairs. We do not therefore recognize any right of the United States of America to instruct us on who we may develop relations with and who we may not.

From day one of the revolution we have always striven to have and develop the closest and friendliest relations with the United States, as well as with Canada, Britain, and all our Caribbean neighbors — English, French, Dutch, and Spanish speaking, and we intend to continue to strive for these relations. But no one must misunderstand our friendliness as an excuse for rudeness and meddling in our affairs, and no one, no matter how mighty and powerful they are, will be permitted to dictate to the government and people of Grenada who we can have friendly relations with and what kind of relations we must have with other countries. We haven't gone through twenty-eight years of fighting Gairyism, and especially the last six years of terror, to gain our freedom, only to throw it away and become a slave or lackey to *any* other country, no matter how big and powerful.

Every day we fought Gairy we put our lives on the line. On the day of the revolution we started out with almost no arms, and in so doing we again put our lives on the line.

We have demonstrated beyond any doubt that we were prepared to *die* to win our freedom. We are even more prepared to die to maintain that freedom now that we have tasted it.

We feel that people of Grenada have the right to know precisely what steps we have taken in our attempts to establish relations at various levels with the United States, and the response which we have so far received.

From the second day of our revolution, during our first meeting with American government representatives in Grenada, we were at pains to emphasize the deplorable and ravished state in which the Gairy dictatorship had left our economy and our country. We pointed out then that massive assistance, technical and financial, would be required in order to begin the process of rebuilding the economy. The American consul-general told us that he was not surprised to hear this and assured us that he would encourage his government to give us the necessary assistance, particularly as he had been so impressed by the bloodless character and the self-evident humanity of our prompt assurances in the first hours of the revolution that the safety, lives, and property of American and other foreign residents were guaranteed. Indeed, he freely admitted that his

American residents had all reported to him that they were happy and comfortable and felt secure. However, one month later, no such aid has arrived.

It is true that the ambassador did point out — and correctly so — that his government generally grants aid on a multilateral basis through the Caribbean Development Bank. It is also true that he said his government would prefer to maintain that approach rather than help directly, despite his admission that red tape and bureaucracy could cause delays of up to one year in receiving such multilateral aid.

It is also true that he advised us that his government is monitoring Gairy's movements and that it is against United States law for Gairy to recruit mercenaries in the United States of America. This we appreciate.

However, we must point out that the fact is that in place of the massive economic aid and assistance that seemed forthcoming, the only aid which the American ambassador has been able to guarantee that he could get to Grenada in a reasonably short time would be U.S.$5,000 for each of a few small projects.

Sisters and brothers, what can a few $5,000 do? Our hospitals are without medicines, sheets, pillowcases, and proper equipment. Our schools are falling down. Most of our rural villages are in urgent need of water, electricity, health clinics, and decent housing. Half of the people in our country who are able to and would like to work are unable to find jobs. Four out of every five women are forced to stay at home or scrunt for a meagre existence. $5,000 cannot build a house or a health clinic. We feel forced to ask whether the paltry sum of a few $5,000 is all that the wealthiest country in the world can offer to a poor but proud people who are fighting for democracy, dignity, and self-respect based on real and independent economic development.

Let us contrast this with the immediate response of our Caribbean brothers. We will take two examples: Guyana and Jamaica, countries thousands of times poorer than the United States of America; countries indeed, like ourselves, which are poor, over-exploited, and struggling to develop. These two countries have given us technical assistance and cheaper goods and are actively considering our request for arms and military training. This assistance has included a shipment of rice which arrived two days ago, a six-man team of economic and other experts from Guyana presently in our country, and the imminent arrival of Mr. Roy Jones, Deputy Governor of the Bank of Jamaica and Professor George Eaton, a leading authority on public service structures. And, notwithstanding these concrete and much appreciated acts of assistance and solidarity, they have never once attempted to instruct us to the manner in which we should conduct our own internal affairs or as to which countries we should choose to develop relations with.

The American ambassador is taking very lightly what we genuinely believe to be a real danger facing our country. Contrary to what anyone else may think we know that the dictator Gairy is organizing mercenaries to attack Grenada in order to restore him to his throne. We know the man Gairy. Nobody knows him better than we, the people of Grenada, and we recognize the meaning and implications of the evidence which has come before us.

We say that when Grank Mabry, Jr. and Mustaphos Hammarabi, Gairy's underworld friends, write to him indicating how much and what kind of arms are available, and when Gairy says on radio broadcasts and in newspaper interviews that he will never give up and that he intends to return to Grenada as prime minister, that he can only mean that he will use force in order to achieve these ends. And because our revolution is a popular one supported by the vast majority of our population and because many of our patriots are armed, force here can only mean getting another country to intervene on his behalf or hiring mercenaries to do his dirty work for him. And this in turn could only mean the mass killing of thousands of innocent Grenadians, regardless of which political party they support. It is in these circumstances, and because we have an undoubted right to defend our people, our sovereignty, and our freedom, that we called on the Americans, Canadians, British, our fellow-countries in the Caribbean Community [CARICOM], like Guyana and Jamaica, Venezuela, *and* Cuba to assist us with arms.

And we reject *entirely* the argument of the American ambassador that we would only be entitled to call upon the Cubans to come to our assistance *after* mercenaries have landed and commenced the attack. Quite frankly, and with the greatest respect, a more ridiculous argument can hardly be imagined. It is like asking a man to wait until his house is burning down before he leaves to buy a fire extinguisher. No, we intend if possible to provide ouselves with the fire extinguisher before the fire starts! And if the government of Cuba is willing to offer us assistance, we would be more than happy to receive it.

Sisters and brothers, what we led was an *independent process*. Our revolution was definitely a popular revolution, not a coup d'etat, and was and is in no way a minority movement. We intend to continue along an independent and nonaligned path. We have stayed in the Commonwealth, we have stayed in the Organization of American States and in CARICOM; despite pressures we have stayed in the Eastern Caribbean Common Market and in the expanded West Indies Associated States Organization. We have applied to join the Nonaligned Movement. We will be applying to join the International Labor Organization — the ILO.

We are a small country, we are a poor country, with a population of largely African descent, we are a part of the exploited Third World, and we definitely have a stake in seeking the creation of a new international economic order which would assist in ensuring economic justice for the oppressed and exploited peoples of the world, and in ensuring that the resources of the sea are used for the benefit of all the people of the world and not for a tiny minority of profiteers. Our aim, therefore, is to join all organizations and work with all countries that will help us to become more independent and more in control of our own resources. In this regard, nobody who understands present-day realities can seriously challenge our right to develop working relations with a variety of countries.

Grenada is a sovereign and independent country, although a tiny speck on the world map, and we expect all countries to strictly respect our independence just as we will respect theirs. No country has the right to tell us what to do or how to run our country or who to be friendly with. We certainly would not attempt to tell any other country what to do. We are not in anybody's backyard, and we are definitely not for sale. Anybody who thinks they can bully us or threaten us clearly has no understanding, idea, or clue as to what material we are made of. They clearly have no idea of the tremendous struggles which our people have fought over the past seven years. Though small and poor, we are proud and determined. We would sooner give up our lives before we compromise, sell out, or betray our sovereignty, our independence, our integrity, our manhood, and the right of our people to national self-determination and social progress.

Long live the revolution!
Long live free Grenada!

Women Step Forward

June 15, 1979

The following speech was delivered to the National Conference of Women, held in St. George's. It is contained in Maurice Bishop, Selected Speeches 1979-81 *(Havana: Casa de las Américas, 1982).*

Sister chairperson;
Ministers of government;
Ambassador Dessima Williams;
Ambassador Kenrick Radix;
Comrade Rizo, Cuban chargé d'affaires;
Ministers of religion;
Distinguished guests on the platform;
Sisters and brothers;
Comrades:

It is my very great pleasure and privilege this evening to open this conference hosted by the St. George's Progressive Women's Association. It is a pleasure to welcome to our country so many distinguished people from different islands and countries in the Caribbean. We are very happy in particular to have with us sister Ingrid Kirkwood, because the country she comes from — Jamaica — has been one of the most outstanding countries in coming to our support and assistance in the first few days and weeks of our revolution. I do ask that you recognize her. [*Applause*]

At the same time, it is unfortunate that invited sisters from some other countries have been unable to come. In particular, I think at this point of Guyana, another country that has rendered valuable assistance to our revolution. I think of Cuba for the same reason and I think also of Dominica because of the suffering that is going on their right now and the struggle against oppression and repression being waged by the freedom-loving people of Dominica at this very moment in time. It is also gratifying to note that there are so many persons in this audience from different parts of our country, because I think that the combination of overseas representation and local representation is a very clear indication that the organization of all the working people of our country, including women, is proceeding at a good pace. It is also an indication, I feel, that the women of our country are beginning the serious task of raising their political consciousness, their political level and understanding and of seeing the importance of being here, of hosting in our country a conference to which they have invited people from the Caribbean and indeed from parts of North America; and I believe this is also a reflection of the internationalist approach that our country will increasingly be taking over the next few months and years.

The program, as I look at it, indicates that there are a number of very important subjects that will be discussed over the next few days — subjects that will have relevance to helping the women of our country and of the Caribbean to better identify their role in society, to better identify the problems which as women they face, and to begin to pose solutions to those problems.

We know that historically there have been many reasons for the exploitation of the woman. The domination by the male started from fairly early times and was a product of the fact that the man at a very early period of history looked around him and said: "This is my cow, this is my goat, this is my pig." In other words, he began to identify property for himself and in no time at all he also turned around and said: "This is my woman." And of course, the reason for that was to ensure that an heir to whom he could pass his property was produced. In other words, the woman was essentially meant to serve the interests of the generation that he was fathering and the main significance during that early period of the woman was as an instrument, if I may use such a crude term, of childbearing for the purpose of ensuring that property was passed on.

The exploitation of the woman which can be seen from these early days was evident indeed with all stages and all epochs of history; all the great modes of production known to mankind have seen the exploitation of woman continuing. Just as in the days of slavery, the woman's main function was to produce children so that the slave master would have more human labor that he could exploit; so today in some parts of the world that situation continues. And just as in the period of feudalism the woman continued to be an object and symbol of exploitation, this time of sexual exploitation in that the lord of the manor had the first right to sleep with any new wife before the husband himself had this right. Today, we can see this level of exploitation of the woman continuing in different parts of the world. Again, under the system of capitalism where the interests of capital and profit demand that there is always a large army of unemployed people to act as a reserve pool of labor for business and for capital, the woman is always at the bottom of that ladder being the last to be hired and the first to be fired.

This historical exploitation, sisters, brothers, and comrades, has both a subjective aspect and an objective aspect. In its subjective side, it has to do with the habits, the values, the ideas, the culture that has been handed down right from the earliest days. We look at the Bible, for example, and it speaks of the Trinity, and the Trinity is God the Father, God the Son, and God the Holy Ghost, all presumably being members of the same sex. The woman herself in the Bible is said to have come from the body of man. The Bible speaks very often of the limb of man and therefore even in the Bible, perhaps unconsciously, there was the beginning of the characterization of the woman in an inferior role. But we have it further. The Church today is still a little slow in accepting the idea that woman can also be priests and indeed perhaps be good priests.

The woman continues to take the man's name; only in few societies do you have a situation where the first surname of a child is the name of the father and the second surname is the name of the mother. In most societies around the world only the man's name is relevant. The child indeed, can only inherit from the mother if he is born out of wedlock and the reason for that is to ensure that the father's precious property is not passed on to apparent undesirables.

In the realm of the monarch there is always a preference for the male so even if the queen or king had six girls first they had to wait for the seventh child, a male, to take the precedence before they could hope to have a successor to the crown.

The woman's right to vote is equality circumscribed in many countries. Indeed in Grenada, up until last year you had a situation where juries were unequally made up — a man could become a juror at age twenty-one, but a woman had to wait until age thirty. The presumption, apparently, being that the woman was too undeveloped and too fickle to pass serious judgement on a curse case or in a case where somebody cuts somebody else. That fortunately has been changed.

You should observe also, that if a woman has to travel she must first of all get permission from her husband before she can take up permanent residence; but I have never heard of a case where a man has to apply to his wife for permission to migrate. Separation agreements are something that lawyers know a lot about. There is a clause in these separation agreements which in Latin is referred to as the "Dumcasta Clause," "Dumcasta Sola" and what this means is that the wife can continue to receive alimony and maintenance and payments for as long as she remains chaste, but I have never heard of a man having to remain chaste in order to meet his own obligations.

The very language that we speak on a day-to-day basis reflects the unequal status of the woman. We speak of a "chairman" and a "foreman" and such like and usually it is to the exclusion again of the women in our society. The woman indeed is generally regarded as being inferior by many men and unfortunately by many women themselves who have also not learnt of the importance of fighting these bad cultural values, bad habits, and prejudices and allow themselves to be abused. They allow themselves to be molested by men without showing sufficient respect for themselves so as to call up the man when he makes mistakes like for example comparing her to a Coca-Cola bottle; you know, she looks good, figure eight, the sex mechanic business; the kitchen business; the so-called housewife where the housewife is supposed to be an unimportant person in society but essentially is supposed to be somebody who stays at home to wash the wares; to make up the bed and to wait for the husband when he comes in late at nights. Indeed, most men do not even reward that function with a housekeeping allowance and if the woman is fortunate enough to have a job at the same time but unable to hire help, when she comes home from work, the housekeeping is hers to do without any sharing whatsoever from the husband.

But apart from these subjective factors there are very serious objective factors that have limited the development and the growth of the women in class society, in the social system that we have where everyone is exploited for profits. We find for example, that there are no day care centers so, even if the woman is lucky enough to find a job, there is no place where she can leave the children at home in order to go out to do that job and at the same time feel reasonably confident that, when she gets back home after work, the child would have been well looked after. The business of day care centers therefore is a serious objective factor in limiting the mobility of our women in countries like Grenada. The business also of nursery schools is a serious limiting factor. The business of educational qualifications among many of the women in our country and indeed most of the countries of the exploited Third World is another cause for alarm because it means that if you are not suitably qualified for particular jobs you are going to be sorted always into a particular kind of mold. There are some figures which I came across a few days ago indicating that among the member states of UNESCO there are something like 740 million people around the world who are illiterate and something like 70 percent of that figure is made up of women. The vast majority of these women come from Africa, and other parts of the Third World. This indicates two very important facts: one, that the woman continues to be dominated and exploited; and two, secondly, that the Third World continues in particular to be ravaged and exploited to be raped of all its resources while those who take those resources away continue to develop their own countries; their own culture; their own educational standards without leaving anything behind.

The lack of community laundries, the lack of pipe-borne water, all these too are very serious limiting objective factors in ensuring that our women have time to do more things. Obviously if you have to spend half day washing by hand when there are things called washing machines and they can be provided for the use of the community, then a lot of your time is going to be wasted. If you have to spend the whole day sweeping when you could perhaps use a vacuum cleaner or if you have to cook on a coalpot when there are things called pressure cookers and gas stoves which would mean that you can cook a lot more quickly, much invaluable time is wasted. All of these factors do reduce the amount of time that women find for developing themselves, for developing their undoubted skills and talents, for further educating and qualifying themselves in order to serve a more relevant role in society.

The question of maternity leave is another serious problem. I am ashamed to say that in the Civil Service in Grenada the women are not allowed maternity leave with pay. Indeed, the International Labor Organization, one of the treaties that we are about to sign, requires that women are given three months leave with full pay, one month before the expected birth of the child and two months afterwards. But, in our country apparently that is totally unimportant, totally disregarded and the women who find themselves bearing children would have to take a week or two off and then perhaps another few weeks off and rush back out with all the attendant disadvantages that child raising involves.

There is also the question of equal pay for equal work and we find that in Grenada up to three months ago it was not even proclaimed that the woman had the same right to equality of pay. Once she was doing the same work as the man she has a right to receive the same pay. Of course, it suited everybody in the system not to challenge that because wherever you look around you find that women are engaged in an occupation. Whether it is in the banks, whether it is on the roads, whether it is on the estates or food farms, you find that the same practice obtains. For doing exactly the same work as her male counterpart, she has to receive perhaps 50 or 60 percent of the pay. Precisely because it is well known that most of our people are unemployed many employers have chosen to exploit this situation and to take women from out of the country areas, bring them into the towns, offer them jobs in stores, tell them they will get $150 or $160 a month, and at the end of the month give them in fact $80. If they choose to complain what they turn around and say to them is that: "there are many more like you outside there so I don't care." That sort of exploitation has continued.

The combination of the lack of technological facilities and other amenities together with the economic dependence of the woman has led to a certain insecurity, a certain frustration, has led to a certain destruction of the personality of the woman. This, of course, has also meant that many women have been forced to suffer from unhappy relationships because the man will always turn around and say: "well you could go if you want." But, of course, the question, is if you go, where is the money going to come from? If you go, where is the housing going to come from? If you go, where are the jobs going to come from? In other words, by denying the woman the right to jobs, the right to decent pay, the right to equality in many of the economic areas of activity it has also confined the woman almost to a perpetual state of insecurity.

It is only when we move to change these subjective and objective conditions that the condition of the woman in our society is going to improve. The reason for these problems is the particular social system which exploits all of us, man and woman. Because of this system we find this exploitation continuing and therefore the real answer in the final analysis is that we must move, we must organize — united as men and women — organize to change the social system and to create a new social system that would indeed ensure freedom and equality for all of us. Any serious society and any serious government must move to begin that change and we feel that the most important beginning is when conscious, organized, and united women themselves take the initiative in beginning to identify their problems.

You think of it, there is no uniformity, there is no homogeneity when you speak of the woman; you could be talking about the young woman; you could be talking about the student woman; you could be talking about the peasant woman; you could be talking about the agricultural estate worker; you could be talking about the urban worker; you could be talking about the professional woman; you could be talking about the unemployed woman; you could be talking about the housewife; you could be talking about the domestic who is a woman. In that kind of situation, it is obvious that the best people to begin the process of thinking about what are the problems and their possible solutions must be the women themselves. Therefore, we are particularly happy that the women of our country, united with their Caribbean counterparts and their international counterparts, have begun this very important process of trying to identify what are the problems facing our women in Grenada; of trying to identify a serious and relevant role for the women in our country and of beginning to pose solutions to those problems. It is clear, however, that having found the problems and having identified the solutions that these solutions can only come into effect, can only be brought about, if there is unity of man and woman in the attempt to try to solve the problems that have been identified. The woman cannot do it by herself; the man cannot do it by himself. It is by the combination of men and women together attempting to build a new process; to build a new society; to build a new civilization; attempting to produce more; attempting to find the new value systems to identify ideas and new ways of pushing our country forward, it is only if we achieve this unity of the man and the woman that we would be able to move forward. I know there are some women, particularly in North America, who feel that the enemy is the man and some of them have begun to go around half-naked, calling that liberation, and others have begun to say that to liberate themselves it is necessary for them to stamp on the man. I do not believe that the women of our country will accept this solution. I do not believe that the women who are going to be speaking here for the next few days, and Sister Kirkwood who would be speaking here tonight, will accept that solution, because it is clear that there is a common enemy that faces both man and woman. That common enemy is identifiable and we can fight that common enemy together and it is only when we have fought and smashed the common enemy that we are going to have the liberation of the woman. Without the liberation of the woman there cannot be the liberation of the man, so man also has the responsibility of pushing for the liberation of our women.

The People's Revolutionary Government [PRG], sisters and brothers, since our coming into being (only three months ago) cannot pretend that we have done anything in a serious way at this point, to solve the objective problems facing the women in our society. We have, however, done a number of things to assist in eradicating some of the subjective difficulties tied up with old habits and old culture and old prejudices that women and men have. We have also begun to make certain proclamations. These are proclamations of intent which we intend to follow up and which we believe will go some way towards dealing with some of these problems.

First and foremost we have proclaimed the principle of *equal pay for equal work* and we have made it clear that our position is going to be that wherever and at whatever level in our society where the woman does exactly the same work as the man, then she must receive the same pay as the man.

Secondly, we have proclaimed the *principle of maternity leave.* I cannot tonight give details of how we will legislate this principle. I cannot speak of whether it is going to be full salary or half salary or whether it might be two months only in the first instance with an option to take another month of unpaid leave or what, because these are economic questions in part and we are going to have to sit down with the experts to look to see what the costs of such a development might be. What we have done and what we will not flinch from is the proclamation of the principle because we feel the principle itself is what is important and we can move from that to begin to identify possibilities existent in our situation for realistic implementation.

We have also issued directives that any minister or civil servant, that they must move rapidly to change the wording of laws to ensure that they begin to speak of the equality of men and women in our society.

As you know, many of our laws speak of the woman in a very disparaging way and we are anxious to have that corrected.

We have also issued directives that any minister or civil servant who chooses to engage in the old practice of the sexual exploitation of our women for work — you remember the old practice that used to exist up to a few months ago where the women were sent from hand to hand in exchange for a job? — we have made it clear that anyone caught engaging in that practice will be immediately dismissed and we are very serious about that.

In the Ministry of Education and Social Affairs, a Women's Desk has been established and it is our hope that this desk will be able to monitor and organize improved rights for our women.

I wish to suggest eight important functions that we expect the Women's Desk to carry out in the interest of the women of our country.

(1) We would expect the Women's Desk to be involved in looking at the laws and constitutions, setting up committees which can do that with a view to seeing which laws can be amended, which laws can be improved, which laws must be changed so as to ensure equality at least on the statute book.

(2) We would expect them to make sure that the government adopts the 1969 resolution of the United Nations on the discrimination of women and look seriously at other charters of the United Nations in which the question of women's rights have been raised and discussed.

(3) We would expect them to actively fight and struggle to get representation on all relevant planning bodies at the national and international level so that they will have a voice, they will have an input in every important area, so that they will be in a position to struggle at all times for the rights of women in our country.

(4) We would expect them to continue to monitor the progress that the government has made in its declarations of policy to ensure that the law and its practice at all times approximate, to make sure that the government itself at all times actively strives to implement those declarations and those proclamations that we have made with regard to the women in our society.

(5) We would expect the Women's Desk to also be involved in the organization of the women in our country, to create different bodies, women's bodies and other bodies that can help to set up guidelines and give advice and channel the energy and creativity of our women into productive work.

(6) We would expect them to make sure that the women of our country are participating in decision-making at all levels in the government and in society.

(7) We would expect them to get the women around the country to organize themselves to make sure that certain basic social services and basic amenities are provided. I refer of course, to pipe-borne water. I refer to improving educational facilities. I refer to the question of housing, the question of child care, the question of day care centers. In all of

these critical areas it would be the job of the Women's Desk to make sure that that practice is not lagging too far behind promises and behind declarations and proclamations.

(8) And finally, improving the area of community development. Community development is, of course, a job that is going to be very important for both our women and men to be involved in, given that the country has inherited a situation of bankruptcy, given that we are not going to be able overnight to get many of the facilities and amenities that we would like to have. It must mean that the job of the people of our country is going to have to include, in part, a great deal of self-reliant and independent activity. We are going to have to try to develop a new attitude that says that if a community building needs fixing that the answer is not to rush down to Brother Strachan in the Ministry of Communications and Works and say that we need a community building in Maran. The answer must first and foremost be to organize the people of that area to see what skills can be provided, to see what materials can be found, and then going down to Brother Strachan and say: "well look, we are from Maran, we have this committee, we have found these materials, we have these human resources, what we want from you is technical supervision, what we want from you is some more cement, some more lumber and together we are going to be able to repair that community center." That sort of development would be of the greatest importance.

So sister chairperson at the risk of have spoken too long I want to thank you again for the opportunity of opening this conference. I want once again to particularly welcome our distinguished overseas guests and friends. We are happy to have them — we are happy to have them because we are always pleased when our neighbors from the Caribbean countries come to our shores in Grenada, because we are also always pleased when progressive women or men come to Grenada to help us to define a role for our revolution, help us to define a role for the making of the new Caribbean man and woman. We are also happy to have them here because we believe that once they have seen what is happening in our country, when they return to their respective countries, they will be able to assist us in smashing false rumors; in smashing the lies and slander being spread against the revolutionary process taking place in our country because they have seen. They will be in a position to say: "That is not true, we went to Grenada, we know what is happening in Grenada." And we believe that they will recognize it as their duty and responsibility to assist our revolution in smashing these lies and exposing these people who are spreading lies, these people who are spreading rumors, these people who are out to destabilize and confuse our population and our people.

Therefore, sisters and brothers, once again on your behalf I declare this conference formally open and I ask you to join me in a very solid round of applause for the St. George's Progressive Women's Association, and for our distinguished overseas guests.

Long live the equality of women!

Long live the revolutionary Grenadian and Caribbean women!

Long live the revolution!

Forward ever, backward never!

Education in the New Grenada

July 2, 1979

The following is from the opening address to the National Education Conference, held July 2–3. From a text issued by the Grenadian government, major excerpts of which were printed in Intercontinental Press, *October 27, 1980.*

It is for me a great honor and privilege to have to speak this morning at the start of this very historic conference. This conference, of course, takes place at this time when momentous events are taking place in our country. It is part of a process, and part of an opportunity which we the people of our country and all the different sectors and sections and classes and strata will have in the next few months of examining and looking anew at all aspects of our society. This gives us, of course, the opportunity for the first time in many years of looking inwards at ourselves and our society.

As a colonial people up to a few years ago, it has been our practice to look outward, outward away from the needs of our country and the problems facing our people, and outward instead to the needs, to the problems, to the solutions that the metropolitan masters wish to impose on us.

Perhaps the worst crime that colonialism left our country, has indeed left all former colonies, is the education system. This was so because the way in which that system developed, the way in which that system was used, was to teach our people an attitude of self-hate, to get us to abandon our history, our culture, our values. To get us to accept the principles of white superiority, to destroy our confidence, to stifle our creativity, to perpetuate in our society class privilege and class difference.

The colonial masters recognized very early on that if you get a subject people to think like they do, to forget their own history and their own culture, to develop a system of education that is going to have relevance to our outward needs and be almost entirely irrelevant to our internal needs, then they have already won the job of keeping us in perpetual domination and exploitation. Our educational process, therefore, was used mainly as a tool of the ruling elite.

In the days of slavery, of course, it was not necessary to even have education because slaves were not required to know how to read or write, nor were they required to think for themselves. Indeed, they did not even have the rights to their own lives. Their sole function was to produce for the slave masters and the sole function of the women was to produce for the slave masters; those that were unable to otherwise work, their sole function was to produce more children that could be used as property to send out profits to the metropolitan countries.

It was only, therefore, after the abolition of slavery, or rather just four years before the abolition, that anything was given at all to education in Grenada, and it was in fact in 1834, I believe, that what they called a Negro Education Grant was set up, and this was to assist with the question of establishing the resources and the means of creating a certain form of education that ensured the continued exploitation of the Grenadian at that time.

Our educational system was used in this way to encourage a number of illusions, a number of deep-seated fallacies. It was meant to create the belief that social mobility was the most important factor to be had from education. It was meant to foster the illusion that the most important reason why anyone should receive education was so that he or she could acquire individual wealth. It helped to teach us most of the negative attitudes and values that today we still see in certain sectors of our society. Attitudes of racist beliefs, racism, priorities, and chauvinist attitudes that make many of the men in our society look at the woman as being not an equal partner but as being a tool for personal use and enjoyment; an attitude of narrow nationalism and of isolationism that has taught us to believe that each of us in each of the several Caribbean islands must always remain separate and apart, and our French- and Spanish- and Dutch-speaking brothers and sisters have no relevance to those of us who live in the English-speaking section of the Caribbean. It has taught us to accept attitudes of authoritarian rule, a hierarchical structure that says that the people do not have any right to participate, do not have any right to have their voices heard.

The education process compartmentalized us, made us believe that during the eighteen or nineteen years — for those who are able to get secondary education — that we are so-called students, that our only role is to study, and this study must be completely unrelated to what is happening in our society. An attitude, also, which continued to teach us that our sole function, a hundred and forty something years after the abolition of slavery, was to continue to be producers of raw materials and raw goods for the former colonial masters. These were some of the problems that we inherited. These were some of the myths that were created.

Sisters and brothers, we inherited very many problems on the thirteenth of March. Perhaps the most fundamental problem of all is the one that many people like to pretend does not exist, and that is the problem of illiteracy. People like to wave around certain facts and figures, and glorify it by the name of statistics, and they say that in Grenada the percentage of illiteracy is very small. But what they mean by that is that most people or perhaps many people are able to sign their names, and the process of being able to scratch a signature on a piece of paper is deemed literacy and therefore they say there is no problem of illiteracy.

But the reality that in fact confronts us is that the vast majority of our people are still unable to read or to write in a functional manner, are still unable to take a newspaper and to appreciate what is written on that paper, are still unable to listen to a radio broadcast and to discern in an intelligent, in an inquiring, in a serious way what is being said, because they have not been given the opportunity of such development. And one of the most crying shames of the recent history of our country is the fact that no one is yet able to assess how many thousands of geniuses might have been uncovered, might have been discovered, might have come forth and flowered if they had had the opportunity of receiving some form of further education.

But one of the major problems of a society such as ours, a society that is ruled by an elite, a society that is divided along class lines, a society where the major motivational factor is profit, is that very few people care whether the agricultural worker, or the fisherman, or the road worker, or the mason, or very often even the civil servants can read or write. That is not an important question, because as they see it, in order to make more dollar bills, what is important is not what you have in your head but what you have in your arms. Once you have the physical strength to turn the work out, once you are able to turn the machine or to dig with the fork or the cutlass, or to cut with the cutlass or whatever, that is what is important.

And therefore what our society has encouraged is division between those who have certain mental and intellectual skills, those deemed the elite, those deemed the important people in our society, and the vast majority of people, the ones who are in fact the most important because they are the ones who are producing, because no amount of reading and writing and passing exams for certificates can help us produce the cocoa, or nutmeg, or bananas that our country relies on in order to produce the wealth that we have.

And yet, precisely the people that are most responsible for developing our country, for creating the wealth that we have, are precisely the ones that are most looked upon, the ones that are most regarded as being useless, the ones that are taught to most hate themselves, the ones that can never fully develop their personality, because they do not even have the most basic requirements that any human being should have to acquire further information and knowledge. The right to read, the right to write, the right to be able to communicate in a serious way with one's fellow human beings, the right to receive all the information that mankind has gathered over the past several thousand years, the right to understand one's history, the right to think about one's future, because they might say you have the freedom to speak or the freedom to read, but what is the point of having the freedom to read and our country at the same time can pass a law that bans the right to certain types of books and magazines to come into our country?

What is the point of saying there is freedom to speak when in our country at the same time three and a half months ago [the Gairy regime] prohibited the right to in fact communicate? What is the point of talking about the freedom to develop when what in fact was being encouraged was backwardness, was superstition, the perpetuating of a feeling that only a small elite can rule; that the only purpose of education was to acquire individual wealth?

The physical condition of our schools is a sin crying to heaven for vengeance. Virtually every single pre-primary school in our country is in need of repair. The secondary schools, a fair number of them, are also in pretty urgent need of repairs, and when we come to the situation of the teacher and that of course is the most single important ingredient in any school — the teachers — because in the final analysis even if you do not have books, or exercises to write on, but you have a serious and committed teacher, you can still learn. That is the history of those people who have been fighting their national liberation struggles in Angola and Guinea-Bissau and Mozambique and other countries around the world — the history that you do not always need a classroom to develop the consciousness, to raise the educational and qualificational standards of your people. It is sufficient if you have committed people who are teaching them.

But yet we find that of our teachers at the primary level less than one-third, in fact only 30 percent, have received any form of professional training at all. At the secondary level the picture is even worse; it is something like 7 percent of all the teachers who have received some form of professional training, and at the pre-primary level the vast majority have in fact received no form of professional training.

And therefore, with these problems it means, sisters and brothers, that the solutions we are going to have to propose, the solutions you are going to have to look at over the next few weeks, are going to have to be radical solutions; are going to have to be solutions that are far-reaching; are going to have to be solutions that will deal with the real problems that we have in our country and not the problems we would like to imagine exist, but with the real problems that in fact face us.

The structural problems affecting education and affecting every other sector in our society are of course also very deep-seated problems. I refer here of course to the poverty of our country, to the high transportation cost, to the poor health facilities, to the lack of jobs, to the lack of meals for schoolchildren at lunch time, to the inadequate housing that children must live in, to the poor water facilities that are available.

But what these structural problems should remind us and what it should teach us is that in order for us to move forward, we will always have to remember that there are very serious problems that we face in our country, problems which we could only solve if people and government together come up with creative solutions. Solutions that are not initially going to require a great deal of capital expenditure.

It is easy for any government, it certainly will be easy for the People's Revolutionary Government, to proclaim the principle of free education for all. And this we are of course very happy to do. But it is one thing to say free education, it is another thing to say how are we going to pay for that free education. Where is the money going to come from? Where are the resources going to come from that we are certainly going to need to run schools, train teachers better, provide a more relevant form of education, and all free of cost?

What I think that points to, is that one of the very important lessons that we are going to have to draw — and one of the very important things that we are going to have to embark on as we try to open up the school system to the economically poor and underprivileged in our society — is that we are going to have to learn the lesson that we will have to take our schools to the people. We are going to depend to some extent on a system of volunteers who will be willing to go out into the countryside, where the most serious and endemic problems of illiteracy exist, and try to train our people.

All of us are going to have to strive to become teachers on the job and off the job. All of us are going to have to try to get down to the important task of raising the literacy standard, providing all our people with the basic opportunity of being at least able to read and to write. And this is going to involve a massive task of voluntary work by those who are sufficiently fortunate to have the skills, to have the ability to communicate what we know, who have been able to receive some form of education and therefore are able to pass on what we have learned to those who are themselves unable to acquire any such knowledge.

Secondly, it seems to me that we are going to have to move very quickly to destroy the artificial class divisions of our people into absurd and illogical compartments. We are going to try to get away from the idea of people who are students full time. And we are going to have to move more and more to the idea of getting everybody in our country to regard themselves as both students and workers.

The whole question of the curriculum is going to be a key one. A curriculum that is geared to developing a new philosophy, that is going to stress the important question of self-reliance, the important question of genuine independence, that is going to look at us as we in fact are, as a small, poor, overexploited form of colonial Third World country and what that means in practice for our future, that is going to try to begin to raise national consciousness, that is going to stress the importance of national unity, that will stress the importance of developing an approach, an attitude that says on the one hand all of us must work harder, all of us must produce more, but says on the other hand when we work harder and when we produce more the benefits of that production and that sort of work must come back to all of us collectively.

That sort of thinking we are going to have to develop. A participatory democracy that seeks to involve all of our people: workers, farmers, fishermen, youths, students, women; all of them on a regular ongoing basis in making decisions and coming up with solutions for the problems that we have identified as being the real problems that are holding us back.

To develop that sort of approach requires the creation of a new philosophy, a new thinking which must be reflected in the curriculum that we are going to have to develop.

The question of the appropriate forms of technology that we are going to use to develop our country, all of these problems are problems which our society must look at, which the curriculum that hopefully over the next few months you will begin to draft an outline of, that the curriculum has relevance to these problems and therefore can assist us, that the educational process can then become a tool for our liberation, our development, for us to make social progress; not as it now is, as a tool to alienate people, to frustrate them, to dehumanize them. And the only way in which we can do that is if we in fact begin a very serious and in-depth process of thinking about the many problems that we face.

So to summarize, sisters and brothers, we must move to wipe out illiteracy, we must move to develop a system of work and study in the schools, we must move to make all of us who are capable of being such teachers, develop the concepts of taking education into the countryside on a voluntary basis to those of our unfortunate sisters and brothers who are not even able to come to the town to get that education.

We must use the educational system and process as a means of preparing the new man for the new life in the new society we are trying to build.

Imperialism Is Not Invincible

September 6, 1979

The following speech was delivered to the Sixth Summit Conference of the Movement of Nonaligned Countries, held in Havana, Cuba. From a text issued by the Grenadian government.

Comrade president;
Excellencies;
Colleagues;
Comrades:

Today it is a great privilege and honor for me to deliver my country's maiden address to the Nonaligned Movement on behalf of the People's Revolutionary Government of Grenada and the people of Grenada.

We are particularly happy, Comrade President, to be speaking right after Comrade Ortega of Nicaragua, because the processes in 1979 that had the greatest impact and the greatest effect on our own revolutionary struggle in Grenada were the revolutionary struggles in Iran and Nicaragua. In fact, we are happy to say that on June 22 this year Grenada became only the second country in the world to recognize the Provisional Revolutionary Government of Nicaragua.

We in Grenada, Comrade President, have always had a very deep admiration for the Cuban people and their revolution and as such it is particularly appropriate that the first Nonaligned summit that we are privileged to attend should be in the great revolutionary country of Cuba.

On behalf of our delegation, our government, and our people, I extend our sincerest and most fraternal thanks to the government and people of Cuba for the excellent and outstanding arrangements made for this summit and for their warm and fraternal hospitality. As always, the government and people of Cuba have demonstrated yet again why their revolution is so highly regarded and so deeply admired by all truly progressive and democratic nations.

May I also join with other colleagues in expressing the appreciation of our delegation for the important contribution made by Sri Lanka in coordinating all activities of our movement since the fifth Nonaligned Movement summit was held.

As Grenada enters the Nonaligned Movement, we do so as one of the smallest nations within this great movement. Indeed we enter as a small island of only 133 square miles and with a population of just over 100,000 people. Like almost all our Caribbean friends here today, we have a population that is overwhelmingly African in its descent, the product of that most gross and open form of exploitation — slavery. And for us, like many of the countries here today, this was only the beginning of our process of exploitation. Hence from slavery we moved to the colonial experience under the hand of European colonialism, an ordeal that saw us conquered, hounded, and exploited by France, and finally England — an ordeal that left us with only one secondary school built by the colonialists after 300 years of colonial rule.

From this form of open exploitation our country was shunted into that second and perhaps more dangerous stage of the colonial experience, the stage that we recognize as neocolonialism. This stage saw us exposed to various constitutional manipulations, a neat cover for the underlying reality of economic bondage shrouded by pretensions to constitutional independence. Indeed, in the closing period of this neocolonial stage, we were exposed to the ruthless neofascist dictator, Eric Gairy, whose closest links were with international imperialism and international criminal elements as represented by the Mafia and also with the openly fascist and dictatorial regime of Chile — a country with which we have since broken diplomatic relations.

The legacy of this neofascist regime for the people of our nation was a total dependence on imperialism, a reality that meant extreme poverty, characterized by massive unemployment, with more than half of the work force out of work, high malnutrition, illiteracy, backwardness, superstition, poor housing and health conditions, combined with overall economic stagnation and massive migration.

Such a situation was intolerable and as such the progressive forces of our nation got together in March 1973, under the leadership of our party, the New Jewel Movement, in order to take power so as to revolutionize our economy, our politics, and our society. And the most important stage in that process ended on March 13 this year when our party led a successful and popular revolution to take power in our country — a revolution that Comrade Fidel Castro has referred to both as "a successful Moncada" and "a big revolution in a small country." And from that day, our people, our government, and our party have been trying to build a new, just, free, and revolutionary Grenada.

Our revolution is a people's revolution and as such the cornerstone of our revolution is the development of our people and hand in hand with this aim is the establishment of the people's rights — rights that include the right to social and economic justice, the right to work, the right to equal pay for men and women, and the right to democratic participation in the affairs of our nation.

With these national aims, we also share a firm commitment to the establishment of an international community based on the principles of opposition to colonialism, neocolonialism, apartheid, racism (including Zionism), fascism, and imperialism:

Comrade President, in fact, the fundamental principles of the Nonaligned Movement.

We affirm before this great assembly our resolute and unwavering opposition to imperialism in all its forms.

We affirm equally resolutely and unwaveringly our opposition to colonialism and neocolonialism in all their manifestations.

We affirm the strongest objection to racism, including Zionism and racial discrimination.

We reaffirm our unrelenting opposition to the hateful and despicable system of apartheid, which continues to hold millions of our brothers and sisters in South Africa in the most inhuman bondage. We pledge our fullest continued support for the great struggles for national liberation now being waged at various levels throughout Africa.

We affirm our resolute stand against economic exploitation and foreign occupation or domination in all parts of the world.

We affirm our rejection of all military pacts or blocs designed to bolster or defend imperialism, expansionism, fascism, or racism.

We stand firmly on the side of national independence and sovereignty, territorial integrity, and equality of all races and peoples of the world.

We also affirm our fullest support for an end to the arms race, completion of the process of decolonization, and the achievement of national independence by millions of people in the Third World. But there still remain areas under colonial rule in the Caribbean, as in Africa, Asia, and elsewhere, and we must persevere in our support for the end of colonialism in these last enclaves of colonial rule.

It is for this reason that our delegation joins the chorus of support for the liberation movements in southern Africa which are seeking to free Zimbabwe, Namibia, and the superracist bastion of South Africa from the clutches of colonialism and imperialism. We have also noted and wish to express our sincere appreciation for the courageous and principled stand of the front-line states in their support of the people of Zimbabwe, Namibia, and South Africa.

We record with pleasure the start made at Lusaka at the Commonwealth Conference last month and the United Kingdom's acceptance of her responsibility to deal with the problem of Rhodesia. We welcome the all-party talks which are about to begin in London on Monday. We anticipate that there will be no great difficulty in reaching a constitutional agreement. But we feel and believe that we are obliged to mention here today that there are still key problems that will remain even after the critical question of the new constitution is settled. Two of these questions relate to the white racist army and the timing of and conditions under which new elections will be held.

We recall that as long ago as September 1977, two years ago, the Anglo-American proposals had already proposed that a new army should be constituted and based on the Patriotic Front forces in Zimbabwe; had already made it clear that the peple of Zimbabwe would have the right to build their own process free from outside interference. That, Comrade President, was two years ago.

But what we find in the interim is that after the visits of [Cyrus] Vance and [David] Owen to the Patriotic Front in early 1978, when they made "sincere" promises that within a matter of weeks everything would have been settled, instead of that, as a result of imperialist intrigue and manipulation we began to hear talk of a possible split in the Patriotic Front and we then saw sham elections being held in Rhodesia. So we regard time as a potential problem, because time allows imperialism room to maneuver. We do not feel that we can rest confidently and feel greatly optimistic just because of the talks next week, because our past experience has shown us that imperialism knows how to manipulate and how to divide and rule.

We want to issue the caution that it still remains important for the Nonaligned Movement, for all progressive, democratic, and socialist countries to continue to maintain maximum vigilance and to give maximum support to the Patriotic Front and to the people of Zimbabwe in order to ensure that their victory comes very soon.

We feel, Comrade President, that the Patriotic Front must be encouraged behind the slogan "Peaceful means by elections if possible, revolution if necessary, if the electoral method does not or can not work."

We express also our support for the people of Namibia and lend our unwavering support and solidarity to their authentic representative — SWAPO. We express our firmest solidarity with the people of South Africa and promise to give our continued firmest support to their representatives, the ANC of South Africa.

Comrade President, our government is firm on the principle that there can no meaningful peace in the Middle East without an acceptable settlement of the Palestinian question. It is on the basis of this principle that we reject and forcefully condemn the Camp David agreement. This agreement was engineered by the United States imperialists in their continuing efforts to divide the Arab world.

We reject the agreement because it offers no solution to the Palestinian people. We reject the agreement because United Nations resolutions have made it clear that agreements can only be reached under the umbrella of the United Nations. We reject the agreement because nobody, except the PLO, has the right to negotiate on behalf of the people of Palestine. We reject the agreement because Camp David is against the interests of and is not supported by the Palestinians, by the PLO, by the Arab nations, and, indeed, by the entire democratic, progressive, and socialist world.

Comrade President, as I stand here and look around this assembly, it reminds me that the PLO is here, it reminds me that in the third row the leadership that signed the Camp David agreement is also here. And if we were to ask the assembly to indicate who they regard as the authentic spokesmen for Palestine, the only people who could stand up would be the comrades in the seventh row — the comrades of the PLO.

And, Comrade President, the problem of Palestine goes even deeper. What is at stake here is not just a great betrayal, not just a major sell-out of the principled support of the Egyptian people under Nasser for many years, but also an attempt to compromise the integrity of and an attack on the credibility of our movement. How can we be comfortable about the presence of the present leadership of Egypt here with us as a member of this assembly? How can we be comfortable with any agreement of this character between the leadership of Egypt and Israel and the USA, particularly as it provides for the supply of arms? Any such agreement must be in the interests of imperialism. Is our movement therefore no longer anti-imperialist? Are we to continue to accommodate Egypt and their Camp David agreement?

And when you add a combination of the USA and Israel, you must come up with South Africa, the superbastion of racism and apartheid. And is not one of the fundamental principles of our movement that we are antiracist?

Consider further, that any agreement which sells out the rights of the Palestinian people must amount to a form of colonial subjugation and domination. Yet our movement is anticolonialist.

Consider again that when you affront the Arab countries, most of which are members of the Nonaligned Movement, it is an affront to the movement itself.

Comrade President, the present leadership of Egypt has unwillingly and consciously assisted the U.S. imperialists in undermining the unity of the Arab world and in threatening the unity of the Nonaligned Movement and they must therefore stand condemned before the bar of the movement for these acts of treachery and betrayal.

When today we think of Kampuchea, the deepest feelings of revulsion and disgust come to us. All of us know of the massacres that are part of the shameful history of Kampuchea; the whole world including the imperialists condemned these mass murders. Who were responsible for these acts? Who are the guilty ones condemned by all mankind just months ago? The only answer must be the Pol Pot regime. But now that the people of Kampuchea have risen and liberated their country from this tyranny of naked brutality, now that they have toppled the brutal Pol Pot regime, you hear reactionaries screaming. They forget all their condemnation of the same regime which they now support — condemnations which they made only recently.

Today they are on the same track as they tried in Angola and Ethiopia, when they shouted interference in internal affairs. They used this slogan then, as they are using the slogan now, in order to divide us.

Not once did they remind themselves today of the brutal crimes of the Pol Pot regime. But Comrade President, just as in the cases of Angola and Ethiopia, foremost in our minds must be the justice and well-being of the Kampuchean people. Should we not breathe a sigh of relief now that the mass murders have come to an end? Given the untold crimes that the Pol Pot regime is guilty of, can we freedom-loving peoples ever dream of permitting them to retain a seat amongst us in the Nonaligned Movement? Comrade President, this would be no different to accepting the Zionist Israeli regime in our midst and in our movement.

Why should we keep out the legitimate representatives of the Kampuchean people, when the only crime they have committed is to put an end to the gross brutality of the Pol Pot regime and his gang of murderers? Can we succumb to imperialism when its aim is to divide us on all world issues: Middle East, Kampuchea, South Africa, and so on? We in Grenada say "No"; we say very boldly that the only legitimate representative of the Kampuchean people is the Heng Samrin regime, the government which we recognized on the twentieth of September last.

Comrade President, when the Spanish withdrew from the Western Sahara, they carved up the area, distributing it to Mauritania and Morocco in the usual colonialist-imperialist fashion. Today, I congratulate Mauritania for recently renouncing all claims to Western Saharan territory and we call on Morocco to do the same and to cease all colonialist ambitions in the area. Morocco must, we feel, respect the United Nations and OAU mandates. They must understand that today the vast majority of the world's people recognize the just claim of the people of Western Sahara for their territory.

We are happy to announce that the People's Revolutionary Government recognizes the Democratic Republic of Western Sahara under the firm revolutionary leadership of the Polisario Front.

All of these fundamental principles of the movement have had a most dramatic impact on the development of our own revolution in Grenada. Indeed, the underlying principles of the Nonaligned Movement have had a significant process of which we in Grenada are merely a small part.

This revolutionary process which has seen the emergence of successful and progressive revolutions in countries like Angola, Mozambique,

Guinea-Bissau, Ethiopia, Vietnam, Laos, and Kampuchea and, most recently, Nicaragua and Iran, has had a vital impact on the balance of forces in today's world. Gone are the days of unbridled imperialist control and domination of the world. In place of this anachronism we have now the emergence of the Third World as an important force in the world of today and this development has been significantly aided by the assertive role of the socialist world under the leadership of the USSR, and for this we in the Third World must express our fraternal thanks.

There are also signs of the collapse of colonialism in the region. St. Lucia and Dominica, which we welcomed this week as observers to the Nonaligned Movement, have gained their independence within the past twelve months. Antigua, St. Vincent, and St. Kitts are about to gain theirs. We resolutely support independence with territorial integrity for the people of Belize. We also wish to express our strongest solidarity with the Puerto Rican Socialist Party and the people of Puerto Rico in their struggle for independence. Our profound solidarity goes to the government and people of Panama in their just struggle to recover the Panama Canal and to the government and people of Cuba in their continuing fight to regain control over Guantánamo Bay. We express also our deepest desire for the peaceful reunification of Korea.

We congratulate Malta on the removal of NATO bases from its territory, in keeping with the principles of the Nonaligned Movement. The example of Malta is a good reminder to us that there are still some twenty army, navy, and air force bases in the area. Just in Puerto Rico–Panama–Guantánamo Bay area there are 30,000 men stationed, and now they are even taking over tiny Dog Island in the Caribbean.

The excuse they are using today is the same they have been using over the years — strategic global considerations. And when we examine these considerations we find that first and foremost the question of profits from the more than U.S.$48 billion investment in the Latin America area arises. They also continue to exploit the resources of the people of our area — bauxite, oil, copper, gold, and so on and on top of this, there are geopolitical considerations. And when they speak of this last consideration, what they primarily have in mind is fear of Cuba. And the main fear of Cuba is that another Cuba may arise in the region.

This fear of Cuba has led to attempts to derail and set back the Cuban revolution. Remember 1961, when direct invasion via the Bay of Pigs was attempted; we recall too the numerous attempts on the lives of Comrade Fidel Castro and other Cuban comrades; we recall the cowardly and blatant attempts at mass murder, one of them being successful, when in 1976 a Cubana plane was blown up off Barbados, killing all passengers; we recall numerous attempts at blockades, barricades, and isolation.

But it is fortunate that there was a Cuba. If there was no Cuba, the world would have not seen the first socialist revolution in the West in this century. If there was no Cuba, we would not have been reminded of the very important lesson that blockades, barricades, and isolation cannot stop a serious and determined people from consolidating their revolutionary process. If there was no Cuba, we would not have been reminded that imperialist and reactionary forces or their attempts at murder and sabotage could never stop a people fighting for their freedom and liberation.

Cuba laid the basis for Grenada, Nicaragua, Vietnam, Cambodia, Laos, Guinea-Bissau, Angola, and Mozambique. The example and spirit of the Cuban revolution has therefore had international impact. But, perhaps, most important of all is the fact that it is now the best example of what socialism can do in a small country for health, education, employment, for ending poverty, prostitution, and disease. It is now the best example in the world of what a small country under socialism can achieve. This is what socialism is all about.

The colonialists have spent several centuries dividing our region, as all other regions of the world. They have spent centuries developing the fine art of dividing peoples of the same area. The French, English, Spanish, and Dutch came. They carved up the area, taught us different languages and cultures, and then turned around and got us to hate each other. They told us that those who speak English must regard those who speak Spanish and Dutch as enemies and vice versa. They told us that those who developed one particular cultural background must despise and hate those with a different cultural background. They created regional boundaries and established different borderlines and even ensured that some countries had no right of access to the sea, thus giving birth to territorial disputes in our region.

But one of the historic tasks of the Nonaligned Movement in the late seventies must be to help to break down and destroy all these artificial boundaries — language, culture, or physical partitioning — created by colonialism. We must begin to find a solution that would create one people and one region. And Grenada strongly pledges to struggle as hard and seriously as we can to build one Latin American movement.

We need the support and solidarity of the Nonaligned Movement to build our process in Grenada. From the earliest days of our revolution we found ourselves threatened, we found ourselves bombarded by threats of force and destabilization. After the first weeks of the revolution, after Gairy fled to America to recruit mercenaries to attempt to come back, we put out signals; we requested assistance by way of arms, calling on America, Britain, and Canada. We also made similar requests of our neighbors in the Caribbean — Jamaica, Guyana, Cuba.

U.S. Ambassador Frank Ortiz then came to Grenada to advise us that any attempt on our part to build close links with the government of Cuba would be severely frowned upon by the United States. And we had to remind the ambassador that, although we are a small country and although we are a poor country, the people of our country had spent several years fighting dictatorship. We reminded him that many of our patriots had been brutalized and murdered fighting the dictatorship, and now that we had won our freedom, we would not give up that freedom because the United States or any other foreign power wishes us to do so. We had to remind them that all countries had the right to build their own way, free from outside interference and free from the use or threat of force, that we were not in anyone's backyard and that we were not for sale.

Today we have found that these threats have continued; these attempts to try to set us back have continued. Just before coming to this conference we received a cable from the U.S. secretary of state telling us that if we were going to the Nonaligned summit we should be in the forefront of resisting further attempts being made by countries like Cuba to try to destroy, to try to divide the OAS. They were saying that there were efforts to destroy the OAS, to destroy the peacekeeping role of that organization; and what was expected of us was to join with other forces to make sure that did not happen.

There were several options open to us. We could have replied saying that we had never tried to give any advice to any country and, certainly, not the USA, about how they should conduct their affairs in any organization they belong to. But we did not adopt this course. Instead, we decided to come to this conference to speak out loudly and clearly on the side and in the interests of the suffering and oppressed people of the world and of these countries and regions fighting for their freedom, independence, and national liberation. We feel that the presence of Grenada and the other ninety full member countries here is the loudest response we could make to the suggestion that we should try to set back the advance of the Nonaligned Movement.

Comrade President, it is a changing world. We know that imperialism is not invincible. We know that the balance of forces in the world is changing. We know that today there is being built a new Caribbean — Jamaica, Guyana, a new Grenada, Dominica, St. Lucia — governments attempting to build new societies with the people's support; governments that progressive forces have rallied behind. We also see a new Latin America emerging — Cuba in 1959, Nicaragua now, Chile a few years ago.

We understand today, Comrade President, how imperialism used the inter-American treaties to allow for interventions in Guatemala and Dominican Republic. Today, when a similar attempt was made in a vain effort to stop the revolution in Nicaragua, that attempt was killed because of the new consciousness, cooperation, and solidarity of the people of Latin America.

The emerging new Africa is evidenced by Guinea-Bissau, Mozambique, Angola, Ethiopia, Benin, Madagascar, Congo, São Tomé, Seychelles. The new Asia can be seen from Vietnam, Laos, Kampuchea, Afghanistan, Democratic Yemen.

We can also see slowly developing a new Europe. We can see this from Malta's courageous decision to remove NATO bases from its territory; from workers' struggles in Europe and the growing emergence of progressive sections and groups in France, Italy, and Spain even in the face of aggressive maneuvers by imperialism.

There is also proof of a new world emerging at this time. The struggle for a new international economic order is part of the proof. The grouping together of oil-producing countries into OPEC is a further testament to this development.

So, Comrade President, all around we see evidence that the world is changing. A new world is truly being built and now, more than ever, the Nonaligned Movement has to address itself to the economic aspect of the struggles against imperialist domination. It needs to be reiterated that, important as political, racial, and cultural liberation are, they need to be buttressed by higher and higher levels of economic liberation. For although the world is changing, the present distribution of economic power and living standards still remain manifestly unjust. This derives from the long history of imperialist expansion and control of the Third World. We see to change this order and substitute for it the new international economic order. And we give our wholehearted support to the efforts of progressive and Third World countries that are fighting for a new world based on social and economic justice for the poor of the world.

Comrade President, before ending, I should like to say a word or two about some of the special problems which are faced by small-island and other specially disadvantaged states. These include problems of limited markets, limited populations, limited resources, lack of skills in key areas, heavy dependence on one or two raw materials for export earnings, lack of capital formation, undeveloped money markets, and inadequate infrastructure. These problems affect most small island and other specially disadvantaged states — countries like Dominica, St. Lucia, Seychelles, São Tomé, Grenada, and so on. And for countries like us, we find ourselves doubly hit by imperialism.

Whereas the larger countries of the Third World are today fighting for the right to achieve a better balance in their terms of trade, for many of us the fight is for the right to trade in the first place. And whereas the larger states in the Third World are fighting to have established an international regime which would exploit the resources of the deep sea for the benefit of all mankind and not just for one or two multinationals; for many of us, the first problem is to have agreed and demarcated our 200 miles economic zone.

Our problems are compounded by the inadequacy and inappropriateness of the criteria that are used to determine whether loans can be made, or aid, or other forms of cooperation or assistance can be given. The balance-of-payments test is unfair for these small states. Many do not have their own central banks, so what passes as a balance-of-payments deficit is more often than not really only a budgetary deficit. The per capita test is also grossly unfair. When you see that test you are taking into account the earnings of the millionaires and other bigshots so that when you come to divide your GDP by the total population, the majority of whom live in conditions of abject poverty, you can get a very inaccurate picture of the true earnings of the average citizen.

Likewise, the requirement of prefinancing costs which requires that the local government purchases out of its own resources the required materials for the particular project, to be reimbursed thereafter, also works very unfairly because very often the initial money cannot be found.

Comrade President, these special problems of small-island developing states do need the urgent consideration of countries, not only of the developed world, but also of countries in the Nonaligned Movement.

We will of course continue to struggle with larger states in the Third World to bring pressure for the creation of the new international economic order. But we must point out that even what might appear to be relatively minor assistance for a larger Third World country can have a tremendous impact in a smaller and poorer society. For example, when we requested assistance from the Revolutionary Government of Cuba and they sent us twelve doctors, this very generous assistance immediately had an overwhelming impact on our country. I am sure you will understand the extent of the impact that twelve additional doctors spread throughout an island as small as Grenada would have.

I do not want to be misunderstood. Obviously, the loan of even one doctor is an extremely valuable contribution even if made to a fairly developed country. But the point is that the impact that twelve doctors can make in a small state, as contrasted to their impact in, say, a vast country as Ethiopia where almost literally they could be swallowed up, bears no reasonable comparison. For a small state, Comrade President, relatively minor assistance of all kinds can make an enormous difference and have an enormous impact.

In this connection, we want to express our appreciation to and voice our support for the proposals made by President Saddam Hussein of the Republic of Iraq at this summit for the creation of a long-term world fund to help the developing countries to combat the effects of inflation. We must now organize to pressure the developed capitalist world to contribute meaningfully to this fund.

We want finally to formally support the appeal earlier brought to this distinguished assembly concerning the devastation done to our sister Caribbean island of Dominica by Hurricane David. We are confident that the statement of solidarity from this conference and the firm offers of support already pledged by Cuba, Sri Lanka, PLO, Cyprus, Iraq, Kuwait, and others will be tremendously appreciated by our sisters and brothers in Dominica.

We thank the government and people of Cuba for their gracious hospitality. We thank the people of Cuba for maintaining and consolidating their revolution. We thank the people of Cuba for their revolutionary example, for their courage, for their discipline, and for their many successes. We salute the indomitable leader of the Cuban revolution, Comrade President Fidel Castro.

Long live the Cuban revolution!

Long live the struggle of working people throughout the world for peace, freedom, justice, and social progress!

Long live the Nonaligned Movement!

A Permanent, Standing Commitment to Freedom of Worship and Religion

February 15, 1980

The following is slightly abridged from a speech broadcast nationally over Radio Free Grenada. From a text issued by the Grenadian government.

Sisters and brothers of free Grenada,

As we prepare for the first anniversary of our historic and glorious people's democratic revolution of March 13, there are definite signs of the reemergence of mischievous and dangerously destabilizing activities by minority elements working among our farmers, agricultural workers, and other sections, including the church.

Those elements of whom I speak know who they are and know what they are doing and what they are hoping to achieve. They should also know by now that the position of the government is that such destabilization of the revolution will not be permitted to continue and that the People's Revolutionary Government will always, as it has done in the past, expose their activities to the people of Grenada, confident that the people will take the necessary action.

Tonight, sisters and brothers, I want to let you know of the activities of a few individuals who are trying to use the church and people's love for their church to bring down the revolution.

Since the uncovering of the counterrevolutionary plot last November, the most outstanding characteristic of this period has been the peace, calm, and unity maintained throughout the country. Under these conditions the government has been able to push ahead the development process at a pace never before experienced in Grenada.

As we look forward to the second year of our revolution, we see the construction of our international airport. We see the magnificent $7.5 million housing construction and repair program for the poor working people of our country, as well as for civil servants. We see the prospect of improved education for our children in their newly repaired schools. We see the vast road repair program soon to begin as a result of the $53 million obtained from the European Development Fund, the Caribbean

Development Bank, and the friendly governments of the Arab countries. Over fifteen community centers in Grenada, Carriacou, and Petit Martinique will also be built as a result of these monies. And for the first time, the people of our sister islands of Carriacou and Petit Martinique will share equally in the development process. Not only will their new airport be opened very soon, but they are to have completely new jetties constructed at Hillsborough and Harvey Vale; all their roads will be rebuilt and they also are to have two new community centers in L'Esterre and Petit Martinique.

The peace and calm in our country has also afforded our people an opportunity to unite and rebuild our communities. During the past three months our people have displayed an energy and enthusiasm never before witnessed in the history of Grenada.

With entirely voluntary effort, community centers have been repaired, road signs and billboards constructed, many miles of roads repaired since the flood damage, and our communities maintained at a high level of cleanliness and good sanitation. The recent voluntary school repair program demonstrated at an even higher level the willingness of all our people to work together, forgetting past political divisions, for the good of our children. It is now known that the value of the labor, materials, and even financial donations contributed by our people during the first two intensive weeks of the school repair program amounts to over $1 million.

The rate of progress experienced over the past few months has been the direct result of the peace, calm, and unity existing in our country. And as we approach the first anniversary of our glorious people's revolution, the mood strongly felt throughout the country is one of unity, hope, growing excitement, and joy.

But, sisters and brothers, I come to warn you tonight that there are local and foreign agents, both inside and outside of Grenada, who are very unhappy about the peace, hope, joy, and unity which we are experiencing. They are very unhappy about the tremendous progress which the revolution has been making. They are determined to turn back the revolution, and their strategy to do this is to create divisiveness, disunity, confusion, disruption, and disharmony. They are especially determined to do this in order to dampen, and if possible destroy, the spirit of the first anniversary of our revolution.

Tonight I want to present to you concrete evidence of counter-revolutionary activities by a few individuals seeking to use the church to create just such confusion and disharmony. Before I present this evidence, however, let me remind you that it would not be the first time that we have faced attempts to bring down the revolution.

The first attempts to derail the revolution were experienced when Gairy himself contacted mercenaries in the USA. You will remember that a letter from one of these mercenary types, Frank Mabry, Jr., to Gairy was discovered in the early weeks of our revolution.

The exposure of this attempt only increased the determination of our people to resist any return to dictatorship. You will remember also that for several months leading up to the counterrevolutionary plot last November, a most vicious local and foreign propaganda campaign was launched against the Grenada revolution. We remember the constant lies being printed in the *Torchlight*, the Trinidad *Express*, and other Caribbean and international newspapers. We remember the rumors that were circulated alleging divisions within our party and also regarding plans by the People's Revolutionary Government to seize people's land, houses, goats, pigs, and so on, to ration food, to prevent eighteen- to forty-year-olds from leaving the country. Despite the intensity of the smear campaign, our people remained firmly behind the revolution, and their confidence in the revolution and the revolutionary government was confirmed when papers discovered at the home of one of the plotters revealed that the rumors had been the result of a carefully planned campaign of lies.

Sisters and brothers, you will remember also that during the three weeks before the counterrevolutionary plot there were attempts to manipulate students, rastas, dock workers, electricity workers, and other militant supporters of the revolution as part of the plot to weaken our people's overwhelming support for the revolution. Finally, last October and November, there were two direct attempts, using criminal elements in the police force, to violently overthrow the People's Revolutionary Government and the revolution itself, to burn down the whole of St. George's and St. John's, invade the country, and to execute mass slaughter of the people. The plotters were caught red-handed just two and a half hours before they were due to start their deadly activities. That attempt to crush the people's revolution and return Grenada to the days of Gairyism also ended in total failure.

And so tonight, sisters and brothers, it should not come as a surprise to us that counterrevolution is once again rearing its ugly head. Today, the counterrevolutionaries, a tiny minority of foreign priests, have laid careful plans to sabotage the revolution, seeking to create a quarrel and a conflict between the People's Revolutionary Government and the church *where no such conflict exists*. Seeking to turn our people against the revolution by making the revolution appear to be against religion, *when it is not*, and when these elements know that it is not.

I want to lay before you now some of the evidence of this dreadful plan which the People's Revolutionary Government has discovered.

Recently a number of documents came into our possession. One of them was a letter written in the past few weeks by a few priests belonging to a particular well-known order of the church. We know the names of these priests and they, of course, will know themselves. One of these priests is presently based in Trinidad, but he used to be based in Grenada and now maintains regular contact with this small group here. This letter was addressed to another member of their order in England and amounts to a request for political help to engage in activities of a destabilizing and counterrevolutionary character. . . .

I do not intend to respond to the individual misrepresentations and falsehoods. Nor do I intend at this time to respond to any of the individual points in the nine paragraphs of this letter, but simply want to invite you to examine with me the deep and sinister implications of six specific quotations in the letter. What these quotations show is the clear intention of this handful of priests, while masquerading behind the cloak of religion, to abandon their traditional and perfectly acceptable role of minister of religion to become instead direct political activists and professional agitators. The quotations clearly show that their aim is to create a political organization within the bowels of the church that will use a political newspaper operating under cover of being a religious newspaper to spread their political views. Further, it is clear that their aim is to use our beloved country as an experimental laboratory and base from which their views and their conception of a new role for the church can be exported to the rest of the Caribbean.

Let us consider the six questions. The first reads as follows, and I quote from them:

"The great majority of the people are completely behind the government in their aspiration to construct a new, free society, independent of American and all European influence in which they hope to discover their identity as a people, (as Caribbean people)." What this clearly shows, sisters and brothers, is that these people clearly understand that the aims and objectives of the revolution are to create a new and better life for a new and conscious people to live in the new and progressive Grenada which we are trying to build. The quotation also clearly shows that these foreign minority elements, who are not inspired by feelings of patriotic love and concern for our country and its betterment, understand very well one of the most fundamental characteristics of our revolution — that it is a popular revolution with, as they correctly say, the support of the "great majority of the people." And because they understand these facts, it is very clear that their concern is not with democratically supporting the views of the majority, not with encouraging the tremendous sense of national unity, national pride, national consciousness, national and collective self-reliance which we now have, but instead their concern is at all costs to fight to ensure that their own backward and oppressive ideas continue to be dominant in our country.

The second quotation which I want to read to you is the following: "The population as a whole remains deeply attached to Christianity and *the government is trying hard to show that it has no quarrel with the church."* What this quotation, in the final analysis, means is that these foreign minority elements are opposed to church-state cooperation. What it further shows is that they understand the ever-increasing amount of cooperation between the People's Revolutionary Government and the different churches in our country and are deeply annoyed about that.

I am sure that they remember very well that in the days of Gairy priests were being deported and made to face constant threats of deportation, sometimes even for refusing to attend Gairy's so-called national days of prayer. These priests will, no doubt, remember that Gairy even went to the extent of writing out his own prayers, which he then forced them to read on their pulpits. I am sure that this minority cannot have forgotten Gairy's total contempt for the church, and his constant refusal to meet with the Grenada Conference of Churches and other church bodies unless it was to lambaste them or to beg political favors.

Can these elements have forgotten Gairy's constant abusing of the church on his radio station? Remember, for example, his statements during the 1977 public servants' wage dispute. These elements also surely remember the trips made and the letters sent by Gairy to Archbishop Pantin of Trinidad, the Roman Catholic cardinal of Haiti and to the pope himself in his desperate attempt to remove the bishop of St. George's from Grenada. In the short period of eleven months, they could not have forgotten that Gairy believed he was God, that he encouraged the exhibition of his photographs in churches, that he chastised those priests who were opposed to reading his blasphemous, obscene, and violence-oriented prayers with the words "I read your prayers, why can't you read mine?" They also could not have forgotten his notorious statement in Parliament in 1978: "He who opposes me, opposes God."

But instead of this abuse and noncooperation, the church has received the fullest cooperation, respect, and noninterference from our government and revolution. Our record has been and our position today continues to be one of total cooperation: duty-free concessions; help in fixing church property; help in fixing church schools; full and prompt payment of government grants to church schools; regular meetings between the prime minister and church leaders on a wide range of issues when the discussions have been frank, free, cordial, and constructive; total freedom of religious worship; complete support for religious education in all schools; and so on.

We have cooperated in this way because we recognize and respect the people's desire for moral and spiritual upliftment. This is why we have not attempted to interfere with the church in its function of ministering to the moral and spiritual needs of our people. This is why we have not attempted, like Gairy, to tell priests what prayers they can say or even cannot say, to force them to come to political national days of prayer.

This is the policy we intend to continue to follow, but it is clear that this minority foreign clique wants disunity, noncooperation, and struggle between church and state in order to better achieve their political ambitions.

The third quotation I am about to read illustrates this point even better. Because what it shows is that this minority element is not prepared to accept the guidance and leadership role of even their bishop. This quotation reads: "Faced with this situation the bishop and clergy are in *disarray*." In other words, until these elements are able to achieve their objectives and to assume full control, they will not be prepared to accept the views of democratic elements within the church who are against strife, confusion, and political involvement and activity of the church.

The fourth quotation is really a series of quotations which show that what these priests aim to create is a church led by professionally trained counterrevolutionaries. To quote their letter, the new kind of priests they want to see brought to Grenada is of the type who "are probably better read in modern Marxist ideology than any of the members of the People's Revolutionary Government. Grenada offers to them a tiny but significant field of experiment in which to test out their theories and aspirations . . . an opportunity to put theory into practice in a very small *theater of operations*" note the warlike phrase ". . . an opportunity to form a group of Caribbean Dominicans who will have to live and work in an increasingly Marxist Caribbean." What is intended by these gentlemen is to bring into Grenada a new kind of priest whose concern will not be to minister to the spiritual needs of our people, but who will be specially trained, specially equipped, and specially prepared professional political people using the frock of the priesthood to engage in direct political activity.

Anyone who is in doubt at all about their true intentions should carefully consider this next quotation. "There would be little difficulty, at present, about their entering the country to work as priests, even though it be privately agreed among us that *their work as priests might be very different* from that usually done in the area." Absolutely no room for doubt. What they are clearly doing here is engaging in a conspiracy or, as they put it, a "private agreement" to import priests into our country who would not be engaged in the usual priestly functions but direct political activity. And perhaps this is a good point to remind you, sisters and brothers: Some years ago President Ford and in the last few weeks President Carter both refused, under pressure from churches in America, to stop using priests as CIA agents in other countries. It is obvious that these American presidents recognize the great value and real potential for direct political activity by political agents posing as priests.

Let me read you the last quotation because it shows the methods that these elements will employ to spread their political views and engage in their disruptive activities. This quotation reads:

"There are great opportunities to influence the situation through preaching, adult education, youth work and perhaps even journalism — the church is planning to start a newspaper." I want you, sisters and brothers, to remember that this letter was written in the past few weeks. In fact, at exactly the same time as this letter was being written, discussions were going on in the Roman Catholic church about publishing a local newspaper right here in Grenada. From the quotation above, it becomes obvious that the few priests who wrote this letter were already planning to utilize the opportunities provided by a local church newspaper in order to spread their political poison and sow the seeds of discord and disunity. And this is yet another lesson for us, as it once again shows how easy it is for mischievous or disruptive or opportunist or destabilizing or counterrevolutionary minority elements to manipulate and use unsuspecting groups of people or institutions for their own sinister ends.

As you know, the newspaper referred to in the last quotation did in fact appear on our streets last weekend for the first time. It was called the *Catholic Focus*, and it was sold all around Grenada, not just in churches but even on the streets by newspaper boys. As you also know, by now, the publication of that paper was illegal, as it was printed by the Torchlight Newspaper Company in defiance of People's Law No. 81, which forbids a newspaper company from publishing a newspaper if there are individuals in the company who own more than 4 percent of the shares. When the fact of this illegality was brought to the attention of Bishop Charles, he immediately agreed to withdraw publication.

However, it was made very clear to Bishop Charles that the existing publication of the Roman Catholic newspaper *Dateline St. George's* can continue as usual. We have no doubt and have accepted the assurance of Bishop Charles that neither he nor most members of his clergy had any knowledge of the sinister plan of the minority priests who were planning to use the newspaper for their own political ends.

I must also bring to your attention, sisters and brothers, that the dangerous plan to use the church as a base of political subversion outlined in the letter is already being implemented.

I want to read you a quotation from a very recent top-secret report given to me by the special investigative branch of our police service. The report begins, "A series of publications are being put out by elements in the Church. Most of those published so far are aimed at showing that NJM and the People's Revolutionary Government are communists. According to my sources, one of whom is a priest, it is the deliberate intention of these publications to distort the policies, program, and objectives of the NJM and People's Revolutionary Government so as to make them appear as communistic.". . .

Since the presentation of this special branch report, more and more evidence of this publishing activity has come to hand. For instance, the one page throwaway already referred to entitled "Essential Teachings of Marxist-Communism" pretends to be about communism but its aim really is to show that revolution and communism are the same thing and that both involve class warfare and violence. Notice, brothers and sisters, that these people deliberately link revolution with an attempt to promote warfare and violence between people of different classes, even though they cannot help but be aware of the firm and constant attempts by the People's Revolutionary Government to promote unity, harmony, and peace among all the people of our country.

A large number of small printed tracts in red, blue, brown, and purple colors have also been circulated recently. Most of these are purely religious and others make general political statements about human rights, about Christians not adhering to any human ideology, and so on. Again, I can only repeat that evidence from the special investigative branch of our police indicates that the plan of the minority elements is to create a mass readership for these tracts and then to gradually begin direct attacks on the revolution.

Meanwhile, some direct attacks on the revolution have already begun from one or two priests, both through sermons in the pulpits as well as private conversations with their parishioners. For instance, we have received a complaint from the people in one area of the country that a foreign priest two weeks ago stated from the pulpit that "people are saying that this government is God-sent and praising it but this government is not God-sent because there is no justice in Grenada. The people are not free to say what they want. The people are being silenced." You can judge for yourself what these remarks are aimed at achieving.

Sisters and brothers, most serious is the very possibility that this attempt to use the church against the revolution may very well be coordinated both internally and externally. In fact it is very likely that there is a coordinating plan against the revolution utilizing religion, from both foreign as well as local sources.

The evidence which I have presented to you tonight indicates not only a concrete plan to bring in foreign priests to subvert our revolution, but also that there is another plan to sabotage the revolution through making it appear to be dictatorial, violent, and opposed to the church and religion. Yet the evidence also shows clearly that, far from being opposed to the church, the People's Revolutionary Government has during its year in office cooperated fully with the church, has allowed the church the fullest freedom to conduct its religious activities free from the fear of harassment which it constantly suffered under the Gairy dictatorship, and has assisted the church materially, wherever possible, in its attempts to improve the quality of life for our people. It is our belief that the church and the state have two separate roles to perform. *Our people look to their church for spiritual guidance and to their government for political leadership, and we believe that this separation of church and state is correct.* The biblical phrase "render to Caesar the things which are Caesar's and to God the things which are of God" represents a correct belief that the functions of the church and of the state are and should be different.

We repeat again our fullest commitment to freedom of worship and religion. We make this a permanent, standing commitment — now and forever.

Likewise, we guarantee our fullest, continued cooperation with the church in all areas which will bring social and material benefits to our people, in education, in health care, community activities, and so on. We have not in the past attempted to tell the church how to conduct its religious activities and we have absolutely no intention of doing so in the future.

But by the same token, we are not prepared to allow the church or elements within the church to carve out a new political role for themselves that will provide them the opportunity to use their influence and standing as religious leaders to engage in counterrevolutionary activities against the interests of the people.

We have stated in the past and we repeat again now that destabilization, sabotage and other forms of counterrevolution which threaten the rebuilding of our society will not be tolerated, and this is so regardless of who is involved or where the counterrevolution comes from.

Consider, sisters and brothers: Who will be the losers if the revolution is turned back or overthrown?

What would the end of the revolution mean for our people?

It would mean no new international airport. No more free milk for our schoolchildren. It would mean no more house repairs for our poorest people. It would mean an end to the construction of new roads, houses, and community centers. It would mean an end to the process of development which has begun — an end to the development of our new farms, our emergent fishing industry and agro-industries, and the expansion of our tourist industry. It would mean too the end of freedom and the return to dictatorship, this one even worse than the Gairy dictatorship, for violent dictatorship is the only way in which the majority of our people who support our revolution could be crushed into submission by the counterrevolutionaries. We of the People's Revolutionary Government are determined that this shall not happen, and we call on the people to stand with us in resisting and beating back the unnecessary and artificial crises which counterrevolutionaries are trying to promote. Make no mistake about it, these counterrevolutionary elements are in reality the enemies of both the local church and the state. We call on our people, in this period leading up to March 13: Be alert and vigilant in your defense of the revolution. Do not allow any minority elements — regardless of who they are — to attempt to mislead or confuse you.

Long live church-state cooperation!
Long live the people's revolution!
Long live the people of free Grenada!
Forward ever, backward never!
Good night, brothers and sisters.

The Fighting Example of Sandino Lives!

February 23, 1980

The following speech was given to a rally in Managua, Nicaragua, of 60,000 people to commemorate the forty-sixth anniversary of the assassination of Augusto César Sandino. It is printed in Maurice Bishop, Selected Speeches 1979-1981.

Comrades of the National Directorate of the FSLN;
Comrade Haydée Santamaría;
Comrade members of the Junta of National Reconstruction;
Esteemed ministers;
Distinguished guests;
Revolutionary people of Nicaragua;
Comrades all:

At this moment words cannot adequately express our profound appreciation for the great honor you have accorded us by your invitation to visit your country and to address this gathering; nor can words convey the happiness that we feel in actually being here, and in being able to embrace you and salute you on the magnificent success of your revolutionary struggle against dictatorship and imperialism.

The honor bestowed on us is deeper in that today you commemorate the sixty-fourth anniversary of the death of your great martyr, father, patriot, and revolutionary, Augusto Sandino, el general de hombres libres, victim of a cowardly act of assassination by the hideous Somocista dictatorship.

Augusto Sandino's heroic struggle inspired you, the people of Nicaragua, to continue to fight against the Somozas, led by your valiant vanguard the Frente Sandinista de Liberación Nacional [FSLN] until your ultimate and inevitable triumph in July 1979.

This is the first occasion since your revolutionary victory that you have the opportunity to honor your revolutionary father Augusto Sandino. On this historic occasion, we of the People's Revolutionary Government of Grenada and the people of Grenada salute him and experience a deep feeling of togetherness and comradeship with you.

Our comradeship is real and deep for several reasons. In 1979 the people's revolutions in Nicaragua and Grenada were the outstanding events of this hemisphere. Nineteen seventy-nine was indeed the year of the fall of the dictators worldwide — in Iran, in Uganda, in Kampuchea, and Equatorial Guinea. And here in the Caribbean–Central American region, the people of our two countries, after having endured several decades of the most brutal and corrupt dictatorships, the dictatorships of Somoza and Gairy, our peoples rose up to strike heavy blows for freedom against fascism spawned by imperialism.

Forty-six years of the towering revolutionary image of Sandino today guides liberated Nicaragua. For you, the patriots of the land of Sandino, the blood shed in 1934 has been fertilized to realize the flowering of Sandino's great revolutionary dream. Today as we look at this great sea of freedom fighters we can feel the vision of one Latin America of which Sandino was so dear.

We can see the true meaning of the Nicaragua revolution to the liberation of this region. We can see the link between the Cuban revolution, the greatest event in the history of this hemisphere in this century, and your own revolution. We can feel today the vast potential for the liberation of this entire continent.

We recall with pride that on June 23, 1979, only a few days after the announcement of the formation of your provisional junta, that our country was the second one in the world, after the Republic of Panama, to recognize your junta as the legitimate government of Nicaragua.

Since then with a token and symbolic contribution from our own very limited resources we have sought to demonstrate solidarity with you in the gigantic task of economic reconstruction of your country, ravaged as much by the long years of corrupt dictatorship as by the war of national liberation.

Our comradeship runs deep because of the similarities in our experiences of imperialism and dictatorship. In Grenada, which is a small island of just over 200 square kilometers and 110,000 people, we endured three centuries of colonialism and almost three decades of the dictatorship of Eric Gairy.

Between them, by 1979, imperialism and Gairyism had thoroughly plundered our economy leaving it in a state of ruin. Unemployment had reached 50 percent; for the masses of our population, there were very low levels of nutrition, health, housing, water — all the vital requirements of a decent life for our people. In the midst of all of this suffering, Gairy and a small clique of parasitic businessmen monopolized the importation of vital food supplies, making large profits off our working people. The dictator himself ran a string of night clubs and restaurants which were supplied by produce stolen from government-owned estates.

The dictatorship also made alliances with international gangster and fascist countries both for illicit enrichment and for the expansion of fascism into Grenada. Most notorious of all were the close links formed between Gairy and the murderous, fascist Pinochet regime in Chile. The Pinochet regime undertook to train and supply Gairy's so-called Defense Force, a gang of thugs trained to murder, brutalize, and generally repress our party and our supporters in Grenada at that time. Members of this Defense Force were sent to Chile for training, while Pinochet sent to Grenada a military training ship, *La Esmeralda*, as well as arms and ammunition.

But, like you, we never surrendered. With each blow the dictator struck our determination stiffened; our people mobilized themselves, taking heart from your struggle, from the struggle of the people of Iran, from the historic struggles of the great peoples and parties of Cuba and Vietnam.

Then victory came, as it had to, on March 13, 1979. Our People's Revolutionary Army quickly dissipated Gairy's brutal army of thugs, and in short time we had full control of the country, backed by the overwhelming majority of our population. The People's Revolutionry Government assumed full power to transform our people, our economy, our whole way of life.

The best news we had, shortly afterwards, was of your own victory after a long bloody struggle in which so many thousands of your brothers and sisters died; so many permanently maimed; so many becoming refugees in their own country or abroad. We mourned the loss of those who died and felt the suffering of the injured and destitute.

For both our revolutions 1979 was the Year of Liberation. And for you, 1980 is El año de la Alfabetización, just like for us 1980 is the Year of Education and Production.

Now, to redeem the sufferings of your people and ours, to provide a better life in freedom for our own populations and for their children, we face two monumental and related tasks: *first*, the consolidation of our revolution and the security of our countries against counterrevolutionary plots both internal and external, and *secondly*, the task of national reconstruction — to build our economic sectors, our infrastructure, our social services, to provide real benefits to the masses in our country.

We are also aware of the imperialist intrigues against your own revolution, first to keep Somoza in power, then to maintain Somocismo without Somoza. We recall that these maneuvers were stemmed by your own firmness, determination, and clarity that only you, the brave people of Nicaragua, could determine your own future. Your heroic stance was backed by the solidarity of progressive-minded governments and forces within the region, culminating with the OAS unequivocally calling for an end to the Somoza regime and rejecting efforts to install a so-called OAS peace-keeping force, thus showing that the lessons of the Dominican Republic of 1965 had been learnt. Imperialism had to beat a hasty retreat because of the tremendous and total solidarity shown by progressive and democratic governments, movements, and peoples of the region with your heroic revolution. That solidarity demonstrated once again the historic truth that a united, conscious, and determined people can never be defeated.

Like you, our second major task is one of national reconstruction. The most fundamental of these tasks is the development of our productive sectors — the main ones being agriculture, agro-processing, fisheries, and tourism. The substantial reduction of unemployment rests mainly on the expansion of these sectors.

Tied to the expansion of production is the improvement in the quality of life of our peoples — in their levels of health, in the quantity and quality of their housing, water supplies, sewerage facilities; in their education improvement, involving the removal of illiteracy, the democratization of educational opportunities, and the acquisition of all the technical and scientific skills we need to develop our country.

These basic improvements will provide us with the resources to launch a full program of transformation, including providing for the care of our elderly — the grandmothers and grandfathers — and our very young, the babies, with guaranteed food supplies, day care centers, and more.

The success of our revolution cannot be an isolated event. The very worldwide nature of imperialism attests to the need for revolutionary solidarity among oppressed peoples everywhere.

Hence one of our first major acts of international policy was to join the *Nonaligned Movement.* This great body, begun as a bulwark in the struggle against colonialism, today upholds the major principles of our international policy: resolute opposition to imperialism, colonialism, and neocolonialism; total rejection of fascism and Zionism; rejection of all imperialist military blocs; full support for peaceful coexistence of states; and the endorsement of the principles and aims of détente and in particular the world disarmament and hence for SALT II.

We condemn colonialism or racism wherever they attempt to hold on, hence our unflagging support for our brother people of Zimbabwe, Namibia, and South Africa.

The freedom-loving people of Zimbabwe are in particular need of the support and solidarity of this historic rally in Managua today. The people of Zimbabwe are today days away from achieving their inalienable right of self-determination, their right to be free and not subjected to colonialism and racism in their own land. But days could easily become months or years if the racists, colonialists, and imperialists have their way. We must stop their sinister plan to reverse the liberation of Zimbabwe by their intimidation, by their continuing murders of the freedom fighters, by their shameless use of racist South African troops, by their assassination attempts on the lives of Comrade Mugabe and other leaders of the Patriotic Front. Only our international solidarity and effort can now keep the racists from reinstalling Ian Smith and the puppet Muzorewa in power.

Let our voices from this rally go forth to the racists and imperialists today. Hands off Zimbabwe. Let the peoples' demand for independence, freedom, and majority rule win. Long live the freedom-loving people of Zimbabwe!

We fully endorse the rights of all peoples to self-determination, national independence, and sovereignity; hence our recognition of the Polisario Front as the legitimate government and representative of the people of Western Sahara. We resolutely support the people of Palestine in their just struggles against Zionism, imperialsim, and now capitulationism by Egypt.

Our resolve to stand up to imperialism wherever it rears its ugly head was recently exhibited in the case of the struggle of the people of Afghanistan in the face of imperialist machinations to turn back the Afghan people's revolution. We were one of only two countries in this hemisphere to vote against the recent Western-inspired resolution in the United Nations.

The views of our enemies on this question are of no concern to us. But to our friends who have raised questions with us about how we relate our Afghanistan vote to our stance on nonalignment we say the following: Nonalignment to us is a positive concept embodying beliefs in positive principles. As we see it, our first duty as a young revolutionary country that believes in nonalignment is always to support the further development of the world revolutionary process, always to take consistent positions of principle, regardless of how others might interpret or misinterpret our position, and regardless of what retaliatory actions imperialism might contemplate as a result.

Our international principles have a special meaning for our relations with our neighbors in the Caribbean-American region.

We of the New World were the early creations and victims of imperialism and colonialism and their tool of physical and psychological emasculation and racism. Imperialism not only exploited us: it divided us into various languages and cultures in an attempt to reproduce European chauvinism and hostilities in this hemisphere. For centuries our peoples were fed with the propaganda that we were French or Spanish or English or Dutch and more recently American; that our destinies lay with continued subjugation to our respective colonial masters in Europe and more recently in the U.S.

Today, however, Caribbean and American peoples are for self-determination and genuine independence, in one common, irreversible anti-colonialist and anti-imperialist struggle. We will win and progress together — imperialism will cease to divide and rule over us.

That common struggle must rid our region of colonialism. We stand shoulder to shoulder with the people of Puerto Rico and the rest of the Caribbean in their struggle for self-determination and genuine independence.

There is no better occasion than this rally to restate our continued firm solidarity with the patriots of Puerto Rico in their fight to liberate their country from the grips of imperialism. Reduced to second-class citizens, the people of Puerto Rico are not free to move in their own country. They still see large "Out of Bounds" signs on Vieques and other parts of their beloved homeland. They still see their people jailed for preserving the peace and rejecting illegal military escalation in their homeland and fighting poverty and degradation. But the release of the heroic "Puerto Rican Four" — Lolita Lebrón and the freedom fighters — has given new meaning to the struggle. Today, the people of Puerto Rico are more united than ever and draw closer to their independence.

Our common struggle must free the region of all attempts to seize territory from other peoples. Right here in Central America, the bestial Guatemalan dictatorship aims to deny the people of Belize their national territory, thus delaying their just right to independence and full sovereign control over all their present land.

We welcome your decision since the revolution to join us, other sister Caribbean states, and the vast majority of peoples and states throughout the world, in condemning Guatemala's claims and rendering full support to the Belizean peoples.

We recognize at the same time the just claims of Bolivia for access to the sea.

The success of our revolutions, particularly of our economic transformation, calls for greater and greater cooperation among our governments and peoples in many areas of economic and technical cooperation. Concrete measures for cooperation in these fields can consolidate our revolutions and our democracies, deepen our friendship, stem the forces of imperialism, and bring real benefits to our peoples.

But these benefits can only come if we are allowed peacefully to build our own process in our own way and free from all forms of outside pressures and interference.

On this historic occasion therefore, Grenada would like to restate our position on certain fundamental issues affecting the conduct of external powers in their relation with our region. We believe it is essential to the peaceful and progressive development of our peoples and region for the following principles, at a minimum, to be firmly upheld, promoted, and respected:

(1) The recent resolution passed at the OAS General Assembly meeting in La Paz, Bolivia, in October 1979, declaring that Latin America and the Caribbean region should be recognized as a zone of peace, must

be respected in practice. Military task forces and air and sea patrols of the region must be outlawed. All military bases and installations must be removed from the territories of Latin American countries that do not want them. The people of the region must be free of aggressive military harassment by any military power. There must be an end to the Monroe Doctrine, and all other doctrines aimed at perpetuating hegemonism, interventionism, and backyardism in the region. Likewise, there must be an end to all attempts to use the so-called peace-keeping apparatus of the OAS to intervene militarily in the region to roll back progressive movements. All genuine regional attempts at resolving regional problems and disputes must be accepted, respected, encouraged, and supported.

(2) The right of self-determination for all peoples must be recognized and respected in practice. As we speak here, there are still twenty-five territories being held in colonial subjugation by the British, French, Dutch, and Americans, telling us that region still has a long way to go to achieve political, far less economic, independence. This massive, humiliating, and debilitating insult to our region, represented by the continuing presence of so many colonies, must be brought to an end.

(3) The principle of ideological pluralism must be respected in practice. The peoples of the region must be allowed to build their own processes, in their own way, free from outside interference, free from all forms of pressure, free from the threat of use of force, free from intimidation, undue influence, duress, and bullying. There must be no more invasions, no more landings by marines, no more gunboats, no more Bay of Pigs, no more slaughters and overthrowings of our Sandinos, Allendes, Juan Bosches, Arbenzes.

There must be an end to the financing, supporting, and encouraging of mercenaries. There must be an end to the use of other countries as a sanctuary base and theater of continuous subversive activities for deposed dictators.

There must be an end to propaganda, economic, and violent destabilization; an end to blockades, assassinations, and policies of isolation and divide and rule.

(4) There must be an end to the arming and financing of counterrevolutionaries and antipopular, antidemocratic, or antiprogressive regimes.

There must be an end to the manipulation of regional and world tensions for electoral purposes.

There must be a firm commitment to the ideals of disarmament and world peace. Imperialism must no longer be allowed to hold back forces striving to undertake new forms and processes, to achieve structural transformations, to build new ways of life, to construct new civilizations for their people.

(5) There must be respect for the sovereignty, legal equality, and ter-

ritorial integrity of our countries. Our relations must be characterized by the fundamental principle of mutual equality, regardless of size of country, size of population, or extent of resources. We must be seen and recognized for what we are — big revolutionaries in small countries. Sandino was a big revolutionary; Fidel is a big revolutionary; the leaders of the Sandinista revolution are big revolutionaries, and we of the progressive Third World will produce many, many more big revolutionaries.

(6) Each of our countries must be free to join whatever international organizations we want and to create any regional and subregional groups which are in the best interests of our peoples. Our fundamental right to join with all other exploited countries of the world to form organizations, to press for a new international economic order to bring greater social and economic justice to the poor of the world, must be fully respected.

Aid with political strings or unreasonable conditions aimed at creating economic hardships on the people or consolidating or entrenching the rule of the minority and the transnational corporations, or holding back internal political processes working in the interests of the people must also be banned forever.

We call on all popular, democratic, and patriotic forces in the region to join together to fight for these principles so as to ensure an end to the continued colonialist, neocolonialist, and imperialist domination and exploitation of the region.

We owe it to our peoples, our countries, our region and the world to band together to fight in a firm and principled manner for the achievement of these noble objectives. The alternative is continued exploitation, continued domination, continued indignity, continued loss of pride, continued eunuchization, continued backyardism.

Our revolution is for peace, justice, and social progress: for food, for shelter, clothing, adequate health care, and creative cultural and recreational facilities for our people. We base our struggles on international brotherhood among all anti-imperialist peoples. Among these your people have an honored place.

So now, we look forward to March when esteemed members of your government will come to our country to join with us in the first anniversary celebration of our revolution. Every Grenadian will be looking forward to the presence in our country of our beloved comrades from Nicaragua, because every patriotic Grenadian wants to be a Sandinista. And every Grenadian will look forward to the day, let us hope not too far away, when other members of the leadership of the junta will be able to join us for an official state visit.

We have come to your country filled with expectations. We have seen the evidence of the devastation, the bombs, the fury, the destruction of the vicious Somoza tyranny.

We can now better understand the extent of the work of national reconstruction that lies before you. But we have also felt the warmth, the vigor, the hope, and confidence of your people; we have seen the vitality, the beauty and the courage of your youth and young women as they proudly bear the arms that will defend your country from all forms of external aggression and internal counterrevolutionary maneuvers. And we know that your revolution is safe, sound, and healthy and will go forward to greater and greater victories.

We are truly proud of the extraordinary achievements and advances made by your revolution after only seven months.

We are very conscious of the fact that internal counterrevolutionary elements backed, supported, encouraged, and inspired by external forces will do all in their power to destabilize your government and to roll back your revolutionary process. But we are confident that your people will deal with them and will bring the full weight of your revolution to bear on them. And you can be confident that in our people in Grenada and in our revolution, you will always have a most consistent and sincere friend; a reliable ally that will make any sacrifices to ensure that your revolution goes on and is not defeated.

On this historic occasion, we salute the memory of your revolutionary father, Comrade Augusto Sandino; we salute you the brave revolutionary government and people of Nicaragua. We thank you, the people of Nicaragua, for your outstanding courage, for your exemplary spirit, for your revolutionary determination, for your lasting example to our region and the world.

Down with imperialism!

Down with colonialism!

Down with neocolonialism!

Down with racism!

Down with fascism!

Long live the fighting example, the noble spirit, and the revolutionary courage of Sandino!

Long live the vanguard and progressive role of the Frente Sandinista de Liberación Nacional!

Long live the Junta de Gobierno de Reconstrucción Nacional!

Long live the just struggle of the liberated people of Nicaragua for peace, genuine independence, and social progress!

Long live Grenada-Nicaragua friendship, solidarity, and cooperation!

Long live the revolutionary government and people of Cuba!

Long live the heroic struggles of the freedom-loving peoples of Latin America and the Caribbean for their liberation and an end to tyranny and injustice.

Long live the forces of progress internationally!
Long live the international solidarity of working people!
Forward ever! Backward never!

Forward Ever!
Against Imperialism and Towards Genuine
National Independence and People's Power

March 13, 1980

The following speech was given to a mass rally in St. George's to mark the first anniversary of the Grenada revolution. It is printed in Maurice Bishop, Selected Speeches 1979-1981.

Your excellencies Sir Paul and Lady Scoon;
Esteemed Comrade Michael Manley, Prime Minister of Jamaica;
Esteemed Commander Daniel Ortega, member of the Junta of National
    Reconstruction of Nicaragua;
Esteemed comrades ministers and members of the People's
    Revolutionary Government;
Distinguished ministers of friendly governments;
Distinguished heads of overseas delegations;
Esteemed comrades on the platform;
Distinguished guests to Grenada;
Sisters and brothers;
Comrades of free and revolutionary Grenada:

I want in your name, comrades, in the name of our free people, in the name of our revolution, to welcome to our country on this occasion our distinguished and esteemed guests from overseas. In your name, sisters and brothers, I particularly want to welcome to Grenada our beloved friend, our sincere ally, Comrade Michael Manley, the prime minister of Jamaica.

Our relations with fraternal Jamaica have always been close, comrades, and they have been close for extremely good reasons. Jamaica was the first country, the very first country, as Comrade Coard has pointed out, [that we were in contact with] in the first few hours of the revolution, and it was the first country that immediately and unreservedly pledged its full support for our revolution. Even in the days when our people's struggle had not been officially recognized, had not yet assumed power, Comrade Michael Manley and his People's National Party of Jamaica maintained fraternal relations with us and with our party, the New Jewel Movement. And during those days, comrades, during those days, there were several countries and several people who were in positions of political power who refused to listen to the cries of our people, who refused to listen to our pleas and our call, who instead argued the position of nonintervention and noninterference and looked on quietly while the dictator continued to murder our patriots. Michael Manley did not fall in that mold.

The excellent arrangements which have been made during the last three weeks for the festival of our revolution, that too we can put down in part to the excellent relations we have with our fraternal sisters and brothers of Jamaica, because the Jamaican government, at our request, sent us immediately their top organizer of festivals, Brother Merrick Needham, and we must also recognize this contribution. When, over the next few days and weeks, all of you, and we hope also our overseas guests, purchase a copy of the forty-five record "Forward March Against Imperialism," that too will represent another aspect of the unity of the peoples of Jamaica and Grenada. Because "Forward March Against Imperialism" is sung by the great Jamaican singer, Barry Chevannes, who first sang this song about his country and has now put it to Grenadian words; and we must also recognize that.

It is also for our country a very great honor and a real privilege to have with us one of the outstanding leaders of the Nicaraguan revolution — Comrade Daniel Ortega, member of the Junta of National Reconstruction. As all of us know, the people of Nicaragua have spent more than forty-five years fighting against mass repression, fighting against murders and disappearances in their own country, inspired by their national patriot and national hero Augusto Sandino. Today we can feel in the presence of Daniel Ortega the spirit, the inspiration, and the moving example of Comrade Sandino. Sandino lives today in free Grenada!

We have absolutely no doubt at all, absolutely no doubt, that the process that is developing in Nicaragua is a true, revolutionary process. We have no doubt at all that the people of Nicaragua, notwithstanding the decades of ravaging by Somoza and imperialism, are going to reconstruct their country in their own image and for the greater benefit and glory of all of their people; of that we have absolutely no doubt. In recent weeks when we were in Nicaragua we saw the evidence of a real revolution, we felt the vitality, the dynamism, the youthfulness, the confidence, the courage, the inspiration; we sensed the great spirit of national unity and the great sense of individual and collective participation by the people of Nicaragua in rebuilding their country. Nicaragua will always be for us a major source of inspiration.

Today in your name, comrades, and in the name of our revolution I must also make special mention of the presence among us of another outstanding Caribbean and Latin American patriot, Comrade Jesús Montané, the leader of the Cuban delegation. The relations, the very warm and very fraternal relations which our country and people have developed with the brother people of Cuba, have been one of the major sources of inspiration for our country and our process. In recognizing as we do the tremendous contribution from the very earliest days and continuing today, which the fraternal government and people of Cuba have rendered to the people of Grenada, we must also acknowledge the most important fact about our relations with Cuba; the greatest debt of gratitude owed to the Cubans is that if there had been no Cuban revolution in 1959 there could have been no Grenadian revolution in 1979.

In your name I would like also to specially welcome another of our honored guests, the representative of a country that has spent upwards of thirty years fighting its war of national liberation, fighting against imperialism, fighting different countries during that period, and finally in the middle seventies winning a glorious victory, and moving from there to the stage of socialist reconstruction. I want to especially welcome the representative of the brave, courageous, and inspiring people of Vietnam.

On an occasion like this, comrades, when so many of our people have gathered together to commemorate the most important day on the Grenada calendar, it is not a time for us to extend apologies, but nonetheless I want to ask you to bear with me for one minute as I express our regret, the regret of our people and our government to all of our distinguished visitors that we are not able to offer them even greater hospitality and better accomodation that we have been able to. We recognize that the resources of our country do not allow us to provide the kind of facilities that we would have liked, to ensure that our guests are as comfortable as possible, but we do want to give them our firmest assurance that what we cannot make up for in luxury or in better accomodation and facilities, we will make up by our warmth, our friendliness, our spirit, and our fraternal ties of friendship with their countries.

We would also like to apologize to our guests and to the several hundreds of people who are presently in Grenada to be with us for our festival of the revolution for the inconvenience, and in some cases harassment, to which they were subjected en route to our country. We have received from several of the delegations and visitors extremely worrying reports, extremely unsatisfactory complaints about the way in which they were treated at the airport in Barbados. We want to make it very clear that we know from our communications with the government of Barbados on this question that the government does not support the behavior of some of their officials at the airport. But I have chosen this public occasion to make this comment because in some countries in the Caribbean, among some officials in these countries, an unfortunate attitude has developed, an unfortunate attitude which says that anyone coming to Grenada to see our country and to spend time with us must first undergo a period of tongue-lashing and harassment. And we in Grenada are not happy with that, we are totally dissatisfied at the fact that when people coming to our country have to pass through another airport they first have to put up with so much inconvenience and so much harassment. The minister from Seychelles, a brother country almost on the other end of the world, a brother country that has chosen to send a minister from so many thousands of miles away, because of delays, unnecessary delays at the airport, was forced to miss his plane and had to stay overnight. We want to apologize to the comrade and we want to apologize to other sisters and brothers who have similarly experienced such inconveniences or harassment.

Similar reports, and I must say this for the record because I want to get it out of the way, similar reports have come to us of like treatment being handed out to our people coming to Grenada and to visitors coming to our country by some of the officials at the Trinidad airport. And again, sisters and brothers, we want to use this public occasion to make it clear that the people and government of Grenada regard it as our right as a member of the Caribbean community to have better treatment handed out to people who are coming to our country; we regard it as our solemn right.

The Grenada revolution was a revolution for democracy, for justice, for social progress, for equal participation by the people of our country in all the decisions which affect their lives. The Grenada revolution, sisters and brothers, has reminded us over the past year of several historic truths that some of us may have forgotten.

The revolution has reminded us, for example, of the great truth of history that a united people, a conscious people, an organized people, can defeat dictatorship, can defeat repression, can defeat imperialism and other forces that try to hold back progress. It is significant that in this region of Latin America and the Caribbean 1979 saw two of the most important developments which took place around the world happen right here in our region. In the space of four months, there was the Grenada revolution in March 1979 and then on the nineteenth of July, 1979, the people of Nicaragua were also able to move finally to throw out Somoza and his henchmen.

The revolution has also reminded us that there are great possibilities for bringing benefits to a people and for a people even in the absence of a lot of resources. The revolution has reminded us that when we put our confidence in the people, when we are honest with the people, when we tell them objectively what the problems are, when we propose solutions they can relate to, when we make it clear as a government that our intention is to address the basic needs and the basic problems of our people, when we tell them that our intention is to stop looking outward for solutions from the metropolitan centers that have dominated and exploited us for so long but instead to begin to turn our eyes inwards to our country, to look at the problems ourselves, to try to find solutions for our problems based on our needs and based on our resources, that when these things are done a lot is possible. We have been amazed, we have been inspired, we have been encouraged by the tremendous unleashing of creativity and of energy by our people.

We have been inspired by the response of the people of Grenada to the call which we made in the first few weeks that they should work with the government to voluntarily rebuild our country. The response has been beyond our wildest dreams. Before the rains came in November last year, there were Sundays when 85 percent of the villages of our country were out there involved in voluntary community mobilization and community rebuilding and that, we feel, is an extraordinary development. The school repair program which ran for two weeks in January, and during which time the people of Grenada were called upon to repair and to beautify the schools in which their children have to receive their education, at the end of that two-week period nearly sixty-six schools had been repaired or beautified entirely on a voluntary basis by the people of our country.

The possibilities for beginning a real process of building a genuine democracy from the grassroots up has also been another lesson of the revolution. We have found over this past year that the people of our country have never been more united, have never been more vigorous, have never been more energetic. The people of our country have never participated more in taking decisions about their lives and in being involved on a regular, daily basis in helping to rebuild our country.

There are those (some of them our friends) who believe that you cannot have a democracy unless there is a situation where every five years, and for five seconds in those five years, a people are allowed to put an "X" next to some candidate's name, and for those five seconds in those five years they become democrats, and for the remainder of the time, four years and 364 days, they return to being nonpeople without any right to say anything to their government, without any right to be involved in running their country. We in Grenada do not regard that as being the real proof of democracy. Instead, we ask ourselves: When decisions have to be taken that are going to affect the lives of the people, are there mechanisms, are their institutions and organizations that allow for the people to participate and to express their views? Are there organizations on the ground that give the people a real opportunity of expressing how they feel and on a daily basis of being involved in taking decisions about their lives?

We say that when in a particular country the question of a new health policy has to be formulated and the people of the country are involved in discussing that policy, and organizations and mechanisms are introduced to ensure that the people will be able to participate in bringing that new policy into existence, we say *that is a real democracy*. When it can be said that the working class in your country, the working people in your country who had been unable previously to exercise the right to join or to form a trade union of their choice had that injustice corrected when in the first month of the revolution legislation was enacted giving to every worker in our country the right to form or to join a union of their choice — and more than 80 percent have done so — we say that is democracy.

Or consider the case of the women of Grenada. The unemployment situation under "Hurricane Gairy" was that over 50 percent of the national work force was unemployed, and among women over 70 percent were unemployed, and those few who did eventually manage to get a job, many of them in return for the job had to sell their bodies before they could get the job. And with the ending once and for all in our country of the sexual exploitation and victimization of our women, we say a real democratic basis for the participation of our women has been laid.

The national unity, the great sense of national pride, the new spirit of patriotism which the people of our country feel, that has to do very directly with their correct assessment that for the first time in the history of our country a government that represents their interests has taken power and is moving in their interest to bring benefits. That national unity has to do with the fact that our people now recognize that the days of job victimization are over; our people now recognize that the days of secret police and Mongoose Gang and Green Beast brutality have been ended once and for all.

That national unity is now possible because our people understand clearly that if they go out there and they do the work on a voluntary basis, if they unite and they organize to help rebuild our country, that their sweat, their labor, that the fruits of that labor will not be picked up by a tyrant and his parasites and passed to Evening Palace or Rock Gardens or some other place owned by the dictator. The people now understand that the leadership of the country is an honest and committed leadership, that the property owned or formerly owned by the dictator Gairy, Evening Palace, Rock Gardens, Tropical Inn, and the rest of it, all of that is now owned by the people of Grenada.

The Grenada revolution, comrades, has been an important learning experience for the people of the Caribbean and Latin America. Notwithstanding the hostility of some governments in the region, we are satisfied, and the presence of so many people of the Caribbean in our country is proof of this, we are satisfied that the people of the Caribbean understand that a new experiment, a new process, a new attempt at building a life of dignity and a new civilization is being attempted right here in free Grenada, and they want to see that go forward.

We know, and we know only too well, that just as with Chile in the early 1970s, just as with Jamaica since 1975, just as with Nicaragua today, just as they are continuing today with revolutionary Cuba, we understand that the forces of imperialism and reaction are going to work overtime to destabilize our process, are going to try to roll us back, are going to try to prevent the further gains of the revolution, are going to try to turn us back because the forces of imperialism, like the forces of colonialism before and still, are not interested in seeing a people move forward with dignity, are not interested in seeing a people and a country build a process that has relevance to their own lives. Their concern is with dollar bills, their concern is with profits, their concern is with ensuring that their big multinational corporations have the correct atmosphere and conditions for continuing their historic exploitation of a country and a people's resources. That is the concern of imperialism. And therefore the imperialists are not going to be happy.

Those who do not want to see a country take control over its national and natural resources are not going to be happy with the Grenada revolution or with the Nicaraguan revolution or with the process being built in Jamaica. These things are going to worry them and we know that they are going to continue to use people inside of our respective countries, local opportunist elements, local counterrevolutionary elements, to try to stop our processes from moving forward. And one of the major lessons of the past twelve months has been the fact that we have discovered and discovered clearly that one of the best ways to defeat destabilization, to defeat imperialism, to defeat counterrevolutionaries, is to be honest with your people, to tell them what is happening, to tell them who is trying to do what, so that destabilization does not come like a thief in the night.

The irony of the situation in the specific conditions of Grenada is that all of the conditions, all of the objective conditions, for maintaining that spirit of national unity which now exists, are present. The workers have reason to feel satisfied, the farmers of our country have reason to feel satisfied, the youth, the students, the women of our country, those engaged in the private sector, in the business community, also have reason to join with the rest of the population in fighting imperialism in our country. The basis for national unity is undoubtedly present.

When we made our first statement of policy after March 13 we made it perfectly clear that we were not interested in taking away rights, that our concern instead was to add new rights. For example, to give workers the right to form a union; to return to our farmers the right to run their own cooperative bodies; to ensure that the women of our country — through equal pay for equal work and through ending sexual exploitation — are able to enjoy an equal place with their menfolk in building our country. We made all of these proclamations and pronouncements and everything that has been done over the past year has been in furtherance of these principles. But the one right, the one right that we made clear that we were going to end once and for all — and that right we have abolished — is the right to exploit. The right to exploit has been killed dead in Grenada. Therefore, when we see elements willing to work hand in hand with external agencies and individuals to try to destabilize the revolution, we can always be sure of the fact that these are people who are annoyed about the fact that the one right which is most precious to them — the right to exploit — has been removed from them.

It is the exploiters, the parasites, the opportunists, these are the types who are likely to be engaged with foreign elements in trying to turn back our process, and if we are to make sure that our country nonetheless continues to move forward, we have to be able always, comrades, to maintain our unity, to maintain our vigilance, to continue to raise our levels of consciousness so that we will always be fully aware of what is happening and what the possibilities for our country are.

Some people are under the mistaken impression that we are trying to make enemies with some governments in the region and internationally. Some people are under the mistaken impression that the revolution in Grenada is anxious to get everybody in the region to act like we do, to attempt to follow the same principles that we do, to attempt to build the same process that our people are now trying to build. That is not correct. We recognize and respect the right of all people in the region and outside of the region to determine for themselves what kind of process they want to build in and for their own country. We do not want to be enemies with anybody.

In Grenada, our population is some 110,000 people; there are perhaps another 500,000 who live outside of Grenada. Perhaps, more than the population of Grenada now lives next door in Trinidad. There are something like 75,000 Grenadians in Venezuela, there are equal or greater number in the United States of America, a fair number in Canada, many others in the United Kingdom. Grenadians are scattered throughout the world. More American tourists come to visit Grenada every year than the entire population of Grenada, so we don't want to be enemies with anybody. Equally, we want to make a sharp distinction between the people — particularly progressive elements — and the government of the United States. But what we say to reactionary elements in the USA, and we say clearly and it must be understood because we are serious, is that small as we are, and poor as we are, as a people and as a country we insist on the fundamental principles of legal equality, mutual respect for sovereignty, noninterference in our internal affairs, and the right to build our own process free from outside interference, free from intimidation, free from bullying, free from the use or threat of force. We say this is our right as a country and as a people and we will fight and die for that right.

To those who continue to believe that the world begins and ends next door in America, to those who continue to believe that the United States or elements in the United States have the right to regard this entire area as a lake, as an extension of America, as part of their backyard, we say "No, we are not in anybody's backyard." The martyrs of our struggles, those patriots who died and who were murdered, those who gave their lives in the cause of the liberation of our people, those patriots in Latin America and the Caribbean who have been assassinated over the years, they have a right to say to us — and as revolutionaries we cannot be cowards — that as revolutionaries we must stand on our feet and face the world, that as revolutionaries we are entitled to say that there must be no more murdering of the Sandinos of this region; there must be no more assassinations of our Allendes; there must be no more overthrowings of the Juan Bosches and the Arbenzes of our region.

We are entitled to say that this region, this Caribbean Sea, this Latin American region has a right to build its own process, has the right to look at its own conditions to decide who we must be friends with, to decide which countries in the region and internationally must be our allies. One of the supreme ironies, one of the most amusing aspects of the situation is that the very country that wants to come to Grenada to tell us who we can be friends with, that country today is offering the least assistance to our process. The very country that wants to come to Grenada and tell us that we have no right to be friends of revolutionary Cuba, that country, when it suits its own interest, is trying and will continue to try to build relations with the government of Cuba. These people who do not understand anything about our history and our past, these people who came down to the Caribbean and to Latin America and took our region and chopped it up like a loaf of bread, in some countries teaching Dutch, elsewhere French, elsewhere Spanish, elsewhere English and most recently American; these people now want to turn around and tell us, we who are basically one people, that because we now speak different languages we can no longer be friends, that we must begin to hate each other, that we must begin to fight each other so that they can better exploit us. But the people of the Latin American and Caribbean regions are now moving fast to end these attitudes of narrow nationalism, of isolationism, of racism, of chauvinism. We as a people in the region are moving fast to build a collective sense of identity, conscious of the fact that we have one basic history, one basic cultural background, one geographical region, and we do undoubtedly have one basic future as a people.

To those who would like to believe that we do not have the right to shape our own future, we want the answer to be clearly understood, we want to say very clearly and very firmly that there are certain basic prin-

ciples which we believe that the people of the region are entitled to have
respected in their conduct with external powers. Recently as party and
as government we have studied the question of the conduct of foreign
powers in their relations with the region and have come up with some
proposals which I would like to quickly put before you.

In our view, first of all, comrades, we believe very firmly that the
Caribbean Sea must be recognized, regarded, and respected in practice
as a zone of peace; we believe that is fundamental. Our view is that military task forces and air and sea patrols of our region must be outlawed.
We believe that military bases and installations must be removed from
the territories of the Latin American and Caribbean countries that do not
want them. The people of the region must be free from aggressive military harassment by any military power. There must be an end to the
Monroe Doctrine, and to all other doctrines including the most recent
one, aimed at perpetuating hegemonism, interventionism, or backyardism in the region. There must be an end to all attempts to use the so-
called peacekeeping apparatus of the Organization of American States to
militarily intervene in the region to hold back progressive movements.
That too must stop. All genuine regional attempts at resolving regional
problems and disputes must be accepted, respected, encouraged, and
supported. That too is our position.

We believe, secondly, comrades, that the right to self-determination
for all peoples in the region and internationally must be recognized and
respected in practice. It is a sad fact about the history of our region that
we had the unfortunate honor of creating racism as a result of having
been used in that vicious system called slavery, because it is out of the
slave system that racism became institutionalized and entrenched in certain countries around the world. And because this region helped to create
racism and big capitalism which in turn led to imperialism, we undoubtedly have the double historic task and duty of being in the forefront of
the fight against racism, colonialism, neocolonialism, and imperialism.

An unfortunate fact is that there are still twenty-five territories right
here in the Caribbean that are not yet independent, twenty-five colonial
territories. Some people look at the fact that St. Lucia, Dominica, and
St. Vincent moved to achieving their independence recently and forget
that there are still twenty-five territories right here in our Caribbean still
under colonial domination, and we are not happy about that. But we are
happy that a representative of Puerto Rico is here with us today at this
rally, as once again we give our firm and unswerving support to the
people of Puerto Rico in their fight for the independence of their country. This massive and humiliating insult to our region represented by so
many colonies cannot be a good thing for the region and we offer our
firm commitment and support to all countries in the region that are willing to stand up and declare that they are ready for their independence and

ready to move their people forward to the twenty-first century.

Our third principle is that the principle of ideological pluralism must be respected in practice. Every single country in the world, including racist apartheid South Africa, will speak in theory of accepting the principle of ideological pluralism. But theory is not enough; we want to see in practice that the people of this region are in fact allowed to build their own processes in their own way, free from outside interference and free from all forms of threats or attempts to force them to build a process that somebody else likes. This principle today must be recognized and practiced. It is a fundamental principle that reflects the reality of today's Caribbean. If that principle is respected, sisters and brothers, comrades, then there could be no more invasions, no more landings by marines, no more gunboats, no more Bay of Pigs, no more slaughters and massacres of our Sandinos and Allendes, and that is why this principle is so fundamentally important. It's a principle we must fight to get accepted. And we want to give our fullest support to Comrade Michael Manley in his articulation of that principle and his brilliant analysis of the reasons why that principle must be accepted. And we share fully the views of our esteemed and illustrious Jamaican comrade and his party on this question.

There must be an end to the financing, supporting, and encouraging of mercenaries; those "dogs of war" must be outlawed once and for all in our region. There must be an end to the use of other countries as a sanctuary, base, and theater of continuous subversive activities for deposed dictators. When dictators run, let them find some obscure little spot to hide on; stop putting them up, stop letting them use other countries to continue to try to destabilize the government of the country whose people were the ones in the first place to run them out.

There must be an end to propaganda, economic, and violent destabilization; and end to blockades, to assassinations and policies of isolation and divide and rule. Every country has a right to exist. Every people has a right to earn its living and to build its own process; everyone without exception. And for this reason we could never support in Grenada and have always opposed as a party and today will continue to oppose continuing attempts at isolation and blockading going on against the Cuban revolution.

We believe, comrades, that there must be an end to the arming and the financing of counterrevolutionaries and antipopular, antidemocratic, or antiprogressive regimes. That sort of interference must also end. There must be an end to manipulation of regional and world tension for electoral purposes. The future of the region and the future of the world, the question of world peace, cannot be compromised because of any election, no matter whose election. There must be a firm commitment to the ideals of disarmament and world peace. Imperialism must no longer be allowed to hold back popular forces striving to undertake new forms, to achieve structural transformations, to build new ways of life, to construct new civilizations for their people. We must have the right to be allowed to do this.

The fifth principle is that we believe very firmly that there must be respect for the sovereignty, legal equality, and territorial integrity of the countries of our region. Our relations must be characterized by the fundamental principles of mutual equality, regardless of size of country, regardless of size of population, regardless of extent of resources. Regardless of how small any country is, such a country and its people do have an inalienable right to build their own process.

Sixthly and finally, we must be free to join whatever international organizations we want, to create any regional or subregional groups which are in the best interests of our people. Our fundamental right to join with all other exploited countries to form organizations to fight for a new international economic order that could bring greater social and economic justice to the poor of the world must be fully respected. Aid with political strings or unreasonable conditions aimed at creating economic hardships on the people, or consolidating or entrenching the rule of the minority and the transnational corporation, or holding back internal political processes working in the interests of the people, must also be banned forever.

It is our very firm conviction, comrades, that the new world that is emerging, this new world that we can see in Africa through Angola, Ethiopia, Guinea-Bissau, and today Zimbabwe; in Southeast Asia through Vietnam; in countries like Madagascar and Benin, São Tomé, the Seychelles; this new world that we also see in our own region through Cuba in 1959, the Chile of the seventies and in the new Nicaragua and Grenada of 1979, in the attempt being made by our brother people of Jamaica to build their own process, we are sure that the meaning of this new emerging world is that imperialism can be defeated, that imperialism is not invincible. It is clear that the people of the region can in fact unite and organize together to begin the serious task of taking control of our own national resources.

Comrades, it is getting late, there is street dancing in the next few minutes, our guests must be tired, not all of them might be accustomed like the people of free Grenada to standing for so many hours. So we must allow our guests to get some rest. We must thank them again for coming to our country because it is our firm belief and for that reason it is one of the main slogans of the revolution: "Do not listen to the propaganda abroad, come and see for yourself."

Those who claim that we have cut down on the forests in Grand Etang and have now pitched the roads where the forests used to be and have missiles aimed at neighboring islands, let them go to Grand Etang and when they return home report what they saw. Those who claim that there is a naval base in Carriacou, let them travel to Carriacou — it is only ten minutes by plane — and if they find any naval base we would like to see it ourselves. Those who publish photographs that show barbed wire blocking off our beaches, we invite them to go to all of our beaches and if they find one with barbed wire tell us, we want to see it. Those who ask "what are the Cubans doing here," those who ask "why do we need an army," those who say "why do we have a militia," those who say "why are we always talking about destabilization," those who feel that they must come here and question us about how much arms we have and where the arms come from and what we need the arms for, let us give them the answer that the free people of Grenada have been giving. Let us give them the answer that whenever Gairy or mercenaries or any other counterrevolutionary elements land on our beaches they will discover the size of our army, how many guns we have, where the guns came from, and whether we can use the guns.

Let reaction understand that this is a people's revolution and therefore when they speak of our army they should not just look at our revolutionary comrades in green, the revolutionary army or the militia, but they should look at all of the people before them because these people are the revolution. Not all of our people are our people in uniform, but all of our people are the eyes, the ears, the conscience, the spirit of the revolution, and the vast majority will fight and die for the revolution.

As a people we recognize today the historic duty that Comrade Daniel Ortega and Comrade Michael Manley have been speaking about, our duty to express our firmest solidarity and support with oppressed humanity. This is why we are so happy today to have with us the representative of a people who have borne the greatest sacrifices over the past three decades, the representative of a people who were forcibly thrown out from their homeland, the representative of a people whose cause is so important and so noble that without a solution to their problem, there could never be any guarantee of world peace. We welcome today in free and revolutionary Grenada the Palestine Liberation Organization and the people of Palestine.

We also welcome to our country, comrades, and are happy to do so, and are honored to do so, representatives from a people, whose country sells the blood of its own citizens for money, representatives of a people whose so-called government allows children to be sold for U.S.$20 and $25, a dictatorship that is an insult and a shame to the region; we welcome today and we pledge our firmest support with the liberation movement and the people of Haiti who are fighting against the Duvalier dictatorship.

Our government was the second in the Western Hemisphere to recognize a particular liberation movement which has now established its own republic and today is still engaged in a bloody war against Morocco which is being supported as usual by the forces of imperialism. But we are confident that that liberation movement and the republic that they have established will undoubtedly go forward to achieve their national liberation. Today we are happy to welcome with us representatives of the Polisario Front that is fighting in Western Sahara for the liberation of their country.

No atrocity, no atrocity in the history of the assassinations, in the history of the gunboats and the marines and the invasions and destabilization of this region, no atrocity was more deeply felt by the people of the entire region, than the atrocity which occurred on September 11, 1973, when that great patriot and martyr, Salvador Allende of Chile, was brutally and cowardly murdered. Today we are also happy to welcome in free Grenada the representatives of the people of Chile who are still fighting against fascism in their homeland.

We express our continuing solidarity with the people of Belize in their just struggle for independence with territorial security. Theirs is another struggle we have supported in the past and will continue to support. We express our firm solidarity and support for the people of Panama as they continue their struggle to reclaim all of their national territory; with the people of Cuba in their just struggle to reclaim Guantánamo; with the people of Puerto Rico in their fight for independence, in their fight against the presence of military bases on their soil and in their fight to end the nightmarish misuse of Vieques Island on which military experiments are being conducted — our fullest support to our Puerto Rican comrades!

We also want to warmly welcome and pay tribute to the representatives of the government and people of Guyana. We place on record that Guyana was the second country on March 13, 1979, that responded to our call for assistance and solidarity, and was the first country to give us material assistance — including critical military assistance — in the first weeks of the revolution.

The people of Guyana can always rely on the solidarity and support of our revolution.

To the brother people of Democratic Yemen and of North Korea who are struggling for the peaceful unification of their countries, we also express our support with them in their struggle.

To the countries of the Middle East that are represented here today, the brother peoples of Libya, Syria, Algeria, Iraq who have given so much to the Grenada revolution and have done so unselfishly, with no strings attached, with no laying down of unreasonable conditions but recognizing their own debt to humanity and recognizing the contribution that they must make to countries attempting to build revolutionary processes; the brother people of these countries have given gifts in the past few weeks amounting to more than EC$27 million to the people of Grenada and we thank them for it.

Right here in our own region, we must also thank another oil-producing country for the unselfish assistance which they have given to us. We warmly welcome to free Grenada the representatives of Venezuela, including the ambassador-designate from Venezuela to Grenada, and look forward to working closely with them in the interests of the people of the region.

We thank too the countries that make up the European Economic Community — the nine member countries — for their continuing assistance to the people of Grenada. We believe that theirs is an example that is worth watching by any country that believes that aid or assistance or cooperation is something that must always be tied to the demand that their exploitation be allowed to continue. We believe that it is a great example to them to discover that these countries — the nine member countries of the European Economic Community — have continued to assist the people of Grenada in the same principled way as before, and we want to welcome those of them who are here and to thank them for their assistance.

Another country that has, like the countries of the European Economic Community, continued to maintain a principled relationship with our government has been Canada. We deeply appreciate their continued asistance to our country and today are very happy to extend a warm welcome to their representatives to our country.

Finally, our brother people of Cuba, the people and the government that have stood by us over the entire period of the last twelve months, and have given medical assistance, assistance with our infrastructure, assistance with our productive sector in fisheries, assistance with our new international airport project, we of free Grenada salute once again the revolutionary people of Cuba. We salute the living legend, their great and indomitable leader, Comrade Fidel Castro.

Comrades, for the decade of the 1980s as a country, as a people, and as a revolution, we must today pledge to all of our guests from overseas that we in free Grenada will never compromise principle, that we will stand with all peoples in all parts of the world that are being oppressed, that, regardless of the consequences, those struggling for their freedom, for their independence, for their national liberation, will always be able to count on us in Grenada as their faithful friends and allies because of our determination to see the world revolutionary process go forward. As a people, our greatest regret — and we must move rapidly to correct that — our greatest regret must be that our contribution to oppressed and exploited humanity to date has been so small, and we must work hard to make sure that as soon as possible we too in free Grenada will reach the stage where we can truly begin to repay our debt to humanity and begin in a massive way to ensure that other oppressed peoples and other revolutions move forward.

Long live the friendship of Grenada and Jamaica!

Long live the friendship of Grenada and Cuba!

Long live the friendship between Grenada and Nicaragua!

Long live the friendship between Grenada and Guyana!

Long live the friendship between Grenada and St. Lucia!

Long live the friendship between Grenada and the people of Puerto Rico!

Long live the friendship between Grenada and other Caribbean countries!

Long live the friendship between Grenada and Libya, Syria, Algeria, Iraq!

Long live the friendship between Grenada and Vietnam!

Long live the friendship between Grenada and the people of Palestine!

Long live the friendship between Grenada and the Polisario Front!

Long live the friendship between Grenada and the national liberation movements!

All power and glory to the working people of the world!

Forward ever, backward never!

Cuba, Nicaragua, Grenada:
Together We Shall Win

May 1, 1980

The following speech was delivered to a rally of 1.5 million people in Havana's Revolution Square. Bishop spoke along with Fidel Castro, Nicaragua's Daniel Ortega, and others. The text was printed in Granma Weekly Review, *May 11, 1980.*

Esteemed Comrade Fidel Castro;
Esteemed Comrade Daniel Ortega;
Beloved revolutionary comrades of free and revolutionary Cuba:

I bring you today warm revolutionary greetings from the people of free Grenada. [*Applause*] This morning, comrades, I was addressing a rally in my own country to honor International Workers Day, and I left my country some time after eleven o'clock this morning to travel more than 1,000 miles to come to your country. But even if the distance was 10,000 miles, no force on earth could have stopped me from being here today. [*Applause*]

The unity, the militant solidarity which unifies our countries, our peoples' struggles — it is this unity and this solidarity which is today making imperialism tremble, because we recognize in Grenada just as imperialists recognize, that without the Cuban revolution of 1959 there could have been no Grenadian revolution, nor Nicaraguan revolution in 1979. [*Applause*]

They therefore have good reason to tremble when they hear the masses of Cubans saying: "Cuba, Nicaragua, Grenada, together we shall win." [*Applause and shouts of "Cuba, Nicaragua, Grenada, together we shall win!"*]

It is the Cuban revolution that has taught the peoples of Latin America and the Caribbean how to face blockades, how to defeat criminal invasions of their territories. The people of this region have looked at Girón, they have looked at *La Coubre*, they have looked at Escambray, they have looked at assassination attempts on their leadership; they remember the October 1976 destruction of their Cubana airliner, they have seen your struggles; they have been inspired by your victories; and they have observed that even in the face of these difficulties revolutionary Cuba was able to wipe out illiteracy, prostitution, drug-taking, and unemployment. They were able to see you build socialism in your small country. They have seen your strides and achievements in health and education. They have seen that today, twenty-one years after your revolution, your country is able to assist more than thirty countries around the world. And countries like Grenada and Nicaragua will always feel grateful to the people of Cuba and to the Cuban revolution for their assistance with their doctors, with their teachers, and with their selfless workers.

Certainly we in Grenada will never forget that it was the military assistance of Cuba in the first weeks of our revolution that provided us with the basis to defend our own revolution. [*Applause*] And when imperialism and reaction keep saying to us in Grenada, why do we need arms, where are the arms coming from, why should such a small country need so much arms, we always give them the answer our people have given. Whenever mercenaries or foreign aggressors land in our country, they will discover how much arms we have, whether we can use the arms, and where the arms came from as we shed their blood on our soil. [*Applause*]

Your revolution, comrades, has also provided the region and the world with a living legend with your great and indomitable leader, Fidel Castro. [*Applause*] Fidel has taught us not only how to fight, but also how to work, how to build socialism, and how to lead our country in a spirit of humility, sincerity, commitment, and firm revolutionary leadership. [*Applause*]

It is important to be in revolutionary Cuba at this period in world history. Today we can see another crisis in international capitalism. Today we can see them complaining that their superprofits are falling. We can see their interest rate running towards 20 percent. The school lunches they have been providing for their children, even that, they have had to reduce by over $500 million. Their workers are daily finding that jobs are disappearing. But their more than $33 billion profit on investments around the world demand that they create new tension in the world, so that their economy, which is based on war and armament, would once again flourish.

They are also terrified by the victories of the national liberation movements in Africa, in Asia, in the Middle East, and right here in Latin America. They have looked around and they see that today the struggles of the people of the region are continuing to reach new heights. They look at El Salvador and they recognize that while yesterday it was Cuba, Nicaragua, and Grenada, tomorrow it will undoubtedly be El Salvador. [*Applause*]

So they have decided to step up on their arms supply and their arms race. They have decided to scuttle SALT II and détente. They have decided to spend this year more than $142 billion on arms. At the same time, the invasions which have characterized their relations with our region over the years starting with the Monroe Doctrine in 1823, they are shaping now to create new doctrines, to plan new maneuvers, to obtain new bases to strengthen and deepen their military presence in the hope that this will crush the rising wave of national liberation consciousness that is sweeping our region and the world.

Their interventions in Mexico, in Nicaragua, in Colombia, in Panama, in the Dominican Republic, in Haiti, in Honduras, all of these invasions which they have had over the years — they are now preparing once again to embark on a new campaign of terror and intimidation of the people of our region.

But sometimes it is no longer by direct intervention, sometimes they rely more on control and manipulation, on the use of threat of force, on the techniques of destabilization, on the use of diplomatic pressure, on the use of propaganda destabilization, on the policy of economic isolation. But in each case all of this is meant to lay the basis for a United States-organized or -backed coup d'etat.

In 1954, they succeeded in overthrowing Arbenz in Guatemala. In 1973, they succeeded in overthrowing Allende in Chile. But the one lesson that they have never forgotten and will never forget is that in 1961 they failed when they tried at Girón right here in revolutionary Cuba! [*Applause*]

Today we can hear them setting up their cries against the revolutionary processes in Nicaragua and Cuba. You can hear them talking about human rights, you can hear them calling for elections even though they won't understand that our revolutions are popular revolutions. You can see them encouraging the ultraleftists in our countries to take violent action against our peoples. Their propaganda has reached the point where our countries have become electoral issues in the presidential campaign in that country. And at the same time, as usual, the threats against revolutionary Cuba, the continuation of the criminal economic blockade against revolutionary Cuba, the creation of artificial crisis after artificial crisis. First the question of the Soviet troops in October last year, and now the question of so-called refugees at this point in time. All of this is part and parcel of the imperialist campaign to try to defame the Cuban revolution, to try to isolate the Cuban people, to try to lay the basis for an armed invasion or other form of intervention of your beloved country. But in Grenada we have been using a slogan and that slogan has been saying that "If they touch Cuba or if they touch Nicaragua, then they touch Grenada too." [*Applause*]

Comrades, as the people who own this region, as the people who belong to these countries, it is for us to decide what we want to do with our lives in our countries. It is for us, the people of the region, to demand whether or not we want to have military bases on our territory. It is for us to decide whether or not we want other peoples' planes to fly over our countries. And one of the most contemptuous and arrogant acts of imperialism is today to presume that in 1980 not only do they have the right to have a base in Guantánamo but that they also have a right to operate military maneuvers on the very soil of free and revolutionary Cuba.

That is an insult and a piece of contempt that the people of the region will never forgive or forget. And the people of this region are going to continue in our demand calling for an end to military bases in Guantánamo, in Puerto Rico, and in all other countries in the region where these bases exist.

We, the people of this region, demand that our region is recognized and respected as a zone of peace. We demand an end to all military task forces and air and sea patrols of our region. We demand that the people of the region must be free from aggressive military harassment of any military power. We demand an end to the Monroe Doctrine and to the Carter Doctrine and all other doctrines which are aimed at perpetuating interventionism or backyardism in the region. There must be an end to all attempts to use the so-called peacekeeping apparatus of the Organization of American States to militarily intervene in the region, to hold back progressive and patriotic movements.

We also call today that the right to self-determination for all peoples in the region must be recognized and accepted.

We today renew our call for the independence of the sister people of Puerto Rico. [*Applause*]

We today insist that all of the people of the region in the twenty-five colonial countries which still exist — English, Dutch, French, or American territories — we demand the right to independence for the peoples of those countries. We demand that a principle of ideological pluralism must be respected and practiced by imperialist powers.

We must have the right to build our processes in our own way, free from outside interference, free from all forms of threats or attempts to force us to accept other peoples' processes.

Today we insist that there must be an end to the invasions, an end to the landing by marines, an end to the gunboats, an end to the Playa Giróns, an end to the slaughters and massacres of our Sandinos, our Ches, and our Allendes. [*Applause*]

We call also for an end to the arming and financing of counterrevolutionary and antipopular, antidemocratic or antiprogressive regimes. There must be an end to the manipulation of regional and world tension for electoral purposes. The future of the region and the future of the world, the question of world peace cannot be compromised because of any election, no matter whose election.

There must therefore be respect for the sovereignty, legal equality, and territorial integrity of the countries of our region.

It is clear today, comrades, that the desperate plans of imperialism can be defeated once again, once we remain organized, vigilant, united, and demonstrate firm and militant anti-imperialist solidarity.

We look to the people of Cuba, we look to your revolution and your leadership to ensure that the revolutionary process in the Caribbean and Central American region continues to go forward with strength.

We salute you, the freedom-loving people of revolutionary Cuba. We salute your great and revolutionary leader, Comrade Fidel Castro. [*Applause*]

Long live the freedom-loving people of revolutionary Cuba! [*Applause and shouts of "Long live!"*]

Long live the Communist Party of Cuba! [*Applause and shouts of "Long live!"*]

Long live Comrade Fidel Castro!

Long live the Nicaraguan revolution!

Long live the Sandinista Liberation Front!

Long live the national liberation movements!

Long live the socialist world!

Long live the Grenadian revolution!

Long live the militant unity and solidarity of workers internationally!

Cuba, Nicaragua, Grenada, together we shall win! [*Applause*]

Adelante siempre, atrás nunca! [Forward ever, backward never!] [*Ovation*]

The Class Struggle in Grenada, the Caribbean, and the USA

July 15, 1980

The following interview was conducted by U.S. Socialist Workers Party leaders Steve Clark, Andrew Pulley, and Diane Wang in St. George's. It was printed in Intercontinental Press, *August 4, 1980.*

Andrew Pulley: What can supporters of the Grenadian revolution, antiwar activists, and Black activists in the United States do regarding the U.S. government's war drive and slander against Grenada? How can we help combat that?

Maurice Bishop: I think there are a number of areas. Certainly the question of mobilizing the population, particularly the Blacks, the deprived minorities, progressive forces, the working class, around the importance of world peace and détente. There might be some concrete ways of getting that message across. Certainly, for example, using the Vietnam experience and what it has meant concretely for people — not only for those who died, but those who are now permanently crippled or those who have come back war heroes but still cannot find jobs.

Secondly, I think it is very important to try to organize around one or two key slogans that could dramatize and really focus in a very concrete and spectacular way on this war drive. What I'm getting at is this, for example. Everyone knows, but most prople cannot quite articulate, that the reasons for war, the reasons for any warmongering right now, have to do essentially with the developing crisis in international capitalism. The economic problems in the United States even more so.

Witness the $142 billion defense budget or whatever it is. Fifty million dollars cut back on school lunch programs. The retrenchment, the general cutback in social expenditures.

Yet at the same time, it is equally clear that while they are cutting back in those areas, they are stepping up on defense spending. And inciting the countries of NATO, for example, to do likewise.

Now it seems to us that it should be possible to get that message across in a concrete way. To point out that really what the war drive is all about is a means of the transnational corporations, the elite in America, to try to revive their super profits, which have been falling so dramatically. And the best way always of doing that is by getting a war economy moving — step up spending in armaments, step up spending in the area of the military generally.

So the slogan, for example, that makes the point: "We don't want a war. General Motors wants a war. Let General Motors go and fight." I'm saying that it should be possible to step up that kind of message in a very concrete way so that people can understand.

Because I get a feeling — certainly the last time I was in America — last year at the United Nations — that this warmongering was beginning to seep through to the population in general to some extent. I wasn't there long enough, I didn't speak to enough people or to an especially wide cross-section to be sure that what I'm saying is right. But certainly listening to the radio, watching the television shows, and just talking to people here and there, that impression came across very strongly.

I don't think there's any need for that to happen in the United States. I certainly feel that a carefully worked-out program aimed at getting the message across that war is *not* in the interests of the American masses, that it's really only a very tiny minority who wants this war, essentially for economic reasons. Therefore, if they want the war, let them go and fight the war. Why should we go and die for them? It's not helping us.

Third, I think precisely what your party and your newspaper have been doing, and we certainly appreciate it. Focusing on the actual reality in the region and the efforts being made by progressive and revolutionary countries to try to get a better life for their people. And doing it in as concrete a way as they can, in terms of focusing on the basic needs of the population — jobs, health, housing, food, clothing. The concrete attempts to bring these about and therefore the developing perception in the minds of the Caribbean masses that this really is a way to measure progress. Not in terms of how many industries you have or how many hotels you have when the profits are going to a very tiny elite, but in terms of what benefits are truly getting to the masses.

Getting across the point, too, that there is absolutely no doubt that for all of us in the Caribbean who are trying to develop new paths and new processes, our concern is not with America. We have no axe to grind. All we want is to be able to live in peace. To have the opportunity to develop our own processes free from all forms of outside interference, from intimidation, from threats of invasion, from task forces and Solid Shields and whatnot. That's really all that the people of our region are asking — that it is our right to do as we wish in our own countries.

I think, as I said, that your party and your paper have certainly been making an important contribution here. And that, to us, is one very, very key area — continuing that work.

The fourth thing I can think of would be the question of Grenada-U.S.

friendships, Cuba-U.S. friendships, Nicaragua-U.S. friendships — these societies, which exist in the case of the three particular countries I've named.

For Grenada, it's a fairly recent development, but it has begun to spread. It's gotten to the West Coast now. And I know there are plans for pushing it further along. The importance is getting, not necessarily progressive, but democratic forces in America to join organizations like that, so that they get an opportunity of learning at first hand what is really happening and give themselves the opportunity of being able to see the other side and being able to understand what the views of the people in these countries are. So that they would get a different point of view and would not have to have to continue to be saturated by the official American propaganda.

Because, again, one of the things that struck me when I was in America — I hadn't been there in two or three years — was the extent to which the news is canned, the way it's focused. If that's really all people get exposed to — the stuff you see in the *New York Times*, what you see on all the different channels and on the radio — you really have no possibility of developing a different point of view. Because it's *all* just aimed at pushing their point of view.

And these are the same people who talk of the free press, the right to have independent views so that everybody gets to hear what's happening. I mean, I can't think of a more unfree press, a more unfree media than the American media.

Pulley: One big lie that they are perpetrating right now in the United States is that Grenada is an armed camp where every single person walks around with carbines and, therefore, if you fear for your safety, you should not go there as a tourist. The truth is that we see more people armed in a two-block area of Chicago, especially policemen, than I've seen here. Do you have anything to say about this line of propaganda?

The other line is that the new international airport that you are building here is simply a military base.

What do you have to say regarding more Black people and other Americans coming down here just to see for themselves what's happening here?

Bishop: On the first question, the question of everybody walking around with guns, the island being an armed camp, civil commotion, civil war, barricades, the rest of it. Obviously that is part of the whole attempt at propaganda destabilization.

We really have been having that from day one. Obviously the aim of that is to wreck the tourists coming here, in particular. To make tourists generally afraid to come to the country. And they are really pushing that very viciously over the past sixteen months.

Within the first few weeks, they were saying that we had cut down the forests in the middle of the island, in the Grand Etang region, and had missiles aimed at neighboring islands. Then there was another story saying that we had burrowed all the earth from under the island and established pontoons and a U-2 base so that the Soviets could attack. Another one said that there was a Soviet naval base on the offshore island of Carriacou.

Obviously that kind of propaganda cannot affect our people. The island is so small that in a quarter of a second everybody knows that it's a joke and a lie. But on people outside of the country, it can obviously have an effect. And has had some impact.

It's the same with this new line about the island being an armed camp. That's just the latest round of propaganda destabilization. We've had a lot of it. They have of course been linking that to economic destabilization — attempts at wrecking the economy.

To go back to tourism again, there are two recent examples that you might find interesting. In February a hotel owner here, the owner of a hotel called the Calabash, received a letter from one of the travel agents in New York saying that the people who were booked to come down had cancelled out because the travel agency had been advised by the State Department that Grenada was off bounds. We published that letter. The U.S. embassy, of course, denied it.

More recently still, someone did a survey for us in the Washington, D.C. area, and they discovered that of the twenty-five travel agencies *nineteen* advised against coming to Grenada, arguing that it was unsafe, the usual stuff.

So that economic destabilization has certainly continued.

As you know, they have been moving more and more now to the third leg of that system of destabilization, the violent destabilization, and more particularly to assassinations and straight terror. All of this is predictable.

We would certainly see it as important for Black Americans to come down to Grenada, for the rest of Americans generally to come, members of the American working class, American working people in general to come to our country *to see for themselves*. We feel in the final analysis that is the best proof. Don't wait and listen to the propaganda. Come down and see.

I just opened the CARICOM ministers of health conference a while back this morning. In talking to a few of the ministers right after the opening, they were all pointing out that they can't believe that they are in Grenada when they consider the propaganda that they were hearing on *all* of the radio stations, that they were reading in *all* of the national newspapers over the past few months.

One sister from Barbados was saying that two weeks ago she heard on the radio station in Barbados a report that said that the Cuban construction workers at the airport are all walking around in full jungle fatigues with AK-47's on their backs, and that the government ministers are likewise walking around that way. That children eight, nine, ten years old walk around carrying guns in the streets. That children are going to school with guns in their hands. That there was a civil war going on in the country. That a barricade had been established in one part of the island near the airport, and people were saying they would not lift the barricade until all the Cubans were sent back home and all detainees released.

Of course, all of these are figments of the imagination. And this sister from Barbados was just so glad that she was able to come herself.

So one of our main slogans has been, "Come to see for yourself." We really think that's very important. The extent to which more and more people can have the opportunity to come down and judge for themselves. We feel that's one of the very best ways of countering these attempts at propaganda destabilization.

Steve Clark: What has been the response of the U.S. government to your government's request for extradition procedures for Eric Gairy?

Bishop: That has had a varied history. In the first few weeks and months before we even formally applied for the extradition, they were all giving the impression, the U.S. embassy people in Barbados, that it's a formality, a very simple matter and so forth. Then, of course, they told us that we should get down to the formal aspects of it — prepare the warrants, and the back-up witnesses, proofs, and whatnot. We did all of that.

By November, we got a written communication from them, saying that the papers were in order. No problem. Then by January they came back saying that they had discovered the papers were not in order. There is some more information they want.

In between all of that [U.S. Ambassador] Sally Shelton comes to Grenada last December, at our invitation, and her line was that America didn't want Gairy. So, we pointed out that, well then, *we* want Gairy. America doesn't want Gairy. Gairy is saying he is coming back tomorrow morning. So what's the problem. Let him come. [*Laughs*]

Of course, she had no answer to that. Because obviously what was going on was just the usual hypocrisy.

More recently, in the last two or three months, they have come out publicly for the first time — not publicly, but privately to our ambassador — saying that they have lifted all surveillance on Gairy — something that they kept saying that they were doing to some extent within their limited resources and whatnot. And that, so far as they were concerned, the Gairy question was a dead letter.

So it has now come to the point where they had admitted openly that they are not going to bother with our request for extradition.

106 *Maurice Bishop Speaks*

Obviously, this is going to be one of the main stumbling blocks to having any kind of reasonable relations with the United States. Because it is not possible to accept that any country, and one that deems itself to be a friendly country, has the right to harbor fugitives from justice from our country — criminals, people who are using the territory of this other country to incite aggression against our country, to actively plan counterrevolution, to plan for mercenary invasion and all that sort of thing.

Therefore, that certainly is going to be one of the major stumbling blocks to the development of any reasonable relations.

Clark: Going back to a point you made earlier. One of the slogans that very quickly has developed into probably the most popular antidraft slogan is, "We won't fight for Exxon." This relates most directly to the war dangers in the Middle East rather than in the Caribbean. But it shows the beginning developmnent among these activists, who are the backbone of the growing antidraft movement, of a consciousness of the cause of war. In the early stages of the Vietnam War, there were many antiwar activists who thought this was just simply a mistake on the part of the U.S. policymakers. It took quite a while into the war before the consciousness of the role of big business, the consciousness that the war was being fought for a specific reason in the interests of a tiny handful, began to develop. But that's there now right at the beginning of this new fight.

Bishop: That's fantastic.

Clark: We think that another very positive thing in terms of mobilizing solidarity not only with Grenada but with Nicaragua, El Salvador, and the Cuban revolution, and against the CIA destabilization efforts in Jamaica, is the fact that Grenada is the first revolution of this power and scope in an English-speaking country with a largely Black population. So it makes it much easier for at least that segment — which is a large and important segment of the American population — to identify with the revolutions in the Caribbean and Central America.

Bishop: I agree fully. I have absolutely no doubt that one of the major factors responsible for all of the aggression and hostility against the revolution in Grenada being shown by the United States government is precisely the fact that they recognize that being a small Black country, with a large Black population, and as you say English-speaking, that it becomes a lot easier for Blacks and other oppressed nationalities in the United States to identify with our goals and our aspirations. And that *must* be a real problem for them. It must be.

Because what you have in America with the Black situation is already a situation of great oppression. And they have not been able to find any solutions by the usual methods of political prisoners and continued shootings of people, like happened in Miami recently. And to have added to that the example of a Grenada-type revolution must be a frightening thing for them — particularly since they see this place as being in their backyard. And they understand only too well that more and more Blacks are going to hear about Grenada, about what we are trying to do. Many of them are going to join any movement that is opposed to trying to turn back our revolution.

I think your point is a key one. Extremely important.

Pulley: I'm looking forward to being able to pick up Radio Free Grenada soon in Miami.

It will be a very powerful development when its beam is strengthened, especially for the English-speaking Caribbean, of course, but also for the average person in the United States, in order to help refute all the lies. The American people are already suspicious of anything the government says about anything. Their first thought is whether the government is lying.

The more people discover that just out-and-out lies are being told about Grenada, Nicaragua, and Cuba, the more the U.S. government will have a tremendous problem trying to get away with its war drive. As people in the Black movement become aware of what your government and country is up against, they will be outraged. Because they will see it as a racist injustice, just as they have seen with regard to Haitians, the Haitian immigrants.

It was largely pressure from the Black community that forced Carter to change, at least in words, his discriminatory double-standard toward Cuban and Haitian immigrants.

A similar consciousness can be developed with regard to this revolution, the more that Black leaders, activists, and others are aware of it.

Clark: What are some of the gains of the revolution over the past year and four months that you are most pleased with? And what are the biggest challenges that you see ahead in terms of social programs and economic development and reconstruction?

Bishop: Answering that question is not the easiest thing, because people's perspectives on that really differ very dramatically.

If you went into the countryside and you spoke to an elderly sister, her response to a question like that might be something like, "I feel free. I feel good. I feel like a Grenadian for the first time." Intangible things.

As for those of us in the party and government, our view is that the greatest single achievement, the thing that we are happiest about, is the community mobilization, community development, community participation. That has really impressed us most.

I can tell you, over and over again, month after month, we keep saying, "It can't continue." [*Laughs*] And then month after month, you make a call and people still come out.

When the rains came in November last year, it did us tremendous damage, more than $50 million worth of damage to the economy, twenty-three inches in one month. Before those rains came, there were some weekends when we'd have 85 percent of the villages around Grenada involved in community efforts. That's an extraordinary development. I tell you that in other English-speaking countries, I don't think they'd get 2 percent of villages to be involved. And I'm not saying this in a boastful way, I'm saying it in a factual way.

In January, we closed down the schools for two weeks so as to hold seminars for all the teachers to talk about the work-study approach, curriculum reform, and so on. And during those two weeks, we asked people to organize themselves to repair, repaint, refurbish all the schools, because they were in disastrous condition. And sixty-six primary schools got refurbished and repainted in that two-week period as a result of that drive, saving the country a tremendous amount of money. Really quite extraordinary.

We see it also in the area of the village health committees that are emerging as part of our drive to move toward a primary health system. Our aim is that doctors, nurses, paramedics, and technicians working as teams will go out into the country and bring medical attention to people where they live and where they need the attention.

The disproportion in the health budget is really quite staggering. In 1978, the last year of Gairy, 70 percent of the health budget was spent on the three hospitals in Grenada and Carriacou. Those three hospitals, in turn, attended to about 25 percent of the sick. But under Gairy only 30 percent of the health budget was spent in trying to keep together the thirty-five health centers and medical clinics around the country where the people actually went for attention.

If you understand the situation in this country in terms of poverty, in terms of the high cost of transportation, in terms of the inaccessibility of many of these health centers and medical clinics, then you can see the problem. People are sick, but they really cannot move. Even if they manage to go once, they cannot return two days later and so forth.

So we see the primary health system as being key. And getting the masses involved in that through village health committees, where they do a number of things. One, involve themselves in public health education. Two, deal with overhangings, deal with unblocking drains, which is one of the main problems with mosquitos outdoors, which means yellow fever and so on.

Third, monitoring the *quality* of health care they receive. Because doctors, naturally, came out of the system of 350 years of colonial oppression and thirty years of Gairy's misrule and neocolonialism. Their education system was preparing a tiny elite and one that was not dedicated to service but to dollar bills and to migrating as fast as they could. And even when they stayed here, they either moved into private practice altogether or insisted on their right, while being paid out of taxpayers' money, to practice privately at the same time, using hospital facilities to do so.

Now that kind of doctor is not going to join up as part of any medical team of nurses, paramedics, and technicians. So it's a real problem getting that struggle, that program going. We have been able to make some limited impact, but we have a long way to go. But we're sure it can be developed because of the community involvement and a new sense of oneness and unity in the country.

The other way I think we can look at the question you asked is to try to identify a little more concretely and specifically some of the actual benefits that have come to the people. More jobs, for example, 2,500 in the first year. That has made a very small dent really in the overall unemployment rate of 50 percent, which we inherited. But obviously it has made a difference. It has helped, reduced it to about 35 percent.

Secondly, in the area of education. Before the revolution, the last year of Gairy, three students went away on university scholarships in 1978. One of the three was Gairy's daughter. After the revolution, in the first six months, 109 scholarships, 109 people are able to go abroad to study.

We've been able to reduce secondary school fees from $37 a term to $12 a term. Next year, we intend to make it entirely free.

We have been able to increase greatly the number of scholarships in the secondary schools so that more children can get in.

We have started a breakfast and lunch feeding program in the schools so that those children who are too poor or are unable to return home for lunch will be able to keep themselves together — while your government is cutting it out.

In the area of health likewise. We inherited a situation where there were eighteen doctors working in the government service — virtually all of them concentrated in the hospitals, one or two moving around the clinics, but mostly doing a few hours every week, once a week for a few hours.

And in the first six months again, we were able to get seventeen new doctors to come to Grenada. In other words virtually the same figure as we had before were added to the system. And that has made an enormous difference in the quality and quantity of health care available.

As you know, twelve of these seventeen doctors and dentists came from Cuba on loan to us and that, of course has been an extremely important contribution, one of many they have made to the revolution.

So you have jobs, you have education, you have health. You also have the question of struggling with the infrastructure. Pipe-borne water has been greatly increased with the opening of the new Mardigras water project, and several others are about to be completed. That should ensure water for the whole of St. George's. There are pipes in some parts of St. George's that have not seen water for four and five years — not days or weeks, but literally four and five years, just rusted up.

We've been struggling with new feeder roads, opening the forests, for example, to get timber. Right now Grenada supplies something like 4 percent of our overall timber needs locally, when there's a lot of forest land just going idle. Without doing any great amount, just cutting a feeder road, not even paving it, just enough for a vehicle to get in using four-wheel drive, buying a sawmill for $20,000, that's all. And doing this now, we expect that in five years, we will be able to supply 90 percent of our timber needs.

There's a lot of little, relatively small things that overall have made quite an impact. These are some of the achievements.

In terms of the challenges. In a situation like ours, given our inheritance and dependent economy, we have an economy that was accustomed to looking outward for solutions, never inwards toward our own needs and problems. We have a country that was misruled for so many years under colonialism and today continues to be exploited by imperialism. The inheritance, the legacy of not just waste and corruption, but the lack of physical amenities, is really quite frightening. Three hundred and fifty years of British colonialism, for example, gave us *one* public secondary school. That's all they could build in 350 years! The other eleven were built by the churches.

When you come into that sort of situation, you obviously have to set yourself goals and targets for the revolution.

As you know, this year in Grenada is the year of education and production. And the two main things involved would be the Centre for Popular Education and the land reform program.

The land reform commission has been established and is laying the basis for eventual agrarian reform. At this point we are mainly trying to identify the idle *lands* in the country, and to see how many of the idle *hands* are willing to work in cooperatives, so as to bring about that marriage.

Clark: And that also involves the development of a fishing industry?

Bishop: Right.

Clark: What are some of the main political features of the Grenadian revolution?

Bishop: I would say that there are three main pillars of the revolution.

First, the organization and mobilization of the masses. That is very key. To always try to fully involve the masses in whatever we are trying to do, to keep them fully involved, to ensure that they understand what the problems are and where we are trying to go.

Secondly, the question of national security and defense — consolidation in those areas.

Thirdly, the question of building a sound national economy and bringing more benefits to the people, improving the quality of their lives.

Those to us are the three key pillars. And we believe that all three have to be worked on at the same time. We cannot afford to let any drop or lag behind.

In any revolutionary situation, in any progressive situation, the question of finding the right mix between the people of the country is key. The people without the guns, after all, is Allende, and we know what happened to Allende. The guns without the people, on the other hand, is Pinochet, and we know what will happen to Pinochet.

So it's a question of striking that balance, ensuring that our people understand the importance of being ready to defend our country from external attack, understand why it is that imperialism *must* attack us — why it is therefore, that assassinations, terrorism, destabilization, mercenary invasions, *must* be a part of their agenda.

That's something that is not as easy as it sounds in our context. Generally speaking, the historical tradition of the English-speaking Caribbean has not been one of a great deal of state violence, or other forms of violence really against the people. It's much easier, I think, for people in Latin America, for example, to understand these realities.

Secondly, remembering the way we took power. While there was a long history of repression by the state, by Gairy, in the days leading up to the revolution, to some extent the people themselves were not really involved in receiving that violence on a personal level.

We don't have, in other words, a situation let's say of Nicaragua, where since 1935 people have been fighting with arms in hand from time to time to try to unseat the various Somozas.

Or a situation like Cuba. The Platt Amendment in 1902 and the constant struggle since then, year after year, the years in the Sierra Maestra. You didn't have that kind of situation here.

The people's consciousness, in other words, did not come out of that objective situation that makes it fairly easy for them to understand what is possible at the hands of imperialism.

In addition, we didn't have the situation that the Cubans and Nicaraguans had, where there is a whole lot of land tied up in the latifundias, in the hands of one or two big exploiters, that you can take and just hand over, making easier the objective basis of proceeding on the subjective level. That is not our situation.

You talk about a big landowner in Grenada, you're talking about somebody with seventy-five acres of land.

So we have had right from day one this tremendous difficulty of getting across to our people, getting them to internalize in their bellies, the fact that we *are* going to be attacked, the fact that economic destabilization *is* going to continue, that the propaganda war *will* continue, that they *are* going to move eventually to assassinations and to mercenary invasions. The objective conditions for getting that message across were not there from before. People did not have that period of socialization, and therefore internalizing this was not the easiest thing.

To that extent, the recent events, unfortunate as they are in terms of loss of life, have gone a long way towards helping to raise consciousness. Because people are now able to say, "Right. From day one the comrades were talking about that." They now see that on June 19, even while [the terrorists] moved to wipe out the entire leadership, they did it in such a way that it didn't matter that hundreds of innocent women and children could get wiped out at the same time.

That has made a qualitative difference in the people's perception of what imperialism, what counterrevolution really means.

From that point of view, it has been an extremely important experience. That certainly is one of the biggest challenges that we face, trying to get that across, trying to get our people to understand that we need to, remain constantly alert, *constantly* vigilant. To understand that the threats are not there in theory, but are there in practice. We have to be ready and prepared to meet that.

You read about Allende, and you know that three months before September 11, 1973, was the last attempt on his life. So that last assassination attempt was a prelude to an actual coup. So we make the point that, in much the same way, an assassination attempt here can easily be a prelude to a mercenary invasion.

What imperialism is admitting now by moving to terror tactics and moving toward assassination attempts is that they have failed. Because all the attempts to build a popular base [for counterrevolution] have failed. Their attempts to push Winston Whyte and his so-called UPP — the United People's Party. The attempts to revive Herbert Blaize and his GNP [Grenada National Party], when the masses literally ran them off the streets; they didn't want to hear what they were saying. The attempts to use the *Torchlight*, the local media, to try to assist them in their propaganda in much the same way as they used *El Mercurio* in Chile or the *Gleaner* in Jamaica.

The attempts to try to find a popular base, using elements in the country who are trying to exploit *genuine* objective grievances of the masses. In other words, conditions *are* bad. There is a lot of unemployment. There is a lot of poverty. They get these people, therefore, to try to incite strikes, to try to whip up sections of the population around issues that *are* pressing issues, that we *are* concerned about, that we *are* trying to do something about. But making them at the same time feel that revolution is like instant coffee; you just throw it in a cup and it comes out presto. That you can negate 350 years of British colonialism and thirty years of imperialism and neocolonialism overnight.

That is really what they have been trying to do, and they failed miserably. Even their attempts to isolate us in the region, that has been a massive failure, notwithstanding all the adverse propaganda against Grenada. While undoubtedly several *governments* are hostile — *they* didn't need propaganda to become hostile; they were hostile from day one — the *masses* in the Caribbean understand well what we're trying to do. They understand that this is a genuine process. That we are really trying to build a new process that may become a new civilization, that could have tremendous relevance as a model to their own lives.

And therefore they have not been put off, and imperialism has seen that. They have seen, too, that their attempts at economic sabotage have not bitten deep enough, partly because America is our number seven trading partner. We get virtually nothing from America in terms of our shops and stores. So they have had problems crippling us in that way.

The only option left was to move to the top of the pyramid. At the top, of course, is the terror, is the assassination, is the mercenary invasions. And I think that's one of the major challenges — getting our people to understand that. Certainly in the last four weeks, that message has gotten across a lot more quickly.

People now see the importance, for example, of joining the militia in larger numbers. The original figures relatively speaking were small; you were talking about the vanguard really in the militia. Now quite a few more thousand have joined up.

People now begin to get a deeper appreciation and understanding that really the People's Revolutionary Army and the small militia that we had at first cannot seriously defend the country in a situation of all-out attack. That we can really only do that through a people's war, to be able to fight on that front. So that when the mercenaries are passing and they look at what appear to be innocent children and women bathing in a river, as they get going they get a bullet in their back. I think our masses are getting to understand that better now.

And a lot of that consciousness has certainly come as a result of recent events, and not just in Grenada. There are the assassinations of Archbishop [Oscar Arnulfo] Romero in El Salvador and Walter Rodney in Guyana; the destruction of the Eventide old people's home by fire in Jamaica on exactly the fourth anniversary of the similar destruction of Orange Lane in 1976; the recent attempt on [Prime Minister Michael] Manley's life and the coup d'etat attempt over there. And then, of course, in Grenada, the June 19 bombing coming right after the April 26 plot.

When you think of it, after just fifteen months, four plots — the October plot, the November plot, April 26 plot, and a few weeks later, June 19. And in each of the plots, what is central is wiping out the leadership. So I think we are beginning to get that clarity a bit more now, and that certainly has been a very important development from our point of view.

At this point, our feeling very strongly is that what is happening in Grenada is really part of a regional plan that imperialism has devised for dealing with progressive forces and revolutionary processes in the region. It's more than regional, it's clearly worldwide — the attempts to roll back the Afghanistan revolution, the continued search for bases in that area, the question of Iran and the attempts to invade that country a few months ago, the military presence in the Indian Ocean and the Persian Gulf area, the floating arsenal at Diego Garcia.

And in our own region, Carter's task force last year, Solid Shield '80 this year, artificial Cuban crisis in Peru, artificial crisis in Nicaragua over the two members of the junta who resigned, continuing destabilization attempts in Jamaica. The pattern is quite clear.

We feel that there are a series of concentric circles that imperialism has drawn up.

Into their first circle they have certainly put Cuba, Nicaragua, and Grenada as being the key countries to get at.

Cuba for obvious reasons. It is obviously the vanguard in this region.

Nicaragua because of its *tremendous* importance for Central America. Everybody in Central America wants to be a Sandinista. It's a massive problem there for them.

Grenada because of our powerful potential example for the English-speaking Caribbean countries, and indeed for the French- and Dutch-speaking Caribbean countries. So that's their first circle.

In the second circle we believe they have countries like Jamaica, Guyana, St. Lucia, Suriname, El Salvador. Countries where either there have been positive developments on the anti-imperialist front, or where there have been important attempts at building new structures for the people and bringing new benefits, or where there are important progressive forces in opposition or in power who are determined to bring about these changes.

Or where, as in the case of El Salvador, there is an ongoing national liberation struggle that clearly will not be settled in any reformist way. All attempts at reformism in El Salvador *must* fail.

Their third circle, therefore, will be aimed largely at all progressive forces, individually and collectively, whether in or out of office. That would explain, for example, the Rodney slaying or the Archbishop Romero slaying. They understand the potential that the left-progressive forces in the region have, and they are determined to crush that potential, using assassinations.

So it's an extremely dangerous period for us in this region.

Clark: The U.S. propaganda around the Cuban emigrants has backfired on Carter, especially following the opening of the port of Mariel, the massive anti-imperialist marches in Cuba, and the racist treatment of the Cubans in the United States. What was the impact here in the Caribbean?

Bishop: Was it in the *Militant* that I saw the Fidel interview with Lee Lockwood from way back in 1965? Did you repeat that in the paper? That I found to be an extremely important interview, particularly as it was fifteen years old, in tracing the history of this whole emigration question.

It was really quite succinct, the way Fidel put it. Pointing out that from the word *go* it was an artificial crisis being created. That people, of course, when they were able to leave freely were leaving freely, nobody was blocking them. It became more convenient eventually for the Americans to force them to escape and then treat them as heroes, so that they can get propaganda out of it.

It was really quite an important article, coming at the time it did, especially as it was done such a long time ago.

That propaganda has really done damage, there's no question about it, in the English Caribbean. Given that there's all this talk about "boat people running from Communism" and so forth. I think a lot of the Caribbean masses have had difficulty in comprehending what is really happening and putting it in a full context.

Because what's the reality? If any of those islands had America's doors opened tomorrow morning, there would be six people left on the island. That's the reality. But they make this song and dance.

The imperialist-controlled media have the resources, they have the skills, everything else. We find that there has been a marked improvement in imperialist propaganda throughout 1980 on virtually every issue. First of all, the speed with which they respond and the amount of ammunition they throw into it has been quite extraordinary.

Consider Afghanistan, in December of last year. Just think of the speed with which they moved and how quick that propaganda built up and therefore how difficult it was to combat and counter it.

But really on every issue. Within seconds of the bomb attack here in Queen's Park, the United States embassy in Bridgetown [Barbados] was already sending reports out. Interestingly, their first reports were saying that members of the leadership had been killed. Very interesting. We want to know, how did they know that?

Or take Iran, the question of these fifty-three hostages. Again, the speed they moved on that question, and the amount of support they were able to muster, made it difficult for people to put it in a full context in terms of the twenty-seven years of oppression under the shah, armed by American guns, and the very deep feelings of indignation as a result of all that by the people of Iran. The feeling that if America is harboring this man, then what is required?

But even more fundamentally, the fact that you have a situation like in South Africa, where there are millions of Blacks being kept as hostages. Yet here they are making so much fuss about fifty-three hostages. Millions of African hostages, imprisoned in a system of apartheid. That's not important. You never hear talk of sanctions about that, but they want sanctions for fifty-three.

It's difficult, because they come over with this powerful emotive line. They put it in the context of the need for international security of all embassies. And it leads many democratic, even some progressive countries to take a firm position against — without ever putting it in any kind of context.

Pulley: One thing that has hurt the imperialists in their drive against Iran has been the attitudes of a good number of the parents of some hostages. Many have come out against the U.S. raid, against the sanctions. A majority favor what Carter is doing, but it's certainly a large number who are vocal and are opposed to it.

They're having a rough time. They've been forced to back away from what was the case at the time of the raid in April, when it looked like imminent war. Everything blew up in their face.

Bishop: The OPEC countries came out with a very strong statement in the last two days. Really good news. I think it was the day before yesterday. Threatening an oil boycott.

Clark: Fidel had urged that in his May Day speech.

Bishop: That's right. That was a first-class speech. It really came over powerfully. What was important to me about that whole trip was the very, very close feelings between the Cuban people and their leader. That was extraordinary. It took Fidel about ten minutes before he could open his mouth. Everytime he tried to say something, the people just kept going again. I really found that extraordinary, because you're talking about a million and a quarter people or whatever it was.

And at the end, their tremendous discipline was another eye opener. Whole waves of people move to the left while others stood still, moved to the right while others stood still. Then the front rows moved out by a few hundred thousand, the back rows by a few hundred thousand. Whole waves of people, left and right, left and right, no pushing. And in ten or fifteen minutes, that square was empty. An extraordinary manifestation of discipline.

Diane Wang: Even the *New York Times* had to comment on that. They wrote with a great deal of consternation about that rally. They had to admit not only the enthusiasm, but the discipline.

Bishop: Yes, it was so striking. You would have had to write your article on the plane before you got there really — which they do sometimes.

Clark: The lies on Afghanistan are often particularly outlandish because it is so geographically remote. The media at one point recently were reporting that an army of 20,000 guerrillas — they always call them "Muslim freedom fighters," failing to point out that there are Muslims on both sides — were surrounding Kabul. But then a few days later, if you turned to the bottom of a remote page, you noticed a little item saying the story turned out not to be true.

One of the things we try to do with the *Militant* and *Intercontinental Press* is simply to counteract the barrage of lies, just to keep reminding people that the capitalist press will stoop to outright deception. Lenin said that they often tell the truth in the little things so that they can lie in the big ones.

Bishop: On the Afghanistan question, we have been pointing out here in Grenada that what we are really concerned with there was the April 1978 revolution, not so much the December 1979 events. And in the intervening eighteen months, what was happening — in terms of the attempts at destabilization, the armed attacks from Pakistan and elsewhere, the plans of imperialism. And that what requires solidarity and support, therefore, is the right of the people of Afghanistan to build their revolution. And people can relate to that over here, because they see it happening to us too. They know we can have a similar type problem.

Clark: One last question. What would you like to say to working people in the United States? To the Black community in the United States? What message would you like us to take back?

Bishop: First of all we would like to stress something that imperialism has been trying to use as a means of dividing and ruling — and this is that we have absolutely no quarrel with the American people. We have nothing at all against the people of America as a people.

Our quarrel is with the system of imperialism. Our quarrel, therefore, is with the American establishment and all its various manifestations — whether it's through the presidency or National Security Council or the State Department or the CIA or the powerful business lobby or the powerful media or whatever. That is who our quarrel is with. And particularly insofar as that establishment seeks to support by violence the right of their transnational corporations to continue to exploit and rape our resources. That is what our quarrel is with.

After all, more Americans come to our country every year than the entire population of Grenada — 140,000 came by ship last year, and I'm not talking about those who came for stay-overs.

So that is not our quarrel and we want to make that clear. Because imperialism has been doing its best to try to sow all sorts of confusion in that area.

Likewise, when you come to the question of the Blacks and other oppressed minorities in America, obviously we have a particularly close feeling, given our own cultural background and our own history. There is a very close sense of cultural identity, which the people of Grenada automatically feel for American Blacks and which we have no doubt is reciprocated by the American Black community.

Because our own struggle is internationalist, we have over the years been giving our fullest support to all international causes that demand such support. We see that as our internationalist duty.

Since the revolution, we have continued in that vein. We were the first country in the Western Hemisphere to recognize the Polisario Front; the second country in the world to recognize the provisional junta in Nicaragua on May 23 last year, fully three weeks before they finally won their victory; our open and consistent support to the PLO, for Puerto Rican independence, and so forth. That is our position.

And therefore we see the importance of progressive forces worldwide joining together. We see that struggle as being *one* struggle, indivisible. And what happens in Grenada, we recognize its importance for all struggles around the world. And we feel that on that basis, the progressive forces and democratic forces in America ought to give their support to our revolution also.

We certainly place a great deal of importance on the activity, the potential, and the possibilities for the American working-class movement. Both in terms of mobilizing and organizing to stop any draft movement, and in terms of the potential of doing mortal damage to the international capitalist and imperialist system from within the belly of the main imperialist power on earth.

And thirdly, in terms of the great possibilities for expressing solidarity with the revolutionary struggles around the world. Something they have done before and can do again. For example, mobilizing and organizing themselves to refuse to load ships heading for particular areas.

So, our basic message would be to get across this sense: That what we are struggling against is the system of imperialism. That we have the greatest respect for the people of America. That we feel a particularly close affinity to American Blacks and other oppressed minorities, to the working-class movement in America, toward progressive forces in America. That we certainly are willing to extend our solidarity with them in their struggles, and we certainly would hope that they would extend their own solidarity to us in our struggle.

Finally, our message would be: We would love to see them. We believe that it is very important that instead of reading the propaganda that is being circulated in America, they should come out to Grenada, come out to Cuba, come out to Nicaragua, and see for themselves. So that they can understand what is happening and as a result be in a better position to appreciate what is going on in this part of the world.

Let me add just one final thing. That is to say that we, without intending to be disrespectful, would very strongly recommend to the Black movement in America the importance of developing the firmest and closest links with the white working-class movement and the white progressive movement. Our feeling certainly is that in order to win that struggle inside of America, it's extremely important that all progressive forces get together and wage a consistent fight against the real enemy. Don't spend time fighting each other, debating trivialities. That's something I think is important and that I would like to get across in the message.

Learning Together, Building Together

July 27, 1980

The following speech, broadcast nationally over Radio Free Grenada, announced the beginning of Grenada's literacy campaign. It is printed in Maurice Bishop, Selected Speeches 1979-1981.

From the earliest months of our glorious March 13 revolution the PRG has stressed the importance of bringing education to all our people and of putting an end to illiteracy in our country. We have placed heavy emphasis on education as a tool for national development. In keeping with this emphasis, the Ministry of Education had established many areas for priority action. From these early months, we have seen some of the results of this work — the lowering of school fees, the granting of more scholarships in the first year of people's power than the preceding five years put together, the introduction of a school feeding program, the beginning of the process of consultation and discussions among teachers of the major problems of the education system, the beginning of work on a new curriculum, the school repair program. All of these areas of activity in education are directed by one fundamental principle: that education is the right of all of our people, the responsibility of our revolution, and a key to the development of our country.

Undoubtedly, among all these initiatives and programs of the Ministry of Education, the Center for Popular Education [CPE] is one of the most important and fundamental. The CPE is a critically important program because through the CPE education, which was previously a privilege for a minority, will now be the right of all our people. Through the CPE we are beginning the long and difficult but vital task of providing education for our working people — many of whom were not able to receive an adequate education for a multitude of reasons, most of which relate to poverty and our colonial experience of exploitation. The revolution has given high priority to education because we clearly understand and recognize that if we are to bring an end to all of the serious problems that we face, education must enable us to confront these problems.

If we are to end unemployment and poor housing, we will have to increase our levels of production by working harder, using better, more scientific methods of production, and using higher forms of technology.

The education of workers is an important dimension in this process.

If we are to defeat disease and poor health conditions, we need to understand their causes and conditions.

If we are to overcome backwardness and poverty, we need to understand the nature of poverty and expoitation.

If we are to overcome superstition, we need to be able to read and write, to understand in a scientific way the environment in which we live.

If we are to continue to struggle against our number one enemy — imperialism — we need to understand its nature. For our own sakes, in our own interests, we need to understand the enemy we are fighting. We need to understand the vicious nature of imperialism, so tragically illustrated in the cowardly and murderous bomb blast of June 19. Our struggle against imperialism and our struggle to build a new Grenada, is a struggle on many fronts in which every patriot and revolutionary has a role to play. We have fought and continue to fight for better terms of trade, better prices for our agricultural produce so that our farmers and agricultural workers can enjoy greater benefits. Education is a tool for understanding this struggle.

Two years after they had removed the tyrant Batista from power, the revolutionary people of Cuba undertook one of the most heroic battles in their history — the battle against illiteracy. In one year this firm and united people were able to teach 1,032,849 Cubans to read and write. In other words, sisters and brothers, the youth, students, workers, and women of Cuba were able, in this short period of time, to teach one out of every four Cubans to read and write. This was a massive and democratic task undertaken by the people to solve one of the major problems of the people. The Cuban literacy campaign was a voluntary task enthusiastically executed by free men and women out of a deep and patriotic desire to build their country, their revolution, and to help their countrymen. It was a stirring challenge posed by the revolution and answered by thousands of students and workers. The youngest volunteer teacher in the Cuban literacy campaign was only eight years old and the eldest student was a woman of 106 years who had been born and grown up as a slave.

In the process of the literacy campaign, the Cuban youth and students learned much more than they taught, the workers received more than they gave. It was far more than an educational exercise, it was a profound human process through which the Cuban people began to know themselves. Students from the cities, by living with the peasants they taught, began to understand (in a manner in which no book could have taught them) the meaning of poverty, the meaning of hard work and sacrifice, and the dignity of honest work.

In Nicaragua since the overthrow of the dictator Somoza, one of the

122 Maurice Bishop Speaks

immediate objectives of the Sandinista revolution has been to teach Nicaraguans to read and write. One out of every two Nicaraguans cannot read and write and in some parts of Nicaragua there is 90 percent illiteracy. The militant and revolutionary sons of Sandino are fighting this battle against illiteracy and have rightly called their literacy crusade "the awakening of the people," because they clearly understand that to teach the people to read and write is to free the people from ignorance, superstition, and cultural backwardness. It is to release the creative and revolutionary potential of the people so that they can continue to be the authors of their history and destiny. In the past couple of months since the literacy crusade began, about 108,000 Nicaraguans have been taught to read and write. That, sisters and brothers, is the population of our entire country. Can we imagine — above everything else — the great enthusiasm, the immense dedication, and the high sacrifices which have made the results possible?

Sisters and brothers of free Grenada, there are some important differences between the Cuban and Nicaraguan campaigns and ours, but there is much that we have to learn from their heroic examples. The unity of action, the determination to succeed, the revolutionary spirit of voluntary sacrifice, are the lessons to be extracted. Only a united and conscious people can move forward. Only an educated and productive people can build a new and just society. Only a literate people can create the new man and woman.

In our literacy campaign conducted by the CPE we have just over 3,500 learners registered and a volunteer teaching force of almost 2,000. We are certain, however, that there are many more people in our country who cannot read and write and many more volunteers need to be found. These figures are small but significant and in any event we know that there are many more people in need of learning how to read and write and many more in need of further developing whatever basic abilities in this area that they have. These figures are small in comparison to the massive figures of the Cuban or Nicaraguan statistics but they are significant.

In Grenada, Carriacou, and Petit Martinique we fortunately do not have as serious a problem of illiteracy as some of our neighbors in Latin America or the Caribbean. But illiteracy does exist in our country, and it exists among that strata of population whose role in the process of production is of vital importance to the economy. The agricultural workers, the manual workers, are the driving forces of the production of wealth in our country. For economic reasons, for moral reasons, for Christian and humanitarian reasons, illiteracy must be eradicated totally from our country. This is the challenge with which we are faced.

How can we respond to this historic and fundamental challenge?

We respond collectively by working together with the CPE village coordinator in our area, by encouraging others to volunteer to teach or to register to learn to read and write. We respond by attending the island-wide training seminar which will be held on Monday and Tuesday in each parish and then by attending the weekly meetings which will be held between the village technician (the professional teacher who will guide the work of the volunteer) and volunteers. Above all, we respond, teacher and students alike, by being consistent and disciplined in our approach to our work.

To teach a brother and sister to read and write is a deeply rewarding task, it is a revolutionary duty for those who know how to voluntarily place their knowledge at the service of those who do not. By undertaking this task with the discipline, the consistency, the enthusiasm that it requires, we will succeed. We will succeed not only in teaching our fellow countrymen to read and to write, but through that process volunteer teachers will also learn a great deal themselves and will help to build a deeper spirit of unity, understanding, and collective endeavor.

We call on all patriotic and concerned Grenadians, potential volunteers and students who have not yet registered, to come forward and to take part in this program now. You can register either by contacting the parish coordinators or one of the volunteer teachers in your area or by contacting the CPE office in Scott Street, St. George's.

I end by repeating that our country cannot go forward if there is a substantial number of our people who cannot read or write. In order to prepare for the kind of society we are trying to build, in order to achieve the greater and greater levels of production we must aim at, all of us have to be developed. We all have to raise our levels of knowledge, our levels of consciousness, our levels of efficiency, our levels of understanding. We cannot build Grenada on the basis where three-quarters of the people could read and write and the other quarter cannot. We cannot build our country on the basis where half of the people can move into higher levels of jobs where you can produce more and the other half cannot. I call therefore on all Grenadians to give their maximum support to this vital project. Let us together develop our collective wisdom, knowledge, understanding, and consciousness. Let us in unity and by learning together move to build our country, to expand our economy and to consolidate our revolution.

Long live CPE!

Long live free Grenada, Carriacou, and Petit Martinique!

Forward ever, backward never!

If They Touch Cuba,
They Touch Grenada

December 1980

The following remarks were given to the Cuban Communist Party's second congress held in Havana, December 17-20, 1980. They were originally printed in Granma Weekly Review, *January 18, 1981.*

Esteemed Comrade Fidel Castro Ruz, first secretary of the Communist
    Party of Cuba;
Comrade delegates;
Comrades:
    On behalf of the Central Committee of the New Jewel Movement, the vanguard party of the Grenada revolution, I bring warm, brotherly, revolutionary greetings to this Second Congress of the Communist Party of Cuba.
    The report presented to this congress by Comrade Fidel Castro shows beyond doubt that the Cuban people have benefited tremendously over the last five years by the successes of the program designed by the party and implemented with great revolutionary zeal by the Cuban people.
    In this room are gathered the finest sons and daughters of revolutionary Cuba, the vanguard of the Cuban people, and the Cuban revolution, the undoubted inheritors of the mantle of Martí, Mella, Camilo, and Che. [*Applause*] You have demonstrated over the past few days a remarkable amount of discipline, patience, organization, enthusiasm, militancy, and deep understanding of the problems which continue to face your country and of the solutions for redressing those problems. But what is remarkable about Cuba is that you comrades assembled here are a symbol of the whole people of revolutionary Cuba.
    I was honored to be present at Revolution Square on International Workers' Day this year and what I saw before me was not just the largest gathering that I had ever seen assembled in one place but in that massive ocean of people, in that extraordinary multitude of one and a half million people, I observed the very same qualities of discipline, enthusiasm, organization, and militancy. [*Applause*] I observed, too, a sense of deep patriotic combativeness and revolutionary fervor. Who could fail to have

been excited by that historic moment and inspired and rejuvenated by that display of enthusiasm? As Fidel said, such a people do indeed deserve victory and a place in history. [*Applause*]

In every corner of our region, the masses joined this unanimous call and demand by the revolutionary people of Cuba for an end to the criminal blockade, an end to the illegal spy flights, an end to the immoral occupation of the Guantánamo naval base. Imperialism can no longer remain deaf to this thunderous call of the people of the region and must end the violation of the sovereignty of Cuba.

Cuba has been a beacon for us in Grenada. It has both taught and reminded us of many important lessons. It has reminded us of the central role of the party in building the revolution. It has reminded us of the critical importance of being the genuine vanguard of the people, building and maintaining close links with the people through the mass organizations.

There can obviously be no doubt that without the leadership and guidance of the Communist Party of Cuba, the heroic vanguard of the Cuban people, there would not have been such dramatic improvements in health, education, economic development and diversification, the raising of political and class consciousness, and the development of a genuine spirit of proletarian internationalism.

Because of this, because of the exemplary success of the Cuban Revolution, imperialism has unashamedly dedicated itself to Cuba's destruction. Those who have attempted it know that the revolution is indestructible. But the newcomers seem to believe that they can turn back the clock of history and therein lies serious danger. We hope that we are wrong, but we see the possibility of dangerous adventurism on the horizon. We know that there are plans to "teach a lesson," as these elements say, to Cuba, Nicaragua, El Salvador, and Grenada.

We know that we are not alone. The people of Cuba unhesitatingly and unselfishly came to our aid in the first weeks of our revolution. When our revolution was at its most vulnerable stage, when imperialism and its mercenary forces threatened to blockade and invade our revolution, Cuba provided us with the military means necessary to defend and secure our young revolution. [*Applause*] That dealt a decisive blow to the designs and ambitions of imperialism.

Consistent with its internationalist principles, Cuba provided urgently needed assistance in the areas of health, education, communications, and fisheries. Today, as I speak to you, dear comrades, there are over 250 Cuban internationalist construction workers working side by side with the Grenadian people to build a modern international airport, a project which will create the basis for the expansion of our economy. This is internationalism in its most profound manifestation.

We have seen internationalism at work thanks in large measure to our steadfast Cuban friends and their allies in the socialist and progressive world. We too have learned the lessons of internationalism, and all our comrades in struggle should know that they are not alone. For once again, in the name of the Grenadian revolution, we give our solemn pledge that wherever circumstances require we shall unhesitatingly fulfill our internationalist responsibilities. [*Applause*] Imperialism must know and understand that, if they touch Cuba, they touch Grenada, and, if they touch Nicaragua, they touch Grenada. [*Prolonged applause*]

From the earliest stages of our revolution, the imperialist powers attempted to dictate with whom we should be friends. They threatened to undermine and destroy our economy, they threatened economic, political, and diplomatic blockade. They encouraged mercenaries to organize invasions of our territory, they launched a vicious propaganda campaign against us.

Over the last twenty months we have, with internationalist aid and support characteristic of this congress, resisted all efforts to destabilize our revolutionary process. We stand firmly on the principle of our anti-imperialist democratic revolution and we work consistently to preserve it. We have taken a wide range of measures to ensure and consolidate our revolution. We have sought to strengthen and diversify our economy and sources of import. We have practiced the principle of peaceful coexistence and stand in full support of world peace and détente. We continue to oppose colonialism, racism, Zionism, and apartheid. We stand in solidarity with all peoples fighting for their national sovereignty and independence throughout the world.

We have mobilized our people at all levels to defend our revolution to the last drop of blood. [*Applause*] The stronger the revolution, the more determined is imperialism to defeat it.

The geopolitical realities of our region make our task even more challenging. Every four years in the month of November the USA elects a president and just after that, on January 20, the president is inaugurated. In 1961, less than three months after John F. Kennedy became president, the CIA launched an attack against Cuba, now known as the Playa Girón fiasco. This led to the first military defeat of imperialism in this region. With renewed efforts in reactionary circles to restore the dirty work of the CIA, we do not rule out the possibility of a similar development. It is clear that already plans have been drawn up aimed against the Cuban revolution, the Nicaraguan revolution, the Grenadian revolution and the revolutionary process unfolding in El Salvador.

We do not possess the full details of these plans, but what we do know is that we must learn from history and take the necessary measures to combat aggression, subversion, and counterrevolution. What we also know is that no revolutionary process can survive, far less go forward, without the building and consolidation of the national economy. No revolution can survive without the political mobilization and organization of the masses, for this teaches them the goals, difficulties, and gains of the revolution. No revolution can survive without the military capacity which provides the people with the honor of defending what they have built. These are the fundamental pillars of any revolutionary process. As we say in Grenada, the people without guns spells defeat; guns without people means facism. Cuba has the guns and the people, that is revolution. [*Applause*]

Long live the Communist Party of Cuba! [*Shouts of "Long live!"*]

Long live proletarian internationalism! [*Shouts of "Long live!"*]

Long live the fighting people of El Salvador! [*Shouts of "Long live!"*]

Long live the revolutionary forces of Latin America and the Caribbean! [*Shouts of "Long live!"*]

Long live Cuba! [*Shouts of "Long live!"*]

Long live Fidel! [*Shouts of "Long live!"*]

Forward ever, backward never! [*Prolonged applause*]

Two Years of the Grenada Revolution

March 13, 1981

The following speech was delivered to a mass rally in St. George's to mark the second anniversary of the revolution. From a text issued by the Grenadian government.

Comrade chairman;

Your excellency Sir Paul Scoon, governor-general of Grenada;

Comrades of the Central Committee of the party and members of the
People's Revolutionary Government;

Esteemed guests;

Beloved sisters and brothers;

Comrades all of free Grenada;

In the name, comrades, in the name of our free people, in the name of our revolution I welcome all of our guests to free Grenada on this occasion of the second anniversary of our glorious and popular people's revolution. We are very happy today, comrades, to have so many guests from all different parts of the world, to share this occasion once again with us. We are particularly happy today to have with us again as we have always had on critical occasions very high, very distinguished representatives from the government and people of revolutionary Cuba. We are also happy today, comrades, to have with us representatives from another country with which we have developed very close, very fraternal ties over the past two years — the government and people of Nicaragua. Comrades, today, too, we have with us some people coming from countries several hundred miles away, people who have had to travel in one or two cases for days before they could reach our country, some of these people who have sent high-ranking ministers to be here with us on this occasion of our second anniversary. I ask you therefore to welcome to our country a minister from the government and people of the Republic of Iraq, a country with which we have been developing very, very close and fraternal ties. [*Applause*] We also have with us ministers from fraternal governments, ministers from friendly governments right here in the region; we have with us a man who has been here on several occasions, a comrade whom the people of Grenada have gotten to know very well. We are very happy today also to welcome to Grenada as an official

128

representative of his government, Comrade George Odlum, of St. Lucia. [*Applause*] And from the government and people of Guyana, has come a minister, a man who is now the minister of national development; I ask you, too, to give a hearty welcome to Comrade Robert Corbin. [*Applause*] And finally from the region, from a country that we have been expressing consistent and firm support for, that we have been demonstrating our total solidarity over the years with their struggle I ask you to welcome, comrades, the member of Parliament and the deputy speaker of the House of Parliament, I ask you to welcome the comrade, Comrade Castillo from the government and people of Belize. [*Applause*] But most of all sisters and brothers, comrades, most of all today in the face of attempts to set back our process from time to time, in the face of attempts to step up the propaganda, to step up the destabilization today, we are particularly happy for us to see before us so many people of free Grenada assembled in their thousands in this park. [*Applause*] The members of our armed forces, the members of our people in uniform, coming from the People's Revolutionary Army, coming from the militia, coming from the Police Service, coming from the Revolutionary Cadets, coming from the Grenada Prisons Service, coming from the women in uniform, today it is a very happy day to see so many of our members of our revolutionary armed forces assembled here with the people of free Grenada. [*Applause*]

As we meet today for the second anniversary, we do so at a time of great crisis in the world, a time of deep international industrial crisis particularly in the Western world, we do so at a time, comrades, when millions of people in the industrialized Western world are roaming the streets looking for work, when all official figures have estimated that perhaps over 14 million people are out of work, a time when people are making comparisons with the periods of the 1920s and 1930s — the period of the great depressions. A time in the world, sisters and brothers, when we are seeing daily runaway inflation, a time in the world when we are seeing a worsening of the balance of trade for developing countries, a time in the world when there is daily deterioration of the conditions of the rural poor of the poorest countries of the world, a time in fact when in some countries illiteracy is actually on the increase, when malnutrition and hunger are actually on the increase, when disease is actually on the increase, a time when it has been estimated that soon there is perhaps going to be over 500 million people who every night are going to bed hungry, with nothing to put into their stomach. A time when the United Nations has estimated that this great crisis in food production will get even worse unless resources are set aside now to begin to deal with this critical problem, a time, sisters and brothers, when there is a serious worldwide environmental decay, when industrial pollution is affecting the air, is affecting the water, is affecting the land, all because some in the pursuit of dollars are doing this indiscriminately without any regard for the health and welfare of the poor people of the world. This period that we are witnessing, comrades, is so bad that in August last year a special General Assembly of the United Nations was convened and at this special General Assembly, which was virtually sabotaged by some of the developed market economy countries, the conclusion was reached that there is going to be, there is going to continue to be, hard resistance to the interest of the countries of the developing world, the countries of the so-called Third World, the conclusion is also reached that the developing countries should not expect any justice or any serious cooperation from the major industrialized Western countries around the world.

This crisis has become so bad that probably before the end of this year a special General Assembly of the Organization of American States is going to be held to examine areas and to structure forms of cooperation for development in energy, in food production, in small island development in Latin America and the Caribbean. This present crisis in the world, sisters and brothers, is so bad that the richest country in the world has taken the decision to close down even hospitals, to close down even schools, to cut back on food stamps that benefit the poor people, to cut back on medical assistance for the poor people, to cut back on subsidies to help the poorest farmers to stay in production, to cut back on students' loans and grants that will assist the poorer students for receiving university education, to cut back in fact on eighty-three poor people's programs, including programs that will benefit handicapped children. This crisis is so bad that this country has decided to allow factories to close, to allow their people to roam the streets in their millions, daily being added to by thousands more looking for jobs that are not available. Comrades, this economic crisis that these countries are facing has had a severe effect on our own country and economy.

Because our country and other countries like ours that are linked to these larger countries in a structural way, our economies are dependent on their economy, when their economies run into trouble, ours also feel the effects of that trouble. When they sneeze we in the Third World catch the cold, when they run into problems we are the ones who feel it even more than their own people do. If it is so tough and difficult and hard for even the richest countries in the world, then imagine the difficulties that the smallest and the poorest of countries must have to undergo. And, comrades, we have to ask ourselves the question, that if it is so difficult for these countries then how is progress going to be possible for the poor and small countries of the world?

We believe in Grenada that it is possible, even in the face of these difficulties, for progress nonetheless to be made, that it is possible for our country to continue to move forward even in the face of these difficulties. We believe that there are ways of achieving these objectives. First and foremost we believe in the need for honesty with the people, we believe it is important to always tell the people the truth, to always give the people the facts even when they are hard facts, to never lull the people into a false sense of security, to never deceive the people, to never make them believe that by some miracle suddenly things are going to improve without greater efforts and greater sacrifice and greater production on our part; to be honest with the people, tell the people the facts, get the people to know the real truth of the situation.

The second formula that we believe could be important is the need to adopt our conscious policy to put the people at the center, put the people at the focus, of all of the activities of the government, the state, and the revolution. To always aim to involve the people, to always aim to get the people to participate, to always aim to mobilize the people, to always seek to deepen the unity of the people because a people that is mobilized is a people that is ready to face the future.

The third formula is that we see it as essential that in a situation as difficult as this one that we take an approach to economic development and we take an approach to building our country that stresses the basic need of our people — an approach that looks inward to the problems of our country and not an approach that looks outward to the need of other people's countries that are already richer than our own. We say it is possible that even with limited resources, even with limited capital formation, even with a limited population, it is possible nonetheless to go forward and to bring benefits to the people if these approaches are adopted.

Because while some people are closing hospitals, we in Grenada are improving and expanding our hospitals; we are building new hospitals, we have already built a new eye hospital that now means that our people can receive attention to their eyes right here in our own country, no longer having to go abroad. [*Applause*] While some are cutting back on hospital care, we are expanding these facilities for our people; we have built a new maternity clinic; we have built for the first time in the history of our country a new intensive care unit; we have added to the casualty department facilities; we have added to the X-ray facilities; we have built a new operating theater in the hospital; we have moved our country from one dental clinic before the revolution to seven dental clinics today after the revolution. [*Applause*] While others are cutting back on medical care and assistance for the poor in their countries, we have moved instead to double the number of doctors who are available to add to the quantity and quality of health care in our country. We have moved to triple the number of dentists in our country, after 350 years, free medical attention for all of our people in all public health institutions. [*Applause*]

While others are choosing to close schools, we are looking to build new schools, and in fact over the past year we have opened a new secondary school named after one of the martyrs of our revolution — the

Bernadette Bailey Secondary School. [*Applause*] And if this sounds like a small achievement, sisters and brothers, I want to remind you that after 350 years of British colonialism and twenty-nine years of Gairyism only one single secondary school was ever built in our country out of public funds — one secondary school after 379 years; but in the first year of the revolution already a second secondary school has been built for the people of our country. [*Applause*] While others, sisters and brothers, are cutting subsidies and cutting grants to their students, we are looking to expand on these facilities for our people; we are now providing in our primary schools a free milk and a subsidized meal system for all of the children in the primary schools who are in need of this attention; we have moved to the point where we have nearly doubled the number of scholarships from primary to secondary schools so that the children of our country, more of them, are aided to receive a secondary education free of cost; we have moved to the stage where, coming out of the last year of Gairy, only three people got university scholarships to study abroad, in the first year of the revolution 109 Grenadian students left to go away to study at universities abroad. [*Applause*] We have moved to the stage where several months from now, sisters and brothers, when the new school year opens in September, secondary education in our country will be entirely free of cost for all of the children of free Grenada. [*Applause*]

While some are looking to cut out the assistance to the poor in their country through cutting back on welfare programs, we are aiming to increase that kind of assistance for our people. We are aiming to keep down the cost of living; that is why we have been able over the past year to keep the price of sugar at sixty-eight cents per pound, while it is selling in neighboring non-sugar-producing islands at $1.22 and upwards a pound, because we are concerned that the masses have their sugar and have it at the cheapest possible cost that they can afford to get it. We in free Grenada, comrades, have been moving to increase the assistance we can provide to the farmers of our country through additional fertilizer, through more plants, through more seeds, through greater and better extension services, through the establishment of a common machinery pool. We have looked at the problem of the poorest of the workers in our country and recognize that for these workers one of the biggest problems has been the rising cost of materials to repair their houses, and therefore we have established a housing repair program for the poorest workers in our country, under which they have over ten years to repay the loan. They pay back only two-thirds of the total amount, they pay no interest at all, and they only pay the sum of $5 a month back towards the cost of the materials they have received to repair their houses. [*Applause*]

The approach of the government has been to try to get the maximum results out of a minimum expenditure of dollars. We always start off from the premise that money will not be available and, looking from that starting point, we move to the situation of seeing in what ways we can mobilize our people, in what ways we can involve them to help to cut back on waste, to help to cut back on corruption, to help to cut back on inefficiency, to help to increase production through their own voluntary contribution. That is one reason why Commander of the Revolution General Austin, the head of the People's Revolutionary Army, has given a directive to the comrades in the PRA that this year the army must feed itself, that this year the army must grow its own food, must develop its own pork, must develop its own poultry, so that the people of our country through their taxes will not have to meet this burden. This is also why, comrades, the way in which the revolution approaches this primary question of defending this country is not just to rely on those comrades who are in the professional army, who are in the professional section of the armed forces, but instead to seek to build a part-time army based on the people who work voluntarily, who work without cost, who work because of their sense of patriotism, because of their consciousness, because of their understanding that the revolution is theirs and they must defend their own revolution. [*Applause*]

The approach of the revolution is also to make a conscious attempt to transform the economy that we have inherited, to seek to break our dependence on outside forces, to lay the basis for planned and progressive development. For this reason dreams and mysticism and lack of information and lack of statistics are replaced now by a Ministry of Planning that functions as a ministry of serious and committed technocrats who understand the importance of building that mechanism in order to achieve the necessary economic transformation. That is also why, sisters and brothers, we have decided and have laid great stress on the need for us to ensure that the productive sector in our country begins to pay for itself in a serious way; that was the reason for declaring 1980 the Year of Education and Production, that is the reason for declaring this year, 1981, the Year of Agriculture and Agro-Industries. That is why in agriculture we have spent so much time and are making sure that more seeds, that more plants, that more fertilizer, that more extension services, that new crops, that agricultural equipment, that new markets are sought after, so that the farmers in our country will be able to receive a better price for what they are producing. That is also why in the areas of agro-industry we have moved to establish the coffee-processing plant out in Telescope, have moved to establish the agro-industrial plant down in True Blue, that now produces juices, that now produces different condiments. That is also why a new Ministry of Fisheries and Agro-Industry under Comrade Kenrick Radix has been created so as to ensure that even more time and more attention is given to pushing production in this year 1981. That is also why, sisters and brothers, in the area of tourism the Hotel Training School has been established; additional plans have been created in the state sector; more tours from abroad have been organized to bring more and more guests to Grenada. More promotion is being undertaken and discussions are going ahead at full speed to see about the immediate construction of new hotels to add to the size of our existing plant. That is also why in the area of fisheries we have now moved to establish the first fish and fish-products processing plant out in True Blue; that is why for the first time in our country today it is now possible to eat entirely locally produced and locally salted salt-fish. That is why we have been moving to get hold of more fishing boats and better fishing boats and to train our fishermen in more modern techniques of catching the fish, and thereafter in processing what they have caught; all of this is aimed at ensuring that the productive sector in fact develops. Further, we believe too, comrades, that progress can continue to be made notwithstanding the difficulties in a situation where we continue to struggle as a people for the new international economic order, continue to struggle for better prices for what we produce, continue to look for new markets for what we produce, continue to struggle to have science and technology transferred to the poorer developing countries around the world. We believe too that in order to keep that progress moving that it can be done through developing closer relations among countries that are themselves developing — to continue to develop what is called South to South cooperation to ensure that we talk to each other and look to find ways of helping each other.

That is why one of the most important aspects of our relationship with revolutionary Cuba is the area of economic cooperation and assistance. That is why, as part of this dialogue between developing countries, revolutionary Cuba has been able to come to our assistance, to help us to construct an international airport, to lend us their doctors, [*Applause*] to lend us their internationalist workers, to lend us their fishermen, [*Applause*] to help us with universities scholarships. Revolutionary Cuba can undertake that kind of assignment because they understand themselves from their own history the meaning of true internationalism. That is one of the things that reaction understands about the relationship between Grenada and Cuba — they understand that this relationship means that the economic development of our country will be pushed even further. And they understand, too, that that means that this will help us to break our dependence on their market and their economies, and that is why they are also so concerned to break those links and bonds of friendship between our two countries. But today again we say what we have always said — that the solidarity, the friendship, the depth of feelings, the unity, the cooperation, the anti-imperialist militancy that keeps us together can never, ever be broken: these bonds between free Grenada and revolutionary Cuba. [*Applause*]

As part of this South to South cooperation, comrades, we have also

developed very great working relations with another country in this region — the country of Venezuela — and with that country we have in
fact been able to develop some good bilateral programs that have sought
to advance the cause of friendship between our two countries. We have
also been able to develop that kind of relation with the government and
people of Nicaragua. That might sound like a strange statement, that
Nicaragua — a country like our own, a country at this stage in a period
of national reconstruction — it might sound strange that areas of cooperation on the economic front are possible. But I must tell you, comrades, that we in free Grenada, as a contribution to the cause of the
Nicaraguan literacy campaign, sent two of our own Grenadian teachers
on an internationalist assignment to help the people of Nicaragua to learn
to read and to write. [*Applause*] Even more importantly, but again showing what is possible between developing countries themselves even
when they are also just struggling and starting off, I must tell you that
only last week the government of Nicaragua sent us a gift that has been
of tremendous importance — a gift that has meant that the militia comrades on duty today are able to have new uniforms, which came as a gift
from the Sandinistas and the junta of Nicaragua. [*Applause*]

In that area too, of South to South cooperation and dialogue, we have
developed excellent working relations and excellent cooperation with
the governments and people of several countries in the Middle East.
From the government of Iraq, we have received tremendous financial assistance both by way of gifts and soft loans, and our government and
people place on record our appreciation of this internationalist support.
[*Applause*] Similarly, we have received tremendous assistance from the
government and people of Algeria, and I ask the representative of that
government to convey our fraternal appreciation. [*Applause*] Such assistance has also come from the government and people of Libya and the
government and people of Syria. [*Applause*] In Africa likewise, among
developing countries on that continent, we have received significant assistance from the governments of Tanzania and Kenya, and that again is
an example of what can be done if we try to help each other. [*Applause*]

Comrades, if we are going to continue to move forward, if we are
going to try to continue to make more progress in the face of these difficulties, the truth of the matter is, we are going to have to work a
thousand times harder in the future. The truth of the matter is, things are
going to get more difficult, not less difficult. The truth of the matter is,
we are going to find that the present dangerous period that we are living
in is going to act as a fetter and a hindrance and an obstacle, trying to
hold back our possibility for peaceful and progressive development.

Today we live in a time of tremendous danger to world peace. The
economic crisis we are seeing reminds us very much of the economic
crisis of the thirties, in the period of the Great Depression, which was

followed very quickly by World War II. This new economic crisis, this new period of international tension and instability, this new round of arms build-up, this new round of psychological preparation and propaganda for war, is extremely dangerous to the survival of our country, the survival of peace in the region and peace in the world. One estimate has it that the present amount that is being spent on arms expenditure in the world is U.S.$450 billion. U.S.$450 billion is equal to EC$1200 billion. I am not saying, comrades, EC$1200 thousand, nor am I saying EC$1200 million, I am saying EC$1200 billion being spent on building arms, on supplying arms.

If you can just think, sisters and brothers, of what EC$1200 billion can do for the hungry of the world, for illiterates of the world, for those in the world who cannot get jobs, for those in the world who are homeless; if you can think of EC$1200 billion imagine what that can do overnight to solve these problems. To give you an example, EC$1200 billion can build 60 million houses of the kind we are now building in True Blue, those two-bedroom houses in True Blue complete with living room, with veranda, with kitchen, with toilet. The two-bedroom houses of that kind — with EC$1200 billion we could build 60 million such houses. And remember the entire population of the CARICOM region is only 5 million people; in other words 60 million houses could be spread to a substantial section of the world.

If you look at those figures another way, if we had EC$1200 billion to spend and if we continued to spend at the rate we are spending in this year's recurrent budget, using the figure of the 1981 recurrent budget, it would mean we would have enough money for 17,143 years to come. For 17,143 more years we could have enough money — that is, the amount of money that has to be spent on this area. And when you consider that war benefits no one, that war is not in the interests of everybody, that war could never help us solve the real burning problems in the world — the problems of hunger, of poverty, of injustice — when you consider today, sisters and brothers, that even food is being used as a tactical weapon, that some people are threatening to hold back on food assistance for developing countries in order to force those countries into submission, it tells you the danger, it tells you the callousness of the present period that we are facing.

And we have observed further that some people have begun once again to talk about dangerous new concepts, to develop dangerous new ideas that will certainly do harm to the peace of the world. Some people are talking about international terrorism, and one may speak of international terrorism; what they are doing is that they are removing the human rights doctrine, what they are doing is that they are conveniently finding a way of no longer having to attack South Africa or Chile or South Korea. What they are doing by this concept of international terrorist is that they are trying to lump together the socialist countries, the nonaligned countries, the national liberation movement, the progressive countries in the Third World, to try to pull all of these countries together, to try to attack the freedom fighters against apartheid in Namibia and South Africa, as being international terrorists and in that way to psychologically prepare their people for action to be taken against these freedom fighters. What they are doing by the use of this label is that they are finding a way of blaming countries like Cuba, like Nicaragua, like Namibia, like Zimbabwe, like Grenada, a way to blame all our countries for their economic difficulties, to argue that those countries that are now trying to build their own countries, to develop their own resources, by their doing so they are holding back the possibility of economic development for them and in that way are causing the problems of unemployment, the problems of cutbacks in social services, and all the other deep problems that their economies face.

It is a very, very dangerous concept, comrades, and that concept is also being linked to another concept. This concept is the one called linkage, where some countries in the world are saying that if something happens in one part of the world that they are not in favor of, then they have the right to take retaliatory action in a different part of the world. That if something happens somewhere else and they don't like it, then they could come down here and, using that as an excuse, attempt to intervene, attempt to attack our countries and other countries like ours. Some of these people are today saying that the people of Panama do not have the right to their own Panama Canal, are saying that the Panama Canal belongs to them, that the people of Panama sold it to them and therefore they have lost their right to it. In this way they are even willing to forget treaty obligations which their own country entered into. Some of these people, looking at the situation in El Salvador, are trying to pretend that in El Salvador it is a case of one small minority of ultraleft forces against another small minority of ultraright forces, when in truth and in fact and in reality it is definitely a case of the vast majority of the people of El Salvador fighting against a tyrannical junta backed up by a military apparatus that is receiving military assistance from other countries abroad. Some of these people are looking to deny even the possibility of a political situation for the people of El Salvador, are looking to deny the people of El Salvador the right to work out their own problem, the right to work out their own difficulties, the right to reach a result inside of their own country without having to be propped up, without having to be repressed by any external force. But we have no doubt at all that the people of El Salvador, because their unity is there, because they understand the meaning of struggling for their freedom, we have no doubt and we give our fullest support to that people as we know soon that the people of El Salvador will win an outright victory. [*Applause*]

Some of these countries, some of these people, seem to believe that we have no rights whatsoever. They speak in terms of the fact that our country is next to the oil routes and the oil lanes that carry their oil, they speak in terms of their foreign investments in the region, they speak in terms of the domino theory that where there is one revolution other revolutions will come. In speaking of these things, they seem to feel that they must expect us to lift up our country and put it in a different location if we must find some way of facilitating their oil routes; like if we must roll over and pretend that the land, that the resources, that the people in this country are not the common property of all of us, the people of Grenada; like if they want us to pretend that we must abandon all our principles, all of our rights, that we must roll over, that we must say that we are sorry, that we must play like an ostrich and cover our heads in the sand and don't continue to stand up for our rights, don't continue to proclaim our sovereignty, don't continue to proclaim our independence and the rights of our people to build our own resources in our own interest and for our own benefit. They seem to expect that these things are part of what they demand. We cannot and we do not, and we will never be able to accept these imperatives and these demands.

We feel that the only way forward for our people and our country is for us to continue with the mobilization of our people, for us to deepen even further the people's grassroots democracy and their grassroots democratic organizations where on a daily basis, where in a relevant way, where in a concrete way the people through their community work brigades, through their community education councils, through their Centre for Popular Education groups, through their mass organizations, their national youth organization, their National Women's Organisations [NWO], their Pioneers Organisations, their ADCs, through the growing and deepening of the trade union movement, through the further involvement of our people in participating in learning about the economy, in helping themselves to run the country, in applying the no-secret rule, where the people in any particular state enterprise are entitled to know all the facts, are entitled to know all the problems, are entitled to know all the projections, are entitled to know whenever difficulties arise, are entitled at the end of the year to have a share in the profits that come out from the enterprise. We feel strongly that our people must know, our people must do, our people must be involved, our people must definitely have a large part in continuing to build our revolution and push it forward.

We feel also, comrades, an urgent need to deepen further the political consciousness of our people, to get them to understand even more the realities of the world, the realities of the economy, the realities of the danger of the times we are now living in. We feel the need to get our people to be involved more and more in productive activity, to ensure that our slogan for the year, the Year of Agriculture and Agro-Industries, is successful, to ensure that the productive capacity of the country continues to go forward even more and at an even faster rate. In going forward for the future too, we certainly will continue to promote the cause of peace, we certainly will continue to promote the cause of disarmament, of détente, of the resumption of the SALT II talks; we will continue to fight to get the Caribbean Sea recognized in practice as a zone of peace, we will continue to push for that concept in all international and regional organizations in which we have a voice. We will continue to urge that no nuclear weapons should be introduced in our region, that all aggressive military maneuvers should be ended in our region, that all foreign military bases should be dismantled in our region when the people of the country do not want them, that colonialism in our region should be brought to an end. We will continue to urge that machinery should be set up to deal with all forms of aggressions, to deal with the threats of assassinations, to deal with the threats of mercenary invasions, to deal with the threats of propaganda and other forms of interventions, to deal with the varying forms of diplomatic and economic aggression, which is waged against small countries like our own. We will certainly continue to struggle to see an end to the aerial spy flights that have been almost nightly going across our country, an end to the military maneuvers of an aggressive character aimed against our country, in nearby territories, an end to economic piracy that has been taking place through some large fishing trawlers that have been coming and pulling all our fish resources out of our seas.

We will continue, comrades, to struggle for peaceful coexistence, for noninterference in each other's internal affairs, for the fight to legal equality, for the right to mutual respect, for sovereignty, for our right to build our own process in our own way, for our right to have ideological pluralism, for our right to develop economic cooperation with all the countries in the world that we choose to develop such relations with, for our right to strengthen our links with the countries of the Middle East, for our rights to strengthen our links with social democracy worldwide, to strengthen our links with friendly countries in Western Europe, in Africa, in Asia, in Latin America, in North America, and particularly of course with our friends from Canada. We will struggle for this right. We will struggle to get this message across and understood: that our country has no reason to want to be enemies with anybody; that our country has no reason to want hostility with any country; that what we want is not enemies; that how we see ourselves is as a small country, but a small country that understands our rights and is willing to struggle for our rights, and is willing to defend our rights to have those rights, that is how we see ourselves. [*Applause*]

There is absolutely no reason at all for us to want to have any hostile relations with our powerful neighbor to the north; there are more Grenadians living in that country than perhaps the entire population of Grenada; there are more of their tourists who come to our country every year than the whole population of Grenada. In terms of trade, in terms of economic cooperation, obviously we must prefer to have good relations. Obviously, we must prefer to be able to live in conditions of complete security and a feeling of no tension and no instability.

But what has to be clearly understood — and this, clearly, is where the problem is — is that on no account and under any circumstances are we going to accept that anyone must tell us that we must trade our principles, that we must sell our beliefs, that we must change our objectives, that we must no longer try to build our own country in our own way and free from all forms of pressure and domination from outside. We could never accept these statements from anyone. And therefore, the kinds of relations that are possible — the relations that we certainly hope to see built, that we believe we have now built, with the nine member countries of the European Economic Community, with our friends to the north, the Canadians, with other members of the world community, the Middle East countries, African countries, Latin American countries, Caribbean countries — we see no reason why, if such relations can be built with our country coming from all different perspectives and positions, there should be any great problem in being able to in fact develop working relations with other countries that right now continue to treat us in a hostile way.

As we close today, sisters and brothers, comrades, I want to leave the message to those here, and to those abroad who doubt our motives, who will suspect that we have plans against them, that we do not want any quarrels with any country in the region. We do not want any quarrel with any bigger countries that have developed their own system, once we are allowed to develop our own process in our country; we do not have any plans or intentions of interfering in other people's countries and their affairs, but equally we demand from them that they do not interfere in our internal affairs; all we want is the right to live in peace. The right to develop our resources, the right to build our economy, the right to have a productive life for our people. The right to develop relations with those with whom we want such relations. The right to be free of tension, of fear of instability, of mercenary aggression, of terrorist activities. To our friends with us here today, we want to say that we appreciate your past support and solidarity, that we appreciate the friendship organizations you have formed; we ask you to form even more friendship organizations and to expand your membership even further in those that now exist in America, Canada, and England. We appreciate the past material support you have given to the revolution. We ask you to continue that support. We ask our people who are living abroad and our friends who are living abroad that they can make a contribution to our economic development through, for example, saving some of their money in our National Commercial Bank. Through getting involved in purchasing our International Airport Bonds and other concrete and practical ways like that. To be of further assistance to our revolutionary process. We ask you to continue to beat back the adverse and negative propaganda when you hear it. We ask you to help us to achieve one of our slogans, the slogan that says "Come see for yourself." Do not let others tell you about free Grenada. Come see it for yourself. When you get back home, encourage your friends, encourage your families, to come see for themselves, to see our people, to see what we are trying to do with our country. We ask you to be vigilant abroad, to help us to expose any attempts, and to organize protests against any attempts at economic sabotage of our revolution, at destabilization, at attempts at bringing isolation and blockage, at attempts at intervention in different forms. To those countries that have supported us, and are supporting us still, we certainly value very highly the cooperation and the hand of friendship you have extended.

We believe that progress is indivisible, we believe that humanity is one and the same, we believe we all have a duty to help each other, to develop our countries, to ensure that in this way all of the world's people will be able to have the fullest and happiest life possible. To the people of free Grenada, we say again we are proud of you, the people of our country. We are proud of your unity, we are proud of your discipline, we are proud of your courage, of your deep commitment, of your character, of your strength. We are proud of your beauty, of your warmth, of your dignity, of your determination to go forward. We say to the people of free and revolutionary Grenada, what we have always said: An organized, conscious, united, and vigilant people can never be defeated.

Long live the people of free Grenada!

Long live the ties of world peace!

Long live the friendship between Grenada and Cuba, Grenada and Nicaragua!

Long live the struggle of the people of El Salvador, the struggle of the people of Namibia and South Africa!

Long live the struggle of our brothers and sisters in Zimbabwe!

Long live the struggle of the Palestinian people!

Long live the struggle of our Caribbean sisters and brothers of St. Lucia, of Suriname, of Belize, of Guyana!

Long live the struggle of our sisters and brothers in Angola, in Mozambique, in Ethiopia, in Zambia!

Long live the struggle of our sisters and brothers in Asia, in Western Europe, in the Middle East, in the socialist world, in the Union of Soviet

Socialist Republics, in Bulgaria, in Hungary, in the German Democratic Republic, in Vietnam, in Poland, in the Democratic People's Republic of Korea!

Long live the progressive people of the world!

Long live our brothers and sisters sharing blood ties with us in the United States, in Canada, in England!

Long live democratic and progressive forces in those countries!

Long live the Grenada Friendship Solidarity Committee!

Long live the women in the Caribbean struggling for their freedom!

Long live the National Conference of Black Lawyers!

Long live the World Federation of Democratic Youth and other progressive youths!

Long live the armed forces of our country!

Long live the workers of our country!

Long live the farmers of our country!

Long live the youths of our country!

Long live the women of our country!

Long live the fighting people of free Grenada!

Long live the Grenada revolution!

Forward ever, backward never!

Forward ever, backward never!

Forward ever, backward never!

Forward ever, backward never!

Together We Shall Build Our Airport

March 29, 1981

The following address was broadcast over Radio Free Grenada. It is printed in Maurice Bishop, Selected Speeches 1979-1981.

Good evening, sisters and brothers of free Grenada. As I talk to you tonight our revolution is just two weeks into its third year of achievements and progress for our people. Yet, as we continue to bring benefits to our nation we equally continue to be threatened by those opposed to progress for our people. The latest attacks on our country have come from none other than the rich and powerful United States of America, which at this very moment is engaged in an all-out massive and vulgar attempt to dissuade various countries and organizations from attending a cofinancing conference to be hosted by the European Economic Community and aimed at raising vital financing for our international airport project at Point Salines.

Sisters and brothers, we must all understand that this conference, due to be held on the 14 and 15 of April in Brussels, is vital for the completion of our international airport. In order to demonstrate how important this conference is, I would like to share with you a few vitally important points about our international airport project. To begin with, sisters and brothers, we must all be clear that this project represents the biggest and single most important project for our future economic development. In fact, as you all know, this represents the single biggest project ever undertaken in the history of our country. More than this, we must understand that the idea for the project has been with various Grenadian governments for twenty-five years or so, a reality that can be proved from the existence of numerous airport study projects dating back several years. However, with our popular revolution of March 13, 1979, the People's Revolutionary Government set out with seriousness and determination to transform the dream of our international airport into a concrete reality.

Needless to say, we understood the monumental nature of this task, and as such, right from the beginning, we have been pursuing various avenues in our effort to see our airport completed. In this regard, from the earliest days, we raised with just about every country and donor organization that visited us, including the United States government itself, our desire for assistance in the building of our international airport. In fact, initially, we met with so little positive feedback that at one stage we even considered at cabinet level the virtual impossibility of a totally self-help approach to the project through the formation of a local task force to tackle this vital project.

Fortunately, this proved not to be necessary as, following conversations that I had with President Fidel Castro, the leader of the Cuban revolution, at the Nonaligned conference in August 1979 and again at the United Nations in October of that same year, the fraternal government and people of Cuba agreed to assist whatever local efforts we could make with their own selfless and critical contributions. In this regard, it was clear from the outset that our fraternal friends in Cuba could help only in certain fields within their possibilities covering four major areas: (1) skilled manpower not available in our country; (2) vital equipment, such as graders, bulldozers, and other such heavy equipment; (3) some technical expertise; (4) some cement and steel.

These were obviously vitally important areas of assistance, and when the promised aid started arriving in November 1979, all Grenadians were sure that our ancient dream of our own international airport was at long last on its way to reality.

At the same time, sisters and brothers, it was clear that despite this vital and important fraternal aid, there were many other areas of need that would be needed for our airport to become a full reality. Thus, it was certain from the beginning that we would still need assistance to complete: (1) the runway — a section needing much oil and asphalt; (2) the terminal and tower complexes; (3) the communications and navigational equipment; (4) the additional infrastructure in terms of roads, electricity, pipe-borne water, etc; and (5) of course, the new hotels that we would need to get built rapidly to ensure that we had a sufficiently large capacity to accomodate the greater number of tourists.

In addition, it was clear that considerable sums of money would be needed to complete the project. This year alone, for example, we will need U.S.$32 million to keep the project going forward on schedule.

Given the reality of all these additional needs, our government has been consistently seeking additional assistance from various sources over the last two years. Hence, you will recall my trips to the Middle East countries of Algeria, Libya, Syria, Iraq — an effort that raised over U.S.$19 million in cash assistance alone, most of which has been earmarked or already used up for the airport project. We have also had valuable assistance from Venezuela, which pledged and has almost completed the delivery of 10,000 barrels of gas-oil towards the project; and even as I speak tonight a Venezuelan team is in our country to explore further areas of assistance.

We are also still hoping that a joint application of Grenada and St. Lucia in 1980 for communications equipment assistance for this project will be approved in due course by the ten member states of the European Economic Community [EEC].

From St. Lucia and Aruba we have also had valuable cooperation from their respective airport authorities in the granting of tours and several evaluation discussions of their airport facilities as guidelines for our own project.

At the same time, we are actively discussing with various local, regional, and international private investors and with certain countries around the world the possibility of building more hotels, either as joint ventures with our government or individually on their own. These talks are going well and some positive results should be announced soon. Similar negotiations are also underway with regard to the creation of an Air Grenada national airline, the granting of route rights to international airlines, and the obtaining of the different types of equipment that would be necessary to ensure the completion of the project.

It must also be pointed out that even after work on the project formally started just over one year ago, we continued to raise the matter of further assistance for the project with the USA, as indeed with several other countries around the world. The meaning of all this is that despite all our efforts we still have to raise much more money and find more technical and other assistance if our airport is to become a concrete reality. It is for this reason that the pending cofinancing conference being hosted by the EEC is so vital. And it is also for this reason that we as a people need to make sure that this conference comes off and is a tremendous success.

Sisters and brothers, we as a people have agreed that the expansion of our tourism industry is vital to the development of our country. We recognize tourism's overwhelming importance in creating jobs for those who are still unemployed as new hotels, restaurants, entertainment facilities, and shopping areas spring up. We recognize the increased market for our agricultural and agro-industrial products. We see the benefits to our artisans proceeding from the expanded sales of handicrafts and other souvenir items. We also recognize the importance of tourism in offering opportunities for the expansion of our private sector as well as the benefits to the people from the public sector's investments in tourism.

In short, the development of our tourism industry will bring with it previously unconceived development to our country and benefits to all our people. And indeed, several studies to date have confirmed the tremendous potential which Grenada has because of our natural and unspoilt beauty, our superb beaches, and our warm, beautiful, and friendly people.

And it is the international airport which will bring all this tourism development, as well as providing vital air-freight facilities for exporting our farmers' perishable produce, providing our own people with a vastly more convenient facility for air travel, and in short, enabling the building of our country in a thousand different ways. One has only to look at our sister island of St. Lucia, where the construction of an international airport was the major turning point in speeding that country's economic development in recent years, to understand what an international airport means to a nation's development potential. That is why our slogan is "The international airport project unites all our people, benefits all our people."

Sisters and brothers, I know that you must be asking yourselves the question: "Why should the United States, the richest and most powerful country in the world, go out of its way to deliberately sabotage the development of our country, one of the smallest and poorest countries in the world? Why should it seek to deny to another country that same development which it enjoys? Why, when it is fully aware of the honesty of our government, our smashing of corruption since the revolution, the genuine benefits which our people have been receiving during the past two years, and the unity of all our people behind this airport project, why should it declare *economic warfare* against our country and our people in this manner, not only denying us economic assistance but even trying to persuade *other countries* to deny us assistance?"

Sisters and brothers, what we must be clear about is that we are living in a dangerous period, a period in which the policies being pursued by the present United States administration pose the world with a real threat to international peace, a period in which aggressive attacks may be mounted against individual countries, a period in fact in which there is a real threat of World War III, affecting all of mankind. And Grenada is not the only target. During the past six to eight weeks, the United States has totally cut off all shipments of wheat to our sister country Nicaragua. In Nicaragua today there is virtually no bread; people face the prospect of widespread hunger. The United States has similarly cut off all food aid to Mozambique. In an even more aggressive stand, the U.S. administration has made clear to the world its desire to support the South African–backed guerrillas in attacks against the Angolan revolution and people and in the face of worldwide shock and anger has strengthened its own relationships with this foul, racist, apartheid regime in South Africa.

Here, in our region again, the United States for the first time in history has begun a policy of providing credits for the purchase of military equipment by Eastern Caribbean governments as part of their global plan of stepping up the arms race. Moreover, we in Grenada have experienced constant illegal "spy flights" by aircraft over our country in recent weeks, and also a stepping up of economic piracy by large fishing trawlers operating illegally in our waters.

Most repugnantly, we have seen the massive stepping up of U.S. military assistance to the brutal junta in El Salvador, and alongside it a new U.S. policy which states that all those who fight for freedom and justice against that repressive government are to be labeled "terrorists" and to be butchered with American military help. This means that increasingly thousands of Salvadoran people will be murdered in coming weeks just as Archbishop Romero and the four nuns were murdered last year. And when the European Economic Community began sending humanitarian assistance on a nonpolitical basis in the form of food and medicines to victims of that war in El Salvador, the United States government demanded that they cease such assistance. Fortunately, this demand was rejected and we in Grenada want to be among those who warmly congratulate the EEC on the principled manner in which, after investigating the situation, they continued their humanitarian assistance to the war victims of El Salvador.

But sisters and brothers, we must face the fact that the present United States administration, even against the will of their own people, is firmly opposed to the rights of all independent countries to act independently and to conduct their affairs in their own way. Indeed, this administration is even trying to force the developed European countries to toe their line and to follow their dangerous and misguided foreign policy positions. Most especially, it is opposed to those underdeveloped countries like ours which are struggling for their national liberation, economic independence, and economic and social development. This administration wants to rule the world alone, they want all countries to bow to the United States; and countries like ours which are firmly nonaligned and determined not to be in anyone's backyard immediately become the target of their aggression. This is the reason why they are attacking us economically and with so much negative propaganda; they hope to cause suffering to our people, so that when our people feel the pain of no work and less benefits they would turn against their government, thus giving the opportunity to overthrow our popular people's revolution and put in a Gairy-type government which would sell out our people's national interests, a government which would permit the increased exploitation of our people and return Grenada to the days of subjugation, oppression, and exploitation.

The United States understands the importance of our international airport and this is why they have declared economic war against us. But we also understand the importance of our international airport, and we as a people must therefore mobilize and fight back to defend our interests. This present situation definitely calls for a massive, all-out effort by all sections of our people to ensure the continuation of our airport project.

The PRG has already begun the process of contacting the member countries of the EEC and all other countries and international organizations invited to the conference to re-emphasize to them the importance of this project to our country. What we are now asking all of our people to do is the following:

(1) First, that all organizations, including those of the hotel sector, the business sector, the trade unions, the professional and service organizations, the churches, the women, youth, student, community, and other organizations — all should immediately issue public statements in support of the airport project. These will not only be published locally on radio and in newspapers, but will also be taken by Grenada's representatives to the cofinancing conference which is to be held in Brussels on 14 and 15 April.

(2) We are also asking our Grenadian nationals and our friends abroad to publicly condemn the U.S.'s efforts to sabotage Grenada economically and seek to put pressure on the U.S. adminstration to change its policy towards Grenada.

(3) Thirdly, the PRG has decided to hold a massive public rally at the international airport site in Point Salines on Sunday, April 12 at 2:00 p.m. This will provide an opportunity for all our people to demonstrate, by their presence, the overwhelming support which the airport project enjoys. Free transport will be provided by the PRG and it will thus also provide an opportunity for our people, especially those from the rural villages, to see for themselves the tremendous progress which has been made on the construction of the airport in one short year and the amazing new face of the Point Salines peninsula.

Sisters and brothers, we owe it to ourselves, we owe it to our country, we owe it to future generations yet unborn to ensure that this project goes ahead. Further, we owe it to our friends around the world, those who have already rendered valuable assistance and those who intend to make a contribution in the future, to continue the struggle for our airport. We certainly owe this to our Cuban sisters and brothers, our Venezuelan friends, our friends in Algeria, Libya, Syria, and Iraq, and most of all at this particular time, to our friends in the secretariat of the EEC and in the member countries of the EEC who are so unselfishly and generously assisting us with the organizing of this conference, as indeed they have assisted us so often in the past.

Sisters and brothers, as we reflect on why the rich and powerful United States of America should try to stop the economic development of our small and poor country, I ask that you reflect on the history of our nation and on the history of our revolution. As you do so, I am sure that you will agree that our history has been a consistent one of determination to struggle and win despite the odds. That was the lesson of Fedon, that was the meaning of the struggle of Marryshow to develop a West Indian identity and consciousness, that was the significance of Butler's victory in firmly establishing the role and importance of the working class and in winning for them the right to have their unions recognized, that was why in 1973–1974 our people struggled so defiantly and so bravely against Gairyism for an end to brutality, corruption, superstition, repression, exploitation, and dictatorship, and that was, of course, why on March 13, 1979, our people finally rose up in a united way to take power into our own hands and to begin the long hard process of national reconstruction, peaceful and progressive development, and economic and political justice for all of our people.

With that in mind, sisters and brothers, I ask that you all join in the battle to make sure that our airport is successfully completed despite the tricks, maneuvers, and threats of the rich and the powerful, for as we always say, no force on earth can stop the forward march of a determined, conscious, organized, vigilant, and united people.

Long live the fraternal assistance of friendly countries!
Long live the principled opposition of the EEC to outside direction!
Long live the fighting and struggling people of our nation!
Long live the unity of our nation!
Long live free Grenada!
Together we shall build our airport!
See you all at the rally on the twelfth.
Forward ever, backward never!

Freedom of the Press and Imperialist Destabilization

June 19, 1981

The following speech was delivered to a mass rally in Queen's Park in St. George's on Heroes' Day, commemorating the revolution's heroes and martyrs. From a text issued by the Grenadian government.

Sisters and brothers, comrades:

The events that took place on this very spot, in this very park one year ago, remind me, comrades, of how close so many of us, perhaps a lot of us who are present again, today, came to losing our lives on that day in the cause of building our revolution, in the cause of furthering the progress of our people.

As I stand here today, comrades, and as I look at you, and as I am conscious of the other comrades on the platform sitting here with me, it is a reminder, comrades, that one year ago, our governor-general also sat with us when the bomb went off; and he has had the courage to return today, not terrified or terrorized by imperialism's bomb. [*Applause*]

As I stand here, comrades, I remember too, sitting on that platform last year was one of the most outstanding leaders of our revolution, a comrade who over the years has done miracles in transforming, in a serious and meaningful way, the economy of our country, a comrade who has done miracles in helping to strengthen the organization of our party and deepening the unity and consciousness of our people. I remember too, that the comrade, who twelve months ago, whose life was nearly taken, but who has continued, who has remained in the struggle, who is today still giving twenty-six hours a day to building our revolution, our party, and our people. I remember today also that Comrade Bernard Coard is also here with us. [*Applause*]

And, comrades, on the platform last year also we had sitting Comrade Unison Whiteman, our outstanding minister of agriculture, a comrade who has known pain and suffering, having been beaten by Gairy's Green Beasts and Mongoose Gang on Bloody Sunday, November 18 [, 1973]; we also have Comrade Kenrick Radix, another outstanding son, another outstanding patriot, another fighter and revolutionary whose blood also was shed, who came within a point of losing his life, another comrade who has remained to carry our struggle forward. And sitting with us too, Comrade Vince Noel, another comrade who was there last year, another comrade imperialism's plan was to remove in one blow, to have deprived the country and the working class in particular of its most outstanding leader, but Comrade Vince also survived and is also here.

And, comrades, I say, our minister of health was also present, he too remains to continue the fight for our people, as a minister of our government, with him also and with him also on that day, Comrade Fitzroy Bain, the leader of the rural working class, the leader of the Agricultural and General Workers' Union, a union that is striving to bring justice to the poor and oppressed agricultural workers in our country; and here with us too Comrade Bernard Gittens, another member of our People's Revolutionary Government, and Comrade Sister Phyllis Coard, the outstanding leader of the National Women's Organisation, the leading mass organization of the women in our country.

And on this platform, also, as last year, representatives of fraternal internationalist friends from Cuba, revolutionary Cuba, that stood by us in the first days and the first weeks, that is standing by us today as we struggle to build our international airport, that stood by us only a few weeks ago when our electricity services were in need of urgent help.

Today with us on this platform also is Sister Simon, a leading member of the Airport Development Committee, a woman who has struggled over these past few years in ensuring that the women of our country play a part in raising funds, to ensure that this airport project, this long-impossible dream becomes a reality.

And on the platform too, comrades, we have Comrade Demo Grant, the dean of our party, the dean of our movement, a comrade who from the earliest days of the party in 1973 came and stood by us, became the national chairman of our public meetings, who was listened to by countless youth in our country who admired the vigor, who admired the firmness, who admired the revolutionary spirit of this living national hero, Comrade Demo Grant. [*Applause*]

And also on this platform, an outstanding representative of our people in uniform, a comrade who today is guiding and trying to shape the army that we are building, is helping to ensure that our popular armed forces, the People's Revolutionary Army, the People's Revolutionary Militia, the Grenada Police Service, another section of our revolutionary armed forces, are built stronger and stronger every day, in preparation for that day we know is coming, the day when we will have to defend our country, defend our people, defend our process, and defend our revolution. A comrade who is also here on the platform Comrade Einstein Louison, he is also here. [*Applause*]

And we know too that today on this platform are women who have lost their loved ones in the cause of our people, in the cause of our struggle, in the cause of making our revolution stronger and stronger. We note today on this platform also is a woman who has known great pain, who has seen her husband taken from her, who has known what is meant when the news comes in the middle of the day that her most-loved one was cut down by a cutlass, felled by a criminal bullet, we note and welcome the presence of my mother, my beloved mother, Mrs. Alimenta Bishop. [*Applause*]

But most of all, on the platform today, comrades, I want you to welcome and to acknowledge the love, the appreciation, and gratitude of those who are still alive, of one of our young sisters, a bright young schoolchild, one of the flowers of our revolution, whose sister was cut down by that murderous bomb blast one year ago in this very spot. That young sister who came here because of a consciousness, because of a love for our people, because of a love for our country, because she was determined to stand up and be counted; a young sister who, when she left her mother's home on that day, the last thing that could have been on her young innocent mind was that that day was going to be her last living day. So I want you to join with us, comrades, in welcoming Jackie and her sister, and mother Rita Bailey, three of the survivors of our young hero Bernadette Bailey. [*Applause*]

But comrades, even among all of them, even among this outstanding revolutionary leadership I have spoken about, even among these courageous patriots, even among these outstanding Grenadian sons and daughters, we have to ask you to realize today something imperialism thought would never have been possible: that one year after their bomb blast, one year after they hoped that they would have frightened and terrorized us into submission, one year after they hoped they would have demoralized our people, one year after they hoped that we would have been frightened and afraid to come to Queen's Park, I want you to welcome yourselves, the brave revolutionary, fighting people of free Grenada. [*Applause*]

Who would ever have believed, who would ever have imagined, two and a half years ago, that a bomb would go off that would send ninety-seven persons into hospital, that would murder three young sisters, and yet, one year after that bomb blast, in the very same spot, not the same size crowd, not a frightened and demoralized people, but a crowd that is bigger than that of 1980. [*Applause*] A crowd that is better than 1980's, a crowd that is more united than 1980's, [*Applause*] a crowd that is more conscious than 1980's, [*Applause*] a crowd that is united in an anti-imperialist spirit of solidarity and defiance. [*Applause*] Today we see the real fighting people of revolutionary free Grenada.

Today, as we stand here and look at these people, I recall that only yesterday, at this very time, in St. Kitts, I stood there and I addressed a proud people in St. Kitts, a people who were happy to have a treaty named after them, the Treaty of Basseterre, a treaty to establish the Organisation of Eastern Caribbean States. There, I saw a proud and disciplined Caribbean people.

As I stand here, I reflect on the fact that, last year on May Day in revolutionary Cuba I stood in Revolution Square with other comrades and addressed over one million fighting, brave Cuban people, a people who have taken on the imperialist giant on several occasions, a people who have demonstrated concretely their unity and their revolutionary spirit.

Today, I also remember the fighting people in Managua, Nicaragua, the fighting and brave people of Nicaragua who fought against the Somoza tyranny for over fifty years but who came out winning in the end, another strong, another conscious, another united people.

But I say to you today, sisters and brothers, there are no people like you in any part of the world, no people like you, and the reason for that is: When you think in terms of what Grenada is, of where we have come from in these past few years; when you consider the fact that if you stand in a big country like North America and you look on a map, you could not even see the name "Grenada" written; when you consider the total population of our country, just over 100,000 people; when you consider the fact that we have to stand here, today, such a small people, such a poor people, yards away from the mouth of the imperialist giant that not only threatened to crush us, but demonstrated in a hundred concrete ways in these past few months their determination to crush us — I say that never before has history ever seen such a small, such a poor people, such a people who are united, who are courageous, who are as determined, and who are as vigilant as the people of free Grenada are.

Our heroes and martyrs — Fedon, Marryshow, Butler, Alister Strachan, Scotilda Noel, Edith McBain, Jerry Richardson, Rupert Bishop, other heroes and martyrs, Evan [Charles] and [Andy] Courtney and the Stanisclaus brothers, Laurice [Humphrey], Laureen [Phillip], and Bernadette [Bailey] — these martyrs to our cause would be proud today.

Our people today have reason to feel proud and confident. Those who have to be concerned today are not our dead heroes and martyrs, not those who imperialism killed; those people who have to stand and tremble in their boots are imperialism itself and the local counter-revolutionaries and the local reactionaries, the local Committee of Twenty-six.

Let the reactionaries and the imperialists tremble today as they see our people standing here, brave in defense, as they bear in mind today that the farmers could not come, it is banana day, the agricultural workers could not come, it is pay day, and thousands of our people are stranded all around the country.

Today we reflect on all the people, united and vigorous, unafraid to face the odds, a people who are determined to go forward to take their destiny into their own hands, a people who will face the future with full courage and full dignity. Let the imperialists tremble today. [*Applause*]

Today, as we get strength and courage from each other, as our vibrations pass through each other, we can say with confidence that if the reactionaries are determined to look for trouble, they are going to get it, [*Applause*] that if the parasites and the puppets play with fire, then the fire will burn them. [*Applause and chants of "You play with fire, fire will burn you. A people united can never be defeated."*]

Comrades, these elements that have chosen, at this particular historic moment, to crawl out from under their beds, to pretend that they are full of vigor and courage, to come out and to pretend, today, after so many dozens of years of exploiting the poor, to pretend, today, that they are conscious of the masses — these elements are using several different covers of pretense to try to confuse the people.

One of the main things that these hypocrites are trying to pretend is that they are involved in a struggle for freedom of the press.

When you hear these elements talk of a free press, when you hear them talk about freedom of the press, you have to ask: Which was the free press that they have ever run, where is that free press that they have ever run? We have to remember, sisters and brothers, that when they speak of a free press, they speak of a press in which their ideas alone dominate, where their exploitative position alone has a monopoly. When they speak of a free press, they speak of the same man or some group of men or companies who run all the newspapers, run all the radio stations, run all the television stations — the same people pretending they are using different voices.

When you think of large countries of this world, you will see that in every other radio and in every other television station and in every other newspaper, they have a hand and they have a voice. When they form an organization like the Caribbean Publishers and Broadcasters Association or the Inter-American Press Association, it is the same small group of exploiters who control the newspapers. These are the same people who run these organizations.

In other words, Pontius Pilate is being called upon to judge Pontius Pilate.

These same elements, when they talk about freedom of the press, mean freedom of the press for themselves, for the small minority they represent, for the exploitative interest that they want to put forward. Their freedom of the press is such that they spend more than nine occasions in one week attacking our country on American television, like that CBS program just four weeks ago, which spent one hour, on nine occasions in one week, attacking us.

When Comrade Radix arrived to reply for our country and revolution, he got only twenty-five seconds' — for freedom of the press — time to reply, twenty-five seconds only.

When these elements think of freedom of the press, we have to remember the number of occasions when we have seen, time and time again, that they carry these nasty, lying, vicious articles about our country. When the Trinidad *Guardian* chose to say we were training terrorists for use in Trinidad and when we published our denial, Trinidad *Guardian* was no longer a free press — at that time the reply could not be seen.

We recall occasion after occasion in the Trinidad *Express*, when all of the major developments of interest in our country are never published by that newspaper. On every occasion possible, they write another editorial; they write another vicious article, full of lies, and they try to confuse our people with that. In the first nine months of the revolution alone, this Trinidad *Express* wrote over fifteen editorials against our country, every one of them in one form or another was a nasty or not-so-nasty attack on the people and our revolution. That is their freedom of the press.

We remember the Barbadian newspaper, the *Beacon*, that was going around carrying these articles, saying how our Cuban comrades, the internationalist workers in our country, were in Grenada exploiting our women. They carry these vicious articles, they carry articles that say our Cuban internationalist workers have gone and arrested a magistrate, and, when the facts were sent to the *Beacon*, that too never got published, because that is what they mean by freedom of the press.

We think of the Jamaican *Gleaner* and its attacks on our friend, Michael Manley, over his two terms in office — vicious article after article, malice after malice, eventually playing one of the key roles in the overthrow of that government last year in the elections in Jamaica.

We remember today, too, the role played by *El Mercurio* of Chile, when that newspaper, paid and financed by the CIA, was used to attack Salvador Allende, to bring down the government of Salvador Allende. *El Mercurio* played a critical role in the collapse of the socialist government of Salvador Allende.

Today we remember too the articles we have seen in *Newsweek* and in *Time* magazine. *Time* comes down here for the second anniversary of our revolution, and they carry a full one-page story on the revolution, and in that one-page story they give the impression that Queen's Park is empty and nobody is listening to the speeches, that by the time the speeches are over half the people are gone home and that the mood of the masses was a dead and demoralized one. They come down to our country, they write their stories on their planes when they are flying down and then even before they spend a good few hours they send their stories back up home, full of the lies. That is what these elements mean by "freedom of the press."

We think of the news reporters, representatives of that exploitative class, and we think of the misrepresentations and the lies. Today we can recall the reporting of Leslie Seon, for example. Last year when the counterrevolutionaries were going around trying to kill our people in St. Patrick's, this man Leslie Seon sent out to the news media in the region a story which said that the country was in civil war, that half of the people were separated and divided from the other half and there were blockages in St. Patrick's. And even when we contacted the Barbados radio station and corrected this statement, we are still waiting today to hear of this correction.

We think of this news reporter, Alister Hughes, a man who has sunk lower and lower over the years, a man who sent out a news report earlier this week, pretending he has been given the news release by the Chamber of Commerce and the Hotel Association, pretending that that news release was just given to him, but it was written up by the Chamber and Hotel Association about six months ago and was never intended for release but meant to be an internal document to be circulated for discussion between themselves and the government. This man Hughes takes it and sends it out to the region, pretending that something new has broken and developed. We think of Alister Hughes constantly reporting on the St. George's Medical School.

We think of the fact that, here is a man who prides himself on being a professional journalist, but we can't see him in a rally; you can't see him at a national event; you can't see him when the first cooperative under the land reform is being established; you can't see him on the occasion when it is being announced that our people now have free health care in our country. You can't see this man when any important national events are taking place because, he says, he is too busy and what is taking place is not important.

This is what these parasites mean by a free press. When they speak of a free press, comrades, we are to understand that they talk of rights to have journalistic license, they have the right to publish freely what they want, but this journalistic license simply means the right to print lies, to slander people, the right to incite people to violence, the right to hold one position only and to pretend that position represents the whole truth. That is what they mean by journalistic license. When they speak of independence, we have to ask what independence and independence from whom. We have to recognize it is the same voice with the one idea, that the voice of the people, the voice of the poor working masses, can never get expression in their journal or their publication.

Think of the *Torchlight* and the role that *Torchlight* played. It was always a good thing, it was always good news, it was always a free press to expose military camps when they were established, it was always a good thing. It was always excellent news to reprint garbage and rubbish from abroad like the article appearing in a West German magazine — the article which said that we had underground submarines in Grenada. That kind of article is in accordance with freedom of the press. But when the masses are meeting, when the masses are engaged in productive activity, that does not require a free press; that then becomes unimportant news for the class and the interest that they represent. We must never forget the role of the *Torchlight* with the Rastafarian brethren in our country, a newspaper that over the years consistently attacked the Rastas, called them all kinds of names, attacked Comrade Radix and myself whenever we went to court as lawyers to defend these brethren. Then remember what we saw in September '79, when the *Torchlight* opportunistically pretended to be a champion of the Rastas, to go around talking how the Rastas were being terrorized and brutalized by the PRG, how they were being killed in the hills and how the time has come for the Rastas to take a response against Babylon. If you could imagine: the *Torchlight* with that level of deceitfulness and hypocrisy taking that kind of position and playing that kind of role.

But, comrades, what I want you to see today, most of all, is that the enemy we face today is no small enemy, it is not just some jokers who are running the *Torchlight*, it is not just some parasites who are running what they call the *Grenadian Voice*. What we are facing today is a much more powerful enemy that has these stooges in their back pockets to do their dirty work for them. What we are facing today, in other words, is the full might of U.S. imperialism. What we are facing is the full fury of the organized CIA, which has made up its mind in the clearest possible way that it is out to overthrow our revolution, and it has told these local elements, these parasites, that they can have the fullest and firmest backing of imperialism in their plan to overthrow the revolution. What we must see today, comrades, is that the CIA has a powerful armory of tricks; they have several different fronts, several different covers, several different tricks that they use. One of their best tricks is called propaganda destablization — when they go around and they spread lies and they slander countries like Grenada, countries which are independent-minded, countries determined to bring justice to their people, countries determined to put through a foreign policy that does not start off from the premise that America is the beginning and the end of the world. They use their propaganda viciously, and they hope by their propaganda to stop the tourists from coming, they hope by that propaganda to get our people confused and to have no confidence. That propaganda trick is one of the best tricks that the CIA has.

A second trick of the CIA — and it is again well documented and well known and we have spoken about it several times — is the trick of economic destablization, the trick of economic sabotage, of economic oppression, of economic warfare against small, poor, Third World countries like our own. We have seen in Grenada over these past few weeks the evidence of this economic war: the attempt to block the financing from European countries for our international airport; the attempt to block our application to the IMF for the extended fund facility; the attempts by the World Bank to sabotage our projects put forward by the revolution; the attempts to pay to come into our regional institution and to try to isolate the Grenadian revolution and block our sources of funding. We have seen this economic plan and sabotage in Grenada.

We have also seen a third of their famous tricks in our country, another popular trick by the CIA, the trick of counterrevolutionary violence and counterrevolutionary terrorism. The trick they use of finding local counter elements, training them how to make bombs, inspiring them with the confidence to plant bombs, stimulating them with the belief that imperialism will be able to save and to protect them, and then getting these unpatriotic scums to come and plant the bomb amidst our people. We have seen terrorism, we have seen counterrevolutionary violence. We have known of the time when our three sisters were bombed, when our five comrades were murdered in one night in the space of over three hours. We know even now of plans some of these elements have to continue this job of murdering poor innocent people in our country.

The fourth trick that imperialism has is the most important trick to be reminded of today, and this is the trick of identifying and then using local stooges, local opportunists, local parasites, local counterrevolutionaries to do their dirty job for them — and in this category are the local reactionaries and opportunists and counters. They have several different forms and shapes and faces and figures. They don't come simply in black or in brown or in white. They don't simply come in forms of fatness or shortness or roundness; they come in all kinds of shapes and sizes and we have to be conscious of all of the different faces, sizes, colors. One of the things they use most often to do their dirty work for them — and that too we are seeing in Grenada — is the corrupt, opportunist trade union leaders. That is one of the most popular categories of the CIA for counterrevolution. We have seen it in free Grenada, over this past two years: a number of different occasions when they reached some of these corrupt trade union leaderships who received the CIA AIFLD [American Institute for Free Labor Development] course when none was justified. We remember Roberts, who today still has that plan. We remember Eric Pierre, who today still has that plan and that ambition. We know of these corrupt trade union leaders, the elements who have received the CIA AIFLD course, these elements who would sell the cause of the revolution for a mess of pottage, for a drop of porridge, for a piece of crumb off the master's table. These elements who would sell their mother's soul for a shilling if not for a penny-halfpenny. These people who don't even have a price because they are so low and so determined to use unpatriotic and criminal methods to try to terrorize our people, to try to stop the benefits and the progress from coming. We have to be conscious of this important category that the CIA loves to use, the category of corrupt trade union leaders. We have not seen the end of them. We are going to see them in action again in the future of our country.

A second category, comrades, you can broadly regard as being the unpatriotic, reactionary, power-seeking national bourgeoisie in our country: in other words, the biggest men, the biggest exploiters, the biggest parasites, the biggest vampires, the biggest blood-suckers in the country. That is another category that the CIA and imperialism always look for because they recognize that some of the elements of that class fear that they have lost their political power, that they are losing their political hold over the masses, and they are afraid that their economic base — which they have built by exploitation and suffering of our people — they are afraid that that too is disappearing.

Those elements represented by the biggest of the big and the baddest of the bad, of the most unpatriotic scum in our country — that is another category that the CIA and imperialism look after. It is no accident, then, bearing this in mind, that so many of the elements of the Committee of Twenty-six come from the biggest and most unpatriotic landowners in the country, those who are opposed to land reform, those who are opposed to workers' participation, those who are opposed to the trade union movement, and when Comrade Coard sends them the annual income tax statement they get a big accountant to fill up a form, to keep two books for them, to pretend they make no profit, and although they are making no profit, they are getting fatter and fatter and fatter and you see more houses go up, you see more land acquired, and you see more and more cars and luxury items — but they never make profits.

Those elements who oppose our National Importing Board because they see that as bringing too many benefits to the poor in our country, because they are accustomed to bringing in the sugar and ripping off the people, accustomed to bringing in the cement and ripping off the people. But the National Import Board, which keeps prices under manners and ensures that the cost of living stays down — these parasites are opposed to that. These are the same elements who are personally opposed to any form of price control, the elements who are always saying that you can't control in a free market — let the forces of supply and demand do the regulation. All kinds of pretty phrases to justify their exploitation. These elements who will have before them five or six price slips showing the price of goods from different countries or different companies and you will see in one case the price of an item is $100; in the next case the price of a dozen is $200; another case the price of the same dozen is $500. And they would not bring in the dozen that cost $100 because the mark-up would be too small, so they bring in deliberately and constantly the dozen that cost $500, regardless of the fact that this means 500 times more oppression and more suffering on the backs of our people. These are blood-suckers who have no conscience.

These same elements who oppose every benefit that the poor in our country receive, who are opposed to free health care because they can always send their wife on a plane to Trinidad or Barbados, those who oppose free secondary education because it means that the little Black man's son will have to go to school to rub shoulders with their nice sons and daughters and transfer some kind of brain disease to them. These elements who oppose the reducing of rent on the backs of our people because they own the buildings and they charge the rent, those who oppose free milk distribution in our country because if there is free milk then the Dano and the Nestles and the Nesquick and all the other brands of milk that they bring in will not be able to be sold anymore. So they oppose the free milk also. Those who are afraid of the benefits the masses are now getting because they recognize and recognize correctly, that what they are facing in this land is a people's revolution, a revolution for the poor and working masses of our country. [*Applause*]

Comrades, another one of these categories we have to look at which the CIA has always used in different countries is the most reactionary members of the bureaucracy in the civil service. They look for the most backward and corrupt elements — whether in the union leadership or elsewhere working in the service — and see if they can get those to join in their plan of sabotage. We have seen that in our country and we will also see it again. And we look out, too, at another one of the potential allies of the CIA: We look for the big foreign multinational corporations.

Some will stand firm. Some will not allow themselves to be bribed or be used or intimidated by imperialism, but others will go along with imperialism and join in imperialism's dirty plan to overthrow the revolution. We must watch these companies also and over the next few weeks and months as we reflect on the fact of the very small support imperialism has in our country. They cannot go to the broad masses of our working people; they cannot approach the vast majority of the urban working class or of the rural working class, the agricultural workers; they cannot approach the small and middle farmers in our country; they will not be listened to by the vast majority of our revolutionary youth and our patriotic women; they will not be listened to by the vast majority of our students. They have a very small minority clique to choose from. Trying to intensify counterrevolution are the biggest, most unpatriotic landowners, the biggest, most unpatriotic businessmen, the corrupt trade union leaders, those in the public service who are attracted by dol-

Havana, May 1, 1980. Daniel Ortega of Nicaragua, Maurice Bishop, Fidel Castro.

Grenadian and Cuban workers march. Above, May 1, 1983; below, May 1, 1980.

Above, Bishop explains progress of airport construction to SWP leaders Steve Clark (left) and Andrew Pulley (right) in 1980. Below, workers building Sandino Housing Plant, made possible by Cuban donations.

Workers' democracy in action. Above, workers' parish council meeting; below, meeting of Technical and Allied Workers' Union.

IP/Pat Kane

Above, militia members at fourth anniversary celebration, March 13, 1983. Below, Centre for Popular Education literacy program.

Above, May 23, 1982, solidarity rally with Mozambique. Mozambique leader Samora Machel at center microphone; to his left, Maurice Bishop. Also visible in this picture are Bernard Coard (third to Machel's left) and Hudson Austin (at far left). Left, Bishop speaks at rally in Managua, Nicaragua, February 23, 1980.

Government Information Service

Grenadians stand up to imperialism. Above, March 12, 1983, rally to protest U.S. threats; below, 1980 rally.

NJM leaders slain with Bishop on October 19, 1983. Clockwise from top left: Norris Bain, Jacqueline Creft, Fitzroy Bain, Unison Whiteman, Vincent Noel.

lars, who will sell their souls and sabotage their country, those in the country working for the big multinational corporations who might allow themselves to be used, the lumpen and the criminal elements in our country, those who want to become millionaires overnight, those who want to use marijuana to become marijuana capitalists. Those lumpen and criminal elements are the few, few elements imperialism has to work among.

In a fighting population of over 100,000 people, you are talking of less than a few hundred people total that imperialism can hope to reach and to induce and to seduce. And we have to recognize, comrades, that it is not a big lot, that it is not a lot we are looking for; it is a tiny minority who choose to go the way of counterrevolution. But they must understand the price of counterrevolution, they must understand that.

We could see as part of this plan, in the next few weeks, moving out from this newspaper that they are hiding behind — the *Grenadian Voice*, as they call it, so bold and fresh and mannish to themselves: the voice of our people, not the ligaroo voice, not the voice of the big bourgeois, not the voice of imperialism or the CIA voice. If they had said any of these, then we could have accepted it, but they so fresh and rude, they say the *Grenadian Voice*. Look at the Grenadian voice right here. But, apart from the first stage of a press, apart from that you will see other developments in the next few weeks.

You might see them try to graduate from the free press to a political organization, a political party; you might see them form a human rights organization; you might see them try to come through a Chamber of Commerce and try to put out some damaging statement; you might see them use their economic base to try to get shortages or to lay off people or to try to close down businesses. You might see them try to use the banks in a particular way. These are all kinds of tricks that are possible, all stages, all elements on the total road to the overthrow of the Grenadian revolution. You might hear Eric Pierre say how he was victimized; you might hear him say how he was picked up and detained and how papers were taken from him. You are to expect all kinds of additional tricks, used to try to back up the action that they have taken because it is but a small part of a total which imperialism has drawn up for those jokers, has put the commas and the full stops and the colons and the semicolons, has underlined the areas to watch, has put the brackets around the important things, and has promised these Judases that if they sell their souls, if they sell their country and their birthright that, in return, they will be backed and blessed by imperialism, that the mighty yankees will make sure that they are all right. This is the nature of the promise that has been made, and imperialism has sat down very carefully and explained to these people exactly how they hope to achieve the overthrow of our revolution.

Imperialism has reminded them of the stepped-up propaganda. Imperialism has reminded them of the economic squeeze on our country, of the World Bank maneuvers, of the IMF stopping of our funds for our international airport, of the plans to refuse to support our regional institutions. Imperialism would have given them a lot of confidence.

We have seen the propaganda attempts of the United States through the CBS television. Imperialism will also have told them of their plans of violence. It would have reminded them that mercenaries are being trained right now in Miami and that TV stations are saying that those mercenaries are for Grenada and Nicaragua. Imperialism would have reminded them of how they taught counters to make bombs to kill our people. It would have reminded them of the job they did in Chile, of the job they did in Guatemala in '64, of the Dominican Republic in 1965, in Jamaica in the '70s. Imperialism would have reminded them of the number of revolutions they have overthrown in the world, and imperialism would have promised them full financial backing, and would have promised them arms, would have promised them men, would have promised them full support if any part of the plan backfired as they went along. Imperialism would have drawn up a complete package for them and given them in their hands. And, therefore, a few weeks ago, when Comrade Radix was in the United States and spoke with the men in charge of Caribbean affairs in the American State Department, a man called Ward was able to tell Comrade Radix that in a few weeks' time a new newspaper will come out in Grenada. This man, working in the American government in the State Department, as head of the Caribbean section, was able to tell Comrade Radix when a new newspaper would go out because he knew that already CIA agents in the region had spoken to these puppets in Grenada and prepared and trained them for this newspaper they were to launch.

Two and a half weeks ago, a man who is head of the American embassy in Barbados, a man called Ashley Wills, the chief of the CIA station there, he too came to Grenada and met with Comrade Louison, he met Comrade Kamau McBarnette, he met comrades in the Ministry of External Affairs, he met comrades in the Ministry of Information and to these comrades he pointed out that the only way in which relations between Grenada and America will improve, the only way they would accept our ambassador to their country, the only way in which we can build new relations is if we meet three conditions. They have the nerve to lay down three conditions for us.

The first condition was, call your elections right away; the second condition was, free all the detainees now or charge them; and the third condition was, break your close ties with Cuba. [*Shouts of No! No!*] They gave us three conditions and in turn we gave them thirteen conditions — condition for condition, we matched every one of them.

The plan of the CIA is to overthrow the revolution in Grenada. The elements they are using are elements like Tillman Thomas and Lloyd Noel, Alister Hughes and Eric Pierre, and other elements like them in this Committee of Twenty-six. The other elements they are using are elements like the "Cold Chicken" — Leslie Pierre, the "peeping Tom" who liked to lift dresses for stolen goods. These elements have been given a plan and this plan has stages.

Stage one was the newspaper.

Stage two, as they analyze it, is when the paper closes down, because they know that we would not allow a counterrevolutionary newspaper. And stage three in the plan was that after the paper was closed down, they use regional and international propaganda against the country and pretend that it is about freedom of the press. Then they were going to try to get a strike going in our country and we know for a fact that even today Eric Pierre and one of them were trying to ignite dock workers to take strike action, even today as I am speaking to you.

We know that the fifth plan that they have is to try to squeeze the economy. We know that this plan can take many different forms and we are going to be looking out for every single one of these forms and every single time we find a single form being implemented, we are going to crush it and confiscate the form.

We have to understand, comrades, that this plan that we are seeing now, the first element of which is this newspaper, is a different plan to all that went before, because this is not the type of plan in which local counters, local opportunists are being used, this is not the kind of plan where the ganja capitalists who are in the employment of the CIA are being used. To understand this plan fully you have to do a piece of magic in your heads, you have to forget the names of the twenty-six and instead of those twenty-six names, you write one single word, you write CIA. That is how you are going to understand this plan. Don't get confused by these twenty-six political prostitutes, don't let them confuse us. To understand this plan, rub out the names on the paper you might have and just write one word: CIA. That is the name of the plan. It is not the Committee of Twenty-six. It is the CIA. This is not about freedom of the press, it is about overthrowing the Grenadian revolution. This is not a harmless accident, it is a wilful stage in a plan. This is not a question of legality or illegality, it is a question of using legality as a red herring to try to pretend that the question is legalization, if legality is about the law. We reject the bourgeois concept in trying to define the law, we reject the meaning the bourgeoisie put to the question of press freedom. We say that — in this country today, in this popular people's revolution — the time of the masses having come, the ideas of the masses must predominate. In counterrevolution under press cover, we reject the fact that it is a legal paper. We say no: The paper is illegal.

It is illegal for five reasons.

The first reason is that they used their own procedure when they tried to create their newspaper company law. That is a legalistic reason, we gave it to them so they can be happy with it. They used the wrong procedure — they must fire Lloyd Noel next time and get a real lawyer.

The second reason is that when the *Torchlight* was closed down the general of the revolution, the Commander of the Revolution Comrade Austin went on the radio and warned these elements that they must not put out a newspaper again until further notice. They have violated the voice of the revolution.

The third reason is that — when, in their second attempt, the *Catholic Focus* was closed down, for the same illegal reasons — we warned them that they must not put out any more papers trying to use illegal means under the Newspaper Act.

The fourth reason is, we have warned them on several occasions that they will have to wait until a media code, a media policy for newspapers, is formulated and implemented before they can bring out any newspaper, and they refused to listen.

And the fifth and most important reason of all: This is a revolution, we live in a revolutionary Grenada, this is a revolutionary condition, and there is a revolutionary legality, and they will have to abide by the laws of the revolution.

When the revolution speaks, it must be heard, listened to. Whatever the revolution decrees, it must be obeyed; when the revolution commands, it must be carried out; when the revolution talks, no parasite must bark in their corner. The voice of the masses must be listened to, their rules must be obeyed, their ideas must receive priority, their needs must be addressed; when the masses speak, they must be heard. When the revolution orders, it must be obeyed. The revolution must be respected.

They are going to have to respect this revolution, because this is a people's revolution and those who won't listen are going to have to feel — those who want to take counterrevolutionary action, those who want to link up with the CIA, those who want to overthrow the revolution — are going to have to learn that the revolution is here to stay. They have to learn that this revolution will not turn over and will not be overturned. We are going to be there fighting. The revolution is the people and the people are the revolution. They are going to understand that counterrevolutionary activity will be met by revolutionary action, they are going to learn that counterrevolutionary violence is going to be met by revolutionary manners. They are going to understand that all counterrevolutionary plots, plans, and schemes will be crushed by revolutionary firmness, revolutionary manners as the comrades say. Manners, revolutionary manners. A people united can never be defeated. If you play with fire, fire will burn you; if you touch the revolution, power is going to break your backs. Don't touch the revo. It is too strong, it is too powerful.

It is one thing when a local counterrevolutionary acts on his own, it is one thing when a local counterrevolutionary tries to make a grab for dollars for personal gain, it is one thing when a local counterrevolutionary is seeking his own benefits. All that is bad enough. But it is another thing when a local counter, like a political Judas, openly and unashamedly links up with the CIA to try to overthrow our revolution.

It is another thing when local counters allow themselves to be used by those people, those political pimps, those political opportunists, those political servants, those political Judases, those parasites, those political foot soldiers of imperialism; those political parasites will not be allowed to stand in the way of the people's revolution of revolutionary free Grenada.

If it is America they love so much, they could go to America. If it is America they love so much, they could instruct the passport office to remain open twenty-four hours a day so that they can fill up as many forms as they want to, as long as they want, so that they can go and join the CIA where they are. [*Applause*] These people are going to have to understand that this revolution must be respected, so this afternoon, comrades, we have passed another law to keep them happy.

Under this law which was passed this afternoon, it is again made clear in the kind of form they like, that no newspaper is to be printed for the period of the next year until a media policy is formulated. They have that in law. [*Applause*] But today you must also understand, coming from our people in Queen's Park on this Heroes' Day, that if they attempt any political industrial strike that is not justified, we are going to manners the strike. [*Applause*] If they come with any terrorism, we are going to manners the terrorists, and those who are paying them are going to get manners. [*Applause*] If they come with any economic sabotage, any time they try, any time they close down as a means of pressuring the revolution, that is going to be the last time they close that door. [*Applause*]

The masses are going to have to get together and discuss the situation. The masses will have to communicate to us through your mass organizations and your groups what your feeling is on this situation, what ideas you have, what you want us to do. We want to hear from the masses, we want the involvement of the masses in this next stage. We feel it very important for our people to be directly involved in deciding what is the best kind of manners to use against those who are insisting on counterrevolutionary behavior.

Counterrevolution will not be allowed. Counterrevolution will not be tolerated. It does not matter who is involved. Whoever and whatever is involved, we are going to put them under firm revolutionary manners. [*Applause*]

Long live the fighting people of free revolutionary Grenada! [*Applause*]

Long live the people of the Caribbean! [*Applause*]

Long live the people of the Third World! [*Applause*]

Long live Heroes' Day! [*Applause*]

Long live the memory of our martyrs! [*Applause*]

Long live the fighting unity of our people! [*Applause*]

Long live the revolutionary spirit of our workers, our farmers, our youth, our women! [*Applause*]

Long live free Grenada! [*Applause*]

Long live the Grenada revolution! [*Applause*]

Forward ever, backward never! [*Applause*]

A people united can never be defeated! [*Applause and chants of "A people united can never be defeated!"*]

For Greater Caribbean Community Integration

June 29, 1981

The following speech was delivered to the Sixth Meeting of the Standing Committee of Ministers Responsible for Foreign Affairs of CARICOM (Caribbean Community) held in Grenada June 29-July 1. From a text issued by the Grenadian government.

Mr. Secretary-General;
Honorable ministers;
Your excellencies;
Members of delegations;
Sisters and brothers:

In the name of the People's Revolutionary Government, and in the name of the people of Grenada, I extend a most cordial and warm welcome to our distinguished friends and colleagues from the sister states of CARICOM to Grenada.

Today you are our esteemed guests and we are happy to have you because your presence here underlines once again the historic, permanent, and ongoing ties which exist between our countries and our peoples. Your presence is also historic because it is the very first time that our country is hosting a meeting of the Standing Committee of CARICOM Ministers Responsible for Foreign Affairs. Certainly we are glad for the opportunity to emphasize once again Grenada's firm and abiding commitment to Caribbean regionalism, to the Caribbean integration process, and to CARICOM as our region's foremost integration institution.

Mr. Secretary-General, only a few weeks ago our regional integration movement lost its stalwart — Dr. Eric Williams, who had been an early proponent of the cause of regional unity and cooperation. We all share this loss. His passing places on our shoulders an even greater responsibility to press on to achieve the noble cause of cooperation and integration in our region. I ask, Mr. Secretary-General, that we pay tribute to the memory of Dr. Williams by observing a minute's silence.

This Sixth Meeting of the Standing Committee of Ministers Responsible for Foreign Affairs takes place amidst a very complex and tense international situation of both political and economic dimensions. Just next door in the neighboring Central American country of El Salvador there exists a focal point of tension and insecurity. Though based on false premises which have now been fully exposed and discredited, the realization of the threat of direct foreign intervention in El Salvador could plunge the Central American and Caribbean area into a state of open conflict in a vain attempt to frustrate the legitimate aspirations of that heroic people. Historically our Caribbean community has always struggled on the side of peace. Today, as these ongoing and new dangers confront us we cannot shirk our historic responsibility, but instead must employ all our resources, however limited they might be, in the noble pursuit of peace. All of our diplomatic and foreign policy work must be geared towards working along with those who are calling for just and lasting political solution of this bloody conflict so close to home; and toward the overall accomplishment of the lofty and vital objectives of peace, justice, and freedom internationally.

This committee must note with deep satisfaction that only three days ago the Organization of African Unity meeting in Nairobi, Kenya, unanimously adopted a resolution which strongly condemned Western support for South Africa's illegal hold on Namibia. In a historic demonstration of unity and collective political will, all fifty heads of state or government denounced the unholy alliance between Pretoria and Washington, and condemned what they described as "sinister moves" by the Reagan administration to circumvent efforts being made to bring about elections under United Nations supervision.

In reiterating our own principled support for the liberation struggles and the call for justice, equality, and self-determination in the southern African region, this committee will certainly wish to take note of the firm, principled, and most recent stand by these distinguished representatives of the people of Africa, a people with whom we in the Caribbean share unbreakable ties of blood, history, and solidarity.

With regard to the Middle East, we cannot afford to continue to ignore the continuing tensions and conflicts generated and perpetuated by territorial injustice. Israel's latest act of aggression against the sovereign and independent Arab state of Iraq aggravates Middle East tensions. The bombing of the Iraqi nuclear installation constitutes a flagrant breach of international law and a gross violation of the national sovereignty and territorial integrity of Iraq. We must place on record our condemnation of Israel's act of premeditated aggression that was vulgarly timed to gain cheap electoral advantage. We must demand that Israel refrain from such acts in the future and insist that Iraq be fully compensated for the material damage and loss of life suffered.

Mr. Secretary-General, two issues of particular concern to all Commonwealth countries are the issues of apartheid in sports and the recent UK Nationality Bill. Because these are matters which, in one way or another, greatly touch and concern our people, this committee will need

For Greater Caribbean Integration   169

to analyze them, assess their full implications and impact, and take firm and principled positions which will ensure that the legitimate interests and concerns of our people and other Commonwealth and Third World citizens are fully respected and upheld. Certain divisive and exploitative forces are attempting to push our countries into a situation of cold war alignment. To us, this is an area in which relations in and out of the region must be founded on the principles of cooperation, peaceful coexistence, mutual respect, noninterference in the internal affairs of other states, and the practice of ideological pluralism.

Policies of confrontations, cold war rhetoric, and military build-up threaten to erode the gains won in the period of the 1960s and 1970s under the guidance of the Nonaligned Movement. It is in the interest of the Caribbean community of nations to struggle for harmonious relations in the region.

This meeting will be followed by the United Nations General Assembly, which opens in New York in September. Coordinated positions and issues of importance to this committee must therefore be ironed out before we face the rest of the international community. Of great significance are the up-coming Mexico summit, the Commonwealth Heads of Government meeting in Australia and the Eleventh General Assembly of the Organization of American States, which will once again be held in the Caribbean, this time in the sister state of St. Lucia in early December.

This meeting should be a useful context for caucusing Caribbean positions regarding the several critical issues which will need close Caribbean collaboration at these extremely important meetings.

Mr. Secretary-General, sisters and brothers, as we review the international political situation we cannot disregard the international economic situation. There is no doubt that the world is facing a serious economic crisis. This crisis begins in the Western industrialized countries and inevitably spreads to the economies of the dependent developing countries. However, although the origin, the basic roots of the crisis rest beyond the border of the developing countries, our subordinate and vulnerable position in the world economic system means that we suffer the most severe effects of the crisis.

This reveals the unjust, inequitable, and anachronistic nature of the present world economic system. As noted elsewhere, this international economic crisis of grave proportions which is unfolding is having a severe impact on our region. Tourism has taken a sharp downward decline for the region as a whole. The prices of most of our major export commodities are declining. The price of basic imports — fuel, food, medicines, machinery — are escalating at a rate that spells danger, if not disaster for our small, open, independent economies. It is against this background, and from this point of view that we observe international economic justice, that the Caribbean community must continue to wage militant struggle for the establishment of a new international economic order first proposed by the developing nations and later endorsed by fair-minded groups from the industrial community. It must be deployed to guarantee better and more stable prices for our exports — better terms of trade. It must democratize the international monetary system, it must terminate domination and manipulation of the international economic system by a few big countries and their multinational corporations. It must increase the transfer of resources, both economic and technological, from the developed to the developing countries. In short, the new international economic order can and should make a contribution to alleviating the existing exploitative world order.

Clearly, also, better commodity prices will give our region — indeed, the developing world in general — purchasing power which can then be used for the purchase of more industrial products. In this way the developing countries will also assist in the recovery of the stagnating industrial economies. It is fundamentally regrettable that agreement on the launching of the round of global negotiations on international economic cooperation was not reached at the Eleventh Special Session of the United Nations General Assembly in 1980. The responsibility for this failure must be placed squarely at the door of the three Western industrialized countries which assumed a very uncooperative and irrational position at the two sessions.

We must devote maximum effort and energy to have these countries change their position and implement the program of action on the establishment of the new international economic order. This committee will therefore want to pay particular attention to the upcoming Mexico summit, which could well represent the last real chance to energize vital discussions around the need for a new international economic order.

Mr. Secretary-General, we must also demand that the tremendous resources employed in the creation of unproductive and dangerous armaments be gainfully utilized in the interest of the developing countries and toiling humanity. This more efficient use of the world's resources will also serve to consolidate international peace and security. This colossal waste of the world's resources could be of tremendous economic benefit to developing countries, and more particularly to the more disadvantaged and small-island developing states such as most of us are. These states are characterized by a variety of features considered normal for poor, underdeveloped countries. These features include a very low and generally [backward] technological development as well as a lack of institutions and organizations designed for modern production.

In addition, small-island states obviously have small physical sizes and small resource bases. The limitations of such a small-island base are many, including the need of a much stricter economic and social use of the limited land available. Land-use policies are therefore often indispensable to orderly housing, agriculture, recreational, and other developmental needs. The other features and unique limitations of small-island states have been elaborated elsewhere.

Grenada, and, no doubt, other sister states, have not spared any opportunity in the international arena to discuss this issue, gaining both understanding and support of the inherent structural difficulties faced in our developmental efforts. The Caribbean community, though relatively small, cannot afford to be isolated from international and regional peace, security, justice, progress, and development. Hence the significance of the agenda before us, which should be examined with due consideration given both to the past and future work of the committee. Before going further, Mr. Secretary-General, I wish to call attention to the recent formation of the eighteenth of this month of the Organisation of Eastern Caribbean States [OECS] as an encouraging and significant development for our subregion and region in general. The closer coordination in fields such as economic and foreign policy which the Treaty of Basseterre seeks will help to further consolidate the integration process started by these seven countries as far back as 1967. This is a positive and correct response to the international situation, which demands the closest cooperation among states, since most of today's problems and issues recognize no borders, and in fact transcend national frontiers.

The OECS treaty, in the light of the relatively weak position of the lesser developed countries of CARICOM, can bolster CARICOM itself, and in this regard is a highly positive factor in the present regional situation. Another positive factor in which this committee must take satisfaction is the ever growing acceptance of, and study devoted to, the concept of the Caribbean as a zone of peace. This concept — first endorsed at the Latin American and Caribbean level by the hemisphere Organization of American States at its Ninth General Assembly in La Paz, Bolivia, in 1979 — was and remains a collective response to the stepped-up military activities initiated in the Caribbean by forces which seek to perpetuate the syndrome of dependency and exploitation. Some of the substantive requirements to be satisfied in order to have our Caribbean effectively become a zone of peace include the following: (1) prohibition of nuclear weapons in the region; (2) an end to all aggressive military maneuvers in the region; (3) the dismantling of all foreign military bases in the region; (4) the decolonization of all of our territories and the establishment of machinery to end all forms of aggression, including assassinations, mercenary invasions, propaganda interventions, and diplomatic and economic pressures.

When these conditions are fulfilled, the most vital prerequisite for progressive development and peace will characterize our Caribbean community. Certainly, our sister state of Belize, now so close to independence yet still beset with a web of issues which threaten to further delay her legitimate attainment of independence with full territorial integrity, stands to benefit from this declaration.

I am certain that this committee will wish once again to pledge our fullest support for and solidarity with, the government and people of Belize. Equally important is our region's deep and continuing concern with the constant threat of mercenary invasions. The cause of peace in the Caribbean can be further reinforced and strengthened if metropolitan countries take urgent and active steps to prohibit the recruitment, financing, training, transit, assembly, and use of mercenaries in violation of established international law. The declaration and practice of the Caribbean as a zone of peace would also undoubtedly help to enhance the security of all Caribbean states.

Mr. Secretary-General, distinguished delegates, this in brief summarizes the nature of the international and regional situation. It is a very grave one and we face many dangers. To improve the existing situation in the region and in the Caribbean community in particular, and to deal effectively with the several problems and issues affecting the regional and integration process, a CARICOM heads of government meeting seems the next logical step in community activities. The CARICOM heads of government have not met since 1975. This is a fundamentally unfortunate reality as many events have occurred which necessitates a meeting of the highest organ of CARICOM.

A CARICOM heads of government meeting will also serve to strengthen CARICOM and will constitute a useful forum in which to exchange views and work out common approaches in light of the complex and tense world and regional situation. We in Grenada and no doubt other countries in the region would like to see this Sixth Meeting of the Standing Committee Responsible for Foreign Affairs recommend strongly a meeting of CARICOM heads of government.

Mr. Secretary-General, almost 150 years after the abolition of slavery, after nearly two decades of formal independence for several countries of our region — we ask ourselves: where are we as a people? What is the state of our housing, our health facilities, our educational institutions, our physical infrastructure? How developed is our agriculture? Our industrial base and our intraregional institutions for cooperation and development? The truth is that, despite progress on some levels, CARICOM countries are still dependent and vulnerable, vulnerable to hurricanes and as vulnerable to international political pressures and economic fluctuations. In an effort to deepen the integration process started eight years ago, my government issues a strong call for unity, solidarity, and further integration among all members of the Caribbean community. Let us face the world as one united region conscious of our collective strength and our individual frailty. As a people we are building a genuine process of fraternal relations based on respect and cooperation. We respect sister countries of the region and expect them to take independent decisions and to pursue, if they so wish, independent paths.

But with your kind indulgence, Mr. Secretary-General, I want to stress that Grenada is obviously not opposed to our sister states receiving assistance from whatever source they wish to receive them from.

Indeed, we urge all donors and potential donors to make positive and substantial contributions to the objective improvement of the material and spiritual conditions of the region's poor. However, what Grenada takes exception to, will continue to reject, is the manipulative and divisive use of funds geared towards compromising our institutions, our solidarity among us, and our people's integrity.

Grenada will always condemn neocolonialist and imperialist tactics whether they are disguised, dressed up, or naked. For our part, Mr. Secretary-General, I pledge the Grenada government's willingness to continue to work in a spirit of fraternal and sisterly cooperation for greater Caribbean community integration. Our record is clear. We are fully committed to even greater and greater unity among us in the region, even greater and greater practical cooperation. These in fact are among our guiding principles!

In the spirit of the region's true pioneer integrationist and in the memory of the outstanding Caribbean statesmen, we once again welcome all of you to Grenada.

Mr. Secretary-General, sisters and brothers, I declare open the Sixth Meeting of the Standing Committee of Ministers Responsible for Foreign Affairs, and wish that our deliberations be constructive, fruitful, and help to advance the process of bringing more benefits to the people of our region — an objective that must always underline *all* of our efforts.

Grenada, Mr. Secretary-General, pledges to continue to work towards a stronger, brighter, and more united Caribbean.

Thank you very much.

The Present Stage of the Grenada Revolution

July 1981

The following interview conducted by Grace Dana was printed in Granma Weekly Review, *July 12, 1981.*

Grace Dana: On the eve of March 13, 1979, what were the conditions faced by the people of Grenada that led you and the New Jewel Movement to overthrow Eric Gairy by force?

Maurice Bishop: There was a situation of total political, social, and economic bankruptcy. The result of this, naturally, was a very united population, united in their desire to have the Gairy dictatorship removed. Fifty percent of the work force of the country was unemployed. About 70 percent of all women who wanted to work were unable to find jobs, and the figure was equally dramatic for the youth.

There was also a stagnant economic situation. In fact, the World Bank report for the last year before the revolution indicated that the economy had actually grown backwards over the previous five-year period. As you know, there were no industries, no factories, no manufacturing sector. There really was absolutely nothing happening, no development at all taking place in the economy.

At the same time, the social benefits coming to the masses had long ago stopped. The condition of the main hospital was quite alarming, and had increasingly come to be regarded as a department of La Qua's Funeral Agency, where in fact you went to die, not to live: no bandages, no medicines, no pills of any sort; pregnant women having their children on the cold floor — really very awful conditions.

This was equally true in terms of the lack of any housing schemes, of pipe-borne water, of the expansion of electrification, and the lack of progress in education. The number of scholarships from primary to secondary schools had not increased for several years, and Gairy had stopped paying the grant to the University of the West Indies, which meant that Grenadian students could no longer go abroad to receive a university education at a subsidized rate. The agricultural workers had not seen an increase in salary for perhaps over ten years. All of these very serious factors made it clear to the masses of people right through the society that the Gairy dictatorship was unable to bring any benefits for them.

In the area of social, political, and economic rights, the situation had deteriorated to a point where we were fast becoming a Caribbean Chile. The right to life had been removed in effect. No one was ever charged or arrested for the murders of many people during the last years of Gairy. No trials ever took place. The criminals were allowed to walk free, and very often, they were promoted, especially if they were policemen. The brutality in the country — police brutality, brutality by Gairy's soldiers — was also very much on the increase, particularly affecting the youth of the country. Disappearances in Chilean fashion had also begun to increase: In the last year, more than seven people disappeared. None of them to this date have been traced.

Gairy also passed different repressive bits of legislation, all aimed at removing further the rights of the people. The Public Order Act of 1974 was his way of ensuring that the people, and the opposition parties and organizations in particular, could not hold public meetings. Because this act required permission to use a public address system, a permission that was never forthcoming. A Newspaper Act was also passed, which in effect made it impossible to publish any newspapers in our country. At the same time, a law from colonial days prohibiting the importation of progressive and socialist literature was applied even more ruthlessly by Gairy, thus making sure that progressive ideas were kept away from the people.

The Essential Services Act of 1978 effectively took away from eleven of the most important categories of workers the right to strike, and that naturally led to very severe dissatisfaction among the working class. The farmers of the country, too, were very dissatisfied. We have had in Grenada a very strong tradition of cooperatives, with cooperative associations running the three major agricultural export crops (nutmeg, cocoa, and bananas) from 1946. Beginning in 1969, Gairy moved to disband these cooperatives by taking control of their elected boards, and removing altogether the rights of electability and accountability, which the farmers had previously been able to exercise on an annual basis.

The foreign poicy of the country was also a matter of very deep concern, and helped to lead to Gairy's total alienation within and outside the country. Foreign policy was based essentially on links with the Mafia, or Mafia-type forces, and with the most repressive regimes around the world. Gairy established diplomatic relations with Chile and then moved to tighten them in terms of military assistance, at precisely the time when most countries in the world were moving to break relations with that fascist dictatorship. He also developed very close relations with South Korea and with Haiti.

Gairy saw our foreign policy in terms of an opportunity to promote his superstitious beliefs. So on every occasion he went to the United Nations, for example, he would spend a lot of time talking about UFOs (Unidentified Flying Objects). Our country, therefore, rapidly gained a reputation of being a number-one comic country in the world.

His approach to running the country also reflected his personal style and his deep mystical beliefs. One result of this was a total lack of planning in the country: Gairy did not have even a five-minute, far less a five-year, plan. Thus, the statistical base in the country, the planning mechanisms which had tentatively begun to grow over the previous years, were all disbanded. This has created a major problem for the revolution.

On top of all this, Gairy was also personally very corrupt and by the time of the revolution had amassed a considerable fortune, by Grenadian standards. Further, his sexual exploitation of our women in return for jobs created deep feelings of resentment among not just the women so degraded but the population at large.

All of these factors naturally led to the increasing unpopularity of the Gairy dictatorship, which the people made a very serious attempt to remove in 1973-74. There was total unity of several organizations in our country, in fact all the key organizations: the workers' organizations, the professional bodies, the Chamber of Commerce, the churches, the service clubs like Rotary and Jaycees, and so forth. All of them got together in what came to be known as a "Committee of Twenty-two." They called a general strike. Every day for three weeks during the month of January 1974, there were massive demonstrations, very often involving a quarter of the entire population, all calling on Gairy to go. Gairy's response was to bring his secret police, his Mongoose Gang, his soldiers, and his police force into St. George's on the occasion of one such demonstration on January 21, and using repression, to crush that particular attempt at revolutionary action. But that only helped to lay the basis for the 1979 March 13 revolution.

A critical factor I should mention, and a large part of the subjective reasons for the revolution, was the strength, the respect, and the trust that the masses had in and for our party, the New Jewel Movement. Over the years, our party had always defended the rights of the people, had always struggled for those rights. As a result, many of our comrades were murdered, several others beaten, many of us were jailed and beaten ourselves from time to time — that sort of thing. But this only gave a very clear indication to the masses that our party was determined to bring about the overthrow of the Gairy dictatorship. And the masses therefore knew they could rely on us. Hence, when the call was made on March 13, 1979, they eagerly responded.

It must be understood, too, that for some time before that, our people had come to understand that the electoral option, the electoral route to removing Gairy, was totally closed. The 1976 elections, which our party contested as part of a three-party People's Alliance, were undoubtedly won by the alliance, a fact that is widely accepted in Grenada and the region. Gairy maintained power on that occasion by virtue of an electoral coup d'etat. And our people understood this, which helped to create the conditions for moving to revolutionary action.

Overall, therefore, I would say there was fairly total unity of all forces to remove the dictatorship; and a broad realization that the country could not go forward under Gairy. The regional and international isolation of Gairy had also been achieved. Because, then, of this combination of reasons, it was possible to make the revolution when we did.

Dana: The People's Revolutionary Government has always said that its first priority is to improve the lives of the people of Grenada. With this in mind, what would you say have been the revolution's main achievements during the first two years?

Bishop: I think one major achievement has been that we have been able to mobilize our people to participate in helping to rebuild the country. If I were pressed, I would say that is the single most important achievement, because it is not something that comes easily; it is not something that many other countries have been able to do.

The second example I would give, and this is the one that a lot of the ordinary masses in Grenada would give, is the fact that our people feel a new sense of pride, a new sense of dignity, a new sense of belonging, a new sense of patriotism, and I think this is definitely a direct consequence of the revolution.

In the area of education, we have been able to double the number of scholarships from primary to secondary school; to reduce secondary school fees from $26 in some cases to $4.50 a term; and as of September this year, secondary education will be entirely free. We have been able to build one new secondary school, the Bernadette Bailey Secondary School — only the second government-built secondary school in 350 years. In the case of university scholarships, we have moved from a situation of three scholarships in 1978, the last year of Gairy, to over 220 university scholarships that our people are now able to enjoy abroad. This has meant, in effect, that university education is also free, because we now have more scholarships offered than we have qualified students to take up.

In health, we have moved from seventeen doctors, to over thirty-seven doctors, which means of course that we have been able to greatly improve the quantity and quality of health care for our people. We now have seven — as compared to one — dental clinics, which means that people are now able to stay in their own parish to have extractions or fillings. Where once people had to pay every time they went to a hospital or to one of our medical centers or visiting stations, now and since October of 1980, medical attention in all public health institutions is absolutely free of cost.

We have been able to open a new X-ray center and build a new operating theater, a new casualty clinic, and a new eye hospital, so that now people no longer have to travel to Barbados or Trinidad for eye operations.

Here, too, the free milk distribution program has been very important, in particular to the mothers of young children of our country.

All in all, the achievements in this area have been extremely impressive, and have accounted for some of the best benefits that our people have received.

In terms of the infrastructure, the new international airport project is of course the most important. The building of new feeder roads has also been significant; and more than eight new community centers have gone up since the revolution, including those now being completed. The new reservoir which was opened recently in Mardi Gras, and another which is being built now, are ensuring that many more people have access to pipe-borne water for the first time.

Our housing repair program, aimed at the poorest of the poor — the agricultural workers, the road workers, and the banana, nutmeg, and cocoa pool workers — has brought substantial relief to those categories of workers who would otherwise never have had the opportunity of having their run-down houses repaired. The workers are required to repay only two-thirds of the loan; no interest is charged; and in fact, they repay only about $2 per month over ten years. We have also made a start with our low-income housing project, a program we intend to step up over the next few years.

We believe we have made progress in agriculture, both in terms of diversifying our produce and also in terms of getting some new markets. Perhaps most critically of all, we have reduced the vast subsidy that used to be paid by the Gairy government to the state farms — from expenditure of well over $750,000 to under $185,000; and by the end of this year, we expect that subsidy to be removed altogether.

In agro-industries, we have opened a coffee-processing plant; an agro-industrial plant (where nectars and juices are being produced); and a fisheries processing plant, where we are now smoking, salting, drying, and filletting our own fish and producing our own saltfish. If that sounds like a small achievement, the fact is that the revolution has been able to do in two years what has not been done in the past 400.

There has been significant progress, too, in tourism. A conscious effort is being made to develop our tourist potential more fully. We have embarked for the first time on a planned promotional drive aimed at raising our occupancy level and also at diversifying our tourist market, particularly in Western Europe. Discussions are presently under way with several countries and individuals with a view at getting more hotels built, particularly through joint ventures. We are also negotiating route and landing rights with several international carriers so that hopefully some of them will come to our country after our international airport is completed. Several different proposals for the establishment of an Air Grenada are also being examined. Additionally, we have just bought an airplane — the first to be owned by our country — and leased it to LIAT, the regional carrier, so as to ensure greater passenger capacity into our country. On top of this, a weekly flight into Grenada by Air Cubana has been a very important factor in terms of helping to solve our communications problem. Over a period of time, we expect these flights to become more regular.

We have characterized our approach to tourism as being the development of a "work tourism." By this, we mean that the tourist sector will be integrated, through vertical and horizontal linkages, with the rest of the economy. Thus, we are planning to have our developing agricultural, agro-industrial, and fisheries sectors supply the necessary food and processed items for the tourist industry. This will mean a greater saving on foreign exchange, more jobs for our people, better prices, and a guaranteed market for our farmers and fishermen. Additionally, our local handicrafts and furniture (areas in which much attention is being given this year) will increasingly replace the items traditionally imported from countries like Taiwan and Hong Kong.

By "work tourism" we also mean the development of a more sociologically relevant tourism. We believe this can be achieved through the organization of package tours aimed at people who are interested in experiencing different aspects of our development process. Thus, people involved in education, say, might wish to come to look at our literacy and adult education programs, our national in-service teacher-training program, and our work-study and community school day program. In this way, while vacationing and enjoying all that our country has to offer, they are also able to be involved in something relevant to their own work interests. Similar possibilities exist for other areas, including sporting and cultural activities. A number of such tours have already been organized, some of them through friendship and solidarity committees abroad. We also believe that tourist travel can help in the pursuit of peace, as it gives people the opportunity of seeing how others live. Particularly in our situation, where we face such massive, negative imperialist propaganda, giving others the opportunity to come to see our developing process for themselves is one of the best ways to counter the aggressive, isolationist, and destabilizing plans of imperialism.

Finally, I should mention on this subject that the state sector in tourism has been developing. The hotels and nightclubs acquired by

Gairy as part of his ill-gotten gains are now the property of the people, and we, of course, have plans for further expansion.

I think too that the country has made progress in the area of deepening the individual and collective consciousness of our people, their greater understanding today of what we are trying to do, of what the problems are, of what the potential is.

The Centre for Popular Education, a project which in the first phase had the aim of eliminating illiteracy, has almost completed that first stage with just under a thousand people learning to read and write. The CPE will now move into its second phase, which will include the teaching of language arts and mathematics.

Finally, I would like to mention the some nine training programs created by the revolution. For example, in the area of education, we have developed an in-service teacher training program, which will train over 500 teachers in the next three years. Under the old system, about fifty teachers were getting trained every two years, about half of whom would then leave the country. We have had very good results with our in-service training program, and the key to its success has undoubtedly been the highly qualified and committed staff we have been able to recruit for it.

A police training school, fisheries training school, hotel training school, public servants' in-service program, and other such programs have also been established. All of these are of fundamental importance since they are aimed at lifting the skills of our people: Because, if our people do not receive training, if they are not exposed to new skills, then there is really no way at all in which the economy can be built and the revolution pushed forward.

Dana: How would you characterize the present stage of the revolution?

Bishop: As the national democratic stage, the anti-imperialist stage of the process we are trying to build. We see this in several ways. Beginning with the economy, we believe that our first task is to lay the basis for moving out of the incredible technological and economic backwardness which we inherited. This means at least four separate things. One is the need to urgently build a strong state sector that for the first time can be used to generate profits which in turn can be used to bring more benefits to the people. As I mentioned, the state sector right now has been developing in agriculture (the various government-owned farms, the agro-industrial plant, the coffee plant); in the fishing and fisheries sector, with the assistance of Cuba; and in tourism.

At the level of the financial institutions, a National Commercial Bank has been established for the first time, and is already the third largest bank in Grenada. A Marketing and National Importing Board, which not only ensures proper handling of exports and the marketing of our products, but also reduces the cost of living through the importation of certain basic essential items, has also been established.

Secondly, we feel that at the same time the state sector is built, we must stimulate the private sector in order to boost production. The state sector alone cannot develop the economy, given the very low level of technology available, the limited human resources, the lack of capital, the lack of marketing expertise, the lack of promotional capacity. So, we must stimulate the private sector in business generally, but also of course in agriculture, and in particular among the small and medium farmers.

A third factor is to create more state organizations to expand the export possibilities of our country as more crops are produced and more industries developed.

And fourth is the obvious need to disengage as rapidly as we can from imperialism. On the international front, this means that we need to struggle with other countries like our own, countries of the "Third World," for better prices, for the creation of a new international economic order. This also means achieving a greater economic control over resources, developing the financial institutions and the financial resources, and achieving tighter fiscal control to lay the basis for monitoring and planning the economy. This process will involve diversifying our trading patterns and developing new trading partners (while not breaking relations with our traditional partners) to bring more benefits to our people, get better prices, and move out of the primitive economy we inherited. This is one reason why we have sought to develop the best possible relations with the socialist world, the socialist-oriented world, and countries which have won their national liberation.

In this attempt to disengage from imperialism, the role of Cuba has been decisive, and the technological transfers that have taken place on a free and disinterested basis have been extremely important. We have received the kind of assistance that enables us to continue to develop our economy on our own — such as the provision of the fishing boats and the assistance with the international airport, the single most important infrastructural project our country has ever undertaken.

The last point I would like to make on the economy is that naturally we are seeking gradually to build cooperatives in the agricultural sector. That process has started, although it has not gone as quickly as we would have liked. But we certainly believe it is going to be the third key sector of the national economy, along with the state and private sectors.

At the level of the state apparatus, the Gairy army which we inherited was completely disbanded. We are now building a new kind of army altogether, an army based on the people, an army at this point largely made up of the formerly unemployed youth of our country, an army with an entirely new set of values, a new approach to their function. Likewise, a people's militia has been established, which is extremely important. It's come about partly as a result of our recognition that we cannot rely solely on the full-time army in a situation of external invasion, but that we must be able also to count on the people themselves to act as a reserve, or wartime army if you wish, that can be mobilized at a second's notice to defend the country.

The police force inherited from Gairy was not disbanded. But here, we have begun a process of democratization under a new leadership, of reorganization and a new round of training. In this way, we hope to reach the stage where the Grenada Police Service, as it is now called, together with the army and the militia and other elements of the armed forces, will become an entirely new kind of armed force that will understand its role as the defender of the revolution, as the defender of the rights of the people, no longer used for repressive purposes.

The bureaucracy which we inherited was extremely demoralized and extremely inefficient, and there, a process of reorganization and training has also begun.

The last broad point I want to make on what we mean by the national democratic stage is related to our approach to the question of democracy. We feel we must build a new grass-roots, people-oriented democracy in our country, from the village level right up to the national level. We see the need to build national organizations of the people, based on the people, relevant to the people's life and to their real problems, to ensure their participation on a daily basis in this revolutionary democracy. This, of course, is the stage we are at: the stage of revolutionary democracy.

Another responsibility of the revolution in this period, given that the legislative and executive functions are right now institutionalized in the People's Revolutionary Government, is to guarantee the widest possible process of consultation with the people on major questions. We have done this, for example, with the Income Tax Law, which came about after some nine months of widespread organized consultation, and with the Maternity Leave Law, that was discussed for some three or four months. And in tourism, one particularly far-reaching proposal made by a largely Canadian firm has been submitted to widespread discussion among the people, to know their views in advance of any decision.

Likewise, the people have been involved in the whole airport question, and in the recent airport struggle we had to fight when the Americans tried to block our funding possibilities from the European Economic Community. Our approach was to update the people fully on exactly what was happening, to give our appreciation of why America was seeking to block the construction of even one international airport in our country. As a result, not only did thousands come out to a rally to defend the building of the airport, but a National Airport Development Committee has also been set up, representing the people in all their organizations, and ensuring that they continue to play a large part in seeing that the airport gets completed.

We feel, too, that it is very important in this period to guarantee that more social benefits are brought to the people. This accounts for the relatively great strides we have made in the areas of health, education, the creation of more jobs, a better water supply — all these critical areas — because we have made the provision of the basic needs of the people a priority for the use of very scarce natural and national resources.

Dana: Could you tell us a bit more about which sectors of the Grenadian population are actively involved in the revolutionary process, and what forms this takes?

Bishop: Most sectors of the population at this point are involved in actively supporting the revolution. I should tell you first that our present analysis is that 90 percent of the people of Grenada are favorably predisposed to the revolution. More than that, this same percentage is favorably predisposed toward being organized by the party and by the revolution. We have found that even those forces that were relatively hostile to the revolution now give us arguments not opposed to what we are doing in any specific area, but very often centered around the fact that they are not seeing the leadership often enough, that the presence of the party is not among them enough, that kind of argument. And we have found a tremendous desire on the part of the masses at large for political education and for organization. I think that's an important general background point.

The youth of our country are becoming increasingly active. Apart from the existing organizations, several new ones have sprung up since the revolution. In fact, many of them arose entirely spontaneously. The leading mass organization for the youth is the National Youth Organisation [NYO], which has been going forward despite tremendous objective problems — the continuing unemployment problem, which in turn leads to frustration; the lack of transport; the lack of sufficient cadres of quality to be involved in the work on a day-to-day basis. (You have to understand that most of the youth who formerly led the NYO are now involved in other very critical areas of work. Over 200 of them are abroad studying in universities; many of them are in leading positions in the party, or have very onerous responsibilities in the state or economy.) But certainly, the vanguard organization for youth in our country is the National Youth Organisation.

The women, too, have become increasingly organized, particularly following the bomb blast in Queen's Park last June 19, which killed three of the women of our country and injured several more. Today, the National Women's Organisation has become the leading mass organization for the women of Grenada.

This has come about in part because of our conscious attempt to tackle the subjective and objective difficulties which our women have traditionally faced. One of the leading women in our party, in fact, a member of the Central Committee and the president of the National Women's Organisation, has been appointed secretary for Women's Affairs and, as such, heads the Women's Desk in the Ministry of Education and Social Affairs. This has given a great impetus, at the level of the state, to the work among women.

With the ending of sexual exploitation and job discrimination and with the proclamation and substantive implementation of equal pay for equal work in the state sector, the women of our country are now involved in every aspect of life and work in the country. Many have received jobs in areas where women have not traditionally been employed; many are working in our developing cooperative sector; several are in the People's Revolutionary Army; many more are in the militia; several dozens are now pursuing free university courses abroad; hundreds more are being trained as welders, farmers, teachers, artisans, fisherwomen, and so forth; and, of course, thousands are involved as students or teachers in the Centre for Popular Education's literacy programs. The Maternity Leave Law of 1980 has also given to our women the right both to paid leave during pregnancy and job security. The women of our country now proudly proclaim that they are rapidly becoming "Equal in production and defense."

The NYO and the NWO have both set ambitious targets for themselves in 1981. These include specific figures for greatly increased membership, more leadership-training programs, and a more interesting, varied, and activity-oriented approach for the base groups. The youth will concentrate a lot more this year on building youth cooperatives, particularly in agriculture, and in providing more sporting and cultural activities. In addition to the above, the NWO will be concentrating on the repair and setting up of pre-primary schools and daycare centers and more active involvement in community projects aimed at providing drains, dustbins, pipe-borne water, and so forth in the more depressed villages.

The NYO aims to quadruple its membership and the NWO to triple its membership during the course of this year — ambitious but realizable objectives.

The National Students Council, which was established since the revolution, has also made impressive strides in its attempts to democratize the school system and to get its membership involved in study emulation programs, work-study courses, and community projects. Likewise, the NJM Young Pioneers, another creation of the revolution, has done excellent work in helping to organize the children of the nation and in beginning the process of instilling in them the necessary qualities of discipline, self-confidence, creativity, commitment, leadership, patriotism, and so forth.

The urban working class has taken great advantage of the trade union recognition law that we passed in the first months of the revolution, which for the first time gave the workers the right to form and to join the trade unions of their choice. From about 40 percent of the working class unionized, we now have about 85 percent unionized. The agro-proletariat, likewise, has been organized in the Agricultural and General Workers' Union, and many of them also work on Sundays in the community work brigades.

The small and medium farmers participate through the various parish councils, which meet on average once a month and bring together those who are willing to work actively on a regular basis for the revolution. They also work, of course, in the community work brigades, in the community education councils, and so forth.

The middle strata of our country are also involved in the parish councils, and to a lesser extent, in the community work brigades; and many are becoming involved in new organizations like the local airport committees. For example, the St. George's Airport Development Committee has done exemplary work over the past two years in helping to raise funds for the international airport project. We certainly expect that the middle strata and the professionals generally will play a leading role in the recently formed National Airport Development Committee.

Our party, of course, is also making sure that not only our active membership but our broad supporters as well (which make up a substantial section of the population) are involved — through selling the newspaper, organizing fund-raising events, participating in seminars, panel discussions, and film shows, party-led education courses, and other activities aimed at developing greater political consciousness. Party supporters are also active in the National Community Development Committee, which has the main responsibility for monitoring what benefits are concretely coming to each village in Grenada.

As the PRG, our role in this process comes in the form of supporting those organizations already in existence and encouraging the formation of new ones; by guaranteeing a legal basis for such participation (as with the trade union law or laws promoting women's equality); and by continuing to bring more benefits for all of the poor and working people. Because, in the final analysis, without those benefits, the possibility of such participation will always remain in the realm of theory.

Dana: Despite the PRG's widespread support, it has been criticized abroad for maintaining political detainees, curtailing freedom of the press, and not formulating a new constitution. Would you comment?

Bishop: The question of detainees first of all. Everyone knows, and even reaction and imperialism when they choose to be honest will admit, that a necessary consequence of a revolution is political detainees. The only way to avoid that is if you chose the route of lining them up and shooting them. I think it is significant that everyone who has come to our country has remarked on the great humanity of the revolution — on, for example, the fact that on the first day of the revolution, the very same unemployed youth who were daily facing the brutality of the Gairy regime were the comrades who went out and picked up the Mongoose Gang, the secret police, the criminal elements in the army and the police force, and all of them were brought into custody without a single scratch. That is quite amazing when you think about it.

It is important to point out, too, that when you consider the hundreds of people who were rounded up during the first few hours, days, and weeks, today there are just fourteen of those people in detention. That tells you the approach the revolution has taken to the question: Whenever and wherever possible, once this is consistent with the interests of the revolution and particularly with national security considerations, people are released. No arbitrariness is allowed or encouraged. People are never picked up merely on hearsay or that kind of thing — but information is double-checked and triple-checked. And thereafter, every attempt is made to monitor the attitude of the detainee while in detention, and to make a careful analysis of whether or not it is safe to release him at that particular time. Again, perhaps I should point out that of Gairy's entire political directorate, ministers and what not, only two of them are now in detention from March 13.

Every other detainee in detention at this point — and there are a few dozen more — are there because they are products of direct criminal activity committed since the revolution. People who were involved in the two major counterrevolutionary plots, for example — those involved in the terrorist activity of June 19 and November 17 last year — people like that. On this, our position is very firm: Once there is any threat of that kind to the revolution, people are going to be detained. But equally, our position is that whenever and wherever possible, they must be brought to trial on specific charges. (We have not created any new or special courts to handle that, though we have created a Terrorism Law that provides special penalties for terrorism.) Likewise, when the circumstances indicate that it would be reasonable to release them, we believe that should be done.

As far as the question of the press is concerned, first of all, the press is not restricted in any way in our country. There were very specific reasons which led to the closure of the *Torchlight* newspaper in 1979. The newspaper was closed at that time because it had begun to incite an important minority section of the population — i.e. the Rastafarian movement — to open counterrevolutionary activity, calling on them to take up arms against the state. Our position is that nobody will be allowed to do that, whether it's a newspaper or whatever else. Once anybody moves to that sort of activity, they are going to be crushed, and that is why there is no *Torchlight*.

However, there is a national newspaper, the *Free West Indian*, which is an objective newspaper, where the views of the masses are printed. In fact, their views are now seen much more than in the days when the *Torchlight* was being published. Now it is quite possible to see how the masses feel on any important subject, including when they are criticizing the government on specific issues.

The National Women's Organisation puts out its own newspaper; so does the National Youth Organisation, the Agricultural and General Workers' Union; as well as several of the urban trade unions, notably the Bank and General Workers' Union. Thus, there is no lack of newspapers in our country. The press is in fact free and allowed to function. Likewise with radio and television — although television we can hardly speak about since it's just beginning to get going again. In the recent dispute we had with the public workers' union over the question of increased wages for them, they were allowed not only to print their pamphlets and to freely circulate them among their workers, but also to hold their meetings during working hours on time off given by the government, and to have all their releases read over Radio Free Grenada. That kind of freedom never existed before in our country, and is certainly not obtained in many of those countries that speak of freedom of the press and freedom of the media generally.

In this region, the hypocrisy practiced by newspapers such as the Trinidad *Express*, Barbados *Advocate*, and Jamaica *Gleaner* is really 'quite outstanding. When our releases go to them, they're not printed. Instead, they choose to rely entirely on rumor. Equally, when our newspaper, the *Free West Indian*, is sent to several of these countries, they are hidden away at the airport or burned. While, on the other hand, their newspapers come to our country every day and freely circulate. *Time* and *Newsweek*, which spend much time slandering and criticizing countries like our own also come into Grenada. But when these people speak of freedom of the press, they obviously speak only of the freedom of a very small minority of the population to push their own views under the pretense of being national and responsible. In fact, what is being peddled is always the same minority views and very often of the same individuals. A man like Ken Gordon in Trinidad, for example, owns or has shares in several newspapers in the region and is also one of the leading figures in the Caribbean Publishers and Broadcasters Association, is also a leading figure in the Caribbean News Agency. He's tied up in every aspect of the media in the region, and that is what they call "freedom."

As far as the constitution is concerned, we feel that the last constitution inherited on independence was a farce. Many important rights were left out, such as the right to work. And even when rights were stated, they were stated in a glib form without any remedies provided. For the so-called fundamental rights and freedoms in Chapter I, there are no remedies provided bar the granting of declarations. Well, the masses can't eat declarations.

Likewise, the responsibilities and duties of the population are not clearly stated, are not stated at all.

We believe the new constitution should entrench the genuine political, social, cultural, spiritual, and economic ideals and values of the society; should indicate very clearly what the rights, duties, and responsibilities of the population are; should provide remedies when these are breached; and should state concrete ways for the masses to be genuinely involved in a grass-roots democracy that will have relevance to them and will help them to deal with their daily problems. Not a democracy that is centered around a parliament, which nobody goes to listen to, or knows what is doing. We certainly feel that the new popular organizations in our country should specifically be referred to or provided for in the new constitution.

Therefore, with the new constitution that we will create in the coming months and years, our approach would be to come up with an appropriate draft, having examined contemporary models around the world; then to submit the draft to a consultative assembly of our people, made up of all their organizations, so they can spend several months discussing it in detail to record their criticisms, their amendments, ideas, and suggestions; and then to incorporate the major changes recommended into a new draft which would be approved by the population through a plebiscite or referendum.

Dana: In the last two years, terrorist attacks aimed at the revolution's leadership and supporters have taken the lives of several young people and even children. How dangerous are these counterrevolutionary elements now to the people and revolutionary process in Grenada?

Bishop: Obviously, even one counterrevolutionary can do substantial damage, even one. Then, to the extent that one such counterrevolutionary exists in our country, and I'm sure there is more than one, they can do very serious damage, certainly of a physical character and certainly in terms of the toll they can take on human lives.

But, I would say at this point that the terrorists are totally isolated; that the masses have become the eyes and ears of our revolution, and it is they who report any suspected terrorist or counterrevolutionary activity. In fact, the evidence shows that every occasion of terrorist activity in our country or of counterrevolutionary activity was discovered not by security forces in the first place, but by the masses. Acting on their information, our security forces were able to move in and make arrests, and ensure that the activity was crushed and the terrorists dealt with. The militia today is involved in an active way in this process, and several of the mass organizations have this as one of their concerns.

I think, too, we were able to use the terrorist activities over the past two years to raise further the political consciousness of our people, because, after all, terrorism is a definite admission of failure. What a terrorist is admitting is that he's unable to reach the people — he's unable to organize them, he's unable to mobilize them, to convince them that he is the answer or that his organization can do something for them. The result is that in his desperation, he turns on the very people that he at one point was trying to reach. And we were able to get this message across.

Naturally, also, in our conditions and in the conditions of countries like our own, terrorists are always encouraged and supported by imperialism — always. And therefore, the link between local terrorism and imperialism is a link that is important for the masses to understand — to see why imperialism, while on the one hand speaking of human rights and even condemning so-called terrorists themselves, on the other hand openly encourages, supports, guides, and directs terrorists in other peoples' countries. On the occasion of terrorism, we have been able to explain to our people once again why it is that imperialism and in particular United States imperialism has been attacking the revolution: Because of the benefits we have been bringing to the people, and because of their endemic fear of any progressive development in the region and worldwide.

Dana: Turning to international relations, Grenada belongs to CARICOM, the OAS, the Commonwealth, the Nonaligned Movement, and the United Nations; and the New Jewel Movement is a member of the Socialist International. Could you tell us what are the main aspects of the PRG's foreign policy pursued on these various fronts?

Bishop: In all of them, we promote very consciously the need for peace in our region and in the world, the need for peaceful coexistence, the need for disarmament, an end to the arms race, for détente, for the resumption of the SALT II talks. We see this whole series of issues, which is really one basic issue, as fundamental to our foreign policy. First, because we believe that the question of peace and peaceful coexistence is at this point the number-one question in the world. And second, because we know that our country, and indeed any country at all, will not be able to develop in a situation of war.

Another common point we stress is our firm position against imperialism, against colonialism, against neocolonialism, and against racism.

And thirdly, we uphold some principles that we believe very strongly in: The right of our country, and of all countries, to use their own resources for the benefit of their own people; the right to build our own process; the right to choose our own friends; and the right to bring about peaceful and progressive development in our country in our own way.

We recognize of course that none of the organizations you have listed are monolithic organizations. In all of them, there are people with differing views of the world and of the issues facing it, and different approaches to building their countries. Thus, in each organization, we articulate as clearly as we can our position, a consistent position, and seek to find as much common ground as we can with those forces represented. There are a number of ways in which I can demonstrate that, coming out of our experience in the last two years.

The first example relates to declaring the Caribbean a zone of peace. That concept has always been very close to us. In the OAS conference in Bolivia in 1979, some six or seven months after the revolution, we put forward a resolution on this idea. And it took our representatives four or five days and several different drafts before they were able to achieve agreement. But the struggle was well worth it. Because they were eventually able to get that resolution passed at the OAS, and in fact unanimously supported, including being supported by the U.S. — which is the strangest of ironies, but nonetheless it happened.

A second example is the concern we have been showing for the problems of small island states and similarly disadvantaged states. We have raised this question in all the different forums in which we participate.

Another example is the position we took for recognition and support for the Polisario Front, a national liberation movement struggling for sovereignty over its national territory. Once we had decided to support the Polisario Front and to extend our recognition to them, our approach was to try to get our friends in the CARICOM area to agree to do this together. When this proved not to be possible, we went ahead and did it on our own, but at a time and in a way that we felt would guarantee that other countries in the region would follow, and in fact that did happen.

The recent airport struggle we have had is another example I can give. As you know, Cuba has been giving us outstanding assistance in building the international airport — in fact, the major reason the airport project was able to start at all is because of the assistance we have received from our revolutionary sisters and brothers in Cuba, in terms of the internationalist workers they have provided, the very critical items of machinery and equipment, the technical experts, the gifts of cement and steel for the project, in several areas like that. The Americans, in their usual way, are "concerned" about this international airport, because they recognize that it is the single most important project that would ensure economic takeoff for our country. And therefore, they are very anxious to crush this airport project. Nevertheless, we have been able to achieve a large degree of international support for it — very good assistance, for example, came to us from the Algerians, the Iraqis, the Libyans, and Syrians, by way of gifts and soft loans; and likewise, we've had assistance by way of diesel oil from the Venezuelans. Then we approached the countries in the European Economic Community, and the Commission of that community agreed to host a co-financing conference in Brussels which took place in April.

The response of the Americans was a massive and vulgar campaign aimed at stopping those countries from taking part, in other words, at trying to dictate Europe's foreign policy, and trying to tell the Europeans how they must use their own national resources. Our counter was to raise the matter in the OAS, in the Nonaligned Movement; to notify the member parties of the Socialist International, our fellow governments in the CARICOM region, and several of the governments in the Commonwealth; and likewise to brief the secretary-general of the United Nations and to ask him to inform all member states of the UN about this. The result was that we received tremendous regional and international support, at different levels, for the project. The African, Caribbean, and Pacific grouping of countries, for example, sixty-one of them meeting in Brussels in April, passed a very firm resolution condemning America's interference and expressing their total support for our right to develop our international airport. Likewise, the meeting of twenty-seven of the SELA countries in Venezuela passed a resolution of support. In other words, our approach was to use our participation in these organizations to alert and notify their members as to what was happening; and at the same time, to seek concrete support from them for the continuation of the project.

Dana: You touched on relations with the United States. Since the revolution, there has been a marked deterioration in Grenada-U.S. relations. What is the basis for this?

Bishop: I think there are several reasons: The United States has historically and traditionally viewed this region as its backyard. They have always believed that their multinational companies have the right to exploit the resources of this region, indeed of the world, at will and with impunity. They have always felt that they have a right to decide the course of economic development that countries like ours should take. In fact, they have always believed it was their right to ensure our permanent underdevelopment.

Historically, this can be seen at least from the Monroe Doctrine in 1823, which gave to different governments in the United States the right to intervene at will in Latin America. And, as you know, acting under this doctrine, virtually all countries in this region at one time or another have been invaded. The Mexicans, for example, in the period of the late 1830s and early forties had most of their national territory stolen from them. The 2.1 million square kilometers taken represents a greater land mass than the total territory of Mexico today.

So, there has been this history of annexation, of invasion, and later still of destabilization and diplomatic pressure which has been used by the Americans over the years. I think, too, that we have to consider the fact that countries like ours — with a particular stance and posture, a nonaligned position in the world, that maintains principled relations with different countries, that maintains excellent relations with countries like Cuba and Nicaragua, that does not see imperialism as invincible, that does not accept that its country is in anybody's backyard, that believes firmly in our right to develop our own process in our own way, free from all forms of outside pressure and interference; that a country like ours that had the honor of having the first revolution in the English-speaking Caribbean — obviously must come in for particular pressure and attack.

The truth is that right from the earliest days of the revolution, we had problems with the Americans. Of the major Western powers involved in this region, they were the last to extend recognition to our government, notwithstanding they knew that the revolution had tremendous, in fact almost total, popular support, that we were in complete control of the country and gave firm undertakings (which have all been respected) to honor our international commitments and to respect the rights and guarantee the safety of all non-Grenadians, and indeed of Grenadians, in our country.

Then, in the first weeks of the revolution, in return for a promise of $5000 "aid," their Ambassador Ortiz tried to dictate to us what our policies must be and in particular was bold enough to warn us against developing "close ties" with Cuba. Naturally, we gave him the answer that we were not for sale and that our internal and international policies were entirely a sovereign matter for us, not subject to any outside negotiation or dictation.

Later on, and still in the first three months, we discovered that the CIA had drawn up a three-pronged "pyramid plan," made up of propaganda destabilization, economic sabotage and destabilization, and terrorist, counterrevolutionary, and assassination activities, to roll back the revolution. And this discovery came after *Newsweek* magazine had informed the world that the National Security Council had considered blockading our country. And I must point out that we have seen *all* aspects of the CIA pyramid plan attempted — some successfully — over the past two years. In fact, some of the counterrevolutionary elements involved in the October 1979 plot confessed that they had been assured of support from mercenaries who would arrive in ships coming from U.S. territory.

The Americans have also refused to extradite Gairy back to Grenada to face trial on charges of conspiracy to murder and attempted murder, among others, notwithstanding the fact that we have complied with all of their legal formalities. From San Diego and Brooklyn, Gairy is today still using U.S. territory and media and other facilities to try to fulfill his impossible dream of recapturing power in Grenada.

The Americans also refused to accredit our permanent representative to the OAS as ambassador to Washington and instructed their outgoing ambassador to Grenada not to come to St. George's last January when we had invited her in for official talks aimed at restoring dialogue.

Recently too, a poll of travel agents in the Washington-Maryland area and in New York revealed that over 90 percent of the forty-odd agencies approached for travel information to Grenada advised that Grenada was an "unsafe" destination. Most of them said that this totally dishonest advice was given to them by the State Department.

Furthermore, after Hurricane Allen caused severe damage to our banana crop last year, an application for rehabilitation assistance by the Windward Islands Banana Association, comprised of Grenada, St. Vincent, St. Lucia, and Dominica, was only granted on the basis that Grenada was excluded. Since then, we have had several more examples of the USA blocking and trying to block our attempts to receive developmental assistance from different international lending agencies like the IMF and from different countries like the EEC to which we had applied for assistance with our international airport project.

Now, they have stepped up their illegal spy flights over our country, have stepped up in a massive way their negative and lying propaganda and who knows for a fact what other plans are on the drawing board or have just been approved.

It seems there is no limit to the vulgarity and grossness of the mighty USA in their attempts to try to stop the peaceful and progressive development of a small and poor but independent-minded country like Grenada. During the election campaign they said that their plan was to teach us a lesson. Our plan is to make sure that our revolution continues and grows stronger every day.

I think we also have to understand that this period is in many respects the most dangerous period in recent times. The Reagan administration has come up with some new concepts — particularly those of "linkage" and "international terrorism" — that are extremely dangerous. This concept of terrorism seeks in one blow to get round the Carter concept of human rights (it is no longer necessary to condemn those countries that have bad human rights records, like Chile), and to give them free reign to call any countries that are opposed to their way of thinking "terrorists." In that way, they are seeking to rewrite recent history; turn back progressive developments around the world; and to create an image and a climate of hostility against those countries that have fought for their liberation and have been successful, countries of course like Cuba and Nicaragua, like Mozambique and Angola.

The concept of linkage likewise is very dangerous. What this doctrine says is that if something happens in some part of the world of which they disapprove then they reserve the right to take a similar action in another part of the world, in Latin America, for example. That would mean that if anything took place in Europe that America disapproved of, that would give them the right to invade Cuba or Nicaragua, El Salvador or Grenada.

This American administration wishes to resume the role of policeman of the world on behalf of imperialism and capitalism. They believe they have the right to rule the world, and this does not seem to extend just to dominating and exploiting small, poor countries like our own, or to trying to roll back the progress that has taken place in the socialist world, but also even to dictating to their so-called allies in Europe what they must do. A very good example of that recently was the attempt they made to stop the humanitarian assistance that the EEC countries were trying to send to the war victims of El Salvador. Another example, which I have already mentioned, is the pressure they brought to bear on these same countries not to give any form of assistance to Grenada for our international airport.

That is the extent to which these people are dreaming — in the White House, in the Pentagon, in the State Department, indeed in the whole military-industrial establishment in America. They would like to redraw the present map of the world. They would like to see an end to the Mozambiques, the Nicaraguas, and the Cubas. They have given open and total support to the racist apartheid regime in South Africa. They are against the national liberation struggle and national liberation movement in Namibia. They have agreed once again that the Chilean dictatorship can receive aid from America, invited them to participate in future military maneuvers with the U.S. armed forces, while at the same time saying the people of Panama do not have the right to their own canal, in open contravention of the Carter-Torrijos treaties.

Really, this Reagan administration — its policies, its postures, its clearly warlike intentions on the world stage — represents a tremendous danger to world peace, has created great new tensions regionally and internationally, and will certainly cause a major regional or global catastrophe in the future if it does not change its warlike aggressive attitude very soon.

From our perspective in Grenada, we have always expressed our desire and interest in having as good relations as we can with whatever government is in charge in the United States. That still remains our perspective. We recognize that several of our own nationals live in the United States and that several of their nationals live in our country; that more tourists come from their country every year to Grenada than the entire population of our country. Therefore, we have absolutely no reason to want bad relations. But we have always said and will continue to say that these relations must be premised on the normal, well-established principles of relations between two sovereign states — that is to say, legal equality, mutual respect for sovereignty, ideological pluralism, and respect for the principle of noninterference in each other's affairs. Now, if these principles can be accepted by the United States, I am certain that a large part of the basis for the problems that now exist between our two countries would immediately and automatically be removed. We will certainly continue working towards achieving that goal.

Dana: "Forward ever, backward never!" is the slogan of the Grenadian revolution. What do you see as the main difficulties that have to be overcome in the present period for the revolutionary process to keep on its forward course?

Bishop: I think that major difficulty centers around the economy, and ensuring that we can do something as urgently as possible about transforming the economy we now have, and developing its productive capacities. There are tremendous problems at this point in time — with the lack of human resources, the lack of technology, the lack of capital, of expertise.

At the same time, there is the continuing problem for countries like ours, primary producers, of the very poor price that we get for the agricultural crops we produce. In 1979, we got $21 million from the sale of nutmeg, cocoa, and bananas; by 1980, for selling just about the same amount, we got $17 million, $4 million less, largely because the price of cocoa fell in a few months from about $4,400 a ton to about $2,400 a ton. There was very little, of course, that we could have done about that. In the longer run, this is part of our struggle for the achievement of a new international economic order, and for diversification of our trading partners and patterns.

There is the problem, too, of the imported inflation that we have to grapple with every year. In a country like ours with a small, open, dependent economy, naturally that's a major problem. In 1979, we spent something like $43 million to import the manufactured items we need from the imperialist countries; by 1980, we had to spend $50 million to get just about the same amount of goods. That tells you that while the price we get for our goods falls every year, the price we have to pay for what they produce goes up every year. It's a massive problem.

As if this weren't enough, we recently experienced outright economic warfare declared on Grenada by three giant transnational corporations which attempted to bring the country to a complete halt by cutting off the electricity supply and plunging our people into darkness. Of course, they hoped that the resulting chaos would make Grenadians lose confidence in themselves to push the revolution forward and lose confidence in their government to solve the burning problems that the country faces.

After more than twenty years of squeezing profits from our people, twenty years of rate increases that even government had no power to control, and twenty years of progressively deteriorating service resulting in massive blackouts during the last months — the Commonwealth Development Corporation of England (CDC) suddenly couldn't obtain further fuel credit from ESSO and couldn't obtain further cash credit from their bankers at Barclay's. Then, on the afternoon of May 21, the government was presented with an ultimatum by these three transnationals: Take over the enormous debts run up by CDC, or the country's generators will stop by 8:00 p.m.

What they did not realize was that for weeks we had been completely informed of their unfolding plot to blackmail our country, that we even knew that attempts had been made to keep the spare parts for the generators from leaving the docks. Faced with this classic example of economic aggression, our government took over majority shares in the electricity company, effectively obtaining control of it; appointed two new directors and a new manager; and met with the workers there, who pledged us their vigilance against any further sabotage. But the generators are in a state of total disrepair, and so it will be some time before we can recover from these past twenty-one years of the exploitation of our people in this essential service, and it will require substantial investment of our economic resources.

Our capital program has also been the target of economic aggression. Just for this year alone, one-third of our capital program was in danger of being sabotaged as a result of last-minute moves by the U.S. representative on the IMF Board of Directors to block a major loan from that institution to our country. And, of course, the World Bank has been busy trying to sabotage our efforts to attain financing from the European countries in the April co-financing conference in Brussels.

The second thing I'd like to say on this is related to our general approach to building the country. What we have been doing over these past two years is relying on three main pillars to build the national economy and to keep the revolution moving forward. These are: one, the need to continue bringing more benefits to the people, through making the economy stronger, through developing as rapidly as we can the productive capacity of our people and productive forces of our country.

Second, to continue to involve our people, to mobilize and to organize them for revolutionary, democratic, and grass-roots-oriented participation in the running of the country and the building of the revolution on a voluntary basis. That has been going quite well in our view.

Third, to develop a capacity to defend the revolution. It is our firm belief that no revolution has a right to call itself that if it does not have or does not develop a capacity to defend itself. This is why the Gairy army was disbanded and a new army, the People's Revolutionary Army, was created. This is also why we have been building the People's Revolutionary Militia so that the people of our country will themselves be involved in the defense of what they have fought for and what they are trying to build.

We feel that once we can continue to find ways of pushing the economy forward, and thus of mobilizing the necessary resources to ensure more benefits for our people, and to build on these three pillars, then whatever obstacles we face we will be able to overcome. As one of our national slogans proclaims: "An organized, conscious, united, productive, and vigilant people can never be defeated."

And we should warn those powers intent upon rolling back our process: As long as this government is here and our party is here and our proud people are here; as long as the revolution is here, whenever we have to make a choice between kneeling down and rolling over, or standing up — we'll always choose to stand up.

Dana: Thank you, Prime Minister Bishop, for the time you have given to *Granma Weekly Review*. One last question — How can our readers learn more about Grenada? And how can they actively show their support for the Grenadian people and their revolution?

Bishop: In terms of learning more about Grenada, it would be important for as many of your readers as possible to get a subscription to our national newspaper, the *Free West Indian*. At this point, this is a weekly newspaper, but we hope soon it will come out twice a week and thereafter daily. But it does offer at this point one of the best ways of receiving regular information on our country. Those people who live in areas where our radio station, Radio Free Grenada, can be picked up could also tune in on medium or shortwave.

Thirdly, in several countries around the world, Grenada friendship associations and solidarity committees are being formed. Where such associations exist, people could certainly consider joining them as a means of getting regular information, and also to take advantage of the trips to our country organized by these societies. And that is the fourth point, of course: to come to Grenada. In that way, they would have the opportunity to see what is happening in our country, and to make up their own minds. Certainly, they can be assured at a minimum of a very pleasant and enjoyable holiday, in really ideal conditions — in terms of the beauty and unspoiled naturalness of our country, of our beaches and climate and of the warmth and friendliness of our people. But also, they would be able to see the new kind of society that is emerging, the committed involvement of our people in the revolution.

As far as concrete support is concerned, one thing we have found particularly effective is when progressive people in any country, through the radio, press, TV, or in any other way, set a true perspective on the situation in Grenada, and raise the consciousness of their people on the true reasons behind the attacks by imperialism against our revolution.

There are many ways in which material support can be expressed. For example, we have received very valuable assistance by way of equipment and materials for the hospitals, community centers, clinics, the Centre for Popular Education program, and the land reform program. Quite a number of people have bought airport bonds to lend support to the international airport project, and many of our nationals abroad have also begun banking some of their savings in our local National Commercial Bank. More specific information on all of this can, of course, be obtained from our embassies or from the friendship societies.

Finally, I would mention that if your readers happen to be living in a country — and I'm thinking of one country in particular — that is especially hostile to Grenada and may well be thinking of sending mercenaries or its own armed forces to invade our country, or if they have reason to believe that such plans are well under way, then actively organizing to show their resentment, their resistance, would be very useful. In fact, that kind of international solidarity has been quite critical to several countries in the past, certainly for Vietnam, where it was one of the decisive factors in ending the war, and also for Nicaragua, and today for El Salvador. We feel the continuation of that kind of opposition by people living in metropolitan centers is of the highest order of importance for the defense of the rights of all progressive countries and peoples engaged in struggles around the world seeking to win their independence or national liberation or to continue to consolidate and build their own internal processes. Certainly such assistance would be one of the most concrete and practical ways in which peace-loving, democratic, and progressive people can ensure the forward march of progressive movements around the world.

Imperialism Is the Real Problem

July 13, 1981

The following address was given to the Organization of American States Conference on the Development Problems of Small Island States, held in St. George's. It is printed in Maurice Bishop, Selected Speeches *1979-1981.*

Distinguished guests;
Sisters and brothers;
Comrades:

It is a great pleasure for me even at such short notice — in fact, about one hour's notice — to have the opportunity of addressing this very important conference this morning.

You should have been hearing Comrade Bernard Coard, our deputy prime minister and minister of finance and planning, but unfortunately Comrade Coard has not been enjoying the best of health in the last few days and as much as he would have liked to be here this morning, he just could not make it. I express his regrets and his best wishes to you.

Comrades, the question before us during this conference will be the question of the problems of small island and other developing states.

The problem of smallness of economies, land sizes, and resources of developing Third World countries like Grenada is a problem which has been addressed on several occasions by several eminent people over the years.

It is a matter that has been looked at exhaustively in the United Nations, in the Organization of American States, the Nonaligned Movement, and at several other international forums. But it is a matter which has not lost its importance and I am sure you will agree that there are several ways in which the subject can be approached.

My approach this morning will aim fundamentally, not at looking once again at the numerous structural problems which small countries like ours face, but at trying to look underneath that, to see what are the underlying realities, what are the real reasons for the difficulties that small developing Third World states, which are very often also nonaligned states, have to face.

My own approach this morning will probably not be an entirely orthodox one, but we feel very strongly that this approach is nonetheless a valid and indeed the correct one.

We contend, comrades, that the real problem is not the question of smallness per se, but the real problem is the question of imperialism. The real problem that countries like ours face is that on a day-to-day basis we come up against an international system that is organized and geared towards ensuring the continuing exploitation, domination, and rape of our economies, our countries, and our peoples. That, to us, is the fundamental problem.

We certainly can see that if, even briefly, we look at the history of exploitation of countries like ours; this will give us a clearer idea as to why we in Grenada maintain this position.

If we examine our region carefully, we will see that as long ago as 1812, the ruling circles in the United States of America, in pursuit of more land, in pursuit of expansionist ambitions, declared war on Canada and tried to seize all of the country to add to their own country.

A few years later, in the 1840s, the ruling circles in the United States were at it again. On this occasion, they invaded Mexico and seized over half of the territory of the people of Mexico. What is today known as California, Texas, New Mexico, and parts of some other states were once part of the sovereign territory of Mexico. In fact, on that occasion, the actual amount grabbed — if my memory serves me right — was 2.3 million square kilometers of Mexican territory.

In pursuit of these expansionist ambitions, in 1898, the ruling circles in the United States bombed their own battleship in the harbor of Havana in Cuba, which was then a Spanish colony. They used that crime to argue that Spain had committed an act of aggression against the United States, and on this fabricated pretext, war was declared on Spain with the true aim being to seize Cuba, Puerto Rico, the Philippines, and other areas in the world.

In World War I, which started in 1914 and ended in 1918, the United States waited until it was clear as to who would win the war, and then they joined the war against Kaiser Germany in 1917, to see how they could share in the booty of that interimperialist war.

During World War II, powerful elements within the United States ruling class were debating seriously on which side they should enter the war — whether to join the fascist Nazi Hitler against most of humanity, or to join the allies. The decision was eventually made for them when the bombing of Pearl Harbor occurred, when the Japanese fascist allies of Hitler attacked the United States itself.

Later on, still in the 1940s, they tried to seize North Korea and even toyed with the idea, under General MacArthur, of invading China in the early 1950s, but the people of those two countries gave them a sound beating and sent them back to South Korea.

They took over colonialist control of Vietnam from the French colonialists in the early 1960s, having helped to finance the French wars against the people in Vietnam, Laos, and Kampuchea. And, as we know, after years of heroic struggle the Vietnamese people were able finally in 1975 to run the United States imperialists back to their country.

In more recent times, in alliance with South Africa, they tried through CIA puppets to seize Angola in 1975 and 1976, but once again they faced defeat.

Right here in our region in Latin America and the Caribbean, the U.S. has intervened through direct military force in different Latin American and Caribbean countries over 135 times in the past 100 years, a situation which historically was reinforced by the Monroe Doctrine of 1823. We can recall Arbenz in Guatemala in 1954, Cuba in 1961, and the Dominican Republic in 1965, as examples of U.S. military intervention.

History is full of such examples, recent and not so recent, of these aggressive imperialist invasions.

What can we conclude from all of the above?

We believe it is fair and correct to draw the conclusion that the ruling circles in the United States, the big monopolies, the military-industrial complex, and the different ruling parties which have fronted for them have always sought and continue to seek to seize everybody's land, to exploit everybody's wealth, and to rule everybody's country. Where they do not rule directly, like in the case of Puerto Rico, they rule through stooges and puppets like Gairy and Somoza, the Duarte junta in El Salvador, Duvalier, Pinochet, Park Chung Hee, Holden Roberto, Jonas Savimbi, Bokassa, or like so many other similar names that we could go on calling for the rest of the morning.

They stop at absolutely nothing to achieve this in all countries of the globe, but what I think is particularly important for us to observe this morning is that their methods have had to change over the years.

The dramatic change in the world balance of forces was brought about by the triumph of socialism in many countries, the success of the decolonization process and the victories of the national liberation movement worldwide, and the growing importance of the working class in the capitalist countries. These factors combined together have meant a shift — a fundamental and irreversible shift — in the political, diplomatic, economic, and military balance of forces in the world, and have strengthened the voice and role of world public opinion. This has forced the imperialists to move from direct overt action (from the direct landing of marines) to covert action, to the development of different techniques of destabilization which are used against countries like ours.

These techniques of destabilization, which have been shaped and developed to a fine art by the Central Intelligence Agency, have been well documented over the years. They have taken several different forms;

there has been propaganda destabilization, there has been political destabilization, there has been industrial destabilization, there has been economic aggression, mercenary invasion, and of course, there has been the assassination of several leaders of progressive countries or parties.

The new last resort, which once again is becoming very current, is the use of mercenary forces instead of regular troops, while pretending these mercenaries have nothing to do with the country which has allowed them to use its soil as a base. But, we know that no mercenary force can mobilize, train, procure supplies, find arms, or leave the particular base from which they have been training, without the knowledge of the particular country which has allowed them to use their soil for training.

In recent months, our country Grenada, a small, poor, developing, nonaligned, Third World country has been feeling the full brunt and impact of these techniques of destabilization aimed against us.

Economic warfare, as is well known, has been openly declared against our country. In fact, United States imperialism has embarked on a coordinated campaign of economic strangulation of Grenada. This is designed to deprive our country of access to financial resources from bilateral, regional, and international sources.

The tactics used by the imperialists include the following:

Firstly, we saw the attempted sabotage of the European Economic Community–hosted cofinancing conference to raise U.S.$30 million that were and still are vitally needed for the completion of Grenada's international airport project. The United States in this case vulgarly pressured Western European governments to boycott the conference.

We saw, secondly, direct interference by the United States director on the Board of Directors of the IMF, resulting in the blocking of Grenada's application for an IMF extended loan facility. These funds are absolutely necessary for the implementation of numerous capital projects in agriculture, in agro-industry, in tourism, in housing, and in other important areas of the economy.

Thirdly, due to political interference by the Reagan administration, the World Bank has refused to endorse Grenada's public investment program, thus preventing the country's access to International Development Agency (IDA) funding — totaling over U.S.$3 billion — funding which was earmarked for the international airport.

Additionally, U.S. machinations have contributed to the vetoing of Grenada's application for a loan under the IMF funds, as earlier mentioned.

Everybody in this room will certainly remember the obvious fourth example. Everybody in this room will certainly know that recently the United States tried to exercise political pressure on the Caribbean Development Bank [CDB], pressure aimed at getting the bank, in violation of the principles of its own charter, to accept money on condition that Grenada be excluded.

It must be noted here that there was absolutely no reason why such money could not have been given on a bilateral basis, a position that Grenada fully supports. But instead, an attempt was made to subvert a multilateral regional institution, an institution that was developed over a period of several years of struggle by small developing Caribbean countries seeking to attain greater collective force and strength in the world. In other words, the aim was divide and rule, the aim was to try to subvert and divide regional institutions; the aim was not really to provide assistance to any of these countries.

We know too, comrades, that recently a major propaganda campaign has been mounted against our country. Perhaps the very best example of the grossness and vulgarity of this campaign can be gauged from the CBS television program, a program in which this United States television crew came to our country, pretending that they were interested in filming the international airport rally held here two months ago, when instead their real aim was to come to try to find the material on which they could spread their filthy, preconceived propaganda, propaganda which was aimed at trying to stop tourists from coming to our country. Further, it was aimed at psychologically preparing the people of the United States for the eventual invasion of our country. This massive campaign also has the objective of seeking to isolate Grenada in the region and the world.

A major reason for the propaganda campaign is to block our possibilities for external assistance. The evidence for this is massive. We have seen it in relation to a project earmarked for Grenada that was being organized by the Caribbean Tourism Research Centre. We have seen it in the attempts made by the United States to block the EEC cofinancing conference. We have seen it in relation to the request for hurricane rehabilitation assistance when, once again, the United States, in offering money to the Windward Islands Banana Association (an association comprising Grenada, Dominica, St. Vincent, and St. Lucia), offered that money only on terms that excluded Grenada, which was also damaged by the hurricane.

And it must be pointed out that this request was made, not by our government, but by a regional organization of banana farmers in the Windward Islands. We have seen it, of course, in the recent CDB attempt which I have just mentioned.

But we should also note, and some of us may not know, that over the past four to six weeks this United States administration has taken to summoning different Latin American and Caribbean governments to Washington and there put pressure on them, using on the one hand bribery, and on the other hand threats to try to force them to agree to their plan to isolate our country.

We have also seen recently that two governments in the region were offered money for a particular project on condition that they would only receive this money if they first made a public statement agreeing that Grenada should be excluded. It is to the merit of those governments that they refused to go along with that call.

We have also seen in our country, as part of these techniques of destabilization, a massive campaign of terrorism against our people. This was evident in the June 19 bomb blast, a blast which was in fact aimed at the entire leadership of our party, government, and revolution. There is absolutely no doubt at all that the hand of the CIA was in that bomb blast.

We saw it too, on the 17 of November last year, when terrorists financed and supported by the CIA, in one night, killed five of our patriots, four in an ambush of their car, and the other comrade a few hours later, in a militia camp in St. Patrick's.

We have also seen recently, comrades, as part of this campaign of terrorism, an organized plot hatched in the United States that sought to use local reactionary and unpatriotic elements as the first stage in a wider plot aimed at overthrowing the revolution. They were made to pretend that they were launching a new newspaper, when, in fact, the newspaper was but stage one in that wider plot which had at least eight separate but related stages, all aimed at overthrowing our government and revolution.

We have seen recently also a campaign to stir up political and industrial unrest within the country; to mobilize the parasites, the opportunists, the criminal elements which every country in the world would have, elements who, over the years, have shown their willingness to be used by the CIA.

We believe very strongly in Grenada, and our government very fervently maintains the position, that the time has now come when economic warfare must also come to be regarded as a serious breach of international law. In just the same way that when countries send their marines and troops into other people's countries, it receives international condemnation and is regarded as an outlaw act, we feel that the time has now come when economic warfare and economic aggression must also be elevated to the same level, must also receive similar condemnation from all forces internationally.

We feel that a number of important international principles are violated whenever there is a concerted, systematic campaign of economic aggression against any country. Certainly, the well-known principle of noninterference in the internal affairs of other states is being violated. Certainly the principle that every country has a right to its full independence is being violated; certainly more than one aspect of the meaning of self-determination, another principle of international law, is also being violated. But perhaps most fundamentally of all, and the most hidden principle of all, is the violation of the right of all countries to develop their own processes, free from all forms of interference, all forms of duress, and all forms of intimidation by any outside country. At least, these four basic and fundamental principles of international law and international custom are being violated, whenever acts of economic warfare are waged against any country.

We certainly believe very, very strongly that economic warfare is increasingly being developed as a substitute for, or at least a major complement to, the direct landing of troops, and therefore it is as bad as the landing of troops.

We feel equally that the entire world must begin to condemn propaganda destabilization as also being against the principles of international law, international custom. This is so because propaganda war can never be taken in isolation, and propaganda destabilization, violence, and terrorism, usually help to lay the psychological and material basis for an invasion to come. Propaganda warfare inevitably must affect the economic development of poor developing countries like ours.

Certainly, in the context of Grenada, a CBS television documentary containing as many lies and as much filthy propaganda as this one did, must have the effect in the short run of helping to keep tourists away from our country.

We also believe that the world must move to condemn attempts at political and diplomatic isolation aimed at trying to force other countries to toe their line; this form of political and diplomatic attack must equally receive the condemnation of the international community.

Needless to say, our position also is that the same must apply to those who allow their countries to be used to train and supply mercenaries. In such situations, not only must the mercenaries be condemned as international outlaws, as pirates in the international community, but also those who harbor the mercenaries, they too must feel the full weight of international public opinion.

We can well ask the questions: How can we plan? How can we develop? How can we economically grow and satisfy the needs of our people when we are under several types of warfare directed by the biggest and mightiest country, which is right at our doorstep, and when we ourselves are one of the smallest and poorest countries of the world? With fascist cynicism, this mighty country of over 220 million people, with the greatest wealth and armory of any single nation, decides, consciously and openly, to crush our tiny nation of Grenada. Can we do anything in this situation?

We believe that even in this grim situation that we face, a fight back is possible, and we feel that that fight can take place on two fronts.

In the first place, it will come from the unity and the determination of our people to fight to make a better life for themselves. That is extremely important, the unity of our people. This unity, this organization and mobilization of our people, this raising of the consciousness of our people, this increasing vigilance of our people; this unity, this organization, this consciousness, this vigilance is our first and greatest weapon.

We can also fight back successfully if, instead of having to face Grenada, a small country of just over 100,000 people, the imperialists are made to face a force of 3 billion strong as we build a powerful, worldwide anti-imperialist alliance in defense of our independence, our freedom, and our right to choose our own path. This, we feel, is certainly possible and is precisely what is required to deal with the situation that countries like ours face today. The full weight of world public opinion and international solidarity can and will make a big difference.

Some of you may still be asking the question: How is all this relevant to an OAS-PRG conference on small states, and the problems of such states? Our answer is that it is relevant because the key obstacle holding back the aggressive development of our countries is not the physical fact of smallness. The key obstacle is imperialism. That is the major problem.

We say it is relevant because whilst it is undoubtedly important to focus on the problems which small countries like ours have to face, that it is useless, that it is a total waste of time unless we also acknowledge the fundamental truth we will never break out of dependence until we work out joint strategies to break our dependence on imperialism.

We feel it is relevant because, whilst we will all agree that objectively, smallness is a problem, that while we will all agree that our lack of access to markets is a problem, and that there are several other problems, serious problems, which hinder the development of our economy, nonetheless, we insist that none of these are the real problems. The real problem is that United States imperialism, the United States ruling class, has always wanted to rule the world, has always wanted to grab everybody's land, has always wanted to grab everybody's resources; and that, with every shift in the balance of forces in the world, they have had to come up with new techniques, they have had to shift their tactics, they have had to move to overt action, like the landing of marines, to covert action — like the development of economic, propaganda, and mercenary techniques of destabilization and aggression. To us these are the real problems.

To us, therefore, in Grenada, while we are very, very happy to welcome you all, while we certainly look forward with great anticipation to the technical results of your conference, we nonetheless issue this caveat from the beginning, that if this conference were to produce yet again only more documentation of a technical character, emphasizing the usual structural difficulties which small countries like ours face, then the conference would not have achieved enough. For this conference to be truly successful, to be really meaningful to the people of the region and people of the Third World who find themselves in these difficulties, we must begin to show a new way forward by addressing what is the underlying and substantial cause of the problem that countries like ours face; and that problem is not the fact of smallness per se. That problem is the fact of imperialism.

I therefore formally declare open your conference and wish you the very best in your deliberations. I certainly hope that you will find the time during the period which you have in our country to enjoy our modest hospitality, to experience the warmth and friendliness of our people, and to feel and see the beauty of our country, and to see for yourselves the popular participation of our people in the new process that we are struggling to build.

Thank you very much. [*Applause*]

The U.S. Has Embarked on a
Massive Offensive

July 23, 1981

Opening address to a meeting of the Socialist International's Latin American and Caribbean Committee, held in Grenada July 23-24.

Comrades:

In the name of our party and our people, I welcome you all to our country; I welcome our member parties, observer member parties, and guests of the Socialist International Regional Conference.

We in Grenada, comrades, we of the New Jewel Movement, value very highly this opportunity to host a meeting of the Socialist International committee for Latin America and the Caribbean, in our free country. Our party is a party of patriotic, democratic, progressive, revolutionary, and socialist Grenadians, and we certainly consider it a high honor and a privilege to host this meeting at a time so critical for the region. In doing so, our party is fulfilling our duty as an internationalist, revolutionary, working people's party of the Grenadian masses.

We regard this conference as significant because it is the first time that the Socialist International committee for this region is meeting in the English-speaking Caribbean. This demonstrates, on the one hand, the truly international character of the Socialist International and, on the other hand, meeting here in Grenada demonstrates once again the fact that the English-speaking Caribbean is becoming more and more integrated into the worldwide social, economic, and political anti-imperialist movement.

We believe that this meeting at this historical juncture is also significant for a second reason. And that is because it is being held at a time when there are determined popular uprisings in Latin America and the Caribbean. The fundamental character of these upheavals is that they are the people's cry; the people's fight for democracy; for democratic participation and decision-making; for world peace and genuine development; for justice and for the overthrow of bankrupt, decadent, colonial, neocolonial, and imperialist domination.

This meeting comes at a time when not only our region, but the world in general is facing a tremendously difficult period. The present United States administration, as all of us know only too well, is set at this point on trying once again to rule the world; on trying once again to dominate the region totally; on trying once again to reintroduce an atmosphere and a position of cold war in this region and in the world. The desperate attempts we have seen recently to launch a mini–Marshall Plan, together with the numerous special trips to this region by U.S. government officials instigating Caribbean disunity and trying to bring about the isolation of the Grenada government and people; the increases in military, paramilitary, and so-called security aid in the form of credits and otherwise; the near-panic rush to give unlimited license to the private sector in the region; the numerous spy flights, certainly over countries like Grenada; the increase in military intelligence and other covert action; the open and active wooing of select Caribbean leaders; the increased CIA support for industrial, political, and counterrevolutionary action in some capitals — all of these, I think, can help to underline the present massive offensive which is being made against the Caribbean region at this time.

Comrades, all sorts of different pretexts are being used to justify these present attacks. We have heard concepts of "international terrorists." We have heard concepts of "enemies of democracy." We have seen that there are attempts to reintroduce a concept of "linkage," a concept that is itself linked to the "spheres of influence" idea, that so many progressive peoples and countries around the world have been seeking to throw out of history.

On the international front we have seen stepped-up pressures in southern Africa, particularly at this time, where a Western alliance led by the United States is presently trying to stop the people of Namibia, under their vanguard SWAPO, from attaining their true independence. We have seen continued racist and imperialist attacks against the sovereign territories of Angola and Mozambique, we have seen too the recent maneuvers around the question of the Springbok rugby tour from South Africa to New Zealand, and the right given to these Springboks to freely transit through the United States. We have seen warm visits being made to the United States by leading South African officials. In fact, on several fronts, it is quite clear that the difficulties that our comrades are facing in Africa, particularly in southern Africa, are difficulties which they will continue to face for some time. Therefore, the continued militant support and solidarity of the Socialist International and other democratic, peace-loving, and progressive forces are demanded more than ever at this time.

Again on the international front, we have seen in recent times the stepped-up attacks against the Lebanese and Palestinian people; we have seen the illegal bombing of Iraq's territory by Israel — all of these, no doubt, as a direct result of the fact that they have received the "go ahead" to move in this direction.

For all of these reasons, internationally and, of course, regionally — where the situation in El Salvador continues to be a major concern for the people of the region, and more and more it is becoming clearer every day to the Latin American and Caribbean masses that the majority of the people of El Salvador are definitely opposed to the junta and the military which are presently waging this war of genocide against them — it is more and more obvious that these are dangerous days. In this situation, daily solidarity for the people of El Salvador and their leading organizations, the Revolutionary Democratic Front and the Farabundo Martí National Liberation Front, is an absolute necessity.

Comrades, the economic situation in the region is also a matter of serious concern. Apart from the usual problems that we face — problems associated with unseasonal weather; problems associated with hurricanes; problems associated with the outbreak of disease — for example, right now many countries in the region are once again threatened by another outbreak of dengue fever. But, over and above all of that, certainly the major problem in the region today, on the economic as on the political front, is the question of United States imperialism and the exploitation that imperialism continues to impose on the people of this region. The blatant, the vulgar, the crude attempts to try to stop the peaceful and progressive development of the region can certainly be laid firmly and squarely at the door of imperialism.

The agenda that we are going to be looking at over these next two days is therefore an agenda that has tremendous concrete and immediate relevance to the actual situation in our region. This morning over the next two and a half hours, as we examine the question of present developments in the region on the economic and political front, we will be looking in a very concrete way at some of these problems, and the New Jewel Movement certainly hopes to make a contribution to that discussion later on in the morning.

This afternoon, likewise, when we consider the question of democracy and different aspects and concepts of democracy, and in particular as we focus on the question of ways of involving our people in a popular participatory manner in the running of the affairs of their own country, we believe that once again the experiences that we will share and exchange will be very valid and important experiences. These will, no doubt, help all of us to work out better approaches, better strategies, better structures and forms and methods for ensuring that our people can be involved, not just on an occasional five-year basis, but on a daily basis in running the affairs of their own country.

Tomorrow, when we get to the third agenda item and look at the present situation in Grenada, we will attempt to review the concrete reality of today's Grenada. We will examine in historical terms what we had to contend with on the morning of the revolution; what the continuing problems and difficulties are; and what are the attempts being made by our party and government to try to bring about a rapid increase in the quality of life of all of our people. We will in that period attempt to show that certainly the United States has embarked on a massive offensive against our country.

This has taken several different forms. One aspect of it is propaganda destabilization, and there has been a really massive campaign going on for the past six months in particular. We have some examples of it in recent times. A CBS television team came to our country pretending to be filming the new international airport being constructed here. In reality, the intention of that television team was to put together a massive piece of fabrication, aimed at trying to discredit our people, our government, and our country.

Also, in a film produced by the American Security Council in January called *Attack on The Americas*, not just Grenada, but also Nicaragua, Cuba, and other progressive countries in this region were viciously libelled in an attempt to try to discredit them; and in the case of El Salvador, in an attempt to make the heroic freedom fighters of that country appear like terrorists, something that is of course far from being the reality.

As part of this propaganda destabilization, we have also seen that recently the United States International Communications Agency summoned to Washington Caribbean journalists from every English-speaking Caribbean country except two — one of them, of course, being Grenada. In that meeting, the attempt was made to try to establish a basis for getting some of these journalists to embark on a massive negative propaganda campaign against the Grenada revolution. And the success of that attempt can be gauged by the fact that within days of their return from this conference, called by the United States International Communications Agency, several of these newspapers in the region — the *Guardian* and *Express* of Trinidad, the *Advocate* of Barbados, the *Chronicle* of Dominica, the *Gleaner* of Jamaica — embarked on another round of vicious editorials, aimed at trying to discredit the Grenada revolutionary process.

Only three weeks ago in New York, in Brooklyn and Manhattan, the third survey since the revolution was done by our comrades in New York. This survey took the form once again of getting people to contact different travel agencies and tour operators in the New York area inquiring about holiday trips to Grenada. Twelve of the eighteen agencies approached made it clear that Grenada was not a safe place to come, that Grenada (as they put it) was a Soviet and Cuban proxy, and went out of their way to try to stop these tourists from coming to our country. When pressed, several of them admitted that this information was given to them by the State Department. There is absolutely no doubt at all that on the propaganda front there is a total offensive. This is also true on the economic front.

Not only has the American government moved to block assistance to our government, but even to the banana farmers in our country — banana farmers who belong to a Caribbean association called the Windward Islands Banana Association made up of Dominica, St. Lucia, St. Vincent, and Grenada. Through this association, a request for hurricane rehabilitation assistance was made and that assistance was given only on the condition that Grenada was excluded!

We have seen too that when we approached the European Economic Community countries in an attempt to get further financing for our international airport, the United States administration embarked on a massive campaign in European capitals. This was aimed at trying to stop the EEC countries from attending the conference; at trying to dictate foreign policy for these European countries; at trying to tell these European countries how they must use their own resources. This campaign was not only aimed at stopping the international airport, but at ensuring that all attempts made by our government and our people for obtaining economic assistance to develop our country in this period of national reconstruction must be smashed.

We have seen this also through successful attempts by them to get the World Bank not to approve capital programs for our country, programs that are undoubtedly very sound technically. We have seen it also in U.S. attempts to stop the International Monetary Fund from giving an extended fund facility to our country. Notwithstanding the fact that this application had gone right through the entire system of the International Monetary Fund and the technical experts in the IMF had made it clear that our proposals were extremely sound technically, yet only two days before this application was due to get to the Board of Directors, the United States member on the Board of Directors vetoed the project and had it taken off the agenda.

In the last few weeks the United States administration made a direct approach to the Caribbean Development Bank, a regional institution created after years of struggle to serve the people of this region, to accept U.S.$4 million in grant monies to what is called the lesser developed countries of this region on the basis that Grenada be excluded. So far this attempt has been unsuccessful. Our friends in the region, different countries in CARICOM, stood up to this latest blatant attempt on the part of the United States administration to divide and rule the region and to attempt to subvert this Caribbean regional institution. We certainly want once again to thank our sister islands for the solid stand that they have taken on this occasion. These different attempts have extended not only to the areas I've described but to several other areas and to virtually every organization to which we belong. Attempts are now being made by the United States to block whatever sources of funds or possibilities of technical assistance we can obtain from different regional and international agencies or organizations. Truly what we are now experiencing is an all-out economic aggression plan, a plan of total economic warfare directed against our country.

Linked to all of this is the continuing problem that not just Grenada but other countries in the region face (both progressive and nonprogressive) — that is, the problem of mercenary invasion. We have seen in the past few years different attempts against the government of Barbados and more recently against the government of Dominica. We have seen too the attempted use of mercenaries against our friends in Suriname in 1980, and of course right now on United States territory in Miami, mercenaries being openly trained in camps are giving interviews on radio and television boasting that they are being trained for possible use in Cuba, Nicaragua, and Grenada. It is quite clear that this threat of mercenary invasion is a real handicap, a real fetter, a real obstacle in the path of peaceful and progressive development of the people of our region.

We must believe very strongly that the time has now come when we must move to elevate the question of propaganda destabilization, of economic aggression, of mercenary invasion or the threat of mercenary invasion, to the same level that world public opinion has already elevated the question of the direct landing of marines. The time has now come, in our view, when international public opinion must be so mobilized that not only when marines land in somebody else's territory, but also when there is evidence of a systematic and concerted plan of propaganda destabilization, of economic aggression, or of political and industrial destabilization, or of mercenary threat, there must also be a great outcry. Even if that mercenary threat consists only in allowing your territory to be used for the training of mercenaries or for them to solve their logistical problems, for them to procure their supplies, and as a possible base from which they can move to invade a particular country. We feel that the time has now come when international public opinion must also launch a similarly strong protest, and take strong, firm, and decisive action in condemning any such attempt; because, given the realities of today's world, it is not as easy for aggressive warlike forces to send their marines directly. Now they can no longer use overt action as much, but more and more they are forced to use covert or more hidden action in the form of one or the other of their various techniques and tactics of destabilization and aggression.

The world balance of forces has changed because of the emergence of the socialist world, the victories of the national liberation movements, the strength and growing force of the working class in the capitalist countries internationally. For factors and reasons like these, the voice of international public opinion is now raised on a regular basis whenever it is alerted to any serious threat or any serious danger to progressive forces around the world.

Certainly one of the major tasks that the Socialist International will have in this period is to devise the most creative methods and ways of exposing covert attempts by imperialism to try to subvert, to sabotage, to destabilize, and to roll back popular processes around the world.

We in Grenada, comrades, we in our party are very happy in particular to welcome the member parties that have traveled hundreds of miles and have come from Europe and North America. We are particularly happy to welcome Comrade Blanca from the French Socialist Party — we welcome you to our country and again salute the victory of your party in the recent election. We have no doubt that your historic victory will be a positive force for peace and progress. We welcome too our friend and comrade from Sweden. The Swedish Socialist Party has over the years played a very dynamic role in the Socialist International and we are confident that that role will continue. To our friend from Canada, from the New Democratic Party, we also extend a special welcome, and likewise to the member parties from the United States of America.

From our own region, like Comrade Carlsson, secretary-general of the Socialist International, I hope that I will be forgiven if I single out one particular delegation for special mention and that is the delegation from Suriname. For several reasons, Suriname, like Grenada, is a country that is beset by many problems; it is a country that is undoubtedly at this time facing several threats of aggression; it is a country that at this time is trying under the new administration to build a progressive, meaningful, popular, and democratic process inside of its country. And in our country today we have not just ordinary members of the leading forces in Suriname, but we have in fact the leader of the Surinamese revolution, the commander-in-chief of the armed forces of that country, so therefore I particularly want to welcome Lieutenant Colonel Desi Bouterse and his delegation.

Comrades, I am sure during the period that you will be here, apart from these deliberations, important as they are, you will have the opportunity of seeing our country. Certainly we would make every effort to ensure that you are able to move around as much as possible and therefore to experience on the ground in a real light what our people are trying to do in Grenada today; to see in a real light the new democracy that we are trying to build; to experience with our ordinary working people the new processes and the new structures which they have established over these past two years. I certainly hope that all of you will attend the public meeting which our party is hosting at the Market Square in St. George's tonight. On that occasion, not only will you be able to meet with our people, to experience their warmth, their friendliness, their unity, their discipline, and their militancy, but equally, we know that our people will be very anxious to give you all a very warm welcome, and to hear from you personally about the problems and some of your own experiences in your particular country.

I would therefore end by thanking the comrade secretary-general of the Socialist International, Comrade Bernt Carlsson, an outstanding comrade, who has been over several years the leading force in the Socialist International administratively and in other ways. We thank the comrade not only for all of the efforts he has made over these past few months in helping to arrange this conference, but also for all of the work he has done in the past two days in ensuring that the meeting itself over the next two days will be a success.

We thank the secretariat of the Socialist International and the members of the regional committee who have come to our country, and in particular, Comrade Héctor Oqvelt of El Salvador, another comrade who has been quite outstanding in the Socialist International over these past two years, and who we have no doubt at all will continue to make a great contribution in helping to ensure that the Socialist International continues to have relevance, not only to the people of this region but to the people of the world.

We certainly believe that the Socialist International is held in the highest esteem by progressive parties and forces of Latin America and the Caribbean because of the critical and crucial role that it has been playing over these past years in supporting and defending progressive and just causes in the region. We certainly recall the support that the Socialist International gave to the Panama Canal Treaty and to the struggle of General Torrijos in Panama during that very difficult period of several years ago. We recall too the very critical support given to our friend and comrade, Michael Manley, and the People's National Party of Jamaica when the United States led an offensive against his party and government over the past five years.

We also salute today the unwavering and massive national support for free and revolutionary Nicaragua — support which the comrades in Nicaragua very highly value and cherish — and, of course, the continuing attempt being made by the Socialist International to bring about a negotiated political solution in El Salvador. We also note the tremendous support and assistance which Willy Brandt personally, and other comrades in the Socialist International have given to patriotic, progressive, democratic, revolutionary, and socialist forces in El Salvador, who are today fighting for their national liberation and their right to run their own country.

I want to thank you all for coming, and I want to say that it is a very great pleasure on behalf of our party and our government, to welcome you here and, of course, to declare the conference open.

May the Socialist International continue to play a positive role in the struggle for world peace, for disarmament, an end to the arms race, for peaceful coexistence, and for the peaceful and progressive development of all peoples!

Thank you very much.

Education Is Production Too!

October 15, 1981

The following speech was delivered at the formal opening of the 1981-82 academic year of the National In-Service Teacher Education Programme, Grenada Teachers' College. It is printed in Maurice Bishop, Selected Speeches 1979-1981.

Comrades:

Approximately one year ago we gathered in this same place to participate in an event that is now part of the history of education in the Caribbean — the launching of a new concept of teacher education. The NISTEP [National In-Service Teacher Education Program] program represents a fundamental departure from the tradition of teacher education that we have inherited in the English-speaking Caribbean. There are two main differences: (1) for the first time in our history we have a situation where the vast majority of our school teachers are either trained or in training; (2) this process of training does not, as in the past, remove the teacher from the day-to-day, practical situation of the classroom, the teacher remains a *practicing* technician, even while in the process of upgrading his or her professional skills.

The NISTEP program is a direct product of a process of consultation initiated by the revolution. In January 1980 all teachers in the primary and junior secondary sector were called together, to reflect critically upon the education system inherited by the revolution and to formulate directions for change. One need that was expressed by teachers again and again, in discussion after discussion, in workshop, and in plenary sessions, was the burning need for increased training opportunities for teachers.

You will undoubtedly recall that at this seminar the conclusions arrived at by teachers every day in their workshop sessions were carefully documented and afterwards disseminated to the schools. You will also recall that the National Teachers' Seminar was followed by a period of ongoing discussions with teachers in the redefinition of education in our country.

The launching of NISTEP just about nine months after the initial consultation with teachers was the fruit of that democratic process, a process that is not limited only to the education system, but represents in fact a major feature of our revolution.

In two and a half years of people's power, we have seen the growth of consultation with the people, a sacred principle of our party. In this period more and more of our people have become organized. There has been a steady growth of membership in the mass organizations — women's organizations, youth, farmers', workers', sporting, and cultural organizations, and a corresponding increase in the activity of the masses: more community work than ever; a phenomenal increase in the number of teams competing in this year's football league; a situation where a massive national program like the distribution of milk is carried out not by paid government employees, but by the mass organizations; the militant participation of our people in the defense of our country, so stirringly demonstrated in the successful maneuvers held recently.

The steady increase in the membership of mass organizations, the increased activity of the masses, the growing consciousness of our people — all of this represents a broadening and deepening of *popular participation*. Some of you will have heard of or actually seen copies of a book (shortly to be launched) which is an excellent documentation and analysis of this process that is under way in Grenada. Entitled *Is Freedom We Making: The New Democracy in Grenada*, and written by two outstanding comrades in the NISTEP program, it represents the type and quality of material we would like to see not just read but used in our education system.

What has this new and popular democracy made evident?

(a) It underscores the fundamental principle of our party and government: the involvement and presence of the people in all aspects of national development.

(b) The replacement of old structures of privilege and elitism by new forms which allow the increasing participation of the people in the revolutionary process.

(c) The involvement of the people increasingly calls for more, not less, education. This is why the revolution moved in the first year to reduce secondary school fees from $37.50 to $12.50, and has now made secondary education free for all students. And this is also why the revolution, in the past two and a half years, has provided over 300 scholarships for our youths to study at universities and technical institutions abroad. Popular democracy does not stand on the same ground as ignorance, myth, and superstition. Genuine democracy — the ability to participate, and the exercise of that right — implies the right to information and the critical mastery of knowledge. That is why one of the slogans of the revolution has been: "Only an educated and productive people can be truly free."

This close link between education and democracy is an obvious but profound one which can sometimes be overlooked, but which is important for you as educators to come to terms with. Can villagers participate in the improvement and control of health standards in their communities if no health education is available to them? Can parents contribute to and have a say in the education of their children if they themselves are illiterate? Can teachers perform at their best, and give our children what they truly deserve, without being trained for their profession?

Our emerging institutions of popular participatory democracy are also, for these reasons, institutions of popular education.

Workers' councils, zonal councils, women's councils are the practice of a new democracy. Just over the last ten days there have been one dozen meetings of zonal councils, parish councils, and the other blossoming organs of popular democracy in the seven parishes. Worker education classes at workplaces and in the communities serve to deepen the collective consciousness of our people — who we are, where we have come from, where we are going. Already, over 3,000 of our workers, small farmers, women, and youth are actively engaged in these classes throughout our country on a regular weekly basis. We now have weekly classes in sixty-five workplaces and thirty communities, and we confidently expect that these figures will double over the next six months.

Our people are the makers of our history, not from a self-alienating viewpoint of imperialism, but from a point of view which affirms our right to self-determination, our proud spirit of resistance, our collective determination.

At the level of the formal system of education, we have spared no efforts to realize our basic goals. Our party has always upheld certain fundamental educational principles:

(a) Education, the right of all — a right, not a privilege.

(b) Education, a continuous and lifelong process.

(c) Education, a key factor in the creation of the new Grenadian man and woman, aptly summarized in the words of José Martí: "To educate is to prepare for life."

What have we done to implement these principles? These three principles underlie all our efforts at developing a new education system.

The Centre for Popular Education extends the right of education to all our citizens who have never before been able to take up this right. It institutes the principle that one is never too old to learn, that education does not end at school leaving. Its basic conception is that the education of our working people is an urgent task of the revolution, if we are to apply new levels of science and technology in the productive process of national development.

The dramatic increase in university and technical scholarships made available by the revolution means that today in Grenada the children of the poor and working people who want to pursue higher studies can do so, at no cost to themselves, once they have the necessary qualifications. In fact it can truthfully be said that today there are more university places available than qualified nationals to fill them. This situation is not likely to persist for a long time, as the establishment of free secondary education for all will in turn make it possible for all university opportunities to be used.

Your own NISTEP is an excellent illustration of these three principles at work. First, it has set aside the idea that only a small number of teachers with "O" levels deserve to be trained for the job that they are doing. It insists that *all* of our children deserve to be taught by trained teachers. NISTEP, like all the other in-service training programs established by the PRG, is based on the principle of continuous education — the need to consistently upgrade one's level of competence in order to keep abreast of innovations and developments in a rapidly changing environment.

As teachers you are called upon to be active participants in the dynamic processes at work within the revolution.

Whom and what should education serve? Whom and what has it served in the past? I understand that in this first year of your training you have discussed this question. You have seen that traditionally education served an elite, the ruling class. It served, it *reinforced*, a whole system of privilege and exploitation.

Today, teachers are understanding that education should be a part of the process of developing a free and just society. Whom should education serve? It should serve the broad masses of working people, the producers of wealth in the society. What should education serve? It should serve the process of transformation from a colonial territory to a liberated, self-reliant nation.

In a modern education system, sisters and brothers, education *must* be related to production. There are a number of reasons why this must be so, and I would like to use this opportunity to highlight three of them.

Firstly, education must be related to production because production is the basis of any society. For Grenada to survive we must produce, and for Grenada to grow we must produce more. Education is production too! It is the worker in the cocoa, the nutmeg, the banana, in agro-industries, fisheries, and tourism that produces the wealth of our country. Without this basic production, government would have no money with which to provide the health care, the roads, the social services, and of course the education of the people. Since the development of our economy is and must be the major goal of all Grenadians, education also must play its part in increasing production. It is only as our economy develops that our education system itself can develop. Do you realize, comrades, that the average age of our farmers is sixty-two and our agricultural workers fifty-six? If our economy is to grow, we must reverse this situation and encourage more and more of our young people to work at the land, our country's true wealth.

Secondly, education must be related to production because the biggest problem facing our society at this time is the problem of unemployment. We can no longer tolerate a situation in which our youths leave school clinging to certificates which make them feel that the only job possible to them is behind some desk. We can no longer tolerate an educational system where, as has been said so often before, a child can pass from kindergarten to university and never see a cocoa tree, or a banana, or a nutmeg. Rather, our educational system must produce the skills that can be absorbed in our economy — we must produce the agriculturalists, the mechanics, the engineers, the hoteliers, the boat captains, etc., that we need to man our agriculture, our agro-industries, fisheries, and our tourism. Equally importantly, education has the function of developing new attitudes to work, new values associated with productive labor.

Thirdly, education must itself be productive because education is a very expensive business. Government expenditure on education increased from $8.8 million under Gairy to $13.4 million last year. And next year you can just imagine what the increase will be, with education in the secondary schools being free to the students, and with the additional costs the government will have to meet for salary increments, as well as for NISTEP increments for our teachers. Think too of the future, when we would have increased the number of students in our secondary schools from the present 40 percent to 100 percent!

Clearly, a country as poor as ours can only achieve these goals if the people who are receiving this education at the same time contribute to the cost of that education — if every school is doing something to teach practical skills and at the same time to earn some monies to support itself. And this is why we attach such tremendous importance to the work-study approach to education in our country.

This is also why we attach such importance to the building of Community Education Councils, involving parents, teachers, students, and the people of the community generally. We recall with particular pride the concrete contribution made by communities all over Grenada in January 1980, when sixty-six of our primary schools were repaired by voluntary labor, thus saving taxpayers well over a million dollars. Heroic as that effort was, I must tell you that an even greater effort is now required, as our schools are at present in need of over $2.5 million worth of repairs. We must now prepare ourselves to assist with the job of complete renovation which needs to be done.

So, comrades, our new education must be productive. Education and production must come together. And that must exist not only as a policy, but in practice in *every one* of our schools. If the school has land, produce crops! If it has a fridge, produce sno-ices! If it has a kitchen, pro-

duce cakes! At this point I would particularly like to take the opportunity
to congratulate the staff and teachers and students of the CSDP for the
excellent handicraft they have produced and which I notice are on display and for sale in GRENCRAFT.

Comrades, just as the old colonial, exploitative system worked to op-
press people economically, using their sweat and labor for the purpose
of bringing profits and dividends to the European powers, so too the colonial education system warped and twisted the minds of the colonized
people. It imposed institutions upon our people that were not our own,
but which were taken directly from London, Paris, or Madrid.

Perhaps the institutions which left the most permanent scars were
those associated with education. For these institutions scarred the minds
and assaulted the intelligence of our people and wore them down for centuries. We were taught to look to Europe for the answers to all our problems. Our own country was overlooked, as we were taught to stare over
the Atlantic Ocean to London for our political institutions, our drama
and songs, our poetry and literature, in the same direction as the boats
steaming north-eastwards full with our nutmegs, bananas, and cocoa,
which were carried to be sold in European markets for the benefit of
European profits. Economic and cultural imperialism became two sides
of the same coin.

So, as we in Grenada gradually build our economic independence and
cut ourselves free from imperialist domination, we are gradually realiz-
ing the need for a *cultural* independence. We are building our own very
unique democratic institutions *alongside* our new economic thrust into
fisheries, agro-industries, and diversified agricultural products. Thus
our education system and its curriculum also need to be transformed. We
need to look to ourselves, our own land and people, to be the base of that
body of knowledge and activity that takes place day by day in our class-
rooms.

Everything we do at school must not only reflect the actual world we
live in, it must create *solutions* for the problems which surround us and
harass us, it must be a *problem-solving curriculum* which zooms in on
us and our world, and no more lingers after Europe or North America. A
mathematics syllabus that gives our children the base for sciences that
can exploit our natural resources, and gives us an apprenticeship in
building our industries and agro-industries; a language-arts syllabus that
teaches our children to love and respect their own people, their workers
and farmers, to give words and meaning to their hopes and aspirations
and the basis to understand, discuss, and criticize the many dimensions
of experience and development around them; a history syllabus that
seeks to analyze the process of emancipation of our working people and
the struggles they have fought over the years, and continues to link that
with the struggles of working people all over the world; and a science

syllabus which sets out to investigate the potential in our own land and people, to establish an inventive, creative technology, whether it be bio-gas, beetle traps, new fishing techniques, the possibilities of hydroelectric power from our rivers, or the development of new strains and flavors of our jams and nectars.

We need a curriculum to practically aid our liberation, not keep us dependent on outside powers that will do nothing but exploit us. Remember, comrades, that the origin of culture itself is the land, the soil, the way we produce and feed ourselves, the way we survive and grow. We need a school curriculum that points directly to those necessities, for if we do not start that process at *school*, our new generations will grow up ignorant and incapable of developing their greatest asset — the rich and fertile soil of our land.

When we use the slogan "A new type of teacher for the new society," what do we mean? We would need to compare the way in which the teacher was told and expected to act under the colonial and neocolonial systems, to the new opportunities for carving out a new model for the teacher in revolutionary and free Grenada.

Under the colonial system, the teacher, like the school, remained isolated and often alienated from the society he or she so much wanted to serve. The school and its Eurocentric core of knowledge stood out like a fortress against the people, pumping out colonial images and values. The teacher was forced to be a propagandist for the colonial system by virtue of the curriculum he had to teach, and thus often became bitter and felt abused and exploited. And although our teachers often struggled relentlessly against this role carved out for them, the colonial grip on the economy and educational system of our country remained — although it often faltered through the live resistance of the people.

The teacher was seen as a keeper of knowledge, often like a "knowledge bank" that is closed to all new deposits. He was thought to be the expert who "knew it all" and could learn no more, particularly from his students. He became an educational overseer of his working-class pupils, one rung up the social ladder in relation to them, yet spurned and often laughed at by those more prosperous than he, those who had gone away and "made it."

The overall career objective was certification, and because certificates were mainly to be found abroad and the higher salaries that went with them, the colonized teacher was racked with a certain kind of consciousness: the visa mentality, with his body in Grenada, but his mind half in Brooklyn or London or Toronto.

And because he was seen as an *intellectual* worker, he divorced his classroom work from physical work, seeing the school as a place solely for the *head* and not for the hand, *brainwork* not work with the hand or the arm. And although, very ironically, at *home* he might work his *own* garden on a daily basis, at *school* he would not lift a single chair or turn over one sod of earth, for the school was entirely separate from physical productive work on the land.

So how does the "new teacher" differ? The new teacher espouses physical work, welcomes the idea of production in his school. He is the first to pick up a cutlass or a hoe. He is no longer an individualist, a king or queen in the classroom with his kingdom of knowledge. He is collective planner, organizing lessons with his colleagues. She is a classroom democrat, encouraging the participation and initiatives of her students. For him, certification is less important than being *useful* and *relevant* to his students. He believes strongly in discipline, but not that of the urine-soaked strap, which carries with it the memories and historical brutality of colonialism. He believes in disciplinary codes and structures that foster criticism and self-criticism, encouraging the participation of the students themselves in the resolving of their own problems. Thus he would give full encouragement to student councils, and their parent body, the National Student Council — yet more democratic creations of our revolution.

The new teacher is deeply embedded in the life of his community. He takes a leading part in the formation and organization of the new organs of democracy that are blooming throughout Grenada. She works in the CPE, he helps organize the workers' parish council, the Pioneers or the NYO. She is active in the NWO and the militia. He lends his skills of organization and discipline to the community, always seeking to raise the level of connection between the school and the community groups. She is a student and scholar of her community — as your own community studies have shown — and seeks to develop a profound and detailed understanding of its proceeds and history, as well as dynamising its future. The teacher systematically, through his active participation in community life and programs such as the CSDP, knocks down the walls and barriers that colonialism erected between the school and the people.

The new teacher knows that the school is not an island in the community, neither must it be barricaded away from the people whom it serves. It must be the *focus* of the community, the communal meeting house, the nursery of the local groups of the mass organizations, religious and community groups, or any group of social, educational, or cultural nature. It must be open to all, it is a people's resource, and the more it is used the better it would be for the community. However, *because* it is the people's property it must be loved and cared for, it must be maintained, cleaned, and treated with the respect and value that all collective property deserves.

But we are saying that we view with great concern the actions of any principals or boards who attempt to cut off access to the schools to the people or groups in their community. In our anxiety to save the wear and tear of our school buildings, we should not allow ourselves to fall into the trap of treating our buildings in the same way as some of our older folk used to treat their new hats or shoes. All of us would remember the days when our parents or grandparents would buy a new hat or a new pair of shoes, and then take them off when rain started to fall, and got a soaking as a result!

Finally, comrades, let us say that although we see the basis of education developing in our own land, our own people, our own *reality* here in Grenada and turning aside from the *mimicry* of London or New York, we are also fundamentally *internationalists*. Our revolution is a part of the international march of progress of working people, and our schools must reflect and affirm this.

We are not only an island, we are part of a region, a part of a continent, a part of a world. If there are people like ourselves, working people who are oppressed and suffering, we must know about them, we must understand that the same enemy, imperialism, is attacking them and us, and our children too must share that knowledge in our schools. Our children are flowers of our revolution, but they are also flowers of the world. Our children must know, for example, that just as we were being threatened a few weeks ago by massive American military maneuvers on the isle of Vieques, near Puerto Rico, the fishermen of Vieques, deprived of their livelihood and suffering from the same threats and tyranny as we were, were making their own protests. One Vieques comrade fisherman, put in jail in Miami for his courage, tragically hanged himself in his cell as his suffering was so great. We can understand that man's desperation, comrades, because he shared with us that same hatred of domination and military arrogance that robbed him of his land and seas and threatened to rob us of ours too. Our children must know such things, discuss such things. When we study geography, let us also study the human geography of our comrade workers and fishermen in Vieques or anywhere else in the world where our classroom concentration falls.

Or let us consider southern Africa, for I see you have mounted a small exhibition of photographs here in the college, explaining and depicting the terrifying reality of the racist apartheid system in South Africa. Do our children know what apartheid is, how it presses down upon every aspect of the lives of the South African children so powerfully expressed in those photographs? When they read or hear about sporting boycotts of South Africa, or the tools of racism like Kallicharran from our own region, serving the racists, do they understand in their brains and on their pulses what that treachery means to the people of South Africa? Do they understand what it means to the survivors of murdered families of the massacres of northern Angola or the patriots behind the wire and the slaughtered heroes of Namibia, occupied by the racist forces since 1918?

We must teach them these things, comrades; our children have a right to know the lives of their brothers and sisters all over the world, in the same way that those children in other countries have the right to know about us and our history and our revolution, as our progress here can give *them* the inspiration and hope that will eventually help to make their own triumph and victory.

In the same way, comrades, we can learn from and take courage from the insights and discoveries that have emerged through the successful struggles of our comrades in other lands. Remember how the JAMAL literacy program in Jamaica and the insights of Paulo Freire, a Brazilian, and also the Cuban experience of literacy campaigns all contributed to the development of our CPE here? And then remember how our successful CPE program immediately dispatched two young Grenadian volunteers to help our Nicaraguan comrades with their literacy crusade there. Internationalism is not just a word or a blank concept; it is an active, living, expanding energy, just like the massive growth of our own international airport, nurtured by the internationalist comradeship of Grenadian and Cuban workers working side by side. That is the truth that must come home to our children in the schools.

And let us finally consider internationalism as it affects NISTEP. Look at your tutors: you have Trinidad, Guyana, Jamaica, New York, Kansas City, London all represented here, a pooling of solidarity and expertise from many origins. Yet another example of how revolution and internationalism are inseparable components of one and the same process.

Comrades, I want to close by reemphasizing the idea that education is production too. All through our history we have produced teachers, and students who have tried, despite the walls of prejudice and domination put up against them, to serve our people, and put their skills and scientific and human learning at the service of our struggling country. These teachers have produced us, and given us the opportunity to continue the work which they achieved, and pass our strengths on to our own childen. They were producers too, producers of knowledge and progress, and it is these educators that we shall soon be recognizing and honoring, together with our most outstanding students, on the 29 of October.

Long live the National In-Service Teacher Education Program!

All power to the new teachers of Grenada!

Forward to education from the cradle to the grave!

Forward ever, backward never!

In the Spirit of Butler,
Unionize! Mobilize! Educate! Democratize!

November 18, 1981

The following speech was presented at the opening of the Third Trade Union Conference for the Unity and Solidarity of Caribbean Workers, held in St. George's. It is printed in In the Spirit of Butler: Trade Unionism in Free Grenada *(St. George's: Fedon Publishers, 1982.)*

Comrades, if we were to study the history of this country, Grenada, we would find that the central theme that has characterized the lives of our people over the centuries has been *resistance.* Our people have struggled at many times and in many ways.

From the stubborn refusal of the Grenadian Caribs to accept any colonial stranglehold over their island; through the consistent pattern of slave revolts which culminated in the mass upsurge led by Julien Fedon in 1795, which for two years brought Grenada a determined, militant independence; through the years of anticolonial agitation and the eloquent leadership of T. A. Marryshow; through the two great popular uprisings of 1951 and 1973-74 to the climax of our struggle in the March 13 revolution of 1979 — Grenadians have always resisted domination, injustice, and exploitation. Our great Caribbean poet, Edward Kamau Brathwaite, himself a Barbadian, has likened this spirit of permanent struggle to the dramatic and sublime peaks which tower along the spine of our island. And it is into this tradition of resistance that we must place the growth and development of our trade union movement.

We have produced here in Grenada perhaps the greatest, the most brilliant and audacious of pioneer Caribbean trade unionists. I am referring, of course, to Tubal Uriah "Buzz" Butler, that huge, monumental igniter of the spirit of the Caribbean masses, who, born in Grenada, moved to Trinidad to accomplish his great deeds of leadership of the burgeoning Caribbean working class. His volcanic influence there sent our entire region throbbing with a new will and resistance, which soon broke out through all our islands. But let it also be said that we produced Eric Matthew Gairy, perhaps the most degenerate and decadent manipulator and corruptor of the trade union movement that our islands have ever spawned.

Butler vs Gairy: To say them with the same breath makes one gasp! But we have seen both their traditions and disciples alive in our Caribbean. Our duty now is to strive to emulate the one and make certain that the other will never be recreated! Certainly we must also remember how Butler was sought, hunted, and hounded by British colonialism and the employing class that saw him as their greatest menace, how they imprisoned him, interned him, but could never smother or even dim his enormous determination and luster! And certainly we must also remember how his opposite lied, bribed, bludgeoned, and murdered in his path to power, and how the consequences of that misrule strewed hurricane wreckage through our nation and working people that he claimed to represent, so much so that nearly three years after the revolution that ended his sordidness forever in our country, we are still cleaning up the devastation he caused to our national life and economy.

So we have known only too well this type of bogus trade unionism in Grenada, and we have lived through the ghastly damage it caused to our country and people. And we also know how much our real, genuine, patriotic trade unionists fought against such deformity when its political arm came to power with the Gairy neocolonial dictatorship, which lasted for over two decades here in Grenada. For right through these years of struggle, our militant, selfless trade unionists fought gallantly against Gairy's terror, squandermania, and neglect of the rights of workers, even though he could also count, through that period, upon certain sections of the trade union leadership to sell out the masses at crucial points of their struggle, as he had done himself in 1951, and as the conciliators did again in April 1974.

Gairy's neocolonial dictatorship introduced several draconian laws that were clearly antiworker and were aimed at muzzling and straitjacketing any threatening action from our trade unions. The 1974 Public Order (Amendment) Act prohibited trade unions, as well as other organizations, from using public address systems. The next year he passed the Newspaper (Amendment) Act, which without just cause effectively forbade trade unionists and other workers' organizations from publishing their own newspapers. Then the Essential Services Act of 1978 was passed, particularly against the prospect of members of the Technical and Allied Workers' Trade Union taking industrial action. Significantly, the leadership of this union, notoriously inactive, did nothing to challenge the passage of a law which was designed to render them impotent. This was hardly surprising when we understand that the leadership of this union was in the hands of the same man who acted as the "research and education officer" of the American Institute of Free Labor Development in the Eastern Caribbean.

But other unions and the political leadership of the NJM fought on behalf of their brothers and sisters in this union, comrades, and when Gairy tried to extend the law to include the dockworkers — who proved to be the most militant section of the urban working class under the dictatorship — they never allowed the amendment to be implemented. For it was a common feature of those years that the workers themselves would take industrial action in the absence of or in defiance of their conciliatory leadership. This was perhaps best seen in the 1973-74 period, when the workers who had to force the hand of their leaders to strike, and simultaneously resist the propaganda and persuasion techniques of the AFL-CIO.

Comrades, it is important to note that all this activity and struggle within our trade union movement was taking place against a backdrop of massive repression that was building up in our country, in all aspects and spheres of the people's lives. The dictator was making a systematic and comprehensive attack on all the rights and freedoms that our people had campaigned for and won over the years of British colonialism. The freedom to express ourselves, the freedom of assembly, in fact the freedom to live any sort of decent life, all this was being ripped from us. The elections that were organized were rigged and farcical, a mockery of the democracy that our people truly aspired to reach. When we moved to protest or organize against the decay of life we saw against us, we were hounded by paid bandits who battered, bruised, and murdered some of our most valued and courageous comrades. Life itself was being torn away from us piece by piece in the growing fear and reality of repression.

Our youth saw desolation around them in a hopeless search for jobs. Our women faced sexual abuse and exploitation in the daily struggle to keep their dignity. A youth like Jeremiah Richardson was shot, point-blank, in the streets of Grenville because he sought to question a policeman's abuse. A boy, Harry Andrews, was killed because he climbed over a wall in a calypso tent. Harold Strachan, Alister Strachan, Rupert Bishop all heroically sought to challenge this ebbing away of freedom and the right to live, and they all fell before the horrendous rule of terror and corruption which characterized our country during those years. Our people lived in an ethos of death and tyranny, when honest people disappeared mysteriously — the fate of Inspector Bishop of the Carriacou police, or the four youths tending goats on Frigate Island. Comrades, to be an active, combative, and militant trade unionist during that portion of our history was to court this danger and violence. Militancy meant a challenge to death and an assertion of everything that was hopeful and positive and which could reconstruct life and happiness for our people.

But as the dictatorship tried to tighten its grip on the lives of the Grenadian people, more and more democratic and progressive fighters were elected to the leadership of our trade unions. By 1978 the executive of the Commercial and Industrial Workers' Union [CIWU] was demonstrating this and Gairy was answering by trying to crush the union. Resolutions were being passed by the executive against Gairy's ties with the butchers of Chile and the visit of Pinochet's torture ship, the *Esmeralda,* to our shores. The dictator realized he was not dealing with the previous pattern of pliable and opportunistic leadership. The only price of these new comrades was freedom! So he went directly to the employers, trying to persuade and bribe them to compel their workers to join *his* union, even though these employers had already signed agreements with the Commercial and Industrial Workers' Union. He also attempted to force CIWU members directly to change unions, but because of the respect they had for the consistent and principled hard work and positions of the new CIWU leadership, they were not moved.

Over the years our Caribbean trade union movement has constantly been the target of that most unscrupulous arm of imperialism: the Central Intelligence Agency. We have had rare instances of our trade union leaders consciously selling out to their silky bribes and offerings, but more usually the CIA, with its sophistication and enormous financial resources, has succeeded in manipulating and infecting unwitting trade unionists who may well have been continuing with their work with the best of intentions. In doing this, the CIA has sometimes directly infiltrated and controlled some sections of our movement, and thus forced the leadership of some of our unions to actually take antiworker positions. This has happened, we know, in Grenada, and more and more of our workers are becoming conscious of this danger to their hopes.

We saw how the CIA actually succeeded in turning back the progress of the organized workers' movement in Chile, by both open and covert activity, and we in the Caribbean must be particularly vigilant in recognizing their poison and subversion of the workers' cause, for imperialism will never rest in its resolution to crush the onward march of the progress and emancipation of our struggling people.

For on the day that the revolution triumphed, March 13, 1979, trade unionists from all over the country showed direct support for and involvement in the revolutionary events. The telephone company workers, for example, were contacting and radioing our security forces to tell them of the whereabouts of Gairy's ministers, and trade unionists and workers generally all over the country left their workplaces to take up arms to end forever the power of oppression that had constantly tried to thwart the free aspirations and genuine and constructive organization of our Grenadian workers.

Since our revolution most of the old, corrupt union leadership has been thrown into the dustbin of history, for because of their growing consciousness, our workers can now contrast and see who is bringing benefits to them and who is not, who is desperately trying to maintain the old pattern of dictatorship and who is in the forefront of the struggle to bring more democracy into our trade unions.

What we are seeing more and more in Grenada is that the objectives of the revolution and the objectives of the trade union movement in our country are one and the same. Thus, any antagonisms between them are gradually lessening and disappearing, for the revolution has set free the opportunities for the trade union movement to accomplish its tasks of building the emancipation, security, and prosperity of the working people, the identical will of the revolution itself.

Let us consider the massive rise in membership since the revolution of the most militant and democratic unions. On March 13, 1979, the Bank and General Workers' Union had some hundred members. It now has about 3,000. It has spread out from its birthplace at Barclay's Bank to the banana boxing plants, the nutmeg pools, the restaurants and hotels, the factories and workshops. Its tradition of honest and consistent struggle on behalf of its members has made it the largest union in the country.

The Commercial and Industrial Workers' Union has had over 50 percent increase in membership, the Technical and Allied Workers' Union a 60 percent increase, and the Agricultural and General Workers' Union has risen from scratch to its present level of 2,300 members.

We had a huge, symbolic demonstration of our increased trade union membership and power in this year's May Day celebrations. It was the biggest-ever May Day turnout in the history of Grenada, and the seemingly endless procession of organized workers wound around the steep streets of our capital.

Along with this sudden explosion in the membership of our unions is the emphasis the new leadership is putting on their democratization. This is very much allied to the general thrust in democracy right through our society since the revolution, in all structures of mass organizations, community groups, and the other organs of our people's power. As we have seen, before the revolution there was a tradition in some unions of few or no general meetings.

Following the revolution, we have seen a massive new interest in trade unionism as Grenadians saw new hope and strength in cooperative and collective democratic solutions to their problems. At the first general meeting of the Commercial and Industrial Workers' Union after the revolution, in July 1979, there was over 100 percent increase in the attendance. Two hundred and ninety members came and voted 246 to 44 in favor of a militant, democratic leadership as against the previous conciliatory and conservative type, even though the latter had organized and conducted the elections.

What is happening now in our country is that everybody is becoming affected by the dialectic of democratic participation that is sweeping through our villages and workplaces. Involvement in one organization or meeting leads directly to involvement in another. A worker who attends a workers' parish council hears something which he wants to bring to his trade union. So he goes to the meeting of his union, although he may not have attended one for years. And when he finds, quite surprisingly, that his union is taking a vibrant, democratic direction, he involves himself on one of its new committees or structures for fundraising, sports, or planning for educational seminars. His confidence is raised through all this activity and the speaking and organizing that goes along with it, and his appetite is whetted to join one of the mass organizations — the local party support group, the militia, house repair program, or for the sisters, the National Women's Organisation. Each organization feeds strength, power, and confidence into the next, and all of them, including the trade unions, grow in real potency and democratic advancement.

And now we see workers' parish councils splitting into zonal councils, in a new sprouting of decentralized democracy right through our nation, a reflection of a similar tendency that is happening within our progressive trade unions.

The People's Revolutionary Government has been swift to take legislative action in favor of the trade unions. All Gairy's antiworker laws were repealed and two months after the revolution, in May 1979, People's Law Number Twenty-nine, the Trade Union Recognition Law, was passed.

For the first time in Grenada's history, our workers had the opportunity to join the union of their choice, and the employer was compelled to recognize the trade union, once 51 percent of his work force were financial members. Under this law, the Ministry of Labor has to respond within seven days of the union's application for recognition, and then call a poll of workers. If the majority is shown to be members, then the union must be certified as the bargaining agent for the workers.

For, apart from Barclay's, before the revolution there were other grotesque examples of nonrecognition of trade unions. The workers at the Red Spot Soft Drinks factory had a 100 percent financial membership of the Commercial and Industrial Workers' Union in 1978, but the company still refused recognition. And it took the workers at Bata some seventeen years of struggle before they finally won recognition, so this law has changed all those old abuses and given the workers real and genuine security in making their trade unions effective bargaining agents on behalf of their workers.

For the sister trade unionists, the 1980 Maternity Leave Law has made an enormous difference to their working and personal lives. Every working woman now has the right to two months' paid maternity leave over the period of the birth of any child. And the trade unions were involved, together with the mass organizations, particularly the National Women's Organisation, and the churches, in the widespread consultation conducted all over the nation before the bill was finally passed. The Equal Pay for Equal Work Decree in the state sector has also had a profound effect on improving the wages of the sisters and leveling them up with those of their brother workers throughout Grenada — as well as increasing their general confidence to organize and struggle, side-by-side, with their brothers. For now both men and women are sharing equally in the improvement in wages and conditions being brought about since the revolution. The old, appalling working conditions and lack of facilities, like no drinking water or workers' amenities in workplaces, compulsory overtime without pay, and no job security, are now doomed. The recent successful strike of agricultural workers in the St. Andrew's parish, waged by members of the Agricultural and General Workers' Union, is proof of this. The comrades achieved their demands of holiday and sick-leave pay under the new democratic leadership of their new union.

At this moment, arising from a decision of a St. George's Workers' parish council, and based on requests from trade unions, the Ministry of Legal Affairs has prepared two pieces of legislation — a Rent Control Law to ease the burden of high rent costs for our people and a new Workmen's Compensation Act, both of which will be circulated to our unions for their comments before enactment.

Of course, you would know how closely higher productivity and trade union organization are connected.

More than two decades of Gairyism produced in our workers many negative attitudes. The new trade unionism in our country is now helping to transform such attitudes by helping to apply new incentives.

Before the revolution, our agricultural estates brought in absurdly low returns. They were making only a quarter of a million dollars, even though their yearly expenditure was nearly three million. Now, from being a national liability, they have become profitable, and the workers themselves have shared in that success, taking one-third of the profits made. This new attitude has grown through the spirit of emulation that the workers have adopted as a result of those seminars. The age of cynicism is gone in Grenada.

Workers in a revolutionary country like ours, who are under a progressive and democratic leadership in their trade unions, do *not* see trade unionism solely in a narrow, economistic sense. They do not see their responsibilities stopping only at their fundamental tasks of improving their members' wages and working conditions. They see themselves deeply involved in *all* aspects of the social and political life of their country, their region, and their world. Our unionized workers have consistently shown solidarity with all other struggling workers of the world. They see this as an internationalist duty to all trade unionists organizing for their rights and fighting for social and political justice, be they in Chile, El Salvador, southern Africa, the Middle East, or any part of the world where the producers of wealth are exploited and oppressed. They see their responsibility, likewise, with other trade unionists of the Third World, in pressing for the new international economic order that will create more favorable terms of trade between rich and poor nations and transfer wealth and technology for the benefit of the masses in countries such as ours.

Comrades, it is clear that the growing economic crisis in world capitalism is having a dynamic effect in the Caribbean. Throughout our region we see the employing class united in its attack upon trade unionism. There have been newspaper advertisements in Barbados calling upon workers there to abandon their trade unions. There have been incidents of multinational companies in St. Vincent forcing workers to sign documents pledging that they will leave their trade union. Clearly, the employers are trying to de-unionize their work forces to make them more pliable and exploitable, so we, throughout the Caribbean, must go beyond all our political and ideological differences and forge the essential unity of our regional trade union movement to combat this reactionary offensive by the employers. This is why we have to work towards the total unionization of our workers and the maximum democratization of our unions, to ensure that they are vigilant and active in the struggles against the employers, and to guarantee that the negativism and passivity that arise from undemocratic trade union structures are forever finished in our region.

We consider that in Grenada we have a critical role to stimulate and achieve this unity, because our revolution has emancipated our trade union movement to fully serve the country and help to build it, along with our party, the mass organizations, and other democratic community structures. For we are benefitting, not only from increased wages and better working conditions, unlocked freedoms, and an explosion of democracy, but also from a massively increased social wage, which makes more and more sure and profound the security of our working people, one of the prime objectives of trade unionism. Free medical treatment, pre-primary care, an eye clinic, free milk distribution, more doctors and dentists than we have ever had before, new low-cost housing and house repair schemes, free secondary education, de facto free middle-level technical and university training for all our untrained primary school teachers, a Centre for Popular Education, cheaper basic food through our Marketing and National Importing Board, loans for productive purposes through our National Commercial Bank, a vastly improved water supply system, cheaper electricity rates and less tax to pay for the poorest workers, a new international airport, a national public bus service on the way — all this has been achieved in the last thirty months. Such concrete benefits are what true trade unionists have always struggled for, and we see our trade unionists too taking a greater and greater part in this huge process of national reconstruction.

For the first time in our history, and as far as we know this step is unique in the CARICOM section of our region, our trade unions have been involved in the exercise of framing the national budget. The Public Workers' Union, the Grenada Union of Teachers, and the Technical and Allied Workers' Union were all involved in this process last year, and this year and in the coming years more of our unions will be involved. Proposals for the 1982 budget will be circularized by the Ministry of Finance in a booklet, and 50,000 of these are being printed, to be given, among others, to the workers at their workplaces for them to study and add their comments and suggestions.

This, of course, is an extension of the already existing policy of our government of *opening all our books to our workers during wage negotiations* with trade unions, giving them access to all accounts and files, so that they can see for themselves what the national budget can afford to give them, and so they can make their own assessment of what could be a realistic and equitable wage demand. This is the absolute antithesis of Gairyism, a total transformation.

This process will underline yet again that the trade union movement must be involved in *all* aspects of national development. This means planning, production, management, distribution of foods, working in the literacy campaign through the Centre for Popular Education, in the house repair program, the school repair program, the community work: democracy in all our popular and democratic programs to ensure that the benefits of the revolution reach not only its own members, but all the people of Grenada.

Finally and crucially, there is the question of national defense, particularly at this juncture when we are facing so many threats from belligerent and vulgar imperialism. Our trade unions and their members are becoming more and more involved in our people's militia, and the Trade Union Council itself, in response to the U.S. "Amber and the Amberdines" provocation and maneuvers in Vieques Island in August, issued a call for all trade unionists to join the militia and be prepared to defend the homeland from imperialist military attack.

So, comrades, what is the way forward? What are the challenges ahead of us and how must we respond? We would not want to leave this conference without having clear ideas and proposals in our heads to secure greater bonds and solidarity between us. What concrete steps can we make as a result of our discussions?

For a start we must exchange information, insights, and experiences to make more profound the trust between us, and more unified the cause and strength that binds us. And let us pledge that in the spirit of trade union democracy we hold more regular assemblies and meetings such as this one, to combine in a more coherent and purposeful way, to consoli-

236 Maurice Bishop Speaks

date our power and unity, and to coordinate our strategies to beat back the offensive against us. Our enemies are intensifying their unity, as has been seen in the recent general inter-Caribbean meetings of Chambers of Commerce, and even more pointedly, in the meetings of various army and police chiefs, with external representatives also involved.

The violence of this offensive has also been made clear in the imperialist-dominated campaign of lies, slander, and disinformation — the deliberate manipulation of half-truths and fabrications — which has been principally directed at the revolutionary countries in our region, Cuba, Nicaragua, and Grenada, and against the progressive movement of workers generally throughout the Caribbean. This campaign intensified to a particularly blatant level in May this year, when the United States International Communications Agency, the propaganda arm of the U.S. State Department, organized a conference in Washington to which were invited the editors of all the major English-language Caribbean newspapers. The editors were counseled and lectured to by reactionary congressmen, and slick American journalists taught them techniques of propaganda destabilization, with "How to Deal with Grenada" as an unlisted item on the agenda.

Within two weeks of this conference we witnessed in the region signs of a coordinated approach by all of these newspapers, in their propaganda attacks against the Grenada revolution. Articles and editorials were swapped and reprinted, and this process descended to its most vulgar depths with the appearance in five regional newspapers — the Jamaica *Gleaner,* the Barbados *Sunday Sun,* the Barbados *Advocate,* the Trinidad *Guardian,* and the Trinidad *Express* — of identical front-page editorials calling upon the governments, peoples and workers of the region to isolate Grenada and expel us from all regional groupings and organizations.

Comrades, this propaganda campaign continues unabated until this very day. We would therefore like to call upon all the delegates here, representing as they do the most active and conscious leaders of the working-class movement in our region, to condemn this monopoly control of the Caribbean media by unprincipled press magnates in league with imperialism, and support the struggle of media workers all over the world for a *new international information order* to serve our movement and our peoples, which can only be made possible through the struggle to achieve the new international economic order, the creation of which will be of particular significance to all workers in the Caribbean and Latin America.

Comrades, very importantly, we must express that all the workers of our region have a clear understanding as to why peace is in their interest and why war is such a high priority on the agenda of Reagan and the ruling circles in the USA.

At present the world capitalist system is in the midst of a serious crisis. Runaway inflation, compounded by ever-rising unemployment, has meant that for millions of workers in the industrialized capitalist economies the cost of living keeps going up, seemingly beyond control, while job security is weakened.

Almost as daily routine, factory after factory is closed down, business after business declares bankruptcy, resulting in hundreds of thousands of workers losing their jobs. Those workers fortunate to retain jobs find that their wages remain stagnant, their unions attacked and undermined by the monopolists, their rights abused, and their hard-won gains eroded.

And as the international capitalist crisis intensifies, it generates increased imperialist aggression, spearheaded by the most reactionary circles of imperialism's military-industrial complexes, who feel that the solution to this crisis is the build-up of arms, the provocation of wars, and the creation of tension spots around the world, the Caribbean region being no exception.

The struggle carried on by the world's workers for peace is strongly linked with the effects of the crisis of capitalism on their living standards. Thus one can say that the economic and social gains won through such struggle are a contribution to the consolidation of world peace, because these gains are an expression of the change in the balance of forces against the roots of all wars: monopoly capitalism and imperialism.

Ignoring the new realities brought about by this change in the world's balance of forces, however, the military and conservative circles of imperialism are trying to return the world to the cold war period and intensification of the arms race, with the planned deployment of many more nuclear warheads in Western European countries, with mad talk of limited nuclear war, and right here in our region with stepped-up military maneuvers and exercises and preparations for military invasions of Cuba, Nicaragua, and Grenada along with massive intervention in El Salvador.

The present level of military efforts puts on the shoulders of Caribbean workers and workers all over the world a very heavy burden of sacrifice, exposing the very existence of humanity to the risk of a catastrophic disaster.

High military expenditures are damaging to economic stability, slow down the rate of development, and make unemployment more acute.

The contemporary capitalist crisis and the arms race are directly connected with each other. In many capitalist countries, arms contracts provide the motive force for the industries connected with arms manufacture.

But workers must not be intimidated or resort to pessimism in the face of this bleak scenario. Hope still exists, and it resides in the struggle of all peace-loving forces for disarmament and world peace, which will make it possible for science and technology to be put fully to work for the material and spiritual enhancement of humankind.

The working class of the world constitutes the principal force of peace. Because of its role in the crucial sphere of social life and production, the working class is also the principal force of social progress.

Thus there is a direct connection between the historical role of the working class and the struggle for peace and disarmament. The Caribbean trade union movement cannot fulfil its mission of emancipating the working people of the region in a situation where imperialism is attempting to make the Caribbean into a theater of war. Genuine social and economic progress can only be achieved in an atmosphere of peaceful coexistence, cooperation, good will, mutual respect, and understanding among the region's peoples.

It is therefore an urgent imperative that the Caribbean trade union movement strongly condemn all efforts by imperialism to bring unnecessary tension to our region, and in equally strong terms support the call for the Caribbean to be declared a zone of peace.

Caribbean and Latin American workers employed by capitalist companies who do not own the means of production, because they are an exploited class, have no stake in war or in the profits deriving from the manufacture of weapons as is the case with the transnational corporations.

Peace is the workers' ideal. Historical experience shows that in the imperialist wars it is the working people influenced by the ideological hegemony of imperialism who are the victims, who shed their blood and sacrifice their lives.

But it is also the working people who have always fought against wars of aggression and who now find themselves in a common front in the struggle for peace.

In fighting against the monopolies, against the transnationals and the military-industrial complexes, the working people of the Caribbean and Latin America carry out a direct offensive against the roots of war.

In this context, the workers and their trade union organizations have a fundamental role to play. In defiance of the imperialist merchants of death, the Caribbean and Latin American trade union movement must make a clear and consistent response to Washington's aggression in this region by the unity and common action of all the trade union forces.

In these times there is an urgent need, comrades, for unity and coordinated action, for cooperation and direct alliance between the region's democratic trade unions, some with different ideological tendencies but all with the same class interests and with similar economic and social aspirations.

Warmongering in our region can only be stopped by a united and decisive workers' struggle for peace and disarmament.

Workers of our region can be heartened and even inspired by the forthright resistance demonstrated by millions of workers who have taken to the streets of European capitals in recent weeks to say a loud "no" to the war policies of the Reagan administration.

So our message today, comrades, to all our workers in our island and throughout the Caribbean, is: In the Spirit of Butler, Unionize! Mobilize! Educate! Democratize! Dynamize the trade union movement throughout our region! Let the spirit of Butler fire and inspire us! Let us seek to emulate his cause and dedication to the most sacred commitment of all — the emancipation and freedom of our working people.

We in Grenada pledge to continue to put our trade union movement at the center of the process in our country, to link all our workers in an organized relationship with democratic structures and practices, and so pump with ever-increasing vigor the vibrant blood that runs through all the organs of our revolution.

Long live the working class of Grenada, the Caribbean, and the world!

Long live the unity and solidarity of working people of the world!

Long live the spirit of Tubal Uriah "Buzz" Butler!

Forward ever, backward never!

Grenada Is Not Alone

November 23, 1981

The following address was given at the opening of the First International Conference of Solidarity with the Grenada Revolution in St. George's. The conference, held November 23-25, was attended by 112 delegates from forty-one countries. It was printed in Intercontinental Press, *December 21, 1981.*

Comrades, in the name of our party, the New Jewel Movement, in the name of the People's Revolutionary Government, and in the name of the people, the workers, the youth, the women, and the farmers of free and revolutionary Grenada, I join comrades in extending to you, our fraternal and esteemed guests from all continents of the globe, a most warm and cordial welcome. We are extremely happy to host you here on our soil and we pledge to ensure that your stay here is both productive and enjoyable.

The importance of this historic conference on international solidarity' with Grenada cannot be overstated. In the first place this conference manifests our continuing strict adherence to international principles. We have always scrupulously avoided viewing our struggle, our revolutionary process, from a narrow nationalist perspective. We have long understood that the world revolutionary process, the struggle of oppressed mankind everywhere, is one and indivisible. Thus, this international solidarity conference holds grave importance as it bears testimony to our commitment to the noble concept of internationalism.

This conference derives additional importance from the fact that your presence here will indicate to imperialism in a clear and forward way that Grenada is not alone. It will tell the imperialists in the boldest terms that their schemes, their machinations, their maneuvers to isolate the Grenada revolution have all failed miserably — as the Grenada revolution enjoys broad popular support, not only at the national level, but also internationally.

Thirdly, for us this solidarity conference is a momentous occasion, as we understand very clearly that the force and weight of international public opinion cannot be dismissed and constitutes indeed a significant factor in the struggles of the people.

Comrades, March 13, 1979, was a bright new dawn for the people of Grenada and the working people of the Caribbean. That dawn marked the end of a long dark night of terror and the beginning of a new day. Our heroic people — the anti-Gairy masses — rose to the challenge of history and, in the words of the Caribbean poet, Edward Brathwaite, "shattered the door and entered that morning, fully aware of the future to come, there's no turning back." As it has been said so often before, when a conscious, determined people rises as a united body and cries "enough," injustice, tyranny, and exploitation are doomed . . . and thus begins a new and glorious chapter in the history of man: the construction of a just and equal society by the poor, for the poor, and with the poor. The people's struggle through time for the realization of that dream is the long march of history. From the very inception of our party, the New Jewel Movement, we have been guided by the clear understanding that the struggle against the dictatorship was not an end in itself, but a necessary precondition for the infinitely larger struggle of building that new and just society.

Building the new society involves a long a difficult process of national reconstruction. Twenty-five years of Gairyism had devastated the social and economic fabric of our society. It had destroyed our country's international standing — Grenada was reduced to the laughingstock of the international community, land of a tin-pot dictator lost in extraterrestrial dreams, [*Laughter*] preoccupied with UFOs, obsessed with his divinity, but brutal and ruthless in the exercise of power. Fifty percent of the labor force of our country was unemployed. Our infrastructure was totally dilapidated. Our tourist industry was one which brought little benefit to the country. Despite our fertile soil, and with Gairy's political interference in the development of agriculture, the production of our main export crops had stagnated. Food crop production had declined, and our food import bill was approximately 40 percent of total imports. Due to the dependent status of our economy and with a combination of ineffective price controls and monopoly profiteering by merchants, inflation rates were very high. Financial mismanagement over many years had reached staggering proportions, and left the national treasury in debt to local commercial banks and in considerable arrears to local, regional, and international agencies.

Our people's revolution was therefore faced with the difficult twin task of economic reconstruction and democratization of the society.

Our fundamental objective has always been, as detailed in the 1973 manifesto of our party, the construction of a new life and new society. In June 1974 we issued a ten-point Statement of Principles. This document reads:

"We stand for: (1) people's participation, people's politics, people's democracy; (2) people's co-operatives for the collective development of

the people; (3) health care based on need; (4) full development of the
people's talents, abilities, and culture; (5) full control, as a people, of
our national resources; (6) employment for all; (7) a decent standard of
living for every family; (8) freedom of expression and religion; (9) the
liberation of Black and oppressed people throughout the world; (10) a
united people . . . a new society . . . a just society."

These principles and objectives were as valid at the dawn of our revolution as they were five years before when they were formulated, and
as they are today — almost three years after that first morning of our revolution. Already we have begun to implement these aims, although in
addition there were certain initial priorities that we set ourselves upon
taking power, based on an assessment of the most pressing needs of the
people — jobs for the thousands of unemployed, health care, the improvement of the agricultural infrastructure, mass education, and above
all, the process which would facilitate all other developments, the democratization of the society. Yet our progress has been hampered by certain objective difficulties which have prevented us from moving as
rapidly as we would wish towards the attainment of our goals.

Like our sister Caribbean islands, we continue to be plagued by natural disasters. Each year since the revolution, hurricanes, high winds, or
torrential rains have caused considerable damage to our agriculture and
infrastructure. In 1979 we suffered U.S.$6 million worth of damage —
in 1980, the total destruction of 27 percent of our nutmeg crop, 40 percent of the banana and 19 percent of the cocoa, amounting to some
U.S.$20 million. In 1981, damage to crops, roads, and bridges totaled
U.S.$5 million.

With an open, dependent economy tied to the economies of the
capitalist world, we have suffered and are suffering from the ongoing
economic crisis in the capitalist world. Demand for our principal commodity exports has dropped. World market prices for nutmegs, cocoa,
and bananas, which account for 97 percent of visible export earnings,
fell by 22 percent in 1980 over 1979. To compound a difficult economic
situation, tourism (our second most important industry) declined by 8.8
percent in 1980. This problem, which is also experienced by our Caribbean neighbors, led to reduction in foreign exchange earnings, employment, and income generation, and some stagnation in economic activity.
The decline in stay-over visits to Grenada fell not only because of the
worldwide economic recession but also because of active propaganda
destabilization by U.S. imperialism. This year, our tourist industry,
poised for recovery with full-house bookings at all the main hotels, was
dealt a major blow with the sudden destruction by fire of undetermined
origin of a substantial part of our largest hotel — the Holiday Inn. Re-
venue losses such as these serve to aggravate an already unfair, unjust,
and unequal balance of trade. Although the total volume of Grenada's

imports remained constant, the total cost of these imports between 1979 and 1980 rose from U.S.$43 million to U.S.$50 million, due largely to steep increases in freight rates and fuel as well as imported inflation from the Western industrial countries.

Another economic difficulty facing us at this moment is the U.S. economic squeeze. U.S. imperialism has embarked on a coordinated campaign of economic strangulation of our country designed to deprive us of access to financial resources from the bilateral, regional, and international sources.

These unprincipled tactics include attempted sabotage of an EEC-sponsored, cofinancing conference to raise U.S.$30 million desperately needed to ensure completion of our international airport. The determination of U.S. imperialism to squash this process is evident in its vulgar and direct interference on the executive board of the IMF and the World Bank to block loans required for vital capital investment and public investment. At the insistence of the U.S., Grenada was recently excluded from receiving financial assistance from the Windward Islands Banana Growers Association from funds provided by USAID [U.S. Agency for International Development] for banana rehabilitation.

Confronted with the belligerence of U.S. imperialism, and having the vicious legacy of twenty-five years of "Hurricane Gairy" to recover from, how has our revolution responded to the urgent tasks of national reconstruction?

In agriculture — the pillar of our economy — our main policy and tactic has been one of diversification. Diversification of agricultural export production to increase the range of agricultural commodities which can earn foreign exchange; diversification of agricultural export markets with the objective of penetrating new markets and lessening our dependence on any one buyer; diversification and expansion of domestic agricultural production for import substitution, as a basis for agro-industrial development, and the linking of the domestic agricultural sector with the tourist sector. Since the revolution, fifty times more money has been allocated in the national budget for agricultural development. In the building of the new tourism, we have also been diversifying our tourist markets through increased promotion in Western Europe, the Caribbean, and Latin American markets, while nonetheless attempting to maintain and indeed to achieve diversification in our traditional North American market.

With a 50 percent increase in our energy costs, energy conservation measures have been put into effect, resulting in a decrease in consumption by private motorists but a 20 percent increase in state consumption (mainly in the operation of equipment) on account of increased developmental activity. Several major infrastructural improvements have been undertaken: a new international airport, highway development of the east coast, the construction and opening up of sixty-seven miles of agricultural feeder roads, improvement of electricity services, vastly increased water supply, major expansion of telephone service, forestry development, and conservation. These efforts at national reconstruction and towards the solution of the main difficulties faced by our economy are the consistent and creative application of the basic program of our party as we set out in our 1973 Manifesto for People's Power and the achievement of genuine national independence. This document states — and I quote:

"NJM has always stood for *real* independence, *genuine* independence, *meaningful* independence. At our People's Convention on Independence on May 6, 1973, at Seamoon, where 10,000 of our supporters were present, our two major speeches were called 'Meaningful vs. Meaningless Independence' and 'New Directions for Genuine Independence.' This manifesto of ours sketches the things we must do as a people under new leadership to achieve *real* independence. For we believe independence must mean better housing for our people, better clothing, better food, better health, better education . . . more jobs . . . in short, a higher standard of living for workers and their children."

The seizure of state power on March 13, 1979, by the people, led by its vanguard party, the NJM, has opened up revolutionary possibilities for the implementation of that program. [*Applause*]

The revolution, with the active participation of our people, has brought concrete benefits to our working people. Unemployment has been reduced from 50 percent of the working population to less than 30 percent by the expansion of the cooperative and state sectors. The people's budget has removed the burden of income tax from the backs of the 30 percent of the lowest-paid workers. Financial assistance to the tune of $4 million has been provided to the poorest sectors of the population for house repair, and a Ministry of Housing with responsibility for a national housing program has been created. Conditions of life in the villages are being progressively improved by the construction of community centers, bath and laundry facilities, and post offices by the voluntary labor of our people in their community work brigades.

In education the revolution has made important gains: the establishment of a national literacy and adult education program, the Centre for Popular Education, the institution of free secondary education, a 300 percent increase in the number of university-level scholarships, the creation of a national in-service teacher training program for the professionalization of all our primary school teachers. The revolution has placed emphasis on the expansion of educational opportunity because our party has always recognized the fundamental link between education, the process of national development, and the construction of a participatory democracy. [*Applause*]

As in the vital areas of housing, jobs, and education, the revolution has brought concrete benefits to the masses in the field of health. A national milk distribution program has distributed 1,100 tons of milk to the elderly, to our youth, and to expectant mothers since 1979. Free health care made possible by increases in medical personnel and the expansion of services, particularly in the rural areas, has transformed the pattern of health.

The transformation of the national economy, begun since the people's revolution, has been guided by the same basic conception of an economy at the service of working people and freed from external domination and control which we proposed since 1973. It is worthy of note that the vast majority of the new programs and bold initiatives embarked upon by the revolution are not bright ideas spontaneously conceived in some moment of inspiration, but the product of collective discussion and analysis within our party and among the broad section of our people of needs, problems, and long-term goals.

On the economic front, new institutions and new programs all aimed at the strengthening of the national economy and the laying down of a sound material basis for future development are being built. The Grenada Farms Corporation — a state enterprise — has been established to coordinate the operations of all government farms. These farms, scandalously mismanaged and their produce shamelessly misappropriated during the Gairy era, are now the centers of a new thrust forward for our agriculture. More important, agricultural workers — the producers of the green gold of our country — on these state farms are learning self-management, and more and more are taking on the responsibility for increasing production. On these farms the arithmetic of exploitation has been replaced with a new language of workers' participation in the establishment of production targets, profit-sharing, and the teaching of the real history of struggle of our working people. [*Applause*]

The establishment of an agro-industrial plant now makes it possible for us to make full use of local crops which in the past were never fully utilized. Mangoes, tamarinds, soursops, guavas, to name a few, are now valuable cash crops because of the demand produced by this agro-industrial plant. Spice Island Products now embraces a proud range of juices, jams, and canned local fruit and vegetables.

Likewise, the Marketing and National Importing Board has reduced the high cost of living and broken the backs of the monopolists in sugar, rice, and cement. This body now has the responsibility to import specified commodities from the cheapest sources and ensure internal distribution at much cheaper prices than obtained previously. Like the Grenada Farms Corporation, the Grenada Resort Corporation was set up to manage government hotels and other tourism enterprises, and has been achieving modest successes!

At the same time, the organization of a national fishing fleet and the establishment of a fishing school and a fish-processing plant are all together serving to build an integrated and sound fishing industry.

Other critical measures and economic programs set up include: a coffee-processing plant to process local coffee for domestic consumption and export; construction of three bio-gas plants and the carrying out of detailed studies of our hydropower, hydrocarbon, and geothermal potential as a possible means of alternative energy; the introduction of scientifically evaluated systems of work planning in government departments and ministries to ensure productive use of government finances and as a basis for budgetary allocations; the setting up of a people's bank — the National Commercial Bank — which after just two years is already the second-largest bank in Grenada.

All of these, comrades, represent some of the initiatives taken in our attempt to place our national economy on a sound footing. We have always given priority to this task because it is a strong national economy that will guarantee the social and material well-being of our people. We have a slogan, comrades, by which the masses understand quite simply this logic, "You can only take out what you put in." [*Applause*]

But more important, comrades, more significant than all the other achievements of the Grenada revolution, because it is the means whereby we achieve all other benefits and will move to achieve even more social and economic benefits as this process unfolds, is the outstanding success of the Grenada revolution in the task of the democratization of our society.

One of the earliest acts of the revolution was the repeal of all anti-worker laws and the enactment of democratic, progressive labor laws such as the Trade Union Recognition Act, which guarantees the right of workers to form and participate in trade unions of their choice. As a result, there are nearly 10,000 workers organized in trade unions today and most of these unions are developing programs of democratic participation and education for their members.

The revolution has also taken several steps to stimulate and make possible the participation of women in the development of our nation. There can be no talk of real democracy if *half* of a nation's population is either disqualified from participation or can only participate in a very limited sense. And there can be no talk of women's participation if the conditions for this participation do not exist. Our sisters cannot participate fully unless the society encourages their participation. And in Grenada, in barely two and a half years of revolution, we have a proud record of measures taken to bring the women of our country fully into the development process.

Consistent with our slogan, "Idle Lands and Idle Hands — An End to Unemployment," in the year two of the revolution we moved to set up a

National Land Reform Commission, with terms of reference to identify existing idle lands and make recommendations for their productive use [by unemployed youth willing to work such lands cooperatively]. In like manner the preparation of our national budget has since the revolution involved the participation of trade union representatives; and this year the process of deciding how our resources will be used for our national development will involve an even wider participation. This year the budget discussion is being take to the people — our national budget will be debated and shaped not by a handful of men sitting in an exclusive "parliament," but by our organized people in their thousands, in their community groups, their zonal councils, their parish councils.

And the mention of these structures, comrades, brings us to the fact of the spectacular growth of mass organizations in our country in the two and a half years of the revolution. Our National Youth Organisation, National Women's Organisation, both founded by the New Jewel Movement, and our NJM Young Pioneers are mobilizing increasing numbers of our youth, our women, and our children. The youth organization is close to a target for this year of organizing one-third of the country's young people. Our sisters in the NWO have passed the 6,000 mark and are fast approaching their target of 7,000 (or nearly one-third of the women of the country) organized for action, participation, and community development.

The revolution has fostered the formation of student councils in every secondary school, linked into the National Students Council.

In the villages you will find community work brigades, which, in fact, determine priority needs and spearhead work on community building, cleaning, and maintenance projects.

Three weeks ago the Productive Farmers Union, one of the most unique organizations that the revolution has produced, held its first annual general meeting with its full membership of just over 1,000 small and medium farmers in militant attendance.

In addition to the many organizations and action groups operating at community, parish, and national level, our people met *regularly* with the leadership of the country in parish and zonal councils and in workers' parish councils, where the twin priniciples of the *accountability* and *responsibility* of the leadership to the people become a reality for the first time in the English-speaking Caribbean. The leadership is accountable because in its face-to-face meetings with the people it must report on the achievements and the difficulties of particular ministries and state bodies, it must answer the questions of the people on those issues which affect their lives. The leadership is responsible to the people because it must take action where the people indicate that action is required.

In Grenada the people do not only listen passively to their leaders, they talk back. They do not only glimpse their so-called representatives now and then in the press, they meet them regularly, they rub shoulders with them. In Grenada, structures have grown up and are developing daily to ensure the real participation of people — a continuous, day-by-day process, not a seasonal exercise which changes nothing. Our democratic process is our strongest weapon for change, for development, for the improvement of life in our country. [*Applause*]

There are many reasons why your solidarity with Grenada is important. There are many reasons why you must not only *feel* solidarity with the Grenada revolution but you must also *express* this solidarity loud and clear.

First of all, our revolution is an attempt to build a new socioeconomic development model. It is an attempt to solve our problems by new methods. It is the boldest attempt, in the history of the English-speaking Caribbean, to tackle the dire problems of underdevelopment which so drastically affect the lives of the mass of people in our region, the problem of poverty, illiteracy and poor education, substandard nutrition, unemployment, and all the other evils. It is an approach which rejects some of the manifestly inadequate strategies which the ruling class in most of our sister islands are still clinging to, because these strategies are guaranteed to safeguard their own position and to yield nothing but the barest minimum of political power and material benefits to the majority of the people.

Therefore, comrades, when you show your support for our revolution, you are asserting with us the right of a small and poor, but courageous and determined, people to build their own process, to solve their problems in their own way, without threatening the sovereignty of any other people, nor compromising their own proud and unshakable principles.

Our people, led by our party, the NJM, are demanding the right to build this new society *in peace*. We desire peace. We know that peace is a precondition for the realization of the people's wish for a better and more just existence. But this wish for peace, this insistence on our right to self-determination, is being denied us. Daily we are threatened by the aggressiveness and the hostility of a power thousands of times our size, thousands of times richer in resources than us. Daily our process is the object of threats both veiled and undisguised, coming from the mighty United States and its string of yardboys and yardgirls in the region. Once again, comrades, we assert that we are the masters of our own house, we stand upright, with dignity, ready to defend this land, this sea, this region.

We need your solidarity, comrades, because this revolution is increasingly a light, a beacon of hope to the poor and exploited masses of the Caribbean. The aims, objectives, and achievements of this revolution are a crystallization of the most profound human aspirations of Caribbean people towards a better life. For 400 years the exploited masses of the region have struggled with dignity for bread, jobs, justice, and peace. Today in Grenada, today in free and revolutionary Grenada, this struggle at last is beginning to bear fruit. And this fruit is not for us alone. It is not the property of ourselves alone. Just as our struggle has been a part of a broader struggle of the working people of the Caribbean and the world, so now our revolution is an integral part of the forward movement of working people regionally and internationally.

We need your solidarity, comrades, because we are conscious of these responsibilities not only to ourselves but to oppressed and exploited peoples everywhere. That is why in every forum, at every opportunity, we have resolutely condemned apartheid, Zionism, and racism, we have unwaveringly accused and unmasked imperialism, and we have added our voice to the condemnation of exploitation, injustice, and inhumanity in all its forms and manifestations. You shall find us marching in your ranks; our voice shall not be stilled. [*Prolonged applause*]

And this important role of the Grenada revolution is clearly recognized by the working people of the region. For whatever the volume and bitterness of the attacks made upon us by the decrepit leadership of the region and its decadent press, however often the voice of Washington is mindlessly echoed by its agents in the region, the real people have again and again demonstrated their confidence in, and support for, this process which they see as theirs, too. Behind the smokescreen of misinformation they somehow perceive the real issues, that this revolution is a unique process in which new benefits are being brought to the people, and a popular process in which the people participate more and more each day.

The Caribbean people refuse to be misinformed about our process. The Caribbean people understand the undemocratic and antiworker position of the regional press. This is borne out by the survey recently conducted by the Jamaican *Daily Gleaner,* itself a tool of international reaction, a survey which revealed that the majority of people are not affected by the negative propaganda put out against our revolution.

There is also the recent example of the strong protest made by workers of the Trinidad *Express* (another regional rag in the service of U.S. imperialism) and other workers in the media in Trinidad. These workers came out in protest against what they correctly identified as a vulgar, concerted anti-Grenada press campaign, they came out and demanded the right of the Caribbean people to undistorted information about a sister island.

There is the evidence of the trade union conference that we have just hosted and which turned out to be the biggest in its three-year history. It was the largest gathering ever of representatives of the Caribbean working class. The hosting of this conference has been for us both a duty and a pleasure. This conference has been held at a time when the working people of the Caribbean are beginning to feel the full weight of the capitalist world economic crisis, and when the regional ruling classes have agreed on common solutions, which can only mean harsher conditions, austerity, more and more hardship, and increased exploitation of the poor.

One of the highest expressions of international solidarity with the Grenada revolution is precisely today's conference. For the first time since our revolution, people like yourselves, who have been consistent friends and allies of our struggle, are meeting all together. You come as friends, as comrades-in-arms, as firm, consistent defenders of the truth of this revolution. The presence of comrades from all continents is not only an indication of the support of the international community for our revolution, but is also a testimony to the oneness of our struggle against a common enemy and to the unity of our aspirations.

Another living example of the regional support that our revolution has attracted is the presence among us of internationalist workers from the Caribbean region as well as from other parts of the world. In all the key sections of our development, these internationalists are co-workers, facing with us the historic challenge of creating the new and just society.

Comrades, one of our most important reasons for calling upon your support is the threat we face from U.S. imperialism. From the earliest days of the revolution we have been subject to threats and attempts by U.S. imperialism to undermine and destroy our process. The strategy of imperialism has been to fight us on all fronts: political pressure, propaganda destabilization, economic warfare, and now, imminently, the military solution.

From the very morning of our revolution, pressure was brought to bear upon us by the U.S. in an attempt to dictate the character and direction of our political process. We were warned, for example, that relations with Cuba would not be countenanced.

The propaganda campaign also began very early, with an impudent plan to use the local media to wage war upon the revolution *from the inside,* like a worm surreptitiously eating away at the heart of a healthy fruit. The lesson that imperialism learned from that early impudence was that this revolution must be respected; and every subsequent attempt, including the recent action of a group of counterrevolutionary planters, merchants, and professionals, has been firmly dealt with. The revolution, having silenced the local mouthpieces of imperialism, faces increased propaganda aggression from outside. This campaign was taken to a new level with the prime-time broadcasts on the U.S. national television network, feeding to the people of the United States of America the most vulgar distortions of Grenadian reality.

On the economic front we have been faced with recurrent acts of sabotage: the vulgar abuse by the U.S. of its dominant position in international institutions like the IMF and the World Bank to stifle the legitimate rights to assistance of small, developing states in the region like Grenada and Nicaragua.

Today the assumption of power by a fascist clique in the U.S. and the failure of imperialism's attempts to destroy our process have brought our revolution face to face with the ugliest side of imperialism — naked military aggression. In the last two months alone there have been two major maneuvers carried out upon Caribbean land and sea by the warlords of the north; "Ocean Venture '81," "Operation Amber and the Amberdines," and "Red X 183" have been shameless rehearsals for eventual invasions of Cuba, Nicaragua, and Grenada and/or preparation for an armed entry into El Salvador on the side of the fascist junta!

But it is not only here in our Caribbean that the enemies of peace have been rattling their sabres. These neutron warmongers have been seeking military confrontation on several continents. The shooting down of two Libyan planes; the military maneuvers code-named "Bright Star"; the South African invasion of Angola; the open attack by Zionist Israel on Iraq, Beirut, southern Lebanon, and the Palestinian people; and the tons of lies being spread today against the revolutionary peoples and governments of Cuba and Nicaragua in preparation for an armed invasion; and the role of the U.S. in El Salvador are all examples of this trend.

The peoples of the world, however, including the people of the United States, conscious of the grave danger to mankind posed by these adventurist actions and policies, are standing up for peace.

Comrades, world public opinion is increasingly a force of international affairs. The voice of the working masses can no longer be ignored. We saw the part it played in the Vietnam War. International public opinion has become more and more powerful in recent times when the balance of forces has been shifting towards anti-imperialism and national self-determination. Again and again we have seen world public opinion respond indignantly to acts of military aggression against small, weak nations; again and again we have seen world opinion condemn and curb the attempts of imperialism to intervene and turn back popular processes.

And this, comrades, is another reason why your solidarity is so important to the *continued forward movement* of the Grenada revolution. But it is important that international public opinion be mobilized not only against the military subversion of popular processes. It is important that we recognize the equally devastating effects of the other forms of aggression. International public opinion must treat with equal gravity attempts to block aid to countries like Grenada, the financing of counterrevolutionary journalism and other propaganda destabilization, and the landing of marines on the soil of other countries. For all of these have the same aim of overthrowing our revolution; all of these are acts of aggression against our people.

So how can you, the friends of the Grenada revolution, continue to help us build and consolidate this process? How can your solidarity safeguard and promote our revolution?

Comrades, solidarity meetings such as this are a vital forum for galvanizing world public opinion. Educating and informing the people of the world about the reality of this revolution is a necessity. This task by itself is part of the general struggle of the poor for the right to information. It is part of the broad struggle against imperialist, monopoly control of the media and for a new world information order.

As a poor, underdeveloped country, our efforts to break the vicious cycle of poverty and exploitation, the programs of the revolution designed to improve the social and economic well-being of our people, depend to a large extent on the material assistance that we receive. And we are therefore always very appreciative of the internationalist assistance which we receive from so many different peoples.

Friends of our revolution, you can help us by organizing Grenada friendship associations in your country. Providing a framework for organized and ongoing solidarity work, providing a framework within which peace forces, friends, and other well-wishers can be drawn into concrete political, educational, and fund-raising activity. Alongside the formation of friendship associations is the organization of tours to Grenada. The most often reiterated position of the revolution in response to the absurd lies and distortions has been to *"come and see for yourself."*

Our revolutionary process is one guided by principles of honesty and integrity; our revolutionary process is one defended and made by the Grenadian masses. We say to our friends, "come, share our experiences," we say to the doubting Thomases, "come see for yourself." [*Applause*]

By coming and seeing for yourself, and by encouraging others to do likewise, you not only dispel the falsehoods of imperialism, but you also help our economy, by contributing to the new tourism.

So here you are among us, brothers and sisters, to witness for yourselves the evolution of what we aspire to build into a new civilization in the Caribbean. What is new about our model, what is different about our process? The answer to this can be assisted by a whole series of questions which might be posed by any visitor to our shores who is struck by the evidence that something is afoot here which does not quite fall into the pattern of life in most of the rest of the Caribbean. Some of the questions that are most usually asked are the following:

● Why did we, as one of the priorities of the revolution, send volunteers into the field to find out how many of our people were illiterate, and then move decisively into developing a national program of adult education?

- Why have we stretched our human and financial resources to set up a training program for all primary and junior secondary teachers, instead of continuing the traditional teachers-college model of training fifty select teachers per year?
- Why are we instituting primary health care?
- Why do we hold so many mass meetings?
- Why do we hold so many solidarity rallies and events with so many national liberation movements and friendly governments around the world?
- Why are we working so hard to expand the NYO, and NWO, and other mass organizations?
- Why are we the only country in the English-speaking Caribbean that has decided to arm our people and create a People's Revolutionary Militia? What has inspired this confidence?
- Why are ordinary, grassroots men, women, and youth being exposed to leadership training and political science courses?
- Why are we developing so many new organizations, and popular democratic organizations such as workers' parish councils, youth and women's parish councils, and community zonal councils within every parish?
- Why is the distribution of milk in every community carried out voluntarily by the organized members of that community?
- Why have we established work brigades to involve our people in the task of rebuilding our country on a voluntary patriotic and unpaid basis?
- Why are our community organizations able to set up and run day-care centers and kindergartens with only minimal input from the government?
- Why, in the face of serious transportation problems, in the face of ongoing attempts to undermine the confidence of the people in their revolution, in the face of serious ongoing objective problems, why, in the face of all this, were we able to bring to Seamoon yesterday a crowd far, far bigger, and far more militant, united, and conscious than the 10,000 who came out to the NJM's first People's Congress held on that same spot around eight years ago?
- Why is the anti-Grenada lobby becoming so strident and hysterical?
- Why does the newspaper of our revolution, the *Free West Indian,* encounter so many obstacles to its distribution in the other Caribbean islands, while their newspapers sell freely on our streets, notwithstanding the lies and distortions which they print about Grenada?
- Why is there no propaganda campaign, no accusations of human-rights violations, no calls for elections, no policy of isolation, no economic blockades, nor any threat of military intervention against a

country like Haiti, where people are literally jumping into the sea every day to escape the unbearable conditions under which they live?

● Why?

We invite you to explore our country, examine our process, experience our revolution, and assess for yourselves the new directions that we have taken.

Comrades, beloved friends, once again we reiterate our pleasure in having you here with us. One hundred and twenty delegates from so many countries from all continents is a definite statement of militant solidarity that "Grenada is not alone."

Comrades, we urge you to enjoy your stay in our country and hope that whatever our modest hospitality lacks will be more than made up for by the warmth and friendliness of our people.

We assure you of our total support in your struggles against injustice, exploitation, and warmongering; and for peace, social progress, and national liberation.

Long live solidarity, friendship, and cooperation among peoples!

Long live the anti-imperialist and antifascist unity of peace-loving and progressive forces worldwide!

Long live the force and weight of international public opinion!

Long live internationalism!

Long live the Grenada revolution!

Forward ever, backward never!

Three Years of the Grenada Revolution

March 13, 1982

The following speech was made to a rally of 20,000 people in St. George's on the third anniversary of the revolution. The text was printed in the March 20, 1982, Free West Indian, *and in the April 19, 1982,* Intercontinental Press.

Comrades, in the name of our party, our government and our people, I want to welcome you all and to welcome all our invited and overseas guests to this historic and massive third anniversary of our people's revolution.

Today, three years have passed since our people's will and giant determination finished with tyranny and fear forever in our country, and these last three years have brought us many transformations, many massive changes.

But seeing this huge assembly before me now, understanding how many of you have come from so many places on earth; from up and down our Caribbean necklace of islands and right through our continent of America; from all over Europe; from Africa, the land of the fighting Angolans, Namibians, and Seychelles Islanders; through Asia to the heroic, struggling nation of Korea, whose shores are washed by the Pacific Ocean; from Australia and the fighting people of the Pacific Islands; all of this great presence has rammed home an extraordinary truth.

In the old days — and now when we speak about the "old days" in Grenada we speak of just three years ago, because we have all matured that much — in the days of darkness that are gone forever, you would find Grenadians leaving their country in their thousands, emigrating by sea and by air to far-off shores to escape the dead end of Gairyism.

Our people were locked inside a mentality of visas, migration, and despair. Grenada was a place to leave, a place to run from, a point of departure to the United States, to Britain, and to Canada.

But our country today has become a symbol of a new reality to oppressed people. No longer are we a point of departure. Today we are a point of arrival for people from all over the world, who have come to celebrate with us our third anniversary of our glorious revolution.

We are certainly proud of what we have achieved over these past three years, but we realize also that we are still on the threshold of the real changes that we want to see in our country. We have only taken the first steps, and we have no room in our process for complacency or premature satisfaction.

Our people, through their history, have always struggled and craved for real transformation, have organized, fought, and died for real transformation, and there is no rest for us until we have built a new life in Grenada that will fulfill all the enormous potential of our people, for our people deserve nothing less.

All of this will of course depend on how quickly we can expand our economy and build the necessary wealth to construct a new life. For we are embarking upon our Year of Economic Construction at a time when the capitalist world which surrounds us, and with whom we trade, has created for itself a whirlpool of economic devastation which is today becoming an economic crisis of worldwide proportions.

Their crisis affects us like a leech, because we are still reliant upon them for exports and imports, and historically, we have been shackled to their economies through a 400-year imposition of colonialism and a quarter-century of neocolonialism.

Our success must, therefore, be measured in how much we can cut through the chains that have bound us to their system, how rapidly we can immunize our economy from their recessions, how quickly we can create our own economic self-reliance that will keep us strong, no matter what happens to the capitalist world.

For, of course, the terms of trade which are favorable to the industrialized countries are inevitably unfavorable to us — that is the great inequality upon which imperialism bases its power. They control the prices at which we sell our crops which have meant life or death for us: our bananas, our cocoa, our nutmegs. They also control the prices of the goods we buy from them. So we are squeezed from both ends.

We are in a vise, and our only way out is real and concrete economic construction. We import their rising prices, we import their inflation, we import everything unhealthy about their economy, and it affects our economy like a cancer.

I know that when I speak to you today of these economic matters, that more and more you are able to understand them. Our last two months of budget consultation have laid bare the economic truths of our country, and the new economy consciousness that has risen so massively among our people has created a new popular understanding of our economy, the second great pillar of our revolution.

If we take the present situation with our nutmegs, for example, we will see that ten years ago, one ton of nutmegs could bring us enough money to buy a car. Now, for a car of the same value, we would have to sell at least five tons of nutmegs. So our nutmegs today are worth only a fifth of what they were worth five years ago. You can imagine how serious that is for our foreign exchange and our imports situation.

And if we look at nutmegs from another angle, we can make an even more important point. A sister cracking nutmegs at a receiving station in Grenada receives a small wage of $7.10 a day, and that sister would need to crack about 150 pounds of nutmegs in order to earn that $7 for the day. Those same nutmegs are sold to a broker — a middleman — and taken off to Europe. Then they are resold to a miller, cleaned, blended, and packaged, and put on the shelves of European supermarkets.

And when one of our sisters or brothers or aunts living in Shepherd's Bush or Brixton or Hammersmith in London goes to buy a one-ounce carton of Grenada nutmeg, the price of that one once of nutmegs is about twenty pence or one of our dollars. One ounce for $1, but 150 pounds of cracking for $7.

So, our worker here earns $7.10 a day cracking 150 pounds of nutmegs in Victoria, Gouyave, or Grenville, but our families in England and the British working people in London pay the equivalent of the same money for seven ounces of the same nutmegs. Those seven ounces represent approximately one-third of 1 percent of what the Grenadian sister earns during one day at one of our receiving stations.

Or to put it another way, the real value of the nutmeg worker's labor is 300 times what she receives in a day's wage. That is what we mean by imperialism at work.

You can see, therefore, what our working people are fighting against every day of their lives, and why we in Grenada are so committed to struggling for the global implementation of the new international economic order.

But all of us know that that struggle will not be finished overnight, and that struggle will be a long and hard campaign, conducted by our comrades all over the developing world, whose peoples are oppressed and battered by the same blood-sucking system of imperialism.

What, therefore, can we do at this moment to wrestle ourselves free of such a stranglehold on our economy? Clearly, we can no longer rely upon our traditional crops alone. The fickle world of capitalist trade owes loyalty to no poor and exploited country, particularly one like ours, which is struggling for its economic independence.

So, we have to find new crops, new products, new exports. We have to diversify. And this is where our people's initiative and creative genius has been, and will continue to be, so vital.

Throughout our weeks of budget participation, we have heard suggestions which our agro-scientists and researchers must take very seriously. We have heard good reasons for processing and canning new products, from Callaloo to sprats, and we have seen over the last three years how neglected fruits have been taken up by our people and cultivated to real economic value and effect.

All those mangoes that used to lie on the ground and rot, that we used to pelt at each other when we were children, those mangoes are now in tins of nectar and jars of chutney! Some people used to think there was no potential for eggplant, but now we are exporting thousands of dollars of eggplants to Britain every year and increasing every month. And we have had a world-winner and international prize-winner in our own nutmeg jelly, which won in our first year of competition abroad. It took the revolution to achieve all this.

For the revolution knows that the richness of our soil is a huge asset to us, and we have as yet only just begun to realize the wealth it can bring to us. Our earth is our treasure, and if we work with it, respect it, love it, and enrich it, it will repay us a thousand times over!

And as we diversify our products and look for more and more ways of making even more appetizing and delicious nectars, jams, and jellies and other agro-industrial products — so that when the people of the world just hear the name "Grenada," they must begin to smack their lips and their mouths must begin to water. Besides this, we need simultaneously and scientifically to search the world for the new markets for our products.

Grenada's "Spice Isle" label must be seen in shops in every continent, and we are asking our internationalist friends here to spread the good news of our tasty products. Take home samples, comrades; for we are not just the Spice Island any more, we are now also the nectar island, the island of vegetables, of fruits, of sauces, of jams.

Tell the world that, and add that our beaches, our hotels, and the hospitality, friendliness and dignity of our people are always ready to receive our overseas guests.

Over the last year we have spoken much about the "social wage" and we have defined it as all those concrete benefits which you receive, but for which you don't have to find the money in your pockets to pay, or for which you pay only a small part of the real cost — those benefits of the revolution: free education; free health care; over 300 free university scholarships abroad; our house-repair program; our new public transport system; our free school books and uniforms for the poorest children; our eye clinic; our free milk program; our new housing schemes for our workers.

These are the benefits that go to make up our social wage.

What we have to make clear, however, is that the money to pay for all these programs has to come from someplace. It doesn't come from the sky, it doesn't come from a fairy godmother, it doesn't come from a money-machine, it doesn't come because Finance Minister Bernard Coard is able to wave a magic wand.

Everything has a cost, everything must be paid for. And as we don't believe in money-machines, and as we have rejected the policy of sinking in a morass of public debt, as we know our people's wages are low and that extra burdensome taxation would not be a just or satisfactory option, then what will be our source, where will we find the money to maintain and expand on these programs?

For maintain them we must, not only for the benefit of our own workers, but because they are an inspiration and a model to the working people the length and breadth of our Caribbean! Comrades, the money we need for these programs and benefits is inside you!

It lies inside your muscle-power and your brain-power, and more than anything else, it lies inside your consciousness and commitment to "Work Harder, Produce More, and Build Grenada" — for it is only with determination and resolution, and the greater production and wealth that it will bring, that there will be a guarantee of the continuation and expansion of all the concrete gains of our social wage.

The same truth rings just as clear in relation to our infrastructural development. For even before the revolution, our New Jewel Movement understood how economic development could only come with infrastructural development, that to create a revolution meant necessarily to create a new infrastructure. And that is why we have it as a number-one priority, a number-one must, for our people and our country.

And the fulfillment of this is beginning to sprout out all around us: completion of the first phase of the Eastern Main Road this year and the beginning of construction of the Western Main Road; development of our Central Water Commission, with a much-improved supply of water all over the nation; the new telephone system which we shall begin to install this year; the new generators we are negotiating to buy for our electricity company so as to bring an end to blackouts; the 67.5 miles of feeder roads that will open up our agriculture to further production this year; our new radio transmitter; our Ramon Quintana Quarry, stone-crusher, and asphalt complex; the Sandino prefabricated concrete unit and block-making plant, which incidentally arrived on St. George's docks this morning, as yet another gift from our internationalist friends of Cuba; a continuation of our international airport and the start of the terminal building in the next few months; construction of warehouses for our Marketing and National Importing Board in every parish — with vital implications for the expansion of our foreign trade and internal supplies; construction of eight fish-selling centers with deep-freeze facilities and the planned dredging of the St. George's Harbor to accomodate larger ships for the advancement of tourism and trade.

This is an impressive infrastructural list to try to bring out in one year, but again, it all has a price, it all has to be paid for. Over the past three years, we have seen magnificent fraternal contributions from our international friends and comrades. Several of these countries are poor, developing countries like ourselves, but that has not affected their generosity.

It is clear that we would be much further back in our development process without this direct help of our sisters and brothers from many nations: from Cuba, from Iraq, from Algeria, from Syria, from Libya, and from other countries in the Organization of Petroleum Exporting Countries, from Korea, from Tanzania and Nigeria, from Mexico and Venezuela, from Canada, from Kenya, from the European Economic Community, and from the socialist countries. All of this assistance has been very, very welcome and heart-warming to our people.

These nations have reached out to us and supported us because they know that we are an honest government, a serious government, a government that will tolerate no corruption, a government that places the welfare of its people as its first overwhelming priority, a government that makes the fullest and most economical use of every cent of assistance that our country receives.

And while we thank these countries from the depths of our hearts, on behalf of all of our people, we are quick to add that none of these countries, not one of them, has ever tried to compromise our freedom or put conditions on their assistance, none of these countries has ever tried to undermine our economic process or pervert our development for their own ends, and we thank them for that also.

So our receipt of their economic aid has taken place in a true relationship of friendship, partnership, and respect for mutual dignity and sovereignty.

But we must realize that many of these countries also have their own problems and that external assistance has to be seen as only a very small part of the solution to our problems. We cannot sit back and become smug and think we can do it only through receiving external assistance. That would be a disastrous mistake.

As always we have ourselves, our own discipline, our organization, our own production, our own self-reliance and recognition that this country is ours and we and we alone have the duty to build it.

And this is why last Monday's historic emulation ceremony, the first of its kind that we have had, was so very crucial for the future of our country. For here were our greatest resources being publicly recognized, here was our greatest power being appreciated, here was the force and dynamo of our future being acclaimed: our incomparable working people, whose determination, commitment, and collective power will add the motor to our production which will drive us victoriously out of economic dependence and towards the self-reliance and prosperity which is the rightful wage and reward of our people's struggling history.

The three years of building the foundations of our revolution have caused us to discover much about ourselves.

March 13, 1979, was crucial for us, in that when we seized that sunrise and dawned our own new day in Grenada, we were suddenly, for the first time in our lives, staring at our true selves, looking at a reflection of who we really were, understanding with additional revolutionary insight who we could become.

We began to see more and more clearly the massive potential of our people, and as we worked together to safeguard and consolidate our victory, our people's genius was set free and began to sparkle with brilliance. For as we began, as a people, to confirm concretely that organization was our greatest weapon, our conviction became doubly reinforced that it was only mass participation and revolutionary democracy that could genuinely move us forward. And that is why we steadfastly believe that our people constitute the first great and indispensable pillar of our revolution.

As we lay to rest in Grenada the Westminster corpse, we recall with admiration the prophetic words, uttered over sixty years ago, by our great democrat and patriot, T. Albert Marryshow, that one day a great spirit of democracy would come to "level up and level down" this Grenada of ours. How happy our T. A. would have been today to have lived to see the fulfilment of his prophesy, that democracy is "leveling up and leveling down" in our country.

And there is another reason why the old patriot's choice of words is vital for us today. Let me try to make them concrete. Perhaps not all of us here will remember Point Salines Estate before the revolution: just bush and salt pond, with ridges and valleys like the fingers of an outstretched hand running down to the sea.

But all of us can now see what our workers and their Cuban internationalist comrades have achieved at Point Salines with their enormous collective effort, cooperation, and discipline. With their own hands and machines they have made Marryshow's dreams come true: they have leveled hills, they have filled in valleys and ponds, they have made land out of sea and created a new Point Salines, so level and smooth that most, if not all the largest aircraft in the world will soon be able to land upon it.

They have transformed our earth, they have concretely and physically leveled our land. If the power of work and collective discipline can achieve all of that in two years, it tells you how far we have moved and the unlimited possibilities for our people in the future. It tells you what our Grenadian people are capable of achieving.

Our zonal councils, our workers' parish councils, our National Women's Organisation, our National Youth Organisation, our Young

Pioneers, our regenerated trade unions of workers and farmers are all mighty achievements: real proof of the progress of our people's revolutionary democracy. They are not talkshops; they are not social clubs or garden parties.

Unless they are causing us to produce more, to build more, to organize more efficiently, to democratize more, to create more wealth for our poor and working people, then they are only ornaments, only luxuries. Their success will, in the final analysis, be measured in the inspiration and ability they give us to produce and the expertise they give us to organize.

The urge and demand for world peace is so dominant that all other issues are dependent on it. The Grenada revolution, all other revolutions, and progressive and democratic forces on earth cannot make progress, cannot move forward, cannot develop, cannot be independent, without peace. It is as simple, as fundamental as that.

The one task that cannot be postponed, the one overriding obligation facing the Caribbean and Latin American region — indeed the challenge that confronts progressive humanity — is the struggle for peace and to safeguard mankind from destruction caused by nuclear war.

We understand today that the struggle for peace and the struggle for development is one and the same struggle. The struggle for people's democracy and economic independence are identical; it is like the relationship with the chicken and the egg, the two things defy separation.

Just thirty-seven years ago, the antifascist movement, led by fighting workers and peasants of many countries, defeated that most notorious mass murderer, Adolf Hitler, and stopped him from murdering humanity and imposing on all nations a thousand years of fascist rule. But what a terrible price was paid to defeat that monster! Millions dead, all cities destroyed, all countries devastated, six years of bitter, bloody, and brutal warfare.

Today, only a few minutes are needed for the world's arsenals of nuclear weapons to completely wipe from the face of this planet the totality of mankind's work.

As a revolutionary people, Grenadians are realists. We know that we have no other recourse, no other alternative but to fight this threat and resolutely mobilize ourselves in preparation to confront this threat. We are under no illusions at all that the responsibility, the real blame for the increase of international tension rests fully with Washington's attempt to seek world domination once more.

U.S. President Ronald Reagan's policy of hostility, of economic and political aggression, of personal interference, of subversion, of counterrevolutionary propaganda, can never be grounds for the sober and constructive dialogue that the world needs at present.

Every day the arms race swallows up over U.S.$1 billion, while every day over one billion men, women, and children continue to suffer from hunger, from disease, from illiteracy, and from underdevelopment. Raw materials which exist in the Third World, and especially the rare ones for which imperialism hungers — bauxite, copper, lead, zinc, nickel, manganese, uranium, oil — are now being squandered for military purposes.

Disarmament will release a quantity of these raw materials for civilian production, and this would make it possible to increase the energy capacity of the developing countries; make it possible for science to discover new sources of energy, and for technology to be placed fully at the service of mankind.

The Grenadian people are convinced that peaceful coexistence and disarmament are the essential conditions for the development of a new system of international economic relations which guarantee the liberation of less-developed countries.

Two years ago, from this very platform, on our revolution's first anniversary, we called for the Caribbean Sea to be regarded and respected as a zone of peace. Two years later, we still hold firm to that call.

Our view remains that military task forces, air and sea patrols, and all military maneuvers by foreign powers in our region, must be outlawed once and for all.

We believe that military bases and installations must be removed from the territories of the Latin American and Caribbean countries that do not want them. The people of Grenada and the region demand the right to be free from aggressive military harassment. We demand an end to the Monroe Doctrine, the Reagan Doctrine, and all other doctrines aimed at perpetuating hegemonism, interventionism, or backyardism in this region of ours.

The people of our region once again demand that their sacred right to self-determination be recognized and respected in practice. We want to see in practice that the people of this region are, in fact, allowed to build their own processes in their own way: free from all outside interference, free from all threats, free from all tic-tacks, free from all attempts to force them to build a process imposed from outside.

We are convinced that peace, independence, and development are inextricably connected. Peace is an imperative precondition for orderly and progressive economic, social, and cultural development of our people.

In addition, to be able to pursue social, economic, and cultural policies which are necessary for its own peculiar developmental requirements, a country must be truly independent and not be subject to any form of outside pressure or dictation. This is an inalienable right of all peoples.

We intend to struggle unceasingly to ensure the widest possible recognition for this concept. Therefore, in the coming months and years, we will continue to raise in every appropriate forum to which we have access that our Caribbean must be recognized and respected as a zone of peace, independence, and development.

Two years ago, we said from this very platform that aid with political strings or unreasonable conditions, which bring about economic hardships on Caribbean peoples, or which consolidate and entrench the rule of the big U.S. companies, must be condemned and avoided like a plague. Today, we are compelled to restate this view in relation to Reagan's version of the Caribbean Basin Initiative [CBI].

Any casual glance at this version of the Caribbean Basin plan would show that it is very different, indeed a prostitution of the original ideas discussed by Mexico, Canada, Venezuela, and the USA in the Bahamas.

It is obvious that is the reason why these other countries are now out of this particular version of the initiative. Right from the outset, these other countries took a principled view that the plan must not exclude any country on the basis of ideological or political deviation, and must not have a military component.

These countries and, in particular, Mexico and Canada, were very, very strong on these points.

Therefore, when on two separate occasions Cuba was excluded from the discussions, it was obvious that the wider plan was dying. And when Reagan's representative at the Santo Domingo meeting in October last year bluntly said that his government was not interested in any "mini-Marshall" idea but rather in promotion of private-sector investment on a bilateral basis, the plan, as originally conceived and involving four original countries, was clearly no longer just wounded and dying, but stone-cold dead!

To get a clearer idea of the extent to which this original plan is dead, and to understand how it was prostituted by this new U.S. plan, let us reflect on the original thirteen points enunciated at the Jamaica and Dominican Republic meetings by the foreign ministers of the region. When we examine these thirteen points outlined by the foreign ministers of the region, we will discover that every single one of the points made by the people of the region has been completely violated, ignored, and broken — every single one:

(1) Participation in the program should be open to all territories in the region.

(2) The program should respect the sovereignty and integrity of states, the integrity of regional institutions and their autonomous character.

(3) Wherever possible, the program should utilize regional institutions and indigenous resources and expertise.

(4) The program to be formulated should be truly reflective of national goals and priority areas for development and the criteria used in

granting aid should not be based on political or military considerations.

(5) The program should respect the right of the people of each state to determine for themselves their own path of social and economic development free from all external interference or pressure.

(6) There should be no diminution in resource flows either to the region as a whole or to individual member states. Rather, there should be additional flows within an agreed time-bound program, and with a major portion being in the form of grants.

(7) Ideological pluralism is an irreversible fact of international relations and should not constitute a barrier to programs of economic cooperation.

(8) Substantial flows of official development assistance and other forms of government-to-government assistance are vitally necessary for essential infrastructural development and to create the conditions for investment, both foreign and regional.

(9) Substantial private investment, both foreign and local, is an essential element if development is to proceed at an acceptable rate.

(10) The flow of resources under the program, whether public or private, should contribute to the maintenance and strengthening of the independence of the countries of the region.

(11) The program should be directed towards strengthening ongoing regional integration and cooperation, and encouraging wider and more intensive cooperation and exchange, particularly in the industrial, financial, technical, and trade areas, in order to get maximum economic and developmental benefits at minimal cost through joint efforts.

(12) The program should respect the commitments of individual member states to regional objectives and to the goals of the developing countries as a whole.

(13) To maintain peace, security, stability, which are essential to the achievement of the social and economic development of the region, the principle of noninterference must be respected.

The Caribbean plan should cover an initial five-year period and be based on the principles outlined in the previous section. It must pay special attention to the balance of payments and the need to remove the foreign exchange and other constraints to development, and to provide: the infrastructural, technological, institutional, skilled, and managerial capability requirements of the production and marketing processes in industry, agro-industry, agriculture, transportation, communication links, and energy. And it should also assist in promoting the diversification of production in the Caribbean countries.

What is now clearer is that this plan is meant only to deal with narrow military, security, and strategic considerations of the USA, and is not genuinely concerned with economic and social development of the people in this region.

Where is the proof? It is contained in Reagan's speech to the Organization of American States on February 24.

"The Caribbean region is a vital strategic and commercial artery for the United States. Nearly half of our trade, two-thirds of our imported oil, and over half of our imported strategic minerals pass through the Panama Canal or the Gulf of Mexico. Make no mistake: the well-being and security of our neighbors in this region are in our own vital interests."

And this sort of justification is repeated more than once in the speech.

We are not surprised, because this has always been the USA's approach, and with Reagan in power, this narrow nationalist approach will not only continue, but will become much more emphasized.

We recall John Kennedy's "Alliance for Progress" plan was U.S.$20 billion, or fifty-seven times more money than what is now proposed for the CBI. And who can forget how dramatically that grandiose Alliance for Progress collapsed?

They speak of U.S.$350 million, but $350 million is equivalent to the profits of a big U.S. company working for only three days of year-round profits.

How shameful it is to reflect that the present military maneuver, announced at the same time as this CBI, costs more than the whole CBI plan.

Reagan says his plan will bring stability to the region. That is only hypocritical nonsense, because what is clear is that Reagan's bilateral aid approach is certainly designed to destroy regional unity.

What is also clear is that the plan will also crush local private investors in the region, while promoting and expanding the role of big U.S. companies. There is no doubt that it is the new strategy of colonization.

In fact, Reagan's ridiculous emphasis on private sector investment downplays infrastructural development, and this is itself a guarantee that private investment will not come.

We observe, too, that in this so-called *Caribbean* Basin Initiative, only two Caribbean islands will benefit in any serious way, and only one of these is a Caribbean Community country. Reagan certainly managed to keep a lot of people dancing to his tune, making dozens of expensive trips and waiting with eager arms outstretched — all for nothing. His basin plan has turned out to be the con game of this century.

The CBI plan reflects the chauvinism and "ugly Americanism" of Reagan, in the vulgar way in which he has completely ignored and discarded the views of Caribbean countries, as to what kind of plan they wished to see.

The concern of his plan is with his warmongering "national security" interests.

The bulk of the CBI is nothing more than money and arms for fascist dictatorships and oligarchies as represented by El Salvador. And giving money to El Salvador today is like sinking money into a hole or flushing it down a toilet. Such money might as well be saved for the massive job of national reconstruction, which patriots of El Salvador in the Farabundo Martí National Liberation Front and the Revolutionary Democratic Front will have to undertake after their certain victory.

On the top of this insult, indignity, charade, masquerade, and pappy-show represented by the CBI, Reagan's speech to the OAS also contains vulgar attacks on Cuba, Nicaragua, Grenada, and the fighting people of El Salvador.

Reagan attacks Nicaragua, he attacks Cuba, he attacks Grenada, he attacks the ordinary working people of El Salvador, who have picked up arms to regain their country from genocidal oppression and imperialist plunder.

But he does so out of desperation, out of the recognition that the people of the region now understand very clearly that there is an alternative to fascism, to nineteenth century capitalism and dictatorship.

That alternative was shown in the glorious Cuban revolution and continued with the Grenadian and Nicaraguan revolutions. Reagan attacks our countries because he understands very well that neither his words, nor his belligerent actions and threats, will stop the heroic people of Cuba from continuing to go forward with their mighty revolution — a beacon, a model of hope, an example of dignity and struggle for the people of the region and of the world to emulate. Reagan understands the power and the impact of the Cuban revolution.

He attacks Nicaragua today, knowing full well that he applauded long and well when Somoza was waging terror. He attacks Nicaragua today, understanding very well that the children of Sandino have made massive strides in their Herculean task of national reconstruction which they so heroically shouldered. He attacks Nicaragua today, understanding very well that neither the November plan of CIA terrorism against Nicaragua, nor the economic warfare and complicity with mercenaries, will ever be able to turn back this glorious people's revolution or stop the ordinary poor and working people of Central America from longing to be noble Sandinista fighters themselves.

And what can we say of Reagan's hypocritical call for elections in El Salvador? The last free election in El Salvador was dozens of years ago, all other so-called elections in that country have been farcical and fraudulent. And on top of that, today conditions are far from normal.

In 1932 over 30,000 Salvadoran patriots were murdered by the then-dictator. In the past two years, another 30,000 patriots have been murdered by Duarte's butchers with the fullest financial, military, and diplomatic backing from the USA. A state of martial law, a state of siege, exists in El Salvador today. What kind of elections could there be in such a state?

Today, we want to repeat once again our fullest support for the Mexican-French declaration calling for a negotiated political solution and for the recognition of the FMLN and the FDR as authentic representative forces.

Today, we also want to repeat our fullest support for the recent statesmanlike offer of Mexican President José López Portillo to act as an intermediary in the Central American situation. We applaud President López Portillo for his statesmanship.

We applaud today, too, the speedy and statesmanlike response of Cuban President Fidel Castro and the Sandinista leadership in accepting this offer and stating their readiness to assist in ensuring a just and negotiated solution to the problems of the region.

Now we wait on Reagan for a serious response. But whether or not the Reagan administration chooses to wake up to the realities of the region; whether or not they choose to come in line with these realities, one thing is certain: The children of José Martí, of Camilo, of Che, of Fidel, the children of Sandino likewise, will continue to write brilliant page after brilliant page in the history of the Caribbean and Latin American region.

Equally certain is the fact that the children of Farabundo Martí will one day soon join the children of José Martí, the children of Sandino, and the children of Fedon, Butler, Marryshow, Rupert Bishop, Harold Strachan, and Alister Strachan in liberating their own territory, and starting on the road to people's power in their own countries. That is certain.

In the presence of our very good friends, outstanding revolutionary Comrade Jorge Risquet, member of the Political Bureau of the Communist Party of Cuba; and of Comrade Carlos Núñez, President of the Council of State and member of the National Directorate of the Sandinista front; and of our comrade representative from El Salvador, we say that the people of Grenada will always give our fullest support and solidarity to your revolutionary process.

Today, we also have to recognize the tremendous work and the great job of nation-building that is being undertaken by a country far away in Asia. This country has sent to our third anniversary festivities their premier, one of the top leaders of their country; a country with a brave heroic people; a country that was victorious over U.S. imperialism in the late 1940s; a country that still continues today to be threatened by the U.S.; a country under a brave and wise leadership. In the presence of the premier of the Democratic People's Republic of Korea [DPRK] and his delegation, we in Grenada pledge to continue to give our fullest support to your struggles for reunifying your country and making once again, one Korea, one people.

Today, we know our comrades in the DPRK are still facing threats from maneuvers right now taking place on their soil and in their region. We want to say to them that they also have our fullest solidarity in their struggle to end those hostile maneuvers, in their fight to have all U.S. soldiers removed from Korean soil.

Coming from almost as far away, from a chain of islands near Africa, with a brave, fighting and heroic people, who had their own revolution a few years ago, and whose president is a very good friend of Grenada, the foreign minister of Seychelles has traveled a long, long distance to be with us here today.

The Seychelles late last year faced a mercenary attack organized and financed by South Africa, with the full backing of the USA. But these brave people, on discovering those mercenaries on their land, with their AK [automatic rifle] in their hand, they drove them off. The South Africans were made to flee as puppy dogs, with their tails between their legs — well beaten.

These comrades have done what our own people in Grenada will do, if any mercenary or outside aggressive force chooses to land on our soil.

We also have here with us our friends from southern Africa, from Namibia, a country that today continues to be denied its independence because South Africa has decided that they should not be independent. The Reagan administration in the U.S. has been the main force pushing to ensure that the timetable and plan for independence in Namibia are made so difficult, so full of ridiculous clauses and conditions, that the elections are bound to be a farce. We, therefore, expect that the people of Namibia, under their authentic leadership, the South-West Africa People's Organization, will continue to fight with arms in hand to win their freedom and their dignity. We again pledge our fullest support and solidarity with the people of Namibia.

We also pledge, on this platform today, our continuing and fullest support for our sisters and brothers in Angola, for our sisters and brothers in the African National Congress in South Africa, and for all of the front-line states that are today facing daily pressure from the South African military. To all our friends in southern Africa, who are today still fighting for national liberation or to consolidate their hard-won independence, the people of Grenada today send their warmest greetings and salutations.

And we also recognize today the struggles of the people of Libya; the struggles of the people of Iraq, who had their nuclear reactor blown up by Israel last year; Syria and Lebanon; of the Western Sahara; and the people of Palestine, who are today continuing to struggle for their homeland. Today, we think of the vicious and wicked annexation of the Golan Heights by Israel, we think of the daily attacks on Lebanon and Syria by the Israelis. Today, we once again send our warmest and firmest handshake to all our friends in the Arab world and particularly to the people of Palestine, who must one day have their homeland returned.

Today, we support on this platform all the struggles of the peoples of the world for national liberation, for the new international economic order, for the new international information order, for peace, for prosperity, for social progress.

And, today, I also want to ask you especially to remember a very brave people who have hit out against local reaction and imperialism, a people who only two days ago had to fight against these forces inside their own country. We want to remember a country [Suriname] that only two days ago was subjected to yet another attack on its process, yet another counterrevolutionary attempt to roll back the new life that is being built for its people.

On the same day that fighting broke out two days ago, we publicly expressed our solidarity to the leadership and the people of that country. We never expected a response because the fighting was still continuing. Nor did we expect to receive a message of solidarity for our third anniversary because of the difficult situation. Thus it was with great pleasure and shock that we received a message from the leader of that revolutionary process, yesterday. The message reads:

"The government and the people of Suriname, although in a situation of distress due to counterrevolutionary threats made by rightist opportunists in the army, want to convey to you, the People's Revolutionary Government of Grenada, and the people of Grenada, the deepest and sincerest congratulations for the results that you have achieved over three years of a genuine people's revolution. The government and people of Suriname follow your development with great attention. We try to learn from you and we know that international solidarity of revolutionary countries is essential to succeed in this day and age, where international imperialist and fascist forces try to destabilize the rightful aspirations of people who fight for genuine sovereignty and development. Long live the Grenada Revolution.

"Signed: Desi Bouterse, Commander-in-Chief of the Army."

If we look at our geography books or consult our atlases, we see that our country, Grenada, is defined as an island, a separate piece of land surrounded by water. But, as I look around this huge multitude this afternoon, and see all the faces from so many parts of our earth, I see quite clearly that while, of course, Grenada remains physically an island, Grenada is no longer really an island! No more can we ever see ourselves as separate, cut off, a little rock in the world's great seas.

For your presence here this afternoon, comrades and friends from throughout the nations of the world, proves to us that we are an integral and individual part of the mainland of the world's people, and that the seas that surround our country can be bridged and leapt over by anyone who wishes to share our process, anyone who wants to see for themselves the freedom we are making, anyone who has the independence of mind and spirit not to be fooled by the imperialist media-monsters and press potentates who spread their lies throughout the world about our revolution.

To all of you who have scorned the distance between your countries and ours, and flown across land and water to reach us and be with us on this, the third anniversary of our people's grasp of power and the irreversible rupture with the brutality and buffoonery of the Gairy dictatorship — our hearts are moved that you have come to us. Our joy at your being with us, we express with our own invitation to share with us everything in our country: our advances, our problems and setbacks, our successes and our mistakes, our achievements and our plans.

We have a national consciousness of the profound need for criticism and self-criticism, and we have nothing to hide. We are justly proud of the steps we have made in three years to wrench our country out of the vortex of underdevelopment into which it was sucked, and through which it whirled in pain, agony, and decay under the dictatorship. We are practically moved at the daily discoveries we are making about the huge capacity and creative genius of our people, and the energy and commitment with which they are fighting the great battle for economic construction, which we are waging in our country.

Every ounce of effort and drop of sweat means investment for us, for our people have learned that nothing will come out unless everything is put in! But we are also continually inspired by our people's ability to pause, analyze and consider their progress, to identify their errors and weaknesses, and to resolve their problems, contradictions, and failures as they move in their masses along the road we are building towards a new society.

If you can help us in that process, come with your suggestions, your help and your criticisms, for the overriding and fundamental principle in our revolution is consultation with all of our people through their structures of democracy, their workers' parish councils, their zonal councils, their trade unions, their NWO, their NYO, and their Young Pioneers. In the spirit of these organs of popular democracy, we welcome your views and your advice.

We also ask you to take the truth of our revolution back to your homeland, for the truth itself is revolutionary and we are confident that it cannot harm us. It is in itself our comrade. It is also the enemy of our enemies and the greatest weapon we have. Our detractors and villifiers have neutron bombs and wage chemical warfare. We hold the truth of our process out towards them: our free health, our free education, our free school books and uniforms, our free milk, our national bus service, our international airport, our clinics, our fishing fleet and saltfish plant, our agro-industries, our house-repair program, our Centres for Popular Education. These are the great truths of the Grenada revolution.

As we begin the fourth year of our revolution, it is very clear that the great strength of the revolution, first and foremost, lies in the unbreakable link between the masses and the party; between the masses and the government; between the masses and the state.

This is what gives our revolution an invincible force, because the masses see the party, see the state and the government as theirs; not something foreign or strange, or apart or isolated from them, but living, throbbing entities that embody their aspirations, their interests and their hopes.

Over the years the leadership of this revolution have learnt much from you, the heroic Grenadian people; over and over again you have renewed and fortified our confidence, our faith, our revolutionary enthusiasm, our resolve; every day you help to educate us, you help the party and the leaders to develop a clearer awareness of our process, you help make us more revolutionary. And we are convinced that these fraternal relationships will expand and endure in years to come.

For together as party, government, and people, we will continue to learn from each other, to share ideas and confidence with each other, to hide nothing from each other, and to love each other. We will continue to work harder together, produce more together, and build Grenada together — a Grenada that will continue to march proudly forward into the bright sunshine of a great future.

The Year of Political and Academic Education

January 3, 1983

The following radio address was printed in the January 5, 1983, Free West Indian. *It has been slightly abridged.*

Sisters and brothers;
Patriots of free Grenada;
Friends;
Comrades all:

On behalf of our party and government I extend to you all warm, fraternal greetings on the first day of 1983 and wish you peace, good health, and success for the new year.

At the beginning of every year it is traditional to throw our vision ahead to the tasks and challenges contained in the upcoming twelve months, to commit ourselves to the fulfillment of those tasks, and to scientifically plan the correct strategy for accomplishing our objectives.

New Year resolutions and recommitments, projected visions and dedications are meaningless if they are not informed and guided by the lessons drawn from the collective experiences of the past year. Therefore, before we open the door to step boldly and forthrightly into 1983 it is necessary to pause and review the road we have traveled, take stock of our successes and setbacks, and honestly evaluate our shortcomings and failures.

Comrades, 1982 was a year when the present economic crisis in world capitalism, which began in 1979, grew worse and this meant that the economies of our region were severely affected.

Sisters and brothers, comrades, in January of last year when our People's Revolutionary Government declared 1982 as the Year of Economic Construction we clearly foresaw the worsening of this capitalist crisis during the year and the negative effects it would have on our fragile, open, and dependent economy.

We were convinced then, and remain convinced today, that the very future of our revolution hinged on our people's struggle to construct a viable economy out of the ruins and devastation inherited from colonialism, Gairyism, and neocolonialism. Economic construction, laying the basis for genuine economic independence and liberation from imperialism, was to be the key focus and major priority for 1982.

At that time we asked ourselves what would the Year of Economic Construction mean to our working people? What challenges will it put to them and what benefits will it bring to them?

We said then and will continue to say in 1983 that real progress for our country will only be achieved through the hard work of our people and that those who labor to construct *must* share in the fruits of their labor.

We stressed then and will continue to stress in 1983 that our working class and our working people must be more involved in the planning and decisions affecting their work, as well as the work itself.

The new revolutionary people's democracy must extend from the community to the workplace. More discussions, more seminars, more structures for emulation, more production committees, must be organized and made to function in the factories, farms and offices of our nation.

We said at the beginning of 1982 and will repeat throughout the new year that our working people must be brought into the process of national economic planning. This heightened democratic activity at the workplace will not only achieve greater production and output, sharpen efficiency, and eliminate waste and corruption but also improve the social wage and thus widen the range and scope of material benefits coming to our working people. . . .

Sisters and brothers, comrades, on March 9, 1982, an unprecedented event in the English-speaking Caribbean took place in St. George's, an event which marked an extraordinary step forward for our people and which has been characterized as the most dramatic single demonstration of the concrete exercise by a whole people of the revolutionary democratic principle of participation.

I am referring, of course, to the presentation to the nation and the world on that day of a genuine people's budget which was formulated out of a process begun on a mass scale when 1,000 delegates from all our mass organizations came together at the Dome on January 29 for an historic conference on the economy.

This was swiftly followed up by a series of twenty-five zonal and workers' parish councils and dozens of other meetings in every corner of our country including meetings with the private sector. Then on March 1 we held another conference on the economy at the Dome, bringing together all those who had not yet aired their views or suggestions, all those who were not yet members of our mass organizations, including our senior citizens, the self-employed, and those working for small enterprises. This was followed by a three-day session, also at the Dome, with the representatives and managers of the state enterprises.

What was being attempted in this democratic exercise, comrades, was a pooling of the ideas and opinions of literally every section and stratum of our people. And what we discovered was a virtual treasure chest of valuable and creative ideas coming out of the concrete experience and social practice of our people and being offered by them in a loud, clear, unequivocal, and unselfish manner, all in the spirit of collective responsibility towards planning and charting the economic construction effort of the nation.

Throughout the year this spirit prevailed as the five component parts of our revolutionary people's democracy — responsibility, accountability, participation, material benefits, and electability — became more entrenched in our society.

In 1982 our working class through their trade unions elected their leaders, and our NWO sisters elected their national executive. People's democracy was evident recently when the general membership of the Technical and Allied Workers' Union and the Agricultural and General Workers' Union made fundamental amendments to their constitutions and when the members of the National Women's Organisation participated over a period of months in a structured manner in drafting, criticizing, and redrafting the highly significant work plan that will guide their work over the next three years.

Furthermore, more new people's revolutionary laws were passed last year, in the ongoing process of enshrining and embedding our people's democratic rights into the laws of the land. The Rent Law, the increased Workmen's Compensation Law, and the Third Party Insurance (Amendment) Law, all of which were announced at Queen's Park on May Day 1982, at the largest gathering of our working class ever assembled in Grenada for May Day, are three particularly significant pieces of legislation that will advance the human rights of our working people. . . .

Comrades, even our right-wing detractors are today being forced to acknowledge the progress we have made. For them it is indeed difficult to dispute a World Bank report which states that our poor, struggling country, with all its natural economic limitations and in spite of the dismal legacy of economic backwardness, corruption, and mismanagement from the Gairy dictatorship, and the well known list of imperialist attempts at economic sabotage, achieved 9 percent cumulative growth in our economy in the first three years of the revolution. Furthermore, what can they say about the reduction of our unemployment from 49 percent in 1979 to 14.2 percent today.

If we stay firmly on the course we have charted then this modest growth will continue in the years to come. And as more economic projects come on-stream, particularly in construction and agriculture, many more jobs will be created and in a few years unemployment will be wiped out in Grenada.

But joyful as that prediction may appear to be on the surface there is an underlying problem that we must recognize and address squarely as we begin the new year. Yes, there will be many new jobs and yes there will be sisters and brothers now unemployed who must take those jobs. But comrades, what is critically necessary is that they must be ready to take up these jobs. They must be prepared and trained and educated for those jobs. We have to recognize that we cannot build a national economy; we cannot reclaim our economy from the grips of imperialism without a well-trained and highly skilled work force. This low training of our people is a major weakness and if we do not move fast to correct it, the progress of the revolution will be held back.

This is yet another fundamental challange that faces our revolution and our people. But it is by no means insurmountable. We can and we will tackle it successfully, but the approach to this challenge must be in keeping with the tradition that we've established since the revolution.

This approach has been one that says: once a major problem has been identified and a top priority attached to it, then we should proceed in a given period of time to channel our resources and concentrate our energies and efforts to the solution of that problem.

Following this approach, since the early days of the revolution we have designated each year a special focus, 1979 was the Year of Liberation, 1980 the Year of Education and Production, 1981 the Year of Agriculture and Agro-industries, 1982 the Year of Economic Construction, and today I am happy to tell you that our People's Revolutionary Government has declared 1983 as the Year of Political and Academic Education.

As in the past, this focus for 1983 was not chosen arbitrarily or as the result of a dream. It is not just a pretty idea that, one day last week, jumped out of the head of a member of the top leadership. It is a scientific and collective conclusion reached after many painstaking hours of analysis and evaluation.

It is true that the political consciousness, awareness, and understanding of the Grenadian people has advanced swiftly since the revolution. It is also true that relative to other countries in the region our people have a fairly high degree of political education.

But, comrades, political education like all forms of education is not static. It does not stop after it reaches a certain level. On the contrary, it is dynamic, always moving, always growing and developing. The complex political and economic situation in the world today demands from all our people greater clarity of understanding, sharper powers of analysis, and broader perspectives.

Our people must develop in the new year a mental grasp on the true nature of the international capitalist crisis which is holding back the progress of our revolution and the development of all poor countries in the world. They must know the causes and origins of this crisis. They must see clearly the link between politics and economics, between imperialist exploitation and persistent poverty, between the mad buildup of arms by imperialism and the economic crisis.

With their political consciousness raised and broadened our people will better understand the necessity to join and strengthen those mass organizations and trade unions that already exist.

Political education will help to identify from the ranks of our working people the future leaders of the revolution, and it will help to prepare the working class to assume its historic role of transforming Grenada from backwardness and dependency to genuine economic independence.

So one of the major tasks that confronts us all in 1983 will be to organize more worker education sessions at the workplaces, and more forums for political discussions in the factories, fields, communities, and schools across the nation.

Comrades, the educational system we inherited from colonialism and Gairyism was geared to exporting our people, not orienting them to tackle the social and economic developmental tasks facing the country. Education and production together with economic construction were never seen to be closely interrelated. The onus is now on us as a free people to redirect this misguided emphasis.

The main academic or educational task for 1983, therefore, must be to push ahead vigorously with the CPE adult education program, to bring thousands more of our working people into this program because of its fundamental relevance to the social, political, and economic development of the masses. CPE certificates will therefore become more of a critical asset in the new job opportunities that will be created and an equally important asset in the areas of training and promotion. A CPE Adult Education Certificate will become a recognized certificate in the society. Those who get it will be able to use it as the qualification for certain jobs and for promotion in exisiting jobs.

Thus, it must be emphasized that adult education through the CPE will be important not only for those seeking jobs, but also for those who already have jobs, and also for the elderly, for the poorest of our people, and indeed for all of our people.

The consolidation and further development of the National In-Service Teacher Education and Community School Day programs, and the further laying of the basis for the establishment of universal secondary education and the creation of more developed technical training programs are all critical priorities for 1983. . . .

What are the main tasks for this Year of Political and Academic Education? The main tasks are the following: (1) Worker education in all workplaces — state and private; (2) CPE in all villages; (3) CPE also for the workers; (4) Total trade union involvement in CPE and worker education; (5) More work-study programs for our students; (6) More seminars and more training programs by the mass organizations; (7) More technical seminars for different categories of workers in order to improve their skills.

Our overall objective in 1983 the Year of Academic and Politcal Education is to make our country and revolution a big popular school. Let study and learning develop into permanent habits of a conscious people. Let us put into full practice that great principle of the revolution that education never stops — that is the fundamental right of all of our people to have more training, to raise ever higher our level of education so as to know and understand ourselves as a people — who we are, where we have come from, where we are going.

Our party and government have set this priority because we firmly believe that it is on the realization of this basic task that our future will be assured. Without education, no genuine people's democracy can be built since real democracy always assumes the informed, conscious, and educated participation of the people. Without education, there can be no real worker participation, no substantial increase in production and productivity, no individual and collective growth, no true dignity, no genuine independence. As a nation we will in 1983 be striving collectively and individually to learn more about ourselves and our condition so that together we can forge ahead to a confident future.

And as we pursue this noble objective with revolutionary zeal and determination, let us also rededicate ourselves to the struggle for world peace, disarmament, peaceful coexistence, and Caribbean integration. Let us continue to push strenuously for the unreserved acceptance in our region of the principle of ideological pluralism and for an end to all forms of oppression, exploitation, and military aggressions against the peoples of the Caribbean, Latin American, and the entire world. . . .

An Armed Attack Against
Our Country Is Imminent

March 23, 1983

The following address was broadcast nationally over Radio Free Grenada. It was printed as a supplement to the Free West Indian.

Sisters and brothers of our beloved revolutionary homeland; Patriots:

Tonight, on behalf of our party and government, I have the responsibility of informing our people that our revolution is in grave danger and that our country is faced with its gravest threat since our glorious March 13 revolution.

From the evidence in our possession, we are convinced that an armed attack against our country by counterrevolutionaries and mercenaries organized, financed, trained, and directed by United States imperialism, is imminent and can come any day now.

Only a few day ago — on March 17, to be precise — at our 1983 Budget-Plan presentation, I revealed the analysis of our party that the warmongering Reagan was becoming increasingly desperate, and in that desperation the possibility of military intervention against the revolutionary processes in the region — particularly Cuba, Nicaragua, and Grenada — seemed inevitable.

This seemed the likely way out for the fascist clique in Washington because their arrogant designs for regional and world domination continue to fail. The continuing economic crisis in the U.S. and its effects, the increasing successes of the popular liberation movements, particularly in El Salvador, the continued deepening and strengthening of the revolutionary processes in Cuba, Nicaragua, and Grenada, the total collapse of Reagan's so-called Caribbean Basin Initiative, and the growing popular opposition to his mad nuclear policy, have made imperialism more desperate and determined to halt revolutionary processes in this region.

Less than thirty-six hours after we publicly revealed what our intelligence sources and analysis suggested, less than thirty-six hours after we alerted our people to this possible danger, an all-out invasion of Nicaragua was launched. A large contingent of Somocista counter-revolutionaries — armed, trained, financed, and directed by the CIA — were dropped by airplanes into Nicaragua, only 120 miles from its capital.

It is important to note also, comrades, that this invasion came exactly three days after the statement by the Chief of Naval Operations, Admiral James Watkins, that the time had come "for the U.S. to put some teeth behind our rhetoric." In other words, the U.S. must back up its threats with military action.

We now have concrete intelligence information which confirms the view that the revolution will be faced with military aggression from imperialism. With the attack against Nicaragua, the dangers facing us are more real and urgent.

For some time now, our intelligence services have been gathering information on counterrevolutionary groups who have publicly declared their intention to overthrow revolutionary governments in the region. What we have discovered as a result are the following facts:

(1) that the key counterrevolutionaries have been meeting more frequently in recent times;

(2) that several of these corrupt, opportunist, and reactionary elements who aspire to grab power have begun to resolve their leadership differences with the aim of creating a more united counterrevolutionary front;

(3) that their coordination with the CIA has stepped up;

(4) that they have received direct assistance from the CIA in the form of money, arms, and training and have also received offers of transportation, logistical support and supplies, and an undertaking that immediately on launching the attack their declared counterrevolutionary government will receive recognition.

(5) We have been able to discover the name and full background of the main CIA case officer responsible for coordinating the present plot. We know his name, where he worked before, his previous activities, and which other revolutionary processes he has attempted to subvert in recent times.

(6) Another CIA case officer involved in this operation is known to have been involved in directing and masterminding the operation to assassinate the leadership that resulted in the fatal June 19, 1980, bomb blast.

(7) These elements have established direct links with the Cuban exile group which was responsible for the Air Cubana disaster and with Somocista counterrevolutionary elements who are right now involved in the invasion of Nicaragua.

(8) With the assistance of the CIA, these elements have been able to get some of the criminal elements they hope to use in the invasion of our country trained in Miami, in some of the same camps in which the

Somocista counters and various mercenaries have been trained.

(9) As part of their planning process, the CIA helped to allocate different sets of these criminal counterrevolutionaries for the physical attacks against Nicaragua and Grenada and decided several weeks ago to attack during this period, in order to coincide with the massive military maneuvers taking place in our region at this time, and as a culmination of the major propaganda offensive of Reagan and his chief lieutenants against the revolutionary processes in the region.

(10) The main base of operation and activity of these elements is one of our neighboring territories, only a few miles away.

(11) As a result of all this work on our part, we have been able not only to uncover actual plans to overthrow our government and to turn back our revolution, but also the appropriate number of men they hope to use, the appropriate number and type of arms they possess, the kind of logistical support they hope to receive. We know, comrades, the targets they intend to destroy. We know many of the persons they plan to arrest, those they plan to kill, and how they plan to strike terror and fear among the broad masses.

(12) It is necessary to doubly emphasize that we know the actual period in the near future that they are hoping to use to launch their murderous attack.

Bearing in mind all the facts mentioned already, considering the clear and disturbing pattern of U.S. intervention and aggression in our region and the world, and noting the invasion of Nicaragua now taking place, we have concluded that the danger which we face in this period is real.

When the president of the United States of America, who is also commander-in-chief of its armed forces, states publicly and clearly that tiny Grenada is a threat to the national security of the mighty and powerful USA, and when his top advisers and military personnel indicate that the time has come to put "teeth into their rhetoric," then it is clear that Goliath has turned his attention to David.

When the commander-in-chief of one of the most sophisticated, most advanced, and largest armed forces in the world chooses to classify a small proud and determined people as a threat to his national security, then this must be cause for serious concern.

We have to ask ourselves why would his most senior officials, including his Vice President, George Bush (former chief of CIA), his Secretary of State, William Schultz, his Secretary for Defense, Caspar Weinberger, and his Deputy Secretary for Inter-American Affairs, Nestor Sanchez, all choose to make slanderous statements, if not to provide the justification for this planned aggression?

The U.S. government has a well-documented history of dealing with countries which it has deemed threats to its national security. The U.S. has intervened militarily in this region well over 100 times in the past

100 years to protect its so-called national security interests.

Although the information on this current threat is, by far, the most detailed and specific that we have had of any plot, and although this threat is by far the most dangerous that we have ever faced, some of our people are saying that there have been other occasions when we have had cause for justified concern that our revolution was threatened.

That is true, comrades, but what is important for us to stress tonight is that on previous occasions we forced our enemies to change their plans at the last minute because we were successfully able to mobilize regional and international public opinion in our defense. In other words, we were able to alert the world of the danger that we faced, and the world stood up with us.

The best example of this that I can give you tonight is the "Amber and the Amberdines" maneuver conducted by the U.S. in August 1981 off Puerto Rico as a full-scale dress rehearsal for an invasion of our country.

Once we had received concrete proof from the mouth of the man in charge of the operation, Rear Admiral McKenzie, that this maneuver was a trial run for the actual invasion of our beloved homeland, we immediately went on a political and diplomatic offensive to alert the world of the threat facing us, to call for international solidarity, and to request our friends to pressure the U.S. not to carry out its aggressive plans.

We informed the United Nations, the Nonaligned Movement, the Organization of American States, and other regional and international organizations of the grave situation. We also informed peaceloving and friendly governments, political parties, pressure groups, and other organizations of the danger. In fact, literally hundreds of cables, telexes, telephone calls, and so on were made to virtually all parts of the world.

It is fortunate for us that the conscience of mankind and the force of world public opinion responded readily on all continents to our call.

In fact, at a recent summit, the head of a particular government informed us of his government's concern at the time of the "Amber and the Amberdines" threat and the action which he had taken in calling in the U.S. ambassador resident in his country to demand an explanation. This particular country is thousands of miles away from us.

As a result of these and other experiences, we now fully understand and appreciate the tremendous importance and impact of international public opinion, and on this occasion we are again taking the necessary steps to alert and mobilize regional and international public opinion.

But, comrades, there is another very important lesson which we have also learnt and this is, whenever our country is in danger, whenever our revolution is threatened, we must always go all out to give our people the facts, to fully alert them as to the precise nature of the danger, and to call upon them to mobilize and organize themselves in defense of our revolution.

That is why, apart from mobilizing public opinion to stand up with us at the time of the "Amber and the Amberdines" threat, we also mobilized our people to respond decisively with the successful "Heroes of the Homeland" maneuver which demonstrated to the world that, in the defense of this land, the freedom of our sea and sky, we stand as a proud, united, conscious, and vigilant people, ready and willing to make the ultimate sacrifice.

Again, in face of grave danger, we need to call our people to arms. Once again, we have to shoulder our fundamental responsibility to defend what we fought for and won after many years of bitter struggle.

We must never forget that the only way in which we can ever guarantee that international public opinion comes to our defense is if we can continue to show to the world that we are willing — as a united people every single one of us — to stand up firmly on our own two legs with arms in our hands to fight and to die, if necessary, in the defense of our beloved homeland.

This land is ours, every square inch of its soil is ours, every grain of sand is ours, every nutmeg pod is ours, every beautiful young Pioneer who walks on this land is ours. It is our responsibility and ours alone, to fight to defend our homeland.

Over the past few days, our people have demonstrated a genuine spirit of internationalism. In the many solidarity statements with heroic Nicaragua coming from all sections of our working people, our women, our youth, the sense of fraternal anguish and shared identity comes very clearly across.

But even so, we have allowed ourselves to slip into complacency and a degree of over-confidence in responding to the present situation. Some sections of our people, while recognizing that dangers do exist, allow themselves to believe that Grenada will not be invaded because we are a small island, or because we share no borders with hostile neighbors as Nicaragua does. Some also feel that because ours is the only revolution that has not yet faced direct military attack, we will continue to be lucky, and some even go as far as saying that with victory on the horizon for our sisters and brothers in Nicaragua, imperialism will not have any mercenaries left to send to Grenada.

However, we cannot, under any circumstances, and particularly in light of the information we now have, lose sight of the dangerous reality at present. The Seychelles Islands and Comoros Islands, smaller in size and population than Grenada, were both subject to invasions from the forces of imperialism in the last few years.

We should also note that prior to the 1961 Playa Girón invasion of Cuba, which resulted in crushing defeat for counterrevolutionary forces supported by U.S. imperialism, there were some Cubans who believed, for all kinds of reasons, that there would be no invasion of Cuba. But it came, and today their revolution is invincible because our Cuban comrades — like our Nicaraguan comrades today — have learnt the lessons of history and the need for permanent vigilance and preparedness of the people.

We in Grenada cannot, like ostriches, bury our heads in the sand and ignore the lessons of history.

How do we respond to the present threat? Our fundamental duty is to defend our homeland, to be psychologically, politically, and combatively prepared to handle an attack in whatever form, and at whatever time Reagan and his warmongers may choose to land on our shores.

This means that for those of us who are not yet in the militia — join now.

For those who are inactive — reactivate yourselves and begin training in a serious, disciplined, consistent, and revolutionary manner.

There is a role for everyone to play in defense — the elderly as well as the young. Remember Reagan and his warmongers will not choose who to kill.

There are trenches to be dug, vehicles to be driven, food to be cooked and distributed, first-aid assistance to be organized, the care of the young and elderly to be guaranteed, and many more specific tasks to be accomplished.

In addition to our number one task of recruitment into the militia, there are other measures to be taken to strengthen our defense capacity.

There will be immediate recruitment into some sections of the PRA and police service.

Our People's Revolutionary Armed Forces, will stage a massive military maneuver from April 21 to 24. This maneuver, which will be called "Jeremiah Richardson Defense of the Homeland Maneuver," will again demonstrate to imperialism that we are a united, strong, and vigilant people who will never give up.

Let us ensure that Reagan and his warmongers never ever turn back the forward march of our people and revolution. The work that we are doing today in the building of a people's economy and the construction of a new infrastructure is laying the basis for a secure future for all our people.

Let us do everything in our power to ensure that that secure future is not unduly disturbed by the terrible loss of life, property, and mass suffering and destruction which any invasion that we are not prepared to withstand is bound to bring.

Notwithstanding the uncertainty posed by this present imminent threat, let us continue to work with discipline, determination, and serene confidence towards the glorious day when there will be no unemployment in our country, when each and every family will have a decent living, when every man, woman, and child is guaranteed their total right to education, health, and social security.

As we prepare to deal with this imminent threat, let us remember that our sisters and brothers, the brave sons and daughters of Sandino's Nicaragua, are continuing their fierce struggle to crush the forces of counterrevolution and imperialism.

According to inside reports, 500 well-trained counterrevolutionaries were parachuted into Nicaragua days in advance of the main force and are right now being supplied by planes from Honduras.

At the same time, 1,500 more are now inside Nicaragua on their way to join the advance group of 500, and a further 2,500 are concentrated on the border with Honduras, awaiting their turn to massacre innocent women and children in their vain hope to turn back the heroic Nicaraguan revolution.

While we in Grenada must unhesitatingly and firmly condemn these acts of aggression against our sisters and brothers of revolutionary Nicaragua, we must at the same time, in a clear, resounding, and unequivocal voice, join the rest of progressive mankind in condemning the active involvement of Israeli and Honduran army personnel, including direct bombing of key positions in Nicaragua by Honduran military forces, in this open and barbarous onslaught on the sovereign soil of Nicaragua.

It is clear to us, however, that no amount of arms and weapons of war can hinder the onward march of the revolutionary process taking place in Nicaragua, and we once again affirm to the sons and daughters of Sandino our full, unswerving and permanent solidarity.

Let us take careful note of the fact that these counterrevolutionary elements were sent in advance of the main force — just like they had done in their attacks on the Seychelles and Comoros Islands — and they are receiving regular supplies by enemy planes and that more elements are waiting to move in.

With our information, with these examples, both historical and present, we ought not to be taken unprepared. Let us together ensure that we come out of this period stronger in unity, fortified in spirit, firmer in our determination, more organized in our democratic structures, responding to future threats like second nature because of our constant preparedness.

Even at this late hour, we want to repeat that our preference is for peace and normal relations with the U.S. administration. We understand very clearly that only an environment of peace will allow us the opportunity to continue to develop our economy, raise our academic and skills' levels and political consciousness, and bring more and more benefits to our people.

We do not want war. We have never wanted war. But equally, we are not prepared to give our birthright or to allow others — no matter how big and powerful they are — to shape our destiny for us or to tell us what we can do, when we can do it, and how we must do it.

Our enemies had better try to understand the deep pride and dignity of our people and the courageous way in which we have always faced up to difficulties. They will do well to recall the heroic history of struggle and resistance of our people from the days of Fedon through Butler and Marryshow, right up to the present.

They had better remember the vanguard role of our glorious party — the New Jewel Movement — which mobilized, organized, and led our people through the years of terror and repression of the Gairy dictatorship up to the seizure of state power and the dawning of the new day of liberation and freedom on March 13, 1979.

There is no doubt that we are a peace-loving people, but there is equally no doubt that we are a proud and courageous people who will always fight to defend our dignity, our freedom, and our homeland.

What is needed from us as a people at this time, is to make sure that we never allow ourselves to slip back into complacency, to make sure that we are always as ready to defend our homeland as we are to continue to build it, to make sure that we never again allow our militia duties to be taken lightly, to make sure that once we regain our fighting strength and vigor of August 1981, that we do not allow ourselves to ever lose that vigor and strength again.

Our watchwords must forever be:

Calm and calculated in our fulfillment of our daily tasks;

Always vigilant;

Always able to work;

Always able to study;

Always able to produce.

Yet ready, prepared, confident, and assured of victory whenever and however Reagan and his warlords strike.

Long live the fighting spirit, unity, and determination of our heroic Grenadian people!

Long live our Revolutionary Armed Forces!

Long live our Revolutionary People's Militia!

Long live the Grenada revolution!

Forward ever, backward never!

Maurice Bishop Speaks to
U.S. Working People

June 5, 1983

The following speech was given to an overflow audience of over 2,500 at Hunter College in New York City. It was originally printed in the July 15, 22, and 29 issues of the Militant. *It has been slightly abridged.*

Thank you very much for that very warm welcome sisters and brothers, comrades all.

May I start out by bringing to you warm fraternal greetings from the free people of revolutionary Grenada. May I also right in the very beginning say how very, very pleasant it is to be back in New York among you, to be in this great hall, where there are so many hundreds of our sisters and brothers. That is going to bring a great deal of pleasure to our free people, and I will certainly report your warmth, your enthusiasm, and your revolutionary support for our process when I return.

I would also like to place on the record our deep appreciation for the people responsible in Hunter College for lending us this facility this evening.

We are here among friends. But looking around, there are two people here who are right now representing their countries at the United Nations — people who are involved in liberation struggles, who are struggling for freedom for their peoples.

It's very important right at the beginning, sisters and brothers, that we acknowledge the presence of Dr. Zehdi Terzi, the representative to the United Nations of the Palestine Liberation Organization, the PLO. [*Chants of "PLO!, PLO!, PLO!"*]

Dr. Terzi can be assured as always that the people of Palestine and their sole authentic representative, the Palestine Liberation Organization, will always have the full support of the fraternal people of Grenada. [*Applause*]

And there is another liberation movement whose representative is present among us. And this one too has been in the news quite a lot recently. Contrary to what some people have been trying to pretend — that this particular liberation organization is not willing to take the struggle to the highest stage — right in the capital city of the racist apartheid country of South Africa, a bomb went off. [*Applause*]

The South African racists who have spent so much time inventing all sorts of ingenious ways of oppressing the people of South Africa, the Black majority, are now discovering that in common with all of the national liberation movements around the world that are forced to move to the highest stage of the struggle, the African National Congress [ANC] is also willing to make that step.

In saluting the deputy permanent representative of the ANC to the United Nations, let us ask him to bring back to his people, to bring back to his organization, to bring back to Oliver Tambo, to Nelson Mandela whose spirit is here with us, to bring back the love, the respect, the concern, the admiration, and the fraternal feelings of all of us: Brother David Ndaba. [*Chants of "ANC!, ANC!, ANC!"*]

The last time I had the opportunity, sisters and brothers, comrades, of being in New York and addressing our Grenadian nationals, other people from the Caribbean and Latin America, and of course the people of the United States was four years ago. Since those four years have passed, a lot has happened in our country. A lot has happened in the world. And one of the reasons that we have come to the United States is to share our experiences of the last four years with the people of the United States.

We were anxious to do this because there has been a major campaign [against Grenada] over the last several weeks and months — starting from last year in November with some remarks by the U.S. vice-president in Miami, continuing with more remarks from the secretary of state, the secretary of defense, the deputy secretary of defense, the admiral of the fleet.

[This included] the president himself, as you know, on the tenth of March addressing manufacturers; on the twenty-third of March in the famous, or infamous, Star Wars speech; and more recently again to the joint session of Congress on the twenty-seventh of April. And in all these, different allegations were made against our country.

And therefore we were particularly happy, comrades, to have the opportunity of an invitation from TransAfrica, the organization based in Washington that has been doing lobbying for Africa and the Caribbean. We were invited to come to address their sixth annual dinner last night, and that was a very successful event. We want to publicly thank TransAfrica, once again, for making this visit possible.

The Congressional Black Caucus, too, was involved as cosponsor of this visit, and we also want to place our appreciation for this on the record. And if anyone has any doubts at all about the growing strength of the Black vote, and of the increasing influence of Afro-Americans in this country, I want to let you know that it was precisely because of the pressures that were brought by our friends in the Black Caucus that a visa was eventually granted for the visit. [*Applause*]

Of course, we set ourselves other objectives for the visit. These included the very important objective of trying to deepen and strengthen the people-to-people relations that have always existed between our two countries, Grenada and the United States. At the level of the people, there has never been any problem. We have always had excellent relations with the people of the United States.

In fact, in some years more American tourists come to our country than the entire population of our country. And if we go around and take a careful count, we may well discover that there are more Grenadians living in the United States than the whole population of Grenada.

And on top of that, there are several Americans who reside permanently in our country. And there is a medical school in Grenada where over 700 young Americans are earning their right to become doctors.

So from our point of view, clearly, bad relations do not make sense. From our point of view, the need to ensure that even more American visitors come to our country every year is a critical and burning need. And the opportunity, therefore, to speak directly to the people of the United States is a very important opportunity.

We also set an objective of trying to make contact with as many sectors and sections of American society as we could during this visit. And to this end, there have been several meetings this past week with congressmen and with other influential people in the society. We have attempted over this period, also, to try to talk to as many people from the media as we could reach. That objective has gone quite well.

And another objective that we had was to use the period to deepen our relations with some of our closest friends in the United States, with our Black American sisters and brothers, with our Grenadian nationals, with those progressive forces right across the United States who have given us so much support unstintingly, to those who lead and are hard workers in the friendship societies and the solidarity committees. We were very anxious to speak to the sisters and brothers, to express our appreciation for the hard work that they have done, and to give them some idea as to what we are doing at this time in Grenada. That objective, also, has gone well.

Another objective was to try yet again to establish some form of official contact, an official dialogue, with the government of the United States. We, of course, cannot decide which government is going to be in power in the United States at any given moment in time. That is a matter for the people of the United States. We believe it is extremely important for us to maintain normal relations so that we are able to conduct proper dialogue in a civilized fashion with whomever happens to be in power at a particular time. [*Applause*]

The question of ideological differences, the question of different paths of socioeconomic and political development, the question of geopolitical perspectives and of strategic consensuses and what not, is really neither here nor there in the final analysis. The fact of the matter is, if there is no established mechanism for holding dialogue, then there is no basis on which relations can be maintained in an effective way. We believe it is in the interests of both the peoples of the United States and of Grenada to have normal relations between our two governments.

We believe it is important because too much is at stake here. Too many of our nationals live in this country. And too many American citizens and students live in our country. There is a need for some kind of mechanism to be established. And that is why we have been struggling so hard to try to get some of the basic norms reestablished.

Let us exchange ambassadors, we have said. They have rejected that. So we have no ambassador accredited to Washington because they refuse to accept the credentials of the ambassador we have suggested. When they replaced their ambassador after the electoral victory of President Reagan in 1980 and a new ambassador came out in 1981, he was not accredited to Grenada. So we have to talk presumably using loud speakers.

In 1981 on two occasions I wrote letters to President Reagan — in March and again in August. The first letter, a short letter, made the simple, obvious point: Look, you are a new president. We had hoped that as a new president you would take a new look at the situation, that you would be anxious to start off on as good relations as you can with all countries around the world. We had hoped, therefore, that you would want relations normalized. And we went on in that letter to make the point that what we are saying is the true bottom line is dialogue; it is talks. Therefore, let us get these talks going. We are proposing no agenda with any preconditions. Let us look at all questions. Let us put them all on the table. Let us see what you perceive as problems, and we will tell you what we perceive as problems. Let us see if in the course of those discussions we can narrow down differences so at least the new beginning that is made will be on the basis of mutual understanding with less distrust and less suspicion. No reply to that letter.

The second letter was August 1981. And this was a very long letter — about twelve typed pages. And the reason there were twelve typed pages was not because there were twelve typed pages talking about an agenda. There were twelve typed pages because by that time, the hostile, aggressive course of destabilization against our government by the Ronald Reagan administration had been well established.

So the letter went into the question of the propaganda destabilization against us. It went into the question of the economic destabilization against us. We were able to speak about a discrimination that is exercised against banana farmers in our country. We were able to speak about the attempt to offer money to the Caribbean Development Bank on the sole condition that Grenada be excluded. We were able to raise a number of these issues, including the fact that in April 1981, when we had organized a cofinancing conference to raise funds for our international airport project, the American administration sent their diplomats to European capitals trying to persuade member countries of the EEC [European Economic Community] not to attend that conference.

We raised in that letter the question of military destabilization, which was already beginning. We pointed out that one well-known mercenary in April of 1981 had gone publicly on television in this country admitting that he was training mercenaries in Miami for an invasion of our country. We said, how can you allow this in your country? There are international conventions against this kind of thing. And sending marines directly to somebody's country is no less a sin than allowing mercenaries to be supplied, to be trained, and to have a logistical base on your own territory.

So we raised all these points. Once again, we said we are willing to talk at whatever level is deemed appropriate — let us make a start. Again, no reply.

The fact is, sisters and brothers, we have had this long, long history of trying to see in what ways relations could be normalized, and we have had very little success in this regard. But I really want to say tonight that we do believe it is important for us to continue that struggle, and therefore, notwithstanding the difficulties in the way, we deem it advisable to continue to press for a full normalization of relations.

But, of course, as we press for normalization, we are also going to continue to build our revolution. We are also going to continue to consolidate our process. In the face of all the difficulties, in the face of the economic destabilization, the political, diplomatic, and military threats and pressure, we are going to stand on our feet and keep going forward.

As you know, sisters and brothers, in these times it is becoming more and more difficult for developing Third World countries to go forward. Because, unfortunately, our economies remain by and large dependent on and tied to the capitalist world economies. And therefore, when the capitalist world goes through their cyclical crises one after the other, it has an immediate effect on us. As we say at home, when the capitalist world catches a cold, we catch pneumonia.

In the OECD [Organization for Economic Cooperation and Development] countries, for example, it is estimated that over 35 million people in the 12-13 countries are out of jobs — 35 million! It is estimated that in the United States there are, perhaps, 12 million people out of work; in Britain, perhaps 4 million people out of work; in all of the developed industrialized countries there is greater and greater unemployment. And as this unemployment goes deeper and deeper into the society, the people who feel it the most are the poor and working people.

There are massive cuts in social welfare. The cuts are not coming in the arms race. The cuts are not coming out of the arms budget. I understand the talk is to spend $3 trillion over five years. The mind boggles. Three trillion dollars is not even three billion, which is three thousand million. But it is three thousand *billion*. And if you work out $3 trillion over five years, you will discover it comes down to a spending of 1.6 billion United States dollars a day.

The arms are swallowing up the money; the people are not benefiting. This crisis in the capitalist world, moreover, has led to a situation where more and more of their countries, especially in 1982, experienced only negative growth.

The effect this has had on us, in turn, has been to create a crisis in the developing world. It is now estimated that our debts exceed $650 billion — that is how much money we owe collectively. And it is not just the amount of money that is owed by one or two well-known cases like Mexico or Argentina where you are talking about staggering debts of over $80 billion. But perhaps over thirty-five countries in the developing world now owe about $1 billion or more in debts in a context where they are still unable to create the necessary surpluses to repay the debts. Last year $131 billion was spent by the countries of the Third World in just servicing their debts, in just paying the interest.

Last year, too, the purchasing power of the countries of the Third World fell again and fell very, very dramatically. It is estimated that over the last two years, Third World developing countries lost $85 billion in purchasing power via the credits we lost, via the real prices for our commodities because the prices keep falling, and via high interest rates.

But on top of that, we are also discovering that it is becoming more and more difficult to engage in trade with the countries of the Western industrialized world. The developing world as a whole in 1955 had 40 percent of total world trade. But by 1969, that figure had dropped to 25 percent. In other words, we lost 15 percent of the world market.

Trade is also increasingly difficult for us because of the high tariff barriers.

The reality is that aid has also decreased quite dramatically for Third World countries. Long ago the United Nations set a target that all the developed industrialized countries should aim to provide as aid 0.7 percent of their gross national product. And so far as I know from the latest figures we have seen, not one single industrialized country has yet attained that target. Collectively they are now giving only 0.45 percent of the GNP as aid.

In the old days, it was possible to supplement some of this through direct investment. In Latin America, about forty years ago, 43 percent of all direct United States investment went to Latin America. But by the beginning of the 1970s, that 43 percent had dropped to 17 percent.

More and more, because of the influence of one or two countries, and in particular of one country, it is now becoming virtually impossible to get loans from the International Monetary Fund [IMF] or the World Bank. In fact, we know that there is a hit list which has been developed with countries like Grenada, Nicaragua, Angola, and Mozambique on it. Once any of these countries makes an application to the IMF, regardless of how good technically its program is, the instructions are to try to find all possible ways of blocking those sources of funding.

They are forcing more and more Third World countries to go directly to the international capital market, to the big commerical banks, to get loans. First of all, you have to have what they call a credit rating, and to get a credit rating you have to go to the same World Bank and IMF — not everybody can get a credit rating. But even after you get a credit rating, you have to then deal with the question of very short repayment terms and very high interest rates.

And while all of this is going on, sisters and brothers, there are so many people in the world who are unemployed, so many people in the world who are going to bed hungry every single night, so many millions in the Third World who are illiterate and whose governments either do not care or feel they cannot do anything to solve that problem. Unemployment, hunger, malnutrition, disease, illiteracy — these are the crimes and the sins that are committed upon the poor developing countries of the Third World while the industrialized countries continue to exploit our resources and keep the profits. [*Applause*]

Consider what happens to the sweat of a banana farmer or a banana worker in Grenada. In Grenada, the particular transnational corporation we deal with is one called Geest Industries. Mr. Van Geest was a man who came from Holland originally, went to England, and opened a flower shop. And then he discovered there was more money in ships than in flowers. He eventually developed a monopoly of transporting bananas from many, many Caribbean countries to the English market. It works out that for every dollar that is obtained from the sale of bananas, the banana workers and banana farmers share ten cents, and the other ninety cents goes in one form or another to Mr. Van Geest and his type. Ten cents for all of that labor and sweat. That will give as good an indication as possible of the inequities and injustice in the system.

But yet, sisters and brothers, in the face of all this the Grenada revolution has nonetheless continued to go forward and to make progress. At a time when even the big powerful industrialized nations were growing backwards last year, we grew forward by 5.5 percent. And coming out of the old history of negative development and retrogression under

Gairy, when year after year it was backward growth, over the last four years of the revolution cumulatively we have grown by over 15 percent.

The revolution in Grenada started from a base under Gairy of 49 percent unemployment — one in every two people who wanted to work couldn't get a job. And among women, 70 percent unemployment, seven out of every ten could not get a job. Therefore at the dawn of the revolution over 22,000 people who wanted to work could not find work. When we did a census last year, April 1982, the unemployment rate had dropped from 49 percent to 14.2 percent. [*Applause*]

In the days of Hurricane Gairy — those twenty-nine years of economic, political, social, and spiritual devastation of our country and of our people — there was no such thing as a plan. There was no such thing as a capital investment program, partly because Gairy was a mystic and therefore he didn't have to plan. But also partly because he was so corrupt that nobody was willing in any event to put even ten cents in his hand unless they sent down ten police to check what's happening to their ten cents. So in those days we had nothing called a public investment program. And when it got going it was on the basis of very small, feeble advances. The last year of Gairy, 1978, the capital investment program was $8 million. The first year of the revolution that figure was doubled to $16 million. The second year of the revolution it was more than doubled again to $39.9 million.

The experts were saying that this is impossible — you don't have the resources, you don't have the management, you don't have enough tractors, you don't have any trucks, you don't have enough engineers, you cannot possibly do it. You are only lucky in 1979 when you doubled Gairy's. And you are only lucky in 1980 again when you doubled your own. And then when we went to 1981 and we doubled it again, they said, we know you has the luck, but something is wrong.

And last year in 1982 it went up to over $100 million, and then we gave them the secret: we told them that in a revolution things operate differently than in the normal situation. [*Applause*] We have been able to make these accomplishments because in Grenada, consistent with our three pillars of the revolution — where the first pillar is our people who are always at the center and heart and focus of all our activities — we are able to mobilize and organize people to cut out waste, to cut corruption, to stamp out inefficiency, to move to planning, to look out for production, to check on productivity, to make sure that state enterprises are not set up to be subsidized but that state enterprises, too, must become viable, must make a profit, and therefore the state sector will have the surplus to bring the benefits.

Our people have gladly been pulled into the economic process because our people see the benefits which the revolution has brought them.

They understand that when thirty-seven cents out of every dollar is spent on health and education that means something.

They look around and they understand that year after year inflation is being held reasonably in check. Last year it ran at 7 percent while wages ran at 10 percent, thus ensuring an overall increase of 3 percent in the standard of living of all our people.

They look around and recognize that year after year production increases. Last year in the state sector, production went up by over 34 percent. And in the private sector, production also rose. Last year, too, there was a tremendous rise in the export of nontraditional products. The increase in the export of fruits and vegetables last year went up by over 314 percent, which is a massive increase in a short period. There are also increases in production in areas like flour and clothing, and there was a slight decrease in the area of furniture.

At the same time there were some increases in the area of our traditional export crops — nutmegs, cocoa, and bananas. Though in the case of nutmegs, there has been a tremendous problem our country has had to face, a great difficulty in obtaining sales for the nutmegs. When you are producing something like nutmegs, which is really meant primarily as a spicing flavor for foods, and when there is a crisis or a recession or whatever the fancy name we use, then people stop putting the spices in the food and therefore your nutmegs accumulate.

But our people in Grenada are not only able to see these economic achievements in the broad terms in which I have described them, but they are able to feel what these benefits mean to them in a concrete and material way. Because today the money that the people of Grenada used to have to spend, for example, when they went to a doctor or a dentist, they no longer have to spend because they now have free health care.

They now understand that the number of doctors in the country has more than doubled, moving from a ratio of one doctor to every 4,000 before the revolution to the present ratio of one doctor for every 2,700 of our population. Moving from a situation before the revolution where there was just one dental clinic for the whole country, today there are seven dental clinics, including one for our offshore islands of Carriacou and Petit Martinique.

Our people understand the value and the benefits of free secondary education. Because they know now that once their children are able to pass a common entrance exam and get into secondary schools, they no longer have to worry about finding those fees, which for agricultural workers, for example, was very often impossible.

But not just free secondary education, but in effect free university education. Moving from a situation before the revolution where in the last year of Gairy, just three people went abroad on university scholarships and they happened to include Gairy's daughter and another minister's daughter. We moved from that situation to the first six months of the revolution, when 109 students went abroad on free university scholarships.

Our people are more and more getting to understand what we mean when we say that education to us is liberation, that education is a strategic concern of this government. That is why this year is the year we have named the "Year of Political and Academic Education." We understand the importance of bringing education to our people, of raising their consciousness, of promoting worker education classes in the workplace, at the same time giving them an academic education, providing them with skills training, ensuring that those who are not able to read and to write are now able to do so.

Following the establishment of the Centre for Popular Education [CPE] program in early 1980, within one year the illiteracy figure in Grenada was reduced to 2 percent of the entire population. And UNESCO, the United Nations body dealing with education, says if you have less than 5 percent illiteracy, you do not have an illiteracy problem.

The fact is, that while illiteracy has now been removed, there is still a serious problem of functional literacy, and therefore the second phase of the CPE program has started. In this phase of adult education — which our people at home call the night schools — for two nights a week, three hours each, in other words, six hours a week, agricultural workers, farmers in our country, clerical workers, factory workers, unemployed youth who have dropped out of school, more and more of them are now going to one of the seventy-two centers operating around the country, bringing this night school education to our people.

I really want the sisters and brothers to understand just how difficult this task is. If you can reflect back on the normal daily habits of the average agricultural worker throughout the fifties, sixties, and seventies, and to a great extent still today — if we are to be frank and honest — we understand how difficult it is to run an adult education program. The average agricultural worker goes to work early in the morning, goes home in the afternoon, does a little back gardening, then maybe heads to the rum shop to play some dominoes or sit down to talk with the partner. To ask such an agricultural worker now to come out twice a week to a night school and for three hours to sit down and go through a formal educational course is really asking a lot.

During the very first experience we had with the illiteracy phase in 1980, I remember holding several meetings from time to time with the CPE mobilizers and CPE educators, and over and over again those comrades would say that the problem is you cannot persuade the sisters and brothers to be consistent. Some nights when they're reaching a house and they knock on the door, and they say, "Where is your husband?" She say, "Not here." And when you look under the bed, you see the man hiding.

In other words, it is a very difficult task. But it is a task we are trying to accomplish.

What is the background and tradition we have had? It is a background and tradition that has, generally speaking, worshipped materialism. It is a background and tradition that has meant that because of the ravages of colonialism, our people have always seen themselves as transients. Our people have always had a visa mentality. And the whole point was to catch the next boat or plane to go abroad.

Coming out of the colonial experience and fed daily all of the rubbish that we are fed through the newspapers, the radios, and the televisions, where they are proclaiming the virtues of materialism. Where they are proclaiming the importance of every single person having a video, and having the latest kind of radio that only came out six months ago, not to mention the newest kind of shampoo. That kind of thing feeds consumerism, feeds economism, and helps to hold a society back. In our country, many people have as a sole aspiration the need to have a motor car. The fact that a motor car means foreign exchange earnings have to go out because we don't produce motor cars; that it means that more money has to be spent on gas — these things are not so easily explainable because of the political education that is daily taking place through the imperialist media.

The reason the people of Vietnam are quite content and happy that virtually every citizen can ride around Vietnam on a bicycle is in part because they have not been exposed to the corrupt and decadent values. But if we ask our people to take up a bicycle instead, of course, that is a problem. In Grenada, it's a double problem because Grenada is one big mountain and bicycles really can't work.

But the point I'm making, sisters and brothers, is the nature of the struggle that we have undergone, not only to raise production and productivity, but to instill new values in our people. As we struggle on the road towards creating a new man and a new woman, living a new life, in what we know will become a new civilization, the old culture, the old habits, the old prejudices are always there struggling against the shoots of the new. That is a struggle that we have to resolutely wage every single day of our lives.

But it is much easier for our people to make those sacrifices. It is much easier for them to accept the importance of doing these things which they have not been in the habit of doing, because now they know that for the first time material benefits are coming. Our people now understand that what they put out will come back, whether through free health care or free education or the number of jobs created.

With the free milk distribution program in our country last year, a small island like Grenada, 73,000 pounds of milk were distributed free every single month to over 50,000 people — nearly half of the population.

Last year, too, under the house repair program in our country, over 17,240 individuals benefited. Under this program, the poorest workers in our country are entitled to a loan to repair their houses, to fix the roofs, to fix the floors to make sure that rain does not fall on a child while he's trying to study. And after the materials are given to the worker, the worker then repays over six years at the rate of five dollars a month out of his wages.

If he had gone to a bank and knocked, let us say, on the door of Mr. Barclays, the first thing Mr. Barclays would ask him is, "Where is your collateral?" And maybe if he understand that big word, he put out his cutlass and say, "Look, no collateral." But even if he got past that word and he was able to find some collateral somehow or the other, there is still another hurdle that he'd have to go over. Because then he discovers that a loan could be only over one year. A $1,000 loan at 12.5 percent interest over twelve months would mean a monthly repayment of over $88 a month. That means that just about no agricultural worker would have been able to afford it.

And that is why today the agricultural workers understand what the revolution is about because they have felt the weight of the revolution.

The people understand that in all areas of their basic needs, attempts are being made to solve these problems. Two and a half million gallons more of water, pipe-borne water, are flowing into homes of our Grenadians at this time. Before the revolution, in many homes and in many parts of the country, pipes had actually rusted up because water had not passed there for years. The pipes just stayed there and corroded. The people understand what it means when electrification is brought to their village. The people understand what it means when they know that by the middle of next year we will have doubled the electricity output and capacity in our country, and therefore more people will have the possibility of using electricity.

Thirty percent of the lowest-paid workers in our country no longer pay any income tax at all. These workers take home all their money. Old-age pensioners had their pension increased by 10 percent last year and this year it is going up again by 12.5 percent. Our people know that last year some $43 million were spent on the international airport project alone, and another $40 million will be spent on that project this year again.

They know that last year over forty-nine miles of feeder roads were built — feeder roads being the roads that connect the farmers to the main roads — so now the produce can be brought out safely. They know that apart from these forty-nine miles of feeder roads, that fifteen miles of farm roads were built, and fourteen new miles of main roads were also built, totaling, therefore, something like seventy-eight new miles of roads in our country last year alone.

Our people, therefore, have a greater and deeper understanding of what the revolution means and what it has brought to them. They certainly understand very, very clearly that when some people attack us on the grounds of human rights, when some people attack us on the grounds of constituting a threat to the national security of other countries, our people understand that is foolishness. They know the real reason has to do with the fact of the revolution and the benefits that the revolution is bringing to the people of our country. The real reason for all of this hostility is because some perceive that what is happening in Grenada can lay the basis for a new socioeconomic and political path of development.

They give all kinds of reasons and excuses — some of them credible, some utter rubbish. We saw an interesting one recently in a secret report to the State Department. I want to tell you about that one, so you can reflect on it. That secret report made this point: that the Grenada revolution is in one sense even worse — I'm using their language — than the Cuban and Nicaraguan revolutions because the people of Grenada and the leadership of Grenada speak English, and therefore can communicate directly with the people of the United States. [*Applause*]

I can see from your applause, sisters and brothers, that you agree with the report. But I want to tell you what that same report said that also made us very dangerous. That is that the people of Grenada and the leadership of Grenada are predominantly Black. [*Applause*] They said that 95 percent of our population is Black — and they had the correct statistic — and if we have 95 percent of predominantly African origin in our country, then we can have a dangerous appeal to 30 million Black people in the United States. [*Applause*] Now that aspect of the report, clearly, is one of the most sensible.

But, sisters and brothers, how do we evaluate other sides of the report? Like when they say that Grenada violates human rights. When they say to us, how come you have detainees, what about the press, what about elections? When they say to us: Where are your elections?, they don't turn around at the same time and say to their friends in South Africa: Where are your elections? [*Applause*]

When they say to us that elections must be held, and if you don't have elections you can't expect support, and unless you have elections we can't give you the normal treatment, we say: Salvador Allende of Chile. [*Applause*] Salvador Allende of Chile was elected in September 1970 by the people of Chile. Allende did not take power through a revolution. Within twenty-four hours of his election, Richard Nixon, [Henry] Kissinger, and [Richard] Helms sat down and devised their plan, "Operation Make the Economy Scream." And even in the first three months after Allende was elected, before he was inaugurated as president, they already tried to kill Allende once. They couldn't even wait for him to be formally inaugurated.

Allende did not form a militia. Allende did not grab any land or property. Allende had no political detainees. Allende did not crush the press. He did not close down the parliament. He did not suspend the constitution. He played by every rule they wrote. But they killed him still.

These people understand very well that a revolution means a new situation. A revolution implies a fracture. It implies a break with the past. It implies disruption of a temporary character. Revolution means that the abuses and excesses of the violent, reactionary, and disruptive minority have to be crushed so that the majority's interests can prevail. [*Applause*]

No revolution that does not have a dislocation can be called revolution. That is an impossibility. When the British had their revolution in the 1650s, it took them 200 years to call their first election. When the Americans had their revolution in 1776, it took them thirteen years to call their election.

In the first week of the American revolution, 100,000 fled to Canada. Thousands were locked up without charge or trial. Hundreds were shot. And the counterrevolutionaries after the American revolution had no right to vote. They had no right to teach. They had no right to preach. They had no right to a job. Their land was confiscated without payment.

So when the falsifiers of history try to pretend that the American revolution was a Boston tea party — it was a very bloody tea party.

The fact of the matter is, sisters and brothers — if we are to be honest about this question — whenever revolution comes, the same questions face the leaders of the revolution. One question always is: what do you do with the bloody-minded murderers, the criminals, the ones who propped up the dictatorship. The ones who led to disappearances of our people. The ones who were beating the people, who were killing the people.

Revolutions answer that question in different ways. Some people take them out in the streets, line them up, and shoot them down. That is one answer. Some other people pretend that they went into the bush, and while they were in the bush as guerrillas, they shoot them down too. Some other people create special courts to deal with them. I am not passing judgment on any of these three models.

The Grenada revolution did not have the appetite for any of those three models. So we took what we say was the humanitarian course. We detained them and treated them well.

And you know it is highly significant that of the 400 to 500 people picked up by our masses on revolution day, on the thirteenth of March, not one of these Mongoose Gang elements arrived in the jail with even a scratch on them. And the only reason that happened is because our people at home understand the principled position that a revolution takes on no revenge, no victimization, no torture, no ill-treatment of anyone, regardless of what they have done. It is because our people understood this, something that very often happens in all revolutions — the spontaneous upheaval of the masses — did not really happen in Grenada.

A church-based organization in Washington called EPICA wrote a book last year on Grenada. They called it, *Grenada: the Peaceful Revolution*. We can understand why.

So when these elements come and make these statements we understand only too well where they are coming from. Because they understand that the processes and procedures for review are ongoing procedures. They understand that in Grenada no one is ever interfered with for what he says. No one is ever interfered with for what he writes. In fact, today criticism is deeper than ever in the society in a constructive way.

Our people also understand that the first law of the revolution is that a revolution must survive, must consolidate so more benefits can come to them.

And because of this fact, the revolution has laid down as a law, that nobody, regardless of who you are, will be allowed to be involved in any activity surrounding the overthrow of the government by the use of armed violence. And anyone who moves in that direction will be ruthlessly crushed. [*Applause*]

But we also feel, sisters and brothers, that the time has come for us to make another step along the way toward institutionalizing the process that we have been building for four years. And that is why only yesterday in Grenada the new chairman of the constitutional commission arrived in our capital city, St. George's, from Trinidad and Tobago, to announce the formation of the constitutional commission that has now undertaken the task of drafting a new constitution for our young revolution.

This constitution is not really going to look like the one that the queen gave us in 1974. That constitution as we remember was one of the main reasons for the struggles of '73 and '74, when so many of us were beaten and jailed. When our families and compatriots were being murdered, one of the main reasons for that struggle was because our people were saying we wanted to be involved in the process of drafting the new constitution. And Gairy did not allow us that right. And the queen of England could have stayed in Buckingham Palace, put it in an envelope, put a stamp on it, and posted it to Gairy. That was the total involvement of Grenada in that constitution.

This time around, the constitution is going to come out of the bowels of our people and out of our earth. Our people will have their input and will decide what they want to see go into that constitution. This time around, the constitution will not just entrench empty rights, but will entrench rights and also provide remedies for enforcement of those rights.

Chapter 1 of our present constitution has twelve freedoms, fundamental freedoms. But anytime those rights are infringed and you go before the courts to see if you can do something about that: first of all you can only go by way of a constitutional motion. Secondly, that means you can only go in the high court, not the magistrate's court, which of course means money. And thirdly, once you reach the high court, even if the judge agrees with you and you win your case, the most the judge can give you is what they call a declaratory order, which declares your rights.

Now when you bring your declaratory order to the government, you then discover another maxim of the law. You cannot enforce against the Crown. In other words, you have a paper judgment in your hands that you can do nothing with.

We are going to want to put rights into the constitution, rights which can be enforced in a way that the people can themselves manage, and rights which, once the remedies are provided, will in fact be allowed by our government. A constitution with real teeth.

Our new constitution also is certainly going to institutionalize and entrench the systems of popular democracy which we have been building over these past four years in our country. Apart from the usual national elections, which will of course be there too, we are going to ensure that these embryonic organs of popular democracy continue to have a place.

Because to us, democracy is much, much more than just an election. To us, democracy is a great deal more than just the right to put an "X" next to Tweedledum or Tweedledee every five years.

The second principle of democracy for us is responsibilities. So the elected officials must at all times ensure that the mandate they are carrying out, if mandate it is, is the mandate the people want. And part of that responsibility means that the right to recall those we elect must be entrenched.

We don't believe in Grenada in presidents-for-life or elected-people-for-life. We believe in service for life. And when you stop serving, you must be recalled and get out of the way for somebody else to serve.

The third principle of democracy is participating mechanisms, popular participation. We accept the well-known definition of Abraham Lincoln. Lincoln said of democracy that it is government of, for, and by the people. I accept that, it's a good definition. But if it is government of, for, and by the people, then it cannot be just government of the people you elect. It also has to be *for* the people and it also has to be *by* them. They have to have a way of participating — that is what the word "by" means. And if that is absent, you don't really have a democracy.

So we are saying we need to have mechanisms that ensure that the people have a way of giving expression to their own feelings and concerns.

In some of the more developed, industrialized countries that have had hundreds of years to build a democracy, a number of things have developed that are perhaps helpful. Some of them have genuinely free and responsible press. Some of them genuinely allow all sections to express their views. Some of them have very effective lobbies where virtually every interest in the society can find a way to get their matter raised in congress or parliament. Some of them, of course, have a highly literate people and a highly developed public opinion, a people who can interpret for themselves, to some extent.

One form or the other of democracy may or may not be correct in those situations. Westminster parliamentary democracy, let us say, may well be acceptable to the people of England. I cannot speak to that.

But I know that for the people of Grenada, at this stage in our history, Westminster parliamentary democracy is really Westminster parliamentary hyprocrisy. [*Applause*]

We believe that it is very important for the people to have a voice in running their affairs. One way is the creation of mass organizations of our people: the National Women's Organisation, the National Youth Organisation, the farmers' union, and, of course, the labor unions.

Before the revolution, Gairy had passed a law in 1978, the Essential Services Act, which took away the right to strike from the workers of our country. We not only repealed that law, but instead we passed a new law, Recognition of Trade Unions Law, under which anytime in any workplace 51 percent of the workers indicate that they want to form or to join a union of their choice, that union must be recognized by the employer.

Not only were the women of our country without work before the revolution, the women of our country were also the most harassed and victimized of any section of our population. Those few who were granted jobs from time to time, many of them were given those jobs only on the basis of a sexual favor. Our women were being sexually exploited in return for jobs.

The very first decree of the revolution was to outlaw sexual victimization and exploitation of our women in return for jobs. [*Applause*]

And going on from that, sisters and brothers, the revolution then passed a law, which applied to all workers in the public sector, of equal pay for equal work for all women. We also then passed another law more recently, a maternity-leave law. And by this maternity-leave law every woman who is pregnant must be granted three months' maternity leave — two months' full pay and one could be without full pay — and a guarantee of return to employment after the pregnancy.

It is because of these laws and because of the new environment in the country that so many women have begun to step forward, have begun to assert themselves, have begun to go out and find new jobs, have begun to get fully involved in production. And that is why so many of them have joined their mass organization, so that today, at this point in time, one in every three adult women over the age of sixteen years is a member of the National Women's Organisation.

And in this organization, the women are able to experience training in democracy, training in self-rule, training in acquiring a new confidence. Once every two months they hold their parish meetings. They are also broken up into groups around the country where, among other things, they conduct political education and provide training opportunities.

Once in every two years at their congress, all the women have the opportunity of electing delegates. For six months before the congress, they have the opportunity to discuss the new program for the next two years. And then on the day of the congress, they elect their entire new leadership by a secret ballot.

So, within our mass organizations the principle of electorality is already entrenched. And for the people in general, there have been organs of popular democracy that have been built — zonal councils, parish councils, worker-parish councils, farmer councils — where the people come together from month to month. The usual agenda will be a report on programs taking place in the village.

Then there will be a report, usually by some senior member of the bureaucracy. It might be the manager of the Central Water Commission. Or it might be the manager of the telephone company or the electricity company. Or it might be the chief sanitary inspector, or the senior price-control inspector. And this senior bureaucrat has to go there and report to the people on his area of work, and then be submitted to a question-and-answer session. And after that, one of the top leaders in our country, one of us will also attend those meetings, and ourselves give a report, and usually there is question-and-answer-time at the end of that also.

In this way, our people from day to day and week to week, are participating in helping to run the affairs of their country. And this is not just an abstract matter of principle. It has also brought practical, concrete benefits to our people.

I remember a worker-parish council in August 1981. The workers were in a real storm that night. They were complaining about the [private] bus drivers. And they were saying that the problem with the bus service is that all six or seven buses pass at the same time on the same route. Which, by the way, is true, because they are speeding and trying to catch all the passengers. And these bus drivers have been the most difficult people to organize. You could sit down and talk until you're blue in the face about the need for routes and the need for schedules. So the people were complaining that night and they said it had resulted very often in them reaching work late.

And there was a second complaint. They were saying that because of the half price for the schoolchildren, the bus drivers were refusing to pick up their children, so the children had to walk to school in the rain or the sun. So they insisted and demanded that we get some buses to start a public bus service.

Now that is August '81. The financial year is already eight months gone. The budget has been set. But because of the pressure and the demands, we were forced to go and find money wherever we could and buy twenty-six new buses to start a public transport service for the people. [*Applause*]

So this concept of democracy and our approach to human rights is one that has stressed solving these problems and the involvement of our people in a participatory way from day to day and week to week.

[Critics of Grenada's revolution] have also raised over and over again the question of our relations with Cuba as a second one of these red herrings. Every now and then when the red herring of detainees and elections and the press is finished, you will hear them say: Soviet and Cuban satellite.

You hear them say that the links with Cuba are such that it is dangerous to the security of the region.

What do we say on this question? We say first of all that yes, we have warm, fraternal relations with the government and people of Cuba. That is true. [*Applause*]

We say secondly that to us this is a matter of fundamental principle. And there are at least three very good reasons why we will always have good relations with the government and people of Cuba.

The first reason: we see Cuba as part of our Caribbean family of nations. One of the greatest curses of colonialism was that they divided the region according to different metropolitan centers. They taught us different languages. And then they made a great play of the fact that you are Dutch-speaking, you are Spanish-speaking, you are French-speaking, you are English-speaking, and, more recently, you are American-speaking.

And based on this linguistic nonsense, they taught us to hate each other. When we were growing up in school, they used to make us believe that the sun sets only in England. We used to be made to go down to Queen's Park on the queen's birthday and stand up in the hot sun all day. And at the end of the day, we're hot and sweaty and tired, and they give us a bun. And I remember the St. John's Ambulance Brigade stop on the corner in case you faint, they catch you quick.

I know the first time I realized just how deep this foolishness went and the extent to which they were miseducating us and trying to make us into little Black Englishmen is when I arrived in England to study law in 1963. One of my first and greatest experiences — shocking experience, traumatic — was when I went somewhere one day. The national anthem started to play — poor little Black me, I jump up fast. When I look around, me only one standing up. Every Englishman sitting down.

You know like old [calypso singer Mighty] Sparrow. Sparrow is such a great Grenadian, so articulate. Sparrow points out in one of his best songs that the way they were educating us, they were really educating us to make us into fools.

They tell us if you're speaking Dutch, you're the best. If it's English, you're the best, French is the best, Spanish is the best, American is the best. And all of us hating each other.

When in fact we are one people from one Caribbean with one struggle and one destiny. [*Applause*]

We see it therefore as one of our historic duties and responsibilities to pull down these artificial barriers of colonialism and to develop that oneness and that unity that we nearly lost.

We believe it is critically necessary to have close relations with all of our neighbors. That is why I have done state visits to Mexico, to Venezuela, to Panama, to Cuba, to Nicaragua, to Ecuador. The reason has been a conscious attempt on the part of this new government to try to build those bridges and make sure that all of this alienation of the past disappears.

The second reason is, we are a nonaligned country. We believe in nonalignment. And to us, nonalignment means that you have the right to choose your own friends. Nonalignment to us means that we have the right and the duty to diversify and expand our relationships and our friendships around the world. Nonalignment to us is not something that implies neutrality. Nonalignment is not meant to make you into a political eunuch that can't speak.

Nonalignment is meant to make you speak out loud and clear for what you believe in. And we have principles we believe in. [*Applause*]

There is also a third reason we will always have relations — warm, fraternal, close relations — with the people and government of Cuba. And that is our admiration and our respect for the internationalism and the achievements of the Cuban people. [*Applause*] Whether they like it or not, Cuba was the first revolution in this hemisphere to have succeeded. And if there was no Cuban revolution, there could have been no Grenada or Nicaraguan revolution. [*Applause*]

Whether they like it or not, Cuba was the first country in this hemisphere to give a sound licking to U.S. imperialism at the Bay of Pigs. [*Applause*]

Whether they like it or not, Cuban internationalist soldiers have been the first in the world to charge the racist South African monster and to face it with arms in their hands while defending Angola. [*Chants of "Viva Cuba! Viva Cuba! Viva Cuba!"*]

If there were no Cuban internationalist troops in Angola, how long ago would the South African apartheid monster have overrun Angola with the assistance of several Western powers? Cuba is a great stabilizing factor in that Angola equation. And that is why when they come up with this hypocrisy of linkage, and say that for Namibia to get independence, Cuban troops have to leave, we who are in the Third World understand that and have seen their bluff and will fully back the Cuban soldiers and the Angolan people in ensuring that they stay in Angola.

They can choose their South African and their Haitian and Chilean and South Korean and every dictator friend they wish. That is okay. But we can't choose our friends. Because we too small and poor to have the right to choose. They like to talk a lot about backyard and frontyard and lake. Grenada is nobody's backyard and part of nobody's lake. [*Applause*]

The more desperate that imperialism gets, the more it comes up with the most vulgar and hostile measures to try to keep the poor oppressed people of the world, who are trying to win their national liberation and to build their own future, down. Think of Nicaragua. Nicaragua, a country invaded over the years — two, three times in this century — by the United States. Nicaragua, a country that has been under the brutal heel of the Somozas for over forty-five years. Nicaragua, a country that, just like the Americans 200 years ago, finally resorted to their supreme right to overthrow their repressors and murderers and to take their destiny into their own hands. And when the people of Nicaragua, when the sons and daughters of Sandino assumed their liberation, when they won in July of 1979, what was the crime they committed thereafter?

Their crime was to be bold and mannish and fresh enough to say that their resources belong to them, to say that they want to build their country in their own way, to say that they want to choose their own friends, to say that they are going to build their country after their own image and likeness and not after the image and likeness of somebody else.

And because of that, you have this situation where today the most vulgar, shameless acts of the last year or so can pale only in comparison to what is happening in El Salvador, or what happened in the middle of last year in Lebanon when the Palestinian people were slaughtered. The most vulgar, shameless act of open CIA activity in their country.

The most open, vulgar, shameless act of even admitting that not only will they resort to covert actions, but if necessary, they will publicly back overt action against the Nicaraguans. The shamelessness of it can only be exceeded by the way in which sections of the media have chosen to respond. To pretend that the Nicaraguans are losing popular support. To pretend that these murderers, ex-Somocista elements, are some kind of freedom fighters. To pretend that these butchers who will just throw bombs on women and children as they are passing and run when they see the Sandinista soldiers. To pretend that these people deserve to have some opportunity to rule the people of Nicaragua — the shamelessness of it is really extraordinary.

And perhaps the only good thing that has come out of this recent episode, sisters and brothers, is the fact that for the first time in a long time, the people of Latin America themselves have tried to find a solution to the problems. That has been the historic meaning of the get-together of Venezuela, Colombia, Mexico, and Panama on Contadora, to launch the Contadora initiative. Because what this Contadora initiative is all about is really extremely important for us.

It says first of all, that we the people of Latin America and the Caribbean will try to solve our problems ourselves. [*Applause*]

It says secondly that we do not accept the use of violence as a means of settling our disputes.

It says thirdly that we must always sit down and engage in negotiations and discussions before taking any other measures.

And it says fourthly that we are not prepared to accept that any country in our region, far less any country outside our region, has the right to interfere in the internal affairs of another country.

And even though this Contadora initiative is fast becoming all things to all men — you hear everybody saying, yes, they're backing Contadora, which must mean that some people are trying to use Contadora in ways different than the original objectives were intended — nonetheless, it is an historic first step.

But these people have also thrown out another allegation against Grenada. I want to deal with it but I know people want to go home, it's getting late. [*Shouts of "No!, No!"*]

This other allegation concerns the question of our international airport project. This one is of course the most comical one of all.

According to the formulators of this famous theory, Grenada's international airport is now going to become a military base, and will now become a strategic jump-off point from where we can launch an attack on the great big, powerful, mighty United States. It looks as if we have become a superpower. [*Laughter*]

But the reality of the airport, of course, is well known to all those who make those statements. This airport is an ancient dream of the people of our country. [*Applause*] This international airport has undergone a quarter-century of studies. There are more than six voluminous reports and studies on this international airport. All previous governments from 1955 have spoken about the need for the airport.

And if you understand the situation in our country, that would be no surprise to anybody. The present airport is called Pearls. Pearls has a strip 5,500 feet long. That means only turboprop planes can come in. The turboprop planes that come in carry a maximum of forty-eight passengers. And better still, these planes can only land during the day between 6:00 and 6:00 because there are no night lights. And we cannot put night lights there because the airstrip happens to be conveniently located between the mountain and the sea. And unless we knock down the whole of the island, you cannot put an international airport in Pearls.

We had to make a strip of 9,000 feet because of all the manuals that were done by European and American companies — I can think of McDonnell Douglas, people who do the DC-8, I can think of Boeing, and so on. They have produced manuals saying what length of strip is required if their planes are to land. So unless we born big and stupid, you cannot expect us to put down a strip that planes that can carry people, normal jet planes, won't be able to use.

This famous military base [*Laughter*] — let me tell you about it in a different way. I'll give you a little joke about it. After President Reagan's statements, one television crew — ABC in fact — came to the country. And they came and they wanted to do an interview, and they had a big fat file with all the questions. But the main question focused around the fact that we were building a sophisticated military base or at least a sophisticated military strip. So we said, okay, let's go down to the airport and take some photographs.

So these people went down there and they took photographs. They discovered that the airport had become the number one tourist attraction of the country. Every tourist on the island was taking a peek. They discovered at the end of this strip, which is also the end of the peninsula, at least two dozen Grenadians go every single evening to fish. They discovered that right at the beginning of the strip — at a distance of this podium to, let us say, the front row of that balcony, a few inches away — is where the medical school, with 700 American students, live and study. And they discovered that these medical school students, American students, were running up and down the strip, jogging, every day and every night. [*Laughter*]

ABC television also discovered that there was in fact a terminal building being constructed. Because in President Reagan's photograph, the one the spy plane took, there was a nice big cloud covering the terminal building. Quite by accident, of course. But when these people went down, that accident did not take place, so they caught the terminal building.

So they came back to put it on "Nightline" and the people of America were able to see that here genuinely was an international airport, with a full terminal building. But two days later, ABC comes back. Same crew. So I say, what's the problem now, fellows?

They say, all right. They say they agree it's not a sophisticated air base, they won't say that again. They're sorry about that. But, they now discover we have sophisticated communications facilities.

So we say, all right. We don't know anything about them. We don't know where they are. But feel free to go around the country. If you can find them, we also would like to see them. [*Laughter*]

So they spent another day or two going around. They didn't find them. They send the film back again, after asking questions and satisfying themselves that this was also nonsense.

Would you believe, the next day afterward they were back again. In other words, three times in six days. And this time they came back, they said, we have another question for you. It is not sophisticated military base. It is not sophisticated communications facilities. But we understand you all have sophisticated *barracks*. [*Laughter*]

Of course, they discovered that this sophisticated barracks they were talking about was no more than temporary sheds which had been constructed on the airport site in which the Grenadian and the Cuban workers who are building the airport are living.

They also discovered that time that on the same airport site are workers from a British company called Plessey, and workers from a Finnish company called Metex, who are down there right now installing the communications equipment, the navigational aids, the electronics, etc. — all the things you need to get an airport functional. Working and living together.

They also then discovered that last year an American company called Layne Dredging from Miami spent nine months in Grenada helping to build this famous military base. [*Laughter*] That this company was dredging a section of the sea where the strip has to pass. A section called Hardy Bay. And therefore for these nine months they too were working and living with Grenadian and Cuban workers, building this airport.

So I said to these fellows, well look, as you know, Grenada relies in part on tourism. So we don't mind seeing you all again. I don't mind if they send you back down tomorrow. But if you're coming back down tomorrow, try to bring a few more ABC people. [*Laughter, cheers*] And secondly, if they will tell you it's sophisticated something else, at least make sure they come [up with something] better than saying sophisticated pants, or socks, or shoes. It had really become that ludicrous.

This international airport project as we see it is the gateway to our future. As we see it, it is what alone can give us the potential for economic takeoff. As we see it, it can help us to develop the tourist industry more. It can help us to develop our agro-industries more. It can help us to export our fresh fruits and vegetables better.

As every Grenadian who has gone back home and as anybody here in this audience who has ever traveled to Grenada will know, coming to Grenada right now is a literal nightmare. Coming to Grenada right now is like a labor of love. You have to be a martyr to want to come. The amount of trouble will make you sick. And what this airport will do is remove all of that trouble and inconvenience and allow our people to fly straight into our own airport. [*Applause, cheers*]

That is why we have made an exception this year. Usually every year at the end of December we announce what the next year will be called: the Year of Education, or Production, or whatever it is. But last month, six and a half months ahead of schedule, we announced to our people what the name of next year will be. So they can start from now to mobilize, including mobilizing overseas around the name, because 1984, next year, will be called the Year of the International Airport. [*Applause, cheers*]

And the fact of the matter is, next year is also significant for us because on the thirteenth of March, '84, it will be the fifth anniversary of the revolution. And as you know, people always make a fuss about the first anniversary, about the fifth anniversary, about the tenth anniversary, and so on. So we have reason to make an extra fuss next year. And therefore, what we want to do during the fifth festival on the thirteenth of March itself is to open our international airport on that date. [*Cheers*]

And I want to say to you sisters and brothers here and particularly to our Grenadian nationals, there is a tremendous amount of enthusiasm and excitement building all over the world because all of them want to be on the first flight that touches down.

When I was in London last month, addressing a rally much like this one, the Grenadians in the audience were all insisting that they will organize an inaugural flight, but the one condition is they must be the first plane to touch down. So what we have decided to do, because of course we can't have all of them first, is to settle for inaugural flights by zones, or by cities. London will have its own inaugural, Liverpool will have its own inaugural, New York, no doubt, will have its own inaugural [*Applause*], Washington is going to have its own inaugural. And what is going to be important, sisters and brothers, is to make sure you get on that inaugural because, as you realize, you'll be coming down to see the most widely publicized airport the world has ever known. [*Applause*]

I think we should give a special round of applause to those responsible for the free publicity. [*Laughter*] You know some people have even suggested that the best name we can give the airport is the Ronnie Reagan International Airport. [*Laughter, shouts of "No!"*] Of course, they are not serious. But as you know, one of the things that has been launched at home is a competition to find a name for the airport. And we would like our people overseas to also be involved in that competition.

Sisters and brothers, I think it really is time to close, it is. [*Shouts of "No!"*]

Long live the people of free Grenada! Long live the workers, farmers, youth, and women of free Grenada! [*Cheers*]

Long live the people of the United States! [*Cheers*]

Long live Grenada-U.S. relations and friendship! [*Cheers*]

Long live the people of Cuba and Nicaragua! [*Cheers*]
Long live the people of Angola and Mozambique! [*Cheers*]
Long live the people of Palestine! [*Cheers*]
Long live the people of South Africa! [*Cheers*]
Long live the people of El Salvador! [*Cheers*]
Forward ever! [*"Backward never!"*]
Forward ever! [*"Backward never!"*]
Forward ever! [*"Backward never!"*]
One love, one heart! [*Prolonged cheers and standing ovation*]

Appendix I

Statement by the Cuban Government and the Cuban Communist Party

The following is the text of an October 20, 1983, declaration issued in the name of the Cuban Communist Party and the revolutionary government of Cuba, followed by a brief decree by the Council of State. The statements were transcribed and translated by Intercontinental Press *from a broadcast over Radio Havana on October 21.*

As has now become totally clear, for some weeks and perhaps months a deepgoing conflict has been unfolding in the ruling party in Grenada and its leadership.

When Maurice Bishop, the principal leader of the party and the prime minister of Grenada, made a brief stop of just thirty-six hours in Cuba between the evening of Thursday the sixth [of October] and the morning of Saturday the eighth, after official visits to Hungary and Czechoslovakia, he made not the slightest mention in his conversations with Comrade Fidel and other Cuban leaders of the serious discussions and differences that were taking place inside the New Jewel [Movement], the name by which the leading party of his country is known. Thus he provided a great proof of dignity and respect for his own party and for Cuba.

All the topics of conversation revolved around Cuba's collaboration with Grenada, the efforts at cooperation carried out by the Grenadian delegation in Hungary and Czechoslovakia, with the results of which Bishop felt broadly satisfied, and other international themes.

On Friday, October 7, Fidel accompanied Bishop on a tour of important installations that are under construction in Cienfuegos, showing him the progress of our development plans and the excellent quality of our workers, with whom both leaders had lengthy dialogues.

A few days later, on Wednesday, October 12, our embassy in Grenada reported the surprising and disagreeable news that deep divisions had surfaced in the Central Committee of the party in Grenada.

During the morning of that day, Bishop himself communicated [to the embassy] regarding the differences that had arisen some time before. He said that they were being discussed and that efforts were being made to resolve them, but that he had never imagined the seriousness they were going to take on during his absence. He simply stated the differences and did not request any opinion or cooperation on our part in trying to overcome them, once again showing his great respect for Cuba's international policy and for the internal affairs of his own party.

During the afternoon, it was learned that Bishop's adversaries had gained a majority in the Central Committee of the party as well as in the political apparatus of the army and the security force, and that Bishop had been removed from his post in the party and put under house arrest.

As it was a purely internal problem, despite our friendship for Bishop and our confidence in his integrity and his leadership abilities, the Cuban government and party instructed our representatives in Grenada that, complying fully with the principles and norms of Cuba's international policy, they should absolutely refrain from involving themselves in the internal affairs of the party and of Grenada.

News went on arriving continually from our embassy during the following days about the positions and arguments of the two sides involved in the conflict. In our opinion, what was really involved was not principled differences, but rather conflicts of personality and conceptions of leadership method, from which other subjective factors were not absent.

On Saturday, October 15, Comrade Fidel sent a message to the Central Committee of the New Jewel Movement expressing with full clarity Cuba's position, which is guided by the principle of absolutely abstaining from involvement in the internal affairs of a party or country. He expressed at the same time his deep concern that the division that had arisen could do considerable damage to the image of the revolutionary process in Grenada, both inside the country and abroad. In Cuba itself, where Bishop was highly esteemed, it would not be easy to explain the facts. Hope was held out that the difficulties could be overcome with the greatest of wisdom, serenity, loyalty to principles, and generosity.

At bottom, Cuba's concern centered on preventing the events from taking on the character of a violent and bloody confrontation. In his message, Fidel also stated that Cuba's collaboration would be maintained as a commitment to the people of Grenada, independently of changes that might occur in the leadership of the party and the country, since it was a purely internal question.

For several more days, the situation remained at an impasse. At certain moments it seemed that an honorable, intelligent, and peaceful solution could come about. It was clear that the people were in favor of Bishop and were calling for his presence.

The Western press launched all kinds of speculations about the events. We did not say a single word in order to avoid having our public statements appear as interference in the internal affairs of Grenada, in view of our close, broad, and fraternal relations with that sister country.

In that way we had complied rigorously with our principles of respect for the internal affairs of fraternal parties and countries.

Yesterday, October 19, during the morning, news began to arrive that the workers had gone on strike and that the people had taken to the streets in support of Bishop. In a massive demonstration they arrived at his residence where they freed him from house arrest.

It seems — since the reports are still imprecise — that a military installation was occupied by the people. The army sent personnel to the area. It is said that the army fired against the demonstrators, causing deaths and injuries, retook the installation, and arrested numerous persons. Of Bishop's fate, and that of other leaders who were with him, there was no news.

In the afternoon the dramatic outcome became known. An official communiqué announced the death of Maurice Bishop, prime minister; Unison Whiteman, minister of foreign relations; Jacqueline Creft, minister of education; Vincent Noel, first vice-president of the trade union federation of Grenada; Norris Bain, minister of housing; and Fitzroy Bain, general secretary of the agricultural workers' union.

It has still not been possible to determine exactly the actual way in which Bishop and the other leaders died. Bishop was among the political leaders who most enjoyed sympathy and respect among our people, for his talent, his simplicity, his revolutionary sincerity and honesty, and his proven friendship for our country. Besides that, he enjoyed great international prestige. The news of his death stirred the leadership of our party, and we render the deepest tribute to his memory.

It is most unfortunate that the differences among the Grenadian revolutionaries climaxed in this bloody drama. No doctrine, no principle or position held up as revolutionary, and no internal division justifies atrocious proceedings like the physical elimination of Bishop and the outstanding group of honest and worthy leaders killed yesterday. The death of Bishop and his comrades must be clarified, and if they were executed in cold blood the guilty ones deserve to be punished in an exemplary way.

Imperialism will now try to make use of this tragedy and the grave errors committed by the Grenadian revolutionaries in order to sweep away the revolutionary process in Grenada and subject it once again to neocolonial and imperial domination. The situation is most difficult and complex. Only a miracle of common sense, equanimity, and wisdom on the part of the Grenadian revolutionaries, and of serenity in the reaction and response of the international progressive movement, can still salvage the process.

No step must be taken that would aid imperialism in its plans. In Grenada many Cuban doctors, teachers, technicians of various kinds, and hundreds of construction workers are collaborating in providing essential services to the people and in the development of projects that are vital to the economy. Though profoundly embittered by the events, we will take no precipitate step with regard to technical and economic collaboration that could affect essential services or economic interests vital to the people of Grenada, for whom we have sincere and deep feelings of admiration and affection.

After the tragic outcome yesterday, we will continue following the development of events closely. We will maintain the strict principle of not involving ourselves in the internal affairs of Grenada, and we will take into account, above all, the interests of the Grenadian people in matters of economic and technical collaboration if that is possible in the new situation. But our political relations with the new figures in the Grenadian leadership will have to be subjected to serious and profound analysis. Nonetheless, if the Grenadian revolutionary process manages to be preserved, we will do whatever is possible to help it.

Let it be hoped that the painful events that have taken place cause all the revolutionaries of Grenada and the world to reflect deeply, and that the concept prevail that no crime must be committed in the name of the revolution and freedom.

*   *   *

The Council of State, making use of the powers conferred upon it, has decided to issue the following decree:

First, to declare three days of official mourning, beginning at 6 a.m. tomorrow [October 21], for the death of the prime minister of Grenada, Comrade Maurice Bishop, which occurred yesterday afternoon.

Second, that the national flag remain at half-staff at public buildings and military installations during the period of official mourning.

Third, that the ministers of the Revolutionary Armed Forces and of foreign relations take responsibility for carrying out the provisions of this decree.

Fidel Castro Ruz
President of the Council of State

Appendix II

The Truth About Cuba's Role

The following is the complete text of an October 25, 1983, statement by the government and Communist Party of Cuba. It originally appeared in English in Cuba: The Truth About the U.S. Invasion of Grenada, *published in Havana.*

The painful internal developments in Grenada that brought about the death of comrade Bishop and other Grenadian leaders are well known by all the people.

In its statement of October 20, the Cuban government explained in detail the unfolding of events and stated our country's unequivocal and honorable position regarding these developments, while cautioning that imperialism would try to derive utmost benefit from this tragedy.

But, above all, it stressed the rigorous policy of Cuba of totally refraining from any form of intervention in the internal affairs of the Grenadian party and people.

The merits of such a policy of principles can be noted now more than ever, since it has become evident that the Cuban personnel in Grenada had the combat capability with which they could have attempted to influence the course of internal events. The weapons in the hands of the Cuban construction personnel and cooperation workers in Grenada had been given to them by Bishop and the Grenadian party and government leadership so that they could defend themselves in the event of a foreign aggression against Grenada, as has unfortunately been the case. These were mainly light infantry weapons. Our own personnel kept custody over those weapons in their living quarters. They were not meant to be used in any domestic conflict and they were never, and will never be used for those ends. Neither had any type of fortification work been undertaken, since it was illogical to do so in times of peace, at the site of a purely civilian airport. And another thing: when the invasion of Grenada took place, the weapons in Cuban hands had less than one ammunition module per rifle.

After Bishop's death and Cuba's statements, relations between our party and the new Grenadian leadership were very cold and somewhat strained. But under no circumstances were we willing to play into the hands of imperialism, foresaking the Grenadian people by stopping our cooperation and halting the work of our construction crews, doctors, teachers, and other specialists. We did not even immediately recall our military and security advisors.

Future relations with the new leadership would be determined by its conduct, its domestic and foreign policy, and by the hope that the revolutionary process could be saved, even though this appeared to be possible only through a miracle of wisdom and serenity on the part of the Grenadians themselves and of the international progressive movement.

Relations with the new government were yet to be defined. But notwithstanding the aforementioned reasons regarding our cooperation with the people of Grenada, from the moment the news of a powerful U.S. naval force advancing on Grenada was made public, it became morally impossible to consider the evacuation of Cuban personnel in that country.

On the other hand, the new Grenadian leadership, faced with the imminent danger of an invasion and invoking their homeland's security, requested our cooperation, an appeal to which it was not easy to accede in view of the events that had taken place in that country.

Numerous messages regarding these matters were exchanged between Cuba and our representatives in Grenada, who conveyed the Grenadian requests.

Due to the imminence of the aggression, during the afternoon of Saturday, October 22, Comrade Fidel sent the following message to the Cuban representative in Grenada:

I believe that organizing our personnel's immediate evacuation at a time when U.S. warships are approaching might be highly demoralizing and dishonorable for our country in the eyes of world public opinion.

A large-scale Yankee aggression against us can take place at any moment in Grenada against our cooperation workers; in Nicaragua against our doctors, teachers, technicians, construction workers, etc.; in Angola against our troops, civilian personnel, and others; or even in Cuba itself. We must always be ready and keep our morale high in the face of these painful possibilities.

I understand how bitter it is for you, as well as for us here, to risk compatriots in Grenada, after the gross mistakes the Grenadian party has made and the tragic developments to which they gave rise. But our position has been unequivocally and honorably clarified, so much so that it has been received with great respect everywhere. It is not the new Grenadian government we must think of now, but of Cuba, its honor, its people, its fighting morale.

I believe that in the face of this new situation, we must strengthen our defenses, keeping in mind the possibility of a surprise attack by the Yankees. The existing danger fully justifies our doing so. If the United States intervenes, we must vigorously defend ourselves as if we were in Cuba, in our camp sites, in our work places close by, but only if we are directly attacked. I repeat: only if we are directly attacked. We would thus be defending ourselves, not the government or its deeds. If the Yankees land on the runway section near the university or on its surroundings to evacuate their citizens, fully refrain from interfering.

Advisors from the army and the Ministry of the Interior are to stay in their posts awaiting new orders, so as to receive information and try to exert as much positive influence as possible on the behavior of the army and the security forces towards the people.

The *Vietnam Heroico* vessel is to be kept there by all means, and efforts should be made to put children and people who are not essential to indispensable services and work there on the first plane that lands on the island.

Convey to [Gen. Hudson] Austin and [Col. Erwart] Layne the following oral reply to their proposals:

That our force, essentially made up of civilian cooperation workers, is too small to be considered as a significant military factor vis à vis a large-scale U.S. invasion.

That sending reinforcements is impossible and unthinkable.

That the political situation created inside the country due to the people's estrangement on account of the death of Bishop and other leaders, isolation from the outside world, etc., considerably weakens the country's defense capabilities, a logical consequence derived from the serious errors made by Grenadian revolutionaries. That due to the above situation, the present military and political conditions are the worst for organizing a firm and efficient resistance against the invaders, an action which is practically impossible without the people's participation. That they have to find a way to reach a reconciliation with the people; perhaps one way would be to clarify the death of Bishop and the other leaders and seek out those responsible.

That the Grenadian government may try to prevent affording a pretext for intervention by publicly offering and reiterating total guarantees and facilities for the security and evacuation of U.S., English, and other nationals.

That if, however, the invasion were to take place anyway, it is their duty to die fighting, no matter how difficult and disadvantageous the circumstances may be.

That the Cuban personnel have been instructed to remain in their camps and to continue work on the airport. That they are to adopt defensive measures and fortify their positions as much as possible in order to be prepared in case of a surprise foreign aggression. That you are to be in constant communication with our party's leadership, and should an imperialist attack take place, you will receive immediate instructions regarding what you should do.

That, in these circumstances, they should keep utmost equanimity and restraint if they wish to preserve the Grenadian revolutionary process's opportunity to survive.

That Cuba will do its best to promote, together with all progressive countries, a strong campaign to counter the U.S. threats against Grenada.

At 9:00 p.m. on Saturday, October 22, we sent the following message to the government of the United States through its Interests Section:

That the U.S. side is aware of the developments in Grenada; that it is also aware of our position on these developments and of our determination of not interfering in the internal affairs of that country. That we are aware of their concern about the numerous U.S. residents there. That we are also concerned about the hundreds of Cuban cooperation personnel working there in different fields and about the news that U.S. naval forces are approaching Grenada.

That according to the reports we have, no U.S. or foreign national, nor our personnel has had any problems. It is convenient to keep in touch on this matter, so as to contribute to solve favorably any difficulty that may arise or action that may be taken relating to the security of these individuals, without violence or intervention in the country.

Once the agreements adopted by a group of Yankee satellites in the Caribbean area to dispatch troops to Grenada became known, the new leadership in that country renewed its requests for the sending of reinforcements by Cuba. On Sunday, October 23, comrade Fidel sent the following message to the Cuban representative in Grenada:

Jamaica, Saint Lucia, and Barbados have no forces to invade Grenada. If this were to occur, it is a mere pretext by the Yankees for their immediate intervention afterwards. In this case you should strictly abide by the instructions received yesterday.

Convey the following answer orally to the Grenadian leadership:

That Jamaica, Saint Lucia, and Barbados have no forces to invade Grenada, and in that case they could defeat them with their own forces without greater difficulties.

That behind this intervention, were it actually to take place, there might be a pretext for the Yankees to act directly; in that case, the Grenadian revolutionaries should try to win over the people for the defense of the country, be ready to fight until the very last man and create conditions for a protracted resistance to the invasion and foreign occupation.

That Cuba cannot send reinforcements, not only because it is materially impossible in the face of the overwhelming U.S. air and naval superiority in the area, but also because politically, if this were to be merely a struggle among Caribbeans, it should not do so in order not to justify U.S. intervention.

That, on the other hand, the unfortunate developments in Grenada render the useless sacrifice entailed by the dispatching of such reinforcements in a struggle against the United States morally impossible before our people and the world.

That, as a matter of our country's honor, morality, and dignity we will keep the Cuban personnel there at a time when powerful Yankee naval forces are approaching Grenada.

That, if Grenada is invaded by the United States, the Cuban personnel will defend their positions in their camps and working areas with all their energy and courage.

That, due to the limited number of those forces, it is impossible to assign them any other mission.

That Grenadian revolutionaries themselves are the only ones responsible for the creation of this disadvantageous and difficult situation for the revolutionary process politically and militarily.

That within the difficult conditions created, the Cuban personnel in Grenada shall honorably meet the duties our revolution has assigned to them under these circumstances.

That, as regards military advising, they will receive all possible cooperation in the face of this situation.

That it is necessary to continue making adequate political and diplomatic efforts on their part to prevent the intervention without compromising on any principles or backing down. That, on our part, we will do our best in this connection.

The Grenadian side continued to insist on plans that in our judgment, were, in some respects, unrealistic and politically unsound. They even hoped to sign a formal agreement on what each side should do in the military field and intended to subordinate the Cuban construction and cooperation workers to the Grenadian army. On Monday, October 24, the following principal points were conveyed to the Grenadian leadership:

• That the Cuban personnel will defend their positions, that is, the runway up to the Hardy Bay filling and the area between Point Saline and Morne Rouge, in case of a large-scale U.S. invasion.

• That, in the present conditions, our personnel have neither the means nor forces to undertake any other mission, nor the moral and international justification to do so in areas outside their work site.

• It is clear to us that were it just a question of evacuating foreign personnel there would be no invasion, and presumably under those circumstances they would find a solution with the parties concerned. That, due to this, the American university and its premises should be under the custody of Grenadians if they deem it necessary and convenient. [The U.S. university is located at one end of the runway under construction by the Cubans.] Perhaps it would be better if that area were free of military personnel so that it would not be regarded as a battleground which could justify armed actions by imperialism under the pretext of evacuating its citizens.

• That there is no need for any formal agreement between us.

• That the instructions regarding what the Cuban personnel is to do in case of war can only be issued by the government of Cuba.

This message, which should have been delivered at 8 o'clock in the morning, Tuesday the twenty-fifth, did not even reach the hands of its addressees. The intervention of the United States in Grenada occurred at the break of day.

The Cuban representatives and personnel strictly followed the instructions of the party and government of Cuba: to fight if they were attacked in their camps and work areas.

322 Maurice Bishop Speaks

During the early hours of the day, while U.S. troops were landing with helicopters in the university area, there was no combat at all with the Cubans, who had taken strictly defensive positions in the above-mentioned sites. Around 8:00 a.m. local time (7 a.m. Cuban time), U.S. troops advanced from different directions on the Cuban facilities, and the fighting began.

At 8:30 (Cuban time) on the twenty-fifth — almost three days later — the government of the United States replied with the following note to the Cuban message sent on Saturday the twenty-second:

The United States of America Interests Section of the Embassy of Switzerland presents its compliments to the Ministry of Foreign Relations of the Republic of Cuba and has the honor to inform the Ministry that the Organization of Eastern Caribbean States, acting out of the grave concern of its members for the anarchy, bloodshed, and callous disregard for human life of the Island of Grenada, has asked the United States Government to facilitate armed forces of its member states in the restoration of security in Grenada. In response to the request, and taking into due account the need to safeguard the lives of several hundred United States citizens now in Grenada, the United States Government has agreed to this request.

Consequently, armed forces from the member states of the Organization of Eastern Caribbean States, supported by those of the United States, Barbados, and Jamaica have entered Grenada for the purpose of restoring order and public safety.

The United States Government is aware that military and civilian personnel of the Republic of Cuba are present in Grenada. It has taken into full account the message on this subject which was delivered on the night of October 22 from the Ministry of Foreign Relations to the Acting Chief of the United States Interests Section in Havana. It wishes to assure the Government of the Republic of Cuba that all efforts are being and will continue to be made to ensure the safety of these persons while order is being restored. These personnel will be granted safe passage from Grenada as soon as conditions permit.

The Government of the United States agrees to the Cuban proposal of October 22 to maintain contact concerning the safety of the personnel of each side. The appropriate civilian representatives with the United States Armed Forces presently in Grenada have been instructed to be in contact with the Cuban Ambassador in Grenada to ensure that every consideration is given to the safety of Cuban personnel on the Island and to facilitate the necessary steps by Grenadian authorities for their prompt evacuation. The United States Armed Forces will be prepared to assure this evacuation at the earliest possible moment on ships of third countries. Alternatively, should there be a vessel of the Cuban merchant marine — not a warship — in Grenadian waters at present, that vessel may be authorized to conduct the evacuation of Cuban personnel.

In addition, any Cuban views communicated to the Department of State through the Cuban Interests Section in Washington or through the United States Interests Section in Havana will be given immediate attention.

The Government of the United States calls upon the Government of the Republic of Cuba, in the interest of the personal safety of all concerned, to advise its citizens and forces in Grenada to remain calm and to cooperate fully with the forces of the Organization of Eastern Caribbean States and with those of the United States, Jamaica, and Barbados. It asks that they be instructed to avoid any steps which might exacerbate the delicate situation in Grenada. Above all, the Government of the United States cautions the Government of the Republic of Cuba to refrain from sending any new military unit or personnel to Grenada.

The United States of America Interests Section of the Embassy of Switzerland avails itself of this opportunity to renew to the Ministry of Foreign Relations of the Republic of Cuba the assurances of its highest and most distinguished consideration.

When this note from the government of the United States arrived, one and a half hours had elapsed since troops from that country started their attack on Cuban personnel and three hours since they had begun the landings.

Throughout the whole day today, Tuesday, the twenty-fifth, the Cuban people have been informed in as much detail as possible on the development of the fighting and the resolute and heroic resistance of Cuban construction and cooperation workers, who practically had not even had time to dig trenches or to fortify their positions in the rocky terrain, in the face of the sea, air, and ground attacks by U.S. elite troops.

The people are familiar with the contents of the message exchanged between the Commander in Chief and Colonel Tortoló, who is in command of the Cuban personnel. This chief, who had not yet been in that country for twenty-four hours and who was on a work visit, with his actions and words has written a chapter in our contemporary history worthy of Antonio Maceo.

At 5:00 p.m. in the evening, while intense fighting was taking place, the government of the United States, through Mr. Ferch, head of the Interests Section, sent the following message to Cuba:

The Cuban personnel stationed in Grenada are not a target for the actions by U.S. troops.

The United States is ready to cooperate with Cuban authorities in the evacuation of Cuban personnel to Cuba.

The United States is aware that armed Cuban personnel do not have either the weapons or ammunition stocks needed for protracted action, thus maintaining a belligerant position would entail a useless loss of human life.

The United States does not wish to present the departure of Cuban armed personnel as a surrender.

Lastly it regrets the armed clashes between men from both countries and considers that they have occurred due to confusion and accidents brought about by our men's proximity to the area of operations of the multinational troops.

At 8:30 p.m., the following reply was handed over to Mr. Ferch to be conveyed to the government of the United States:

1. That we did our best to prevent the intervention, and that in our note dated Saturday we explained that, according to our reports, no U.S. or foreign citizen was in danger, while at the same time we expressed our readiness to cooperate so that the problems could be resolved without violence or intervention.

2. That the intervention is totally unjustifiable. That we had absolutely refrained from meddling in the country's internal affairs, despite our friendship with and sympathies for Bishop.

3. That the answer to our constructive note delivered on Saturday 22, at 9 p.m., arrived on Tuesday, the twenty-fifth, at 8:30 a.m., when our personnel and installations at the airport had been under attack by U.S. troops for one and a half hours.

4. That we have no soldiers, but actually construction workers and civilian advisors in Grenada, with the exception of a few tens of military advisors who were working with the army and security forces before Bishop's death. Our personnel had been instructed to fight back only if attacked, and they were not the first to shoot. Furthermore, they had been given instructions not to obstruct any action for the evacuation of U.S. citizens in the area of the runway near the U.S. university. It was evident that if any attempt was made to occupy Cuban installations they would clash with them.

5. That our personnel has suffered an indeterminate number of casualties in today's combat.

6. That the attack by U.S. troops came as a surprise, without any previous warning.

7. That although the Cuban personnel that are still in a position to resist stand at an absolute numerical, technical, and military disadvantage, their morale remains high, and they are firmly ready to continue defending themselves, were the attacks to continue.

8. That if there is a real intention to forestall further bloodshed, attacks against the Cuban and Grenadian personnel who are still fighting should stop, and an honorable way should be sought to put an end to a battle that far from honors the United States; a battle against small forces that, though unable to resist the overwhelming military superiority of the U.S. forces, even when losing the battle and sacrificing themselves, could still inflict a costly moral defeat on the United States — the most powerful country in the world, engaged in a war against one of the tiniest countries on earth.

9. That the head of the Cuban personnel in Grenada has been instructed to receive any parleyer that might approach him, listen to his views and convey them to Cuba.

10. It cannot be ignored that some Grenadian units are also fighting, and that the treatment given to the Cubans should not differ from the one they are to receive.

During this evening the Cuban construction and cooperation personnel were still holding some of their positions in an uneven and difficult struggle but with high morale and steadfastness. Later into the night there was little news forthcoming from Grenada, and communications were becoming difficult.

The courageous and heroic Cuban construction and cooperation personnel have written an unforgettable chapter in the annals of international solidarity, but in a larger sense, in Grenada they have been waging a battle for the small countries of the world and for all the peoples of the Third World in the face of a brutal imperialist aggression. They have also fought for the American continent and for their own homeland as if there, in Grenada, they were in the first line of defense of the sovereignty and integrity of Cuba.

Grenada may become for Yankee imperialists in Latin America and the Caribbean what the Moncada garrison meant to the Batista tyranny in Cuba.

Eternal glory to the Cubans who have fallen and to those who have fought and are still fighting to defend their honor, their principles, their internationalist work, their homeland, and their own personal lives threatened by the unjustified, treacherous, and criminal imperialist attack.

Patria o Muerte.

Venceremos.

Appendix III

Fidel Castro on the Events in Grenada

The following speech by Fidel Castro was given in Havana on November 14, 1983, to more than a million people gathered to honor Cuban workers killed during the U.S. invasion of Grenada. The English-language text was distributed by the Cuban government.

Fellow countrymen:

On October 15, 1976, a little over seven years ago, we gathered here, in this same place, to deliver a funeral address for the fifty-seven Cubans who were vilely murdered in the Barbados plane sabotage, carried out by men who had been trained by the U.S. Central Intelligence Agency. Today we have come once again to bid farewell — this time to twenty-four Cubans who died in Grenada, another island not very far from Barbados, as a result of U.S. military actions.

Grenada was one of the smallest independent states in the world, both in territory and population. Even though Cuba is a small, underdeveloped country, it was able to help Grenada considerably, because our efforts — which were modest in quantity though high in quality — meant a lot for a country less than 400 square kilometers in size, with a population of just over 100,000.

For instance, the value of our contribution to Grenada in the form of materials, designs, and labor in building the new airport came to $60 million at international prices — over $500 per inhabitant. It is as if Cuba — with a population of almost 10 million — received a project worth $5 billion as a donation. In addition, there was the cooperation of our doctors, teachers, and technicians in diverse specialties, plus an annual contribution of Cuban products worth about $3 million. This meant an additional annual contribution of $40 per inhabitant. It is impossible for Cuba to render considerable material assistance to countries with significantly larger populations and territories, but we were able to offer great assistance to a country like tiny Grenada.

Many other small Caribbean nations, accustomed to the gross economic and strategic interests of colonialism and imperialism, were amazed by Cuba's generous assistance to that fraternal people. They may have thought that Cuba's selfless action was extraordinary. In the midst of the U.S. government's dirty propaganda, some may even have found it difficult to understand.

Our people felt such deep friendship for Bishop and Grenada, and our respect for that country and its sovereignty was so irreproachable, that we never dared to express any opinions about what was being done or how it was being done.

In Grenada, we followed the same principle we apply to all revolutionary nations and movements, full respect for their policies, criteria, and decisions, expressing our views on any matter only when asked to do so. Imperialism is incapable of understanding that the secret of our excellent relations with revolutionary countries and movements in the world lies precisely in this respect.

The U.S. government looked down on Grenada and hated Bishop. It wanted to destroy Grenada's process and obliterate its example. It had even prepared military plans for invading the island — as Bishop had charged nearly two years ago — but it lacked a pretext.

Socioeconomically, Grenada was actually advancing satisfactorily. The people had received many benefits, in spite of the hostile policy of the United States, and Grenada's Gross National Product was growing at a good rate in the midst of the world crisis.

Bishop was not an extremist; rather, he was a true revolutionary — conscientious and honest. Far from disagreeing with his intelligent and realistic policy, we fully sympathized with it, since it was rigorously adapted to his country's specific conditions and possibilities.

Grenada had become a true symbol of independence and progress in the Caribbean. No one could have foreseen the tragedy that was drawing near. Attention was focused on other parts of the world.

Unfortunately, the Grenadian revolutionaries themselves unleashed the events that opened the door to imperialist aggression. Hyenas emerged from the revolutionary ranks. Today no one can yet say whether those who used the dagger of divisionism and internal confrontation did so *motu proprio* [for their own ends] or were inspired and egged on by imperialism.

It is something that could have been done by the CIA — and, if somebody else was responsible, the CIA could not have done it any better. The fact is that allegedly revolutionary arguments were used, invoking the purest principles of Marxism-Leninism and charging Bishop with practicing a cult of personality and with drawing away from the Leninist norms and methods of leadership.

In our view, nothing could be more absurd than to attribute such tendencies to Bishop. It was impossible to imagine anyone more noble, modest, and unselfish. He could never have been guilty of being authoritarian. If he had any defect, it was his excessive tolerance and trust.

Were those who conspired against him within the Grenadian party, army, and security forces by any chance a group of extremists drunk on political theory? Were they simply a group of ambitious, opportunistic individuals, or were they enemy agents who wanted to destroy the Grenadian revolution? History alone will have the last word, but it would not be the first time that such things occurred in a revolutionary process.

In our view, Coard's group objectively destroyed the revolution and opened the door to imperialist aggression. Whatever their intentions, the brutal assassination of Bishop and his most loyal, closest comrades is a fact that can never be justified in that or any other revolution. As the October 20 statement by the Cuban party and government put it, "no crime must be committed in the name of the revolution and freedom."

In spite of his very close and affectionate links with our party's leadership, Bishop never said anything about the internal dissensions that were developing. On the contrary, in his last conversation with us he was self-critical about his work regarding attention to the armed forces and the mass organizations. Nearly all of our party and state leaders spent many friendly, fraternal hours with him on the evening of October 7, before his return trip to Grenada.

Coard's group never had such relations nor such intimacy and trust with us. Actually, we did not even know that this group existed.

It is to our revolution's credit that, in spite of our profound indignation over Bishop's removal from office and arrest, we fully refrained from interfering in Grenada's internal affairs. We refrained even though our construction workers and all our other cooperation personnel in Grenada — who did not hesitate to confront the Yankee soldiers with the weapons Bishop himself had given them for their defense in case of an attack from abroad — could have been a decisive factor in those internal events. Those weapons were never meant to be used in an internal conflict in Grenada and we would never have allowed them to be so used. We would never have been willing to use them to shed a single drop of Grenadian blood.

On October 12, Bishop was removed from office by the Central Committee, on which the conspirators had attained a majority. On the thirteenth, he was placed under house arrest. On the nineteenth, the people took to the streets and freed Bishop. On the same day, Coard's group ordered the army to fire on the people and Bishop, Whiteman, Jacqueline Creft, and other excellent revolutionary leaders were murdered.

As soon as the internal dissensions, which came to light on October 12, became known, the Yankee imperialists decided to invade.

The message sent by the leadership of the Cuban party to Coard's group on October 15 has been made public. In it, we expressed our deep concern over both the internal and external consequences of the split and appealed to common sense, serenity, wisdom, and generosity of revolutionaries. This reference to generosity was an appeal not to use violence against Bishop and his followers.

This group of Coard's that seized power in Grenada expressed serious reservations toward Cuba from the very beginning because of our well-known and unquestionable friendship with Bishop.

The national and international press have published our strong denunciation of the events of October 19, the day Bishop was murdered.

Our relations with Austin's short-lived government, in which Coard was really in charge, were actually cold and tense. So that, at the time of the criminal Yankee aggression, there was no coordination whatsoever between the Grenadian army and the Cuban construction workers and other cooperation personnel.

The basic points of the messages sent to our embassy in Grenada between October 12 and 25, the day in which the invasion took place, have been made public. Those documents stand in history as irrefutable proof of our unblemished, principled, position regarding Grenada.

Imperialism, however, presented the events as the coming to power of a group of hard-line communists, loyal allies of Cuba. Were they really communists? Were they really hard-liners? Could they really be loyal allies of Cuba? Or were they rather conscious or unconscious tools of Yankee imperialism?

Look at the history of the revolutionary movement, and you will find more than one connection between imperialism and those who take positions that appear to be on the extreme left. Aren't Pol Pot and Ieng Sary — the ones responsible for the genocide in Kampuchea — the most loyal allies Yankee imperialism has in Southeast Asia at present? In Cuba, ever since the Grenadian crisis began, we have called Coard's group — to give it a name — the "Pol Pot group."

Our relations with the new leaders of Grenada were to be subjected to profound analysis, as was set forth in the October 20 statement by the party and government of Cuba. In it, we also stated that, due to our basic regard for the Grenadian people, we would not rush to take any steps with regard to technical and economic cooperation that could affect essential services or economic interests vital to the people of Grenada.

We could not accept the idea of leaving the Grenadians without doctors or leaving the airport, which was vital to the nation's economy, unfinished. Most certainly, our construction workers were to leave Grenada when that project was completed, and the weapons that Bishop had given them were to be returned to the government. It was even possible that our very bad relations with the new government would make it necessary for us to leave much earlier.

The thing that placed Cuba in a morally complex, difficult situation was the announcement that Yankee naval forces were en route to Grenada. Under those circumstances, we couldn't possibly leave the country. If the imperialists really intended to attack Grenada, it was our duty to stay there. To withdraw at that time would have been dishonorable and could even have triggered aggression in that country then and in Cuba later on. In addition, events unfolded with such incredible speed that if the evacuation had been planned for, there would not have been time to carry it out.

In Grenada, however, the government was morally indefensible. And, since the party, the government, and the army had divorced themselves from the people, it was also impossible to defend the nation militarily, because a revolutionary war is only feasible and justifiable when united with the people. We could only fight, therefore, if we were directly attacked. There was no alternative.

It should nevertheless be noted that, despite these adverse circumstances, a number of Grenadian soldiers died in heroic combat against the invaders. [*Applause*]

The internal events, however, in no way justified Yankee intervention.

Since when has the government of the United States become the arbiter of internal conflicts between revolutionaries in any given country? What right did Reagan have to be so aggrieved over the death of Bishop, whom he so hated and opposed? What reasons could there be for this brutal violation of the sovereignty of Grenada — a small independent nation that was a respected and acknowledged member of the international community?

It would be the same as if another country believed it had the right to intervene in the United States because of the repulsive assassination of Martin Luther King or so many other outrages, such as those that have been committed against the Black and Hispanic minorities in the United States, or to intervene because John Kennedy was murdered.

The same may be said of the argument that the lives of 1,000 Americans were in danger. There are many times more U.S. citizens in dozens of other countries in the world. Does this, perchance, imply the right to intervene when internal conflicts arise in those countries? There are tens of thousands of Grenadians in the United States, England, and Trinidad. Could tiny Grenada intervene if domestic policy problems arose that posed some threat to its compatriots in any of those countries?

Putting aside the fallacy and falseness of such pretexts for invading Grenada, is this really an international norm that can be sustained? A thousand lessons in Marxism could not teach us any better about the dirty, perfidious, and aggressive nature of imperialism than the attack unleashed against Grenada at dawn on October 25 and its subsequent development.

In order to justify its invasion of Grenada and its subsequent actions, the U.S. government and its spokesmen told nineteen lies. Reagan personally told the first thirteen:

1. Cuba was responsible for the coup d'etat and the death of Bishop. [*Shouts of "Lie!"*]

2. The American students were in danger of being taken hostage. [*Shouts of "Lie!"*]

3. The main purpose of the invasion was to protect the lives of American citizens. [*Shouts of "Lie!"*]

4. The invasion was a multinational operation undertaken at the request of Mr. Scoon and the eastern Caribbean nations. [*Shouts of "Lie!"*]

5. Cuba was planning to invade and occupy Grenada. [*Shouts of "Lie!"*]

6. Grenada was being turned into an important Soviet-Cuban military base. [*Shouts of "Lie!"*]

7. The airport under construction was not civilian but military. [*Shouts of "Lie!"*]

8. The weapons in Grenada would be used to export subversion and terrorism. [*Shouts of "Lie!"*]

9. The Cubans fired first. [*Shouts of "Lie!"*]

10. There were over 1,000 Cubans in Grenada. [*Shouts of "Lie!"*]

11. Most of the Cubans were not construction workers but professional soldiers. [*Shouts of "Lie!"*]

12. The invading forces took care not to destroy civilian property or inflict civilian casualties. [*Shouts of "Lie!"*]

13. The U.S. troops would remain in Grenada for a week. [*Shouts of "Lie!"*]

14. Missile silos were being built in Grenada. [*Shouts of "Lie!"*]

15. The vessel *Vietnam Heroico* was transporting special weapons. [*Shouts of "Lie!"*]

16. Cuba was warned of the invasion. [*Shouts of "Lie!"*]

17. Five hundred Cubans are fighting in the mountains of Grenada. [*Shouts of "Lie!"*]

18. Cuba has issued instructions for reprisals to be taken against U.S. citizens. [*Shouts of "Lie!"*]

19. The journalists were excluded for their own protection. [*Shouts of "Lie!"*] [*Applause and shouts of "For sure, Fidel, give the Yankees hell!" and "Fidel, give them hell; let's make 'em respect us well!"*]

None of these assertions were proved, none are true, and all have been refuted by the facts. This cynical way of lying in order to justify invading a tiny country reminds us of the methods Adolph Hitler used during the years leading up to World War II.

The U.S. students and officials of the medical school located there acknowledge that they were given full guarantees for U.S. citizens and the necessary facilities for those who wanted to leave the country. Moreover, Cuba had informed the U.S. government on October 22 that no foreign citizens, including Cubans, had been disturbed, and it offered to cooperate in solving any difficulty that might arise, so that problems could be settled without violence or intervention in that country. No U.S. citizen had been disturbed at all prior to the invasion, and if anything endangered them, it was the war unleashed by the United States.

Cuba's instructions to its personnel not to interfere with any actions to evacuate U.S. citizens in the area of the runway under construction near the university contributed to protecting the U.S. citizens residing in that country. Reagan's reference to the possibility that Grenada might turn into another Iran — a reference calculated to appeal to the U.S. feelings wounded in that episode — is a demagogic, politicking, dishonest argument.

The assertion that the new airport was a military one — an old lie that the Reagan administration had dwelt on a lot — was categorically refuted by the English capitalist firm that supplied and installed the electrical and technical equipment for that airport. The British technicians of the Plessey Company, which has made a name for itself internationally as a specialist in this field, worked alongside the Cuban construction workers, to whose civilian worker status they attest. Several countries of the European community that are members of the Atlantic alliance cooperated in one way or another with the airport. How can anyone imagine them helping Cuba to build a military airport in Grenada?

However, the idea that Grenada was being turned into a Soviet-Cuban base is refuted by the proven fact that there wasn't even one Soviet military adviser on the island.

The supposedly secret documents that fell into the hands of the United States and were published by the Yankee administration a few days after the invasion refer to the agreement between the governments of Cuba and Grenada by virtue of which our country was to send Grenada twenty-seven military advisers, which could later be increased to forty — figures that coincide with the ones Cuba published on the number of advisers, which was twenty-two on the day of the attack, to which were added a similar number of translators and service personnel from the mission.

Nowhere in those documents that they have been crowing over is there anything that has anything to do with the idea of military bases in Grenada. What they do show is that the weapons that the Soviet Union supplied to the government of Grenada for the army and the militia were subject to a clause that prohibited their export to third countries. This refutes the idea that Grenada had been turned into an arsenal for supplying weapons to subversive, terrorist organizations, as the present U.S. administration likes to call the revolutionary and national liberation movements. No weapons ever left Grenada for any other country, and, therefore, Reagan can never prove that any did.

The assertion that Cuba was about to invade and occupy Grenada is so unrealistic, absurd, crazy, and alien to our principles and international policy that it cannot even be taken seriously. What has been proven is the absolutely scrupulous way in which we refrained from meddling in the internal affairs of that country, in spite of our deep affection for Bishop and our total rejection of Coard and his group's conspiracy and coup, which could serve only the interests of imperialism and its plans for destroying the Grenadian revolution.

The messages containing precise, categorical instructions to our embassy in Grenada, which have been widely publicized by the government of Cuba, constitute irrefutable proof of the clear position of principle maintained by the leadership of our party and state with regard to the internal events in Grenada.

The civilian status of the vast majority of the Cuban cooperation personnel in Grenada has been shown to the whole world by the hundreds of foreign journalists who saw them arriving in our country and who were able to interview each and every one of them.

Nearly 50 percent of them were over forty years old. Who could question their status as civilian cooperation personnel and workers with long years of experience on their jobs?

When the U.S. government spokesmen asserted that there were from 1,000 to 1,500 Cubans in Grenada at the time of the invasion and that hundreds of them were still fighting in the mountains, Cuba published the exact number of Cuban citizens who were in Grenada on the day of the invasion — 784, including diplomatic personnel with their children and other relatives.

The agencies that sent them and the kind of work they did were also reported, as well as the instructions given them to fight in their work areas and camps if attacked, and the fact that it was impossible — according to the information we had — that hundreds might still remain in the mountains. Later, the names and jobs of all cooperation workers were published, as well as the known or probable situation of each one. The facts have shown that the information provided by Cuba was absolutely true. There isn't a single fact in all that information that could be proven false.

The assertion that the Cubans initiated the acts of hostility is equally false and cynical. The irrefutable truth is that the Cubans were sleeping and their weapons were stored at the time of the air drop on the runway and around the camps. They had not been distributed. There weren't enough to go around, and they weren't distributed until the landing was already underway. And that is when the Cuban personnel went to the places assigned to them for that emergency.

Even so, our personnel, now organized and armed, had time to see the U.S. paratroopers regrouping on the runway and the first planes landing. That was the invader's weakest moment. If the Cubans had fired first, they would have killed or wounded dozens — perhaps hundreds — of U.S. soldiers in those early hours. [*Applause*]

What is strictly historical and strictly true is that the fighting began when the U.S. troops advanced toward the Cubans in a belligerent way.

It is also true that when a group of unarmed cooperation personnel was captured, they were used as hostages and forced to lead the way in front of the U.S. soldiers.

The invasion of Grenada was a treacherous surprise attack, with no previous warning at all — just like Pearl Harbor, just like the Nazis. The note from the government of the United States to the government of Cuba on Tuesday, October 25, in an attempted response to our note of Saturday, October 22, was delivered at 8:30 in the morning, three hours after the landing had taken place and an hour and a half after the U.S. troops began attacking our compatriots in Grenada. Actually, on the afternoon of the twenty-fifth, the U.S. government sent the government of Cuba a deceitful note that led us to believe the fighting would cease in a reasonable and honorable manner, thus avoiding greater bloodshed. Although we immediately responded to that note, accepting that possibility, what the U.S. government did was to land the Eighty-second Airborne Division at dawn on the twenty-sixth and attack with all its forces the Cuban position that was still resisting. Is this the way a serious government behaves? Is this the way to warn of an attack? Was this the way to avoid greater bloodshed?

Mr. Scoon blatantly declared that he approved of the invasion but that he had not previously asked anyone to invade Grenada. A few days after the landing, Mr. Scoon — lodged in the *Guam* helicopter carrier — signed a letter officially requesting the intervention. Reagan could not prove any of his false assertions.

As a pretext for keeping the *Vietnam Heroico* — which was in the port of St. George's on the day of the invasion — from being used as a means of transportation for evacuating the Cuban hostages from Grenada, it was alleged that it carried special weapons. Its captain was immediately asked if by any chance he carried weapons on board, and the only thing that was determined was that it had just one fearful weapon — its name: Vietnam. [*Applause*]

The slanderous charge that Cuba had given instructions to carry out actions against U.S. citizens in other countries was given a worthy, official, and public reply based on the reality, proven by the history of the revolution, that Cuba has always been opposed to acts of reprisal against innocent people.

The government of the United States has not even condescended to make known the number of people arrested nor the figure of Grenadian losses, including civilian losses. A hospital for the mentally ill was bombed, killing dozens of patients.

And where is Mr. Reagan's promise that U.S. troops would withdraw in a week? President Reagan himself in his first address to the U.S. people, at 8:30 a.m. on the day of the invasion, in a speech prepared before the landing, stated that the situation was under control. That same day, his own spokesman described the resistance the invading forces were facing. The military parade the Pentagon had planned to hold in four hours did not take into account the tenacious and heroic resistance of the Cuban cooperation personnel and of the Grenadian soldiers. [*Applause*]

Who, then, has told the truth, and who has cynically lied about the events in Grenada? No foreign journalists — not even those from the United States — were allowed to see and report on the events on the spot. The pretext that this prohibition was a security measure for the journalists is both superficial and ridiculous. What they obviously wanted was to monopolize and manipulate the information so they could lie without hindrance to world public opinion, including the people of the United States. This was the only way they could spread deliberate lies and falsehoods of all kinds — which would be difficult to clear up and refute after their initial impact and effect on the people of the United States. Even in this, the method used by the U.S. administration was fascist.

What is left now, objectively, of those nineteen assertions? Where are the silos for strategic missiles that were being built in Grenada?

But all those lies that the world did not believe, told by the U.S. president and his spokesmen, made a tremendous impact on U.S. public opinion.

Moreover, the invasion of Grenada was presented to the U.S. people as a great victory for Reagan's foreign policy against the socialist camp and the revolutionary movement. It was linked to the tragic death of 240 U.S. soldiers in Beirut, to the memory of the hostages in Iran, to the humiliating defeat in Vietnam and the resurgence of the United States as an influential power on the world scene. A dirty, dishonest appeal was made to U.S. patriotism, to national pride, to the grandeur and glory of the nation.

This was how they got a majority of the U.S. people — it is said that it was 65 percent at first and then 71 percent — to support the monstrous crime of invading a sovereign country without any justification, the reprehensible method of launching a surprise attack, the press censorship and all the other procedures the U.S. government used for invading and justifying its invasion of Grenada.

Hitler acted the same way when he occupied Austria in 1938 and annexed Sudetenland in Czechoslovakia in 1938 in the name of German pride, German grandeur and glory, and the happiness and security of German subjects. If a poll had been taken in Hitler Germany at that time, in the midst of the chauvinistic wave unleashed by the Nazis, around 80 or 90 percent of the people would have approved of those aggressions.

The deplorable, truly dangerous fact — not only for the peoples of the Caribbean, Central and Latin America, but for all the people of the world — is that, when world opinion unanimously denounced the war-mongering, aggressive, unjustifiable action that violated people's sovereignty and all international norms and principles, most of the United States — manipulated, disinformed, and deceived — supported the monstrous crime committed by their government.

There is something even more disturbing: When this about-face was effected in U.S. public opinion, many U.S. politicians who initially had opposed these events ended up by condoning Reagan's actions, and the press — censored, humiliated, and kept at a distance from the events — ended up moderating its complaints and criticism.

Are these, perchance, the virtues of a society where opinion and the political and the informational institutions can be grossly manipulated by its rulers, as they were in German society in the time of fascism?

Where is the glory, the grandeur and the victory in invading and de-feating one of the tiniest countries in the world, of no economic or strategic significance?

Where is the heroism in fighting a handful of workers and other civil-ian cooperation personnel whose heroic resistance — in spite of the sur-prise element, the shortage of ammunition, and their disadvantages in terms of terrain, arms, and numbers — against the air, sea, and land forces of the most powerful imperialist country in the world forced it to bring in the Eighty-second Airborne Division when the last stronghold was being defended at dawn on October 26 by barely fifty fighters? [*Applause*]

The United States did not achieve any victory at all — not political or military or moral. If anything, it was a pyrrhic military victory and a pro-found moral defeat.

As we pointed out on another occasion, the imperialist government of the United States wanted to kill the symbol of the Grenadian revolution, but the symbol was already dead. The Grenadian revolutionaries them-selves destroyed it with their split and their colossal errors. We believe that, after the death of Bishop and his closest comrades, after the army fired on the people, and after the party and the government divorced themselves from the masses and isloated themselves from the world, the Grenadian revolutionary process could not survive.

In its efforts to destroy a symbol, the United States killed a corpse and brought the symbol back to life at the same time. [*Applause*] Was it for this that it challenged international law and won the repudiation and condemnation of the world? Does it feel such contempt for the rest of humanity? Is that contempt really so great that Mr. Reagan's appetite for breakfast on November 3 was not at all affected, as he declared before the press?

If unfortunately all this were true — and it seems to be — the invasion of Grenada should lead us to an awareness of the realities and dangers that threaten the world.

Mr. [Thomas] O'Neill, speaker of the House of Representatives, said that it was sinful that a man who was totally uninformed and ignorant about international problems and who doesn't even read the documents was president of the United States. If we consider that the United States has powerful sophisticated means of conventional and nuclear warfare and that the president of that country can declare war without consulting anyone, it is not only sinful but truly dramatic and tragic for all humanity.

An air of triumph reigns in the Reagan administration. The echoes of the last shots in Grenada have barely died away and already there is talk of intervening in El Salvador, Nicaragua, and even Cuba; in the Middle East and southern Africa. Imperialism's acts of interference and military aggression against progressive countries and national liberation movements continue unabated.

In Europe, the first of the 572 Pershing II and cruise missiles are already being deployed, surrounding the USSR and other socialist countries with a deadly ring of nuclear weapons that can reach their territories in a matter of minutes. Not just the small countries, but all humanity is threatened. The bells tolling today for Grenada may toll tomorrow for the whole world.

The most prestigious and experienced scientists and doctors assure us that humanity could not survive a global nuclear war. The destructive power of these stockpiled weapons is a million times greater than that of the unsophisticated bombs that wiped out the cities of Hiroshima and Nagasaki in just a few seconds. This is what the Reagan administration's aggressive, warmongering policy can lead to.

Meanwhile, the arms race is already a reality in the midst of the worst economic crisis the world has witnessed since the thirties. And, with the problems of development of the vast majority of the peoples in the world still to be solved, who can feel confidence in a government that acts as precipitately, rashly and cynically as the U.S. government did in Grenada?

Reagan did not even bother to listen to the advice of a government as closely linked to him politically, ideologically, and militarily as the British government. It is not strange that, in a poll taken just a few days ago, more than 90 percent of the British people were categorically opposed to the United States having the unilateral prerogative of using the cruise missiles that are being deployed there.

In our hemisphere, just a year and a half ago, a NATO power used sophisticated war means to shed Argentine blood in the Malvinas. The Reagan administration supported that action. It did not even consider the Organization of American States or the so-called security pacts and agreements, but scornfully pushed them aside.

Now, basing itself on the alleged request of a phantasmagoric organization of microstates in the eastern Caribbean, it has invaded Grenada and shed Caribbean blood and Cuban blood.

Nicaragua paid a price of over 40,000 lives for freedom, and nearly a thousand more sons of that noble people have been killed in attacks made by mercenary bands organized, trained, and equipped by the U.S. government.

In El Salvador, over 50,000 people have been murdered by a genocidal regime whose army is equipped, trained, and directed by the United States.

In Guatemala, more than 100,000 have died at the hands of the repressive system installed by the CIA in 1954, when it overthrew the progressive Arbenz government.

How many have died in Chile since imperialism staged the overthrow and assassination of Salvador Allende? How many have died in Argentina, Uruguay, Paraguay, Brazil, and Bolivia in the last fifteen years?

What a high price our peoples have paid in blood, sacrifice, poverty, and mourning for imperialist domination and the unjust social systems it has imposed on our nations.

Imperialism is bent on destroying symbols, because it knows the value of symbols, of examples, and of ideas. It wanted to destroy them in Grenada, and it wants to destroy them in El Salvador, Nicaragua, and Cuba. But symbols, examples, and ideas cannot be destroyed. [*Applause*] When their enemies think they have destroyed them, what they have actually done is made them multiply. [*Applause*] In trying to wipe out the first Christians, the Roman emperors spread Christianity throughout the world. Likewise, all attempts to destroy our ideas will only multiply them.

Grenada has already multiplied the patriotic conviction and fighting spirit of the Salvadoran, Nicaraguan, and Cuban revolutionaries. [*Applause*] It has been proven that the best U.S. troops can be fought and that they are not feared. [*Heavy applause and shouts*] The imperialists must not ignore the fact that they will encounter fierce resistance wherever they attack a revolutionary people. Let us hope that their pyrrhic victory in Grenada and their air of triumph don't go to their heads, leading them to commit serious, irreversible errors.

They will not find in El Salvador, Nicaragua, and Cuba the particular circumstances of revolutionaries divided among themselves and divorced from the people that they found in tiny Grenada. [*Loud applause and shouts*]

In more than three years of heroic struggle, the Salvadoran revolutionaries have become experienced, fearsome, and invincible fighters. There are thousands of them who know the land inch by inch, veterans of dozens of victorious battles, who are accustomed to fighting and winning — when the odds are ten to one against them — against elite troops, trained, armed, and advised by the United States. Their unity is more solid and indestructible than ever.

In Nicaragua, the imperialists would have to confront a deeply patriotic and revolutionary people that is united, organized, armed, and ready to fight and that can never be subjugated. [*Prolonged applause and shouts*] With regard to Cuba, if in Grenada, the imperialists had to bring in an elite division to fight against a handful of isolated men struggling in a small stronghold, lacking fortifications, a thousand miles from their homeland, how many divisions would they need against millions of combatants fighting on their own soil alongside their own people? [*Prolonged applause and shouts*] Our country — as we have already said on other occasions — might be wiped off the face of the earth, but it will never be conquered and subjugated. [*Prolonged applause and shouts of "Commander in chief, we await your order!"*]

In the present conditions of our continent, a U.S. war against a Latin American people would raise the morale of all the peoples of Latin America and turn their feelings against the aggressors. A bottomless abyss would be opened between peoples, who — because they are in the same hemisphere — are called upon to live with one another in peace, friendship, and mutual respect and cooperation.

The experiences of Grenada will be examined in detail to extract the utmost benefit from them for use in case of another attack against a country where there are Cuban cooperation personnel or against our own homeland. [*Applause and shouts*]

The Cubans who were captured and turned virtually into hostages had an unforgettable experience of what a country occupied by Yankee invading troops is like. The physical and psychological treatment given the cooperation personnel who were taken prisoner was insulting and a cause for indignation. Promises of all kinds were made to each of them to try to get them to go to the United States. But they were not able to break their steel-like staunchness. Not a single one deserted his homeland. [*Loud applause and shouts*]

There was no manipulation of the news, nothing was hidden from the people in our country. All reports concerning the invasion that were received directly from Grenada were transmitted to our population just as they arrived, even though the ones on October 26 turned out to be exaggerated.

As a matter of principle, at no time were efforts made to play down the seriousness of the situation or to minimize the magnitude of the dangers facing our compatriots.

We are deeply grateful to the International Committee of the Red Cross [*Applause*] for its interest, dedication, and efficient efforts to identify and evacuate the wounded, sick, and other prisoners and the dead as quickly as possible. We are also grateful to the governments of Spain and Colombia for the immediate efforts they made in this regard. [*Applause*]

In bidding farewell to our beloved brothers who died heroically in combat, fulfilling with honor their patriotic and internationalist duties, and in expressing our deepest solidarity with their loved ones, we do not forget that there are Grenadian mothers and U.S. mothers who are crying for their sons who died in Grenada. [*Applause*] We send our condolences to the mothers and other relatives of the Grenadians who were killed and also to the mothers and other relatives of the U.S. soldiers who died — because they, who also suffer from the loss of close relatives, are not to blame for their government's warmongering, aggressive, irresponsible actions. They, too, are its victims. [*Applause*]

Every day, every hour, every minute — at work, at our studies and our combat positions — we will remember our comrades who died in Grenada. [*Applause*]

The men whom we will bury this afternoon fought for us and for the world. They may seem to be corpses. Reagan wants to make corpses of all our people — men, women, the elderly, and the children! He wants to make a corpse out of all humanity.

But the peoples shall struggle to preserve their independence and their lives! They will struggle to prevent the world from becoming a huge cemetery! They will struggle and pay the price necessary for humanity to survive.

However, they are not corpses! They are symbols. They did not even die in the land where they were born. There, far away from Cuba, where they were contributing with the noble sweat of their internationalist work in a country poorer and smaller than ours, they were also able to shed their blood and offer their lives. But in that trench, they knew they were also defending their own people and their own homeland.

There can be no purer way to express the generosity of human beings and their willingness to make sacrifices. Their example will be multiplied, their ideas will be multiplied, and they themselves will be multiplied in us. No power, no weapons, no forces can ever prevail over the

patriotism, internationalism, feelings of human brotherhood, and communist consciousness which they embody.
We shall be like them, in work and in combat!
Patria o muerte!
Venceremos! [*Ovation*] [*The crowd sings the "Internationale"*]

Index

Trade Union Recognition Law, xxi, 232, 246, 303
Trade unions: before revolution, 5, 8, 14, 21, 149, 175; and democracy, 230-31, 234, 235-36, 246, 262, 271, 275; elections in, 231, 275; growth of, xxi, 138, 185, 231, 246, 303; internationalism of, 233-34; and management, 235; militant, 228, 231, 234; misleaders of, 158-59, 227, 228, 230; recognition of, 14, 85, 232, 246, 303; unity of, 234, 238
TransAfrica, 288
Transportation, xxii, 234, 253, 258, 304-5; under Gairy, 45-46, 108
Trinidad and Tobago, 9, 83
Trinidad *Express*, 62, 155, 187, 211, 236, 249
Trinidad *Guardian*, 155, 211, 236
Trotsky, Leon, xix
Truong Chinh, xlvi

Uganda, 71
Ultraleftism, xvi, xx, xxx-xxxi, 98, 112, 329
Unemployment: under capitalism, 129, 237, 291-92; under Gairy, xvii, 10, 20, 29, 36, 71, 85, 174, 241-42; after invasion, xxvii; as major problem, 112, 221; progress in eliminating, xiii, 73, 109, 244, 275, 294
UNESCO, 35, 296
United Nations, 51-52, 74
United People's Party (UPP), 13, 18, 112
United States: antiwar activity in, viii, x, xlvi, 106, 198, 251; attacks on working class in, 97, 101, 130, 237, 291-92; impact of Vietnam on, ix, 101; interventionism by, 56, 72, 76, 88, 89, 98, 99, 139, 162, 191, 200-201, 263, 281-82, 307, 337; military maneuvers by, 139, 171, 235, 251, 281, 285; nature of ruling class in, ix, 206; planned invasion of Grenada by, xxv-xxvi, 203, 205, 206, 213, 237, 250, 251, 279-80, 282, 283-84, 327; threats vs. Grenada by, xv, 26-28, 55-56, 98, 102, 126, 137, 147, 189, 193, 248, 250, 274-86, 288; war drive of, viii-ix, 101-2, 107, 114, 126, 146, 194, 209, 236-37, 262-63, 266, 279, 337, 339; working class in, viii, ix, x, 101, 117-19
United States International Communications Agency, 211
United States invasion: and attacks on Cu-

bans, 323-25, 331, 334; criminal nature of, 325, 334; and destruction of revolution, xxvi, xxvii; goal of, vii, ix, xxvii, xxxix, 336-37; Grenadians' response to, xxvi, xxxix, 330; justications for, xxvi, 322-23, 330, 331, 332-33, 334, 338; preparations for, xi, xxxix, 318, 320, 329-30; U.S. lies about, 330-35; and U.S. public opinion, ix-x, 321-23, 335-36
Unity, 61, 118-19, 206, 238, 339
University education, xxiii, 174, 176, 219-20, 244
Uruguay, 338

Vance, Cyrus, 51
Van Geest, 21, 293
Venezuela, 30, 94, 135, 144, 190, 260, 264
Vesco, Robert, 19
Vieques, 75, 93, 225
Vietnam, ix, xlvi, 8, 54, 55, 57, 72, 82, 91, 201, 297, 335
Vietnam Heroico, 319, 334
Voluntary work, 46, 61, 84, 107-8, 123, 133, 185, 221, 244, 253
Voting rights, 34

War drive. *See* Imperialism, as cause of war; United States, war drive of
Water supply system, xxii, 29, 35, 39, 46, 109-10, 174, 234, 244, 259, 298
Watkins, James, 280
Weinberger, Caspar, 281
Western Sahara, 53, 74, 93, 269
West Indian, 4
West Indies Associated States Organization, 30
Whiteman, Unison, xii, xxxiii, xxxiv, xxxvii, 9, 11, 150; murder of, xxxviii, 315, 328
Whyte, Winston, 112
Williams, Eric, 167
Wills, Ashley, 162
Windward Islands Banana Association, 203, 212, 243
Women: equal pay for, 36, 38, 184, 233; growing participation of, 21, 183-84, 246, 303-4; liberation of, 37-38; PRG measures for, xxiv, 38-40, 85, 86, 303; roots of oppression of, 33-37; sexual exploitation of, 38-39, 85, 176, 184, 229, 303; and unemployment, 29, 85, 174, 303. *See also* Maternity leave; Na-